AN A–B–C–D OF POLITICS AT THE END OF A ROAD

by
V. J. Chalupa

ISBN 1-887567-10-0

Published by
Central Bureau, CCVA

Printed by
St. Martin de Porres Lay Dominican Community
New Hope, KY 40052

TABLE OF CONTENTS

Dedication

Dedicated to Rev. John H. Miller, C.S.C., S.T.D.,
thanks to whose inspiration, guidance,
encouragement and patience this book has been written.

INTRODUCTION

About half a century ago, two refugees from the communist regime in Czechoslovakia debated the future in Paris. One of them maintained that for men thinking is as indispensable as eating and digesting, and in view of the infinite variety and variability of genes, any attempt to suppress human thinking and to force human society into a society of an antheap, and therefore totalitarian regime, must collapse. The other countered with the observation that ants had not always lived in the same way as they were living at present, that they obviously evolved into perfect coordination from a community of complete and more independent individuals, and that therefore humanity could follow the same path and totalitarian regimes could succeed.

The purpose of this book is (1) to concede that the latest evolution of humanity is proving the second debater right, (2) to describe how this is coming about, (3) to assert that it does not have to be so, and (4) to open the discussion on ways and means to lead humanity in a right direction.

It is common to describe any present situation as critical, decisive and a crossroad in history. This is to a certain extent true: panta rei, history does not stand still, and therefore each of its steps, each historical period, each answer to any situation co-determines what the future will be. But there are differences. As long as such turns and innovations take place within the framework of one civilization, they do not change the basics of things. The shifts in power among Egypt, Assyria, Babylonia, Persia left undisturbed the elements constituting a civilization: the spiritual underpinning and the arrangements between people and peoples and the principles of society and economy.

To a different category belong changes which bring about the destruction and replacement of such fundamental elements and thus the rise of a different civilization. This process is usualy connected with great demographic changes. The rise of Greece and Rome created a new civilization on the ruins of the Fertile Crescent one, and when it perished under the impact of Christianity and the invasion of Germanic and Slav tribes from Eastern Europe, a new, the Christian Western civilization arose victorious and dominated the world.

The rise of a new civilization is a drawn out and costly process, costly in spiritual and material goods and especially in human lives. The signs of its beginning and progress are impossible to hide and under the assumption of human freedom can be avoided by man's reason and will. Such signs are clearly visible in the present situation. They are the challenge to the spiritual foundation of Western civilization's values and institutions by materialistic principles; the denial of the exceptional position and mission of humanity in creation and the view of man as an equal, non-special part of the animal and inert world; the enmity towards family and nation as humanity's main institutions; and the bypassing of its structured political arrangements: the state and its most valued form, democracy, replacement of government as a codified manner of ruling, by governance as an informal and therefore uncontrollable rule; all these changes paralleled by far reaching demographic shifts herald the end of the road for Western civilization.

Dealing with such a complex situation requires a comprehensive understanding of politics. This is the purpose of this book: to enlarge the knowledge of objective truth about politics rather than to express an opinion. Search of the truth is not directed mainly towards the past, but to the present and the future. But its seeking, representing and proving has two disadvantages. It is necessary to explain the terminology and the structure of organizing the acquired knowledge, which is tedious and whose direct connection with the main subject, i.e., politics, is not always obvious. The dealing with the truth must rely on past knowledge commonly known and possibly considered boring and superfluous, although new light is cast on it from new observations.

The contents are presented here in four parts.

The first objective ("A"chapters) is to explain politics as an activity of beings endowed with freedom, i.e., reason and volition, who act purposefully. In the interest of precise and clear terminology, it must be introduced by the book's most tedious part: the first two chapters devoted to the logic of purposive thinking and its two poles: purpose and means. With the help of these instruments, it then follows the creation of purposes, their coalescence into movements, the transformation of movements into political movements and of political movements into political organizations; the utilization of the management of public affairs as means for attaining the sundry purposes, and the types of government. For the purpose of the book, it is necessary that these chapters cover not only politics as they exist in the United States, but generally; therefore this descriptive part is the longest portion on which the rest is based.

The second objective ("B" chapters) seeks to determine generally valid criteria, i.e., absolute standards for judging the facts delineated in the preceding five chapters; such criteria are the feasibility of purposes and the suitability of means. These two qualities depend on the relationship of the observed phenomena towards the two tendencies pervading being: the tendency of unfolding its potentialities into actualities (evolution, development) and their collapse (devolution, entropy). Man can, in his freedom, choose between them; he can choose destruction, even his own destruction. This book follows the principle "being is better than non-being" as the absolute good: evolution over entropy, growth over decline (stagnation is not a third alternative due to the unceasing change of the existent world).

The third objective ("C" chapters) is the application of the established criteria to the present world political scene in order to evaluate positive elements of the present civilization, the nature of the surging new civilization and the eroding of Western civilization by the forces of the new individualistic culture of economic and biological materialism. It also deals with their methods and strength.

The fourth objective ("D" chapters) is the examination of options humanity has for its future development. Not surprisingly, the decision lies largely with the United States due to its unique power position in the present configuration. Thanks to their manipulations of domestic politics, from the United States springs most of the financial and political power of the promoters and realizators of the "global governance" among the world's elites.

After consideration of these factors, the conclusions of this book can be summed up as follows:

Half a billion children have been outsmarted, outmaneuvered and deprived of their main human right: to be born. Billions of "ordinary people" are being outsmarted, outmaneuvered and deprived of a basic human right: to pass on their life to their children. It happens due to their political ineptitude and organizational haplessness. Their numbers and their power immeasurably overwhelm the agents of the "civilization of death," but they need a program and gradual realization of a new world order benefiting humanity, its spiritual and material growth, a program of saving, sharing and using the resources of this planet to serve humanity and to push humanity's new frontier past the limits of this planet into space. The United States has led humanity victoriously in the struggle for democracy; it is also spiritually and technologically capable to lead it in the preservation and perfection of the civilization which gave birth to human rights and democracy. This demands political action, and someone should try it.

This book includes also the experience of over forty years of international banking including the service of chairman of the National Association of the Council on International Banking and representing the American banking community during international conferences at the International Chamber of Commerce in Paris and even more so the traces of fifty years of participation in politics, clandestine and public, under two totalitarian and three democratic regimes, as inmate of a concentration camp in Germany, a political refugee in France and a citizen of the United States to which, at the end of the road, by this summary of a tortuous life, I confess my thanks.

V. John Chalupa

PART A.

POLITICS AS ACTION

— WHAT IS IT?

CHAPTER 1

EXPLAINING POLITICS

Why and how Write on Politics?

Shortly after Communism took over Czechoslovakia, a study entitled *Political Control of Czechoslovakia* by Dutch sociologist of Czechoslovak origin Dr.Ivan Gadourek examined the order of importance of the various spheres of social life in a communist country. This is the result: from the most important to the least important arranged in the order in which each of them influences and impacts others:

1. Politics
2. Economy
3. Science
4. Education
5. Recreation
6. Arts
7. Morals
8. Religion.

This represents a reversal of priorities when compared with the preceding era when life in the West was dominated by religion. The Faith permeated people's entire life: the hope of salvation and dread of damnation ([1]). Religion came first, politics last.

While Communism fell, its order of importance of various spheres of life survived in Western culture that aims to become the prevailing world culture. This is most apparent in the United States. Behavior, language and social life must be politically correct. ([2]) Wars are fought over ideologies and the resulting political and economic structures. Politically correct values dominating the United States are imposed on the rest of the world by international organizations and a globalized economy.

Seeking the Truth

Politics is the most influential factor in our present civilization. This is the reason why it is essential to understand it.

Knowledge presupposes understanding; understanding depends on explanation, explanation is an answer to the question "why"? "Why is something?" or "Why is something the way it is?"

Reason has only two explanatory principles: necessity or freedom. Either something exists necessarily because something else exists, it is the effect of a cause; or something exists, because it is wanted, it is a means to an end. The human mind has always used the one or other explanation intermittently; it has also endeavored always to convert all explanation to the one or other principle.

Being, in the sense of an object of knowledge and/or inquiry, can be understood as a creation of a free and almighty will pursuing its own (mostly unfathomable) purpose, as "nature" obeying and maintained by its Creator who is free to change His will at any time, but is consistent and true to Himself; He does not change His will arbitrarily.

Obedience can be exercised only by beings endowed with freedom, i.e., reason and volition. These are exhibited by men, but neither "nature" nor its parts exhibit reason and free will. This led some thinkers to conclude that reality, once it was given its impulse and its laws were given, is left to itself and is governed by necessity. The answer to the question "why" is to be looked for in the laws of necessity without direct recourse to God's will. This reasoning gave rise to science whose explanation of being as effects of causes, as causal chains, expanded the sphere of human freedom so fast and so widely that the understanding of reality was reduced to the one single principle necessity, of cause and effect. By an integral utilization of this principle also human freedom is explained away — action becomes identified with activity which in turn is explained as result (effect) of biological, environmental, race, class, social circumstances, causes which determine man's behavior and prove his freedom to be an illusion.

This simplification collapses on two accounts. (a) Although human behavior is influenced by cause and effect relationships, there always remains an unexplainable and unpredictable residuum so that the concepts of freedom of will and of purpose (even if disguised as "function") must be reintroduced. (b) The simplification also presupposes an infinite or a circular chain of causes and effects. Such explanation is logically false: it must postulate a "first cause" which means assuming an effect without a cause. It is therefore necessary to reach for the other explanatory principle, that of freedom: the so-called first cause is not an effect, but the result of an act of will.

CHAPTER 2

PURPOSIVE THINKING

An attempt to explain politics through necessity fails because choice is at the very heart of politics.

Understanding of politics is achieved by comprehending its purpose. In its essence, politics is action, i.e. an intended and rational sequence of acts derived from the selection and utilization of means towards the implementation of a chosen purpose. Action is attributed to (presupposes) a subject endowed with reason (acquisition of knowledge and evaluation) and volition (decision and choice).

Purpose and Means

This defines the two focal points of the purposive thinking: The *purpose (= end, goal or objective)* is a wanted phenomenon for whose attainment other phenomena (means) are wanted. Logically, there can be no purpose for whose realization ways are not sought, no means wanted. The *means* is a phenomenon wanted in order to attain another wanted phenomenon, namely the end (goal). The same object can be wanted both as a purpose, if another object is wanted for it attainment, and a means, if it is wanted in order to attain another object. Several purposes can be in two different relationships: They may be ordered *hierarchically* into a purposive system each of them wanted as means for the attainment of the next one, and thus forming a pyramid ending in a purpose which is wanted for itself and not as a means for another purpose. Such a purpose is the *primary purpose*, the other ones are *derived purposes*. The purposes may be in the relationship of *equality*, i.e., none of them is a means for any of the other ones; they compete for the means for their respective attainment. The relationship in which they are allocated the available means, is their *material solidarity* which constitutes their common superior *complex* purpose. A purpose whose fulfillment is wanted to the greatest extent (as much as possible) is a *maximum* purpose; if it is a complex purpose, it is an *optimum* purpose. (Among the most important actions of politics is the deciding of the material solidarity among competing maximum purposes.)

Purposive values are quantities of usefulness or harm; *usefulness* is the ability of an object to attain a purpose; *harm* is the quality of an object to dely, diminish or prevent the attainment of a purpose. They derive their quality from the purpose to which they relate (cultural values, religious values, family values, etc.) They are commonly designated as "good" or "bad" ; some goods can be "good" in relation to one purpose and simultaneously "bad" in relation to another purpose. The quest for an absolute purpose generating absolute good and absolute evil is the subject of Part B of this book.

The want of a means is a *need*. When projected unto the means, it becomes its *passive* need: it is not wanted by the means, but because the purpose is wanted. (A car needs fixing because the car is a means to achieve the purpose of reaching a destination, not because the car wants to be fixed.) The object of passive need(s) is the *object of care* of the purpose from which this need is derived. Among primary actions in politics is to decide which groups of people are to be objects of care and what their passive needs will be.

Such a group is constituted by either *similarity* or *complementarity* and represents a special case of a whole. No description or analysis of any group or any totality escapes generalizations; without abstraction and, to a greater degree, generalization any whole dissolves into its component singularities. Abstraction and generalization, however, cannot avoid exceptions and is therefore open to the reproach of inaccuracy and invalidity, possibly considered as unacceptable. But omitting certain aspects of reality by creating concepts, i.e., only abstractions and generalizations, allows the mind to organize perceptions and out of the chaos of ever changing singularities create knowledge enabling action. One type of generalizations attributes to all members of a group the qualities of the whole group. Generalizations of a different type do not deal with characteristics of a totality, but with its individual members: when many members of a group exhibit certain qualities or behavior, such qualities or behavior are attributed to all members of the group; such generalization can concern intellectual qualities, physical qualities or moral. Such generalizations have practical validity; they are based on probability and experience.

Subjects of Thought and Will

A purposive system, i.e., a pyramid derived from a primary purpose, presupposes its source: a subject endowed with freedom, i.e., with the faculties of reasoning and volition. In experience, such a subject is identical either with a human individual or with a group of human individuals organized for the pursuit of a common purpose.

Individuals

When the subject of freedom coincides with an individual, his primary purpose from which all his wants are derived, is the *purpose of personal subjective satisfaction, of happiness.*

Actions find their explanation in the fact that man uses reason to evaluate, select and utilize means towards the achievement of the purpose of subjective satisfaction, in order to attain *happiness*. This term is not used here to convey a state of bliss, pleasure or well-being; it explains the order of priorities and answers the question why does man prefer this action from another, this situation over another; The answer is because his choice brings him more satisfaction, makes him happier or diminishes his happiness less than another choice.

Man is endowed with a wide scope of potentialities which all have the inherent tendency to become actualities. His potentialities become actualities when and as he adjusts his environment — actively; he adjusts to the environment — unwillingly. The development of his physical potentialities has limits in the structure of his body, but his thoughts and will, especially will, does not know such limits and can encompass, not only all humanity and the entire world, but reaches out to the stars and seek, beyond time and space, the transcendental and eternal. The constraints imposed on these tendencies, the impossibility of actualizing all his potential, is felt by him as dissatisfaction.

The recognition of the resistance to his expansive tendencies does not in itself trigger his reactions, but the feeling of dissatisfaction does: he endeavors to eliminate his constraints, break the chains that hold him back. Some of such reactions are automatic, instinctive; others are rational: the removal of these elements that hem him in becomes his goal, his objective, a purpose for whose achievement he chooses means, and in order to obtain the means he selects other means, so that he constructs through his reason an entire hierarchically ordered purposive system in which he ascribes values to things and actions according to their ability to bring him closer to or to obstruct the achievement of his purpose.

The immediate means everybody has at his disposal are his actions. Here he finds the main obstacle in achieving fully the objective of happiness. Human potentialities and ambitions are such that they can never be completely actualized: because of their scope, but also because they contradict each other. People can have, at the same time, the potential to be poets or scientists, artists or bureaucrats, saints or evildoers. Everyone has the potential to be a saint or a sinner.

Man's actions are limited by his own abilities and external circumstances, especially by time and space. This limitation forces him to select, among his available means, those apt to bring him fullest and fastest satisfaction. But such choices necessarily entail forgoing others. Also among his conflicting potentialities, he must chose — select some and give up others.

To be able to make such choices he defines elements of his satisfaction and ranges them from the basic ones — those which are common to all human beings, such as food, shelter, health, procreation — to those which are his own and distinctive: art, love, religion, science, relaxation, entertainment. Having made these choices he must allocate to each of them a proportion of means which are at his disposal and/or those he can obtain. While many of the derived purposes are common to most people, the allocation of means to them differ; it is this allocation, this setting of preferences, which individualizes men's purposes of happiness.

The composition of the elements of satisfaction as well as the allocation of means to them is not rigid, it is a process of constant change, and because of the scope of human potentialities, the purpose of *happiness can never be fully and permanently achieved*. Therefore, man is fated to strive for achieving as much of the purpose of happiness as possible by achieving as much as possible of the various derived purposes; the purpose of happiness is thus an optimal purpose.

From Individuals to Organization

Because contents of many derived objectives are capable of being communicated, individual subjects of volition whose derived objectives are identical constitute the same movement, they can join their efforts on behalf of the shared objective, and in order to enhance their effectiveness agree to a *division of labor*. They become organized; division of labor creates *organization*.

The essence of organization is that its members give up a part of their freedom and subordinate a portion of their actions to the organization; they exchange a part of their freedom for achieving their common purpose better (faster, fuller). (3) This common goal is the nexus of the organization, its *raison d'etre*, is not subordinated to any other purpose; it is its primary purpose under which derived purposes/ means are arranged hierarchically on the basis of cost effectiveness; therefore organizations are sources of actions, as if endowed by their own reason and will, as subjects of freedom: making decisions, seeking means, evaluating them and utilizing them independently of their constituent members.

Strong individuals, strong personalities play a specific role In the process of creating and transforming a mood in a movement, and a movement in an organization a specific role is played by strong individuals, strong personalities.

The main characteristic of a *personality* is the recognition, positive or adverse popularity, the impact he makes on a more or less restricted circle of people, due to an outstanding performance in a field of human endeavor: Al Capone in crime, Mother Theresa in charity. The status of "personality" does not indicate the personal or moral qualities of an individual; actually, many historical personalities behaved cravenly in their private life. At present, personalities are often created not so much by their outstanding performance as by the notoriety manufactured for them by the media. The recognition of individuals as personalities is not identical with affection.

With recognition goes authority. Authority consists of an individual's ability to have his opinion accepted as valid or his behavior as a model not so much for its contents as for the fact that they come from a personality. The root of authority can be rational, traditional or charismatic. A rational basis of authority is the fact that its bearer has been right so often in the past and that his knowledge is known to be so extensive, that his opinions are adopted on the basis of trust and respect towards his qualities, without a need to be substantiated in any other way. The traditional authority is derived from the fact that its author holds a position, exercises certain function within long established structures of society and acts within the limits of such function. The inertia of society and of people supports and accepts such authority more or less automatically as given until it causes or is convincingly accused of causing significant harm to society or individuals. Charismatic authority stems from the conviction and assertion of a personality that he is the executor of a higher, transcendent mandate, of an imperative of supranational forces: an inner voice, God's revelation, historic mission. Such a conviction endows its bearer with a complete devotion to his mission, a devotion which borders on fanaticism and includes disdain towards existing opinions, institutions and authorities. A charismatic person transfers this attitude to his followers, "disciples", i.e., persons whom he convinces about his mandate and mission and who, therefore, accept his authority even if its consequences imply the dismantling of the given order and the creation of a new one. As the charismatic movement develops, it becomes institutionalized and bureaucratic, which leads to a limitation of the charismatic leader's influence. ("a revolution devours its children").

According to the nature of its primary purpose — or of the movement that gave it birth — an organization can be charitable, cultural, physical education, pro-abortion, homosexual, religious, or other. Each of them can then become a part of a compatible movement, a charitable organization can belong to the movement for sexual freedom, a cultural organization of a movement for human rights in Nigeria, etc. Therefore, an organization can join a movement, and can also join a related organization as soon as it subordinates itself, in a certain area, to the decisions of such organization. It behaves like an independent subject of volition and reasoning independent, divorced from the individual purposes of happiness of the organization's members because they have given up a part of their freedom to the pursuit of its purpose.

Normativity, the relationship of superiority of the organization and subordination of members, distinguishes an organization from a movement. An individual can simply join a movement; but he must be accepted into an organization. A movement is spontaneous and improvised, in an organization, members must accept its structures. In a movement, leaders arise; in an organization they are selected by fixed rules. In a movement, each member is active where and when he likes. In an organization, members act in the manner, time and place assigned to them by the organization as if they were subordinated to the organization's will whose expressions become, for them, norms whose duty-bound subjects they become voluntarily, as indicated above, or sometimes involuntarily if the organization has means to threaten them or inflict them harm. Such pressure exerted by economic or other means in order to enforce obedience to a non-legal norm and outside the law, is *terror*.

Politics and Its Subjects

Subjective satisfaction (happiness) is not identical with selfishness. No one is an island. Man is a social being, a being for whom presence of others of the same species is the natural environment. Therefore his unhappiness (including absence of happiness) can be caused also by the situation of a group of people with whom he identifies. The group whose betterment is the purpose man as the subject of freedom may, but does not have to, be the group to which he belongs; the reason of dissatisfaction of an American can be, for instance, the existence of slavery in the Sudan or suppression of human rights in China.

In both cases, a certain change in the situation of the given group becomes a condition of his satisfaction (a secondary purpose of the purpose of happiness)., and because such a change brings the subject of will closer to his satisfaction, it is, in his value system, an improvement. *Situation* means in this connection external conditions and/or the psychophysical status of the members of the given group and their mutual relationship, its internal structure. It can be, therefore, concluded as a general rule, that one of the conditions (one of the secondary purposes of man's supreme objective) is *the betterment of the situation of a certain human group;* such group becomes his *object of care*. The removal of a danger threatening such group falls also under the term "betterment".

It is impossible to communicate, to measure or compare the magnitude of happiness due to diversity in the composition of individual purposes of happiness, and poets as well as scientists have tried this in vain. It is however possible to communicate its parts, its elements; every person is able to name at least some derived objectives whose achievement is necessary for his satisfaction, as well as means towards their attainment (a means to achieve satisfaction is to assuage hunger; a means to assuage hunger is food; a means to obtain food is money; the means to obtain money is work, the means to obtain work is education, etc.). The contents of such derived purposes are capable of being objectively communicated to others so that they are able to recognize if they are a part of their purpose of happiness too. Individuals who share identical objectives, constitute a *movement.* A movement derives its character from the common derived objectives its members share, such as an ideological, religious, social, ecological etc. movement, reflecting the unlimited variety of human spirit and human appetites. Within a movement, the causes of dissatisfaction and the means towards their elimination are discussed, articulated and aggregated. From diffused and unformed opinions held by individual members of the movement, evolve specific and exact demands (articulation) and the various articulated demands are joined (aggregated) into common goals which become the program of the movement.

Thus the derived purpose of "betterment of the situation of a certain group" becomes articulated from the primary purposes of happiness as a category which includes politics; however, "betterment of the situation of a certain group" is not yet politics. It is a part of the striving for satisfaction, a part which is objectively understandable and which an individual can share with other individuals and organizations. Together with them, he then seeks and utilizes hierarchically lower means towards its implementation.

"Betterment of the situation of certain group of people" as purpose is the logical category immediately superior to the term "politics" and does not define politics because it is common to other actions or activities. A person or an organization can strive for the betterment of the situation of a certain group of people which is the object of his or its interest, individually, through own actions, or jointly with others, but this goal does not make their actions politics. To attain the definition of politics, it is necessary to identify a specific quality which distinguishes politics from other actions aiming at the betterment of the situation of a certain group of people, such as education, welfare, protection of environment, electrification, equalization of incomes, building an army, participation in international organizations.

Ultima Ratio — the State

When those who pursue these goals realize they are unable to achieve them through their own resources, individual or organized, they seek the utilization of an institution which does posses such resources. This institution is the *state* and its organs, because the state has gradually concentrated so many instruments of power as to become sovereign, i.e. on a certain territory its will is commanding and the state is able to make it prevail against any other will. The will of the state is superior to the will of any real and logical subjects of will within the scope of its power, and therefore becomes, in the state's relation to them, a *norm*, namely a *legal norm* which differs from all other norms because *it can be systematically enforced.*

Political action consists in subjects of will (individuals or organizations) striving for the implementation of their political objectives through the utilization of the power of the state because their own means are insufficient and because the implementation necessitates constraint of others which only the power of the state can provide — or at least they came to the conclusion that they can so implement their objective more easily, with less effort or less sacrifices than those that would be required for its implementation by their own means. Usually the changes intended by a political program are so far-reaching that they involve structural changes of the entire society dominated by the state, and therefore the utilization of state power is indispensable. The subjects of political will recognize that the most efficient, least costly way of achieving their political objective is to participate *in the creation of the will of the state* as a means towards the achievement of their political purpose. For politics, it is characteristic that it strives for participation in the *directing of public affairs.* A bureaucratic administration of decisions made by the state is an act of obedience, of subordination, and does not fall under the concept of politics.

Clearly, politics is distinguished from other actions pursuing the same purpose by the choice of means — the utilization of the power of the state through participation in directing public affairs. This is the specific that makes it possible to narrow down politics within the wider category of "betterment of the situation of a certain group of people." *Politics is actions whose purpose is the betterment of the situation of a certain group of people through participation in the directing of public affairs.*

Understanding politics requires examination of its constituent elements: (1) to determine the group of people whose interest is served (object of care), (2) to define the contents of betterment, (3) to utilize state power for its implementation, (4) to obtain a share in the directing of public affairs, (5) to select the ways in which state power is to be utilized, and (6) to utilize it properly.

Subjects of will that are constituted to pursue objective goals of a non-political nature (associations, enterprises, trade unions, churches) become politically acting subjects insofar as they strive for a share in the directing of public affairs as a means towards achievement of their non-political goals. They become members of that political movement whose program coincides most closely with their own purpose (for instance business associations support parties promoting the free market system, unions support political parties stressing social issues). They may even become a part of a political organization.

CHAPTER 3

POLITICAL ORGANIZATION

Politics is actions whose purpose is the betterment of the situation of a certain group of people through participation in the directing of public affairs.

Political activities fall into two categories: one has as its purpose *attaining* (or maintaining) a share of the central means of politics — the share in the directing of public affairs, the other has as its purpose the *utilization* of this means, i.e., the implementation of the betterment of the situation of a certain group of people. Attaining a share in the directing of public affairs and the implementation of the political program are two different purposes which generate two separate systems of derived objectives ascribed to two different subjects of will. Providing the general means of politics is the role of *political organizations;* the utilization of this means — the implementation of the betterment of the situation of a group of people belongs to the *state.* A political organization aims at sharing in the power of the state — this is its primary purpose, actions aimed at implementation of changes without the intervention of state power would not be politics but self-help. Therefore, political organizations do not have their own organs for their program's implementation. The division of labor among members of a political organization, their relationships, their actions make sense only in view of their common goal of attaining the ability to use the coercive power of the state and/or of its autonomous units

A political organization builds its structure as a means of accomplishing its purpose. By following its goal of attaining a share in state power, a political organization selects secondary, tertiary, etc. objectives, and creates appropriate organs for their utilization. Actions of a political organization are not determined by its structure, on the contrary, its structure serves its activities. Structure then becomes one of its instruments, a means in the political struggle and is therefore contingent upon the environment in which the political organization acts (the nature of the state, the structure of society) and upon the means the political organization selects to attain its goal (bombs or ballots).

The organizational structure of political organizations tends to be somewhat vague, the functions of its organs not strictly defined, statutes formulated in generalities or not at all. This applies especially to new political organizations and to those created under pressure. While vagueness brings obvious disadvantages, in certain situations it may be beneficial: it may enhance flexibility and facilitate adjustment to changed circumstances.

A political organization selects its structure to suit its strategy and tactics, its strategy and tactics are determined by changes in the circumstances in which it operates and the changes require the creation or adaptation of the organization's organs. Organizing is thus a precondition of its activities. Because of this subordination of organization to changing strategies, tactics and conditions this section mentions only functions which are indispensable to all political organizations; the variables will be dealt with in connection with the forms of political struggle which produces them, as they appear in various types of government under various operational modes.

Decision making

The goal of a political organization can be defined also as gaining power in order to acquire the ability for implementation of its plans about how to improve the life of society. Those who formulate the image of an improved society and how to attain and use public power *create the will* of the political organization. According to the manner in which this process takes place, the will of the organization is created autocratically or democratically.

Autocracy ("normative heteronomy") is justified either on the basis of a special quality of the decision makers ("leadership belongs to the best"), or by demands of efficiency (an organization executing orders of one leader is more efficient than an organization which at every step must expend a part of its energy and time to obtain a decision from members).

The key question of an autocratic organization is to determine which person or group of persons is "the best." The answer of this question is not left to members; it is decided on the basis of qualifications which do not depend on the will of members. Historically, such standards were origin (reigning family, aristocracy), authority received supernaturally (vision, mission by a supernatural being), in modern times mostly scientific knowledge.

The *democratic forming of will* ("normative autonomy") is justified either on the basis of a fundamental equality of the decision makers ("inalienable human rights and civil liberties") or by demands on correctness of decisions ("more heads are better than one"). In practice, members mostly decide between several opinions and/or persons without proposing their own opinions or candidacy; they entrust the leadership of the organization to those who represent most closely the membership's opinions and desires. The will of members can be expressed either directly (voting, elections) or indirectly (by electing delegates who conceivably elect other delegates). The more levels of delegation there are, the lesser is the influence of members on the final decision. (A memorable example of such process is the "democratic centralism" of the communist parties.)

The system of delegation (indirect democracy) allows a *combination of autocratic and democratic principles* by allocating a certain fraction of delegates to be elected and another fraction to be nominated by the existing leadership or by granting to members of the present leadership the automatic right to be delegates. Another option is to entrust the selection of delegates (or some delegates) to special bodies that are not under control of the membership. Justification for these combinations are the necessity to preserve a continuity of the organization and the fact that, in large organizations, the members do not have access to knowledge sufficient to make an informed decision.

The manner in which the will of the organization is formed is expressed in the organizational statutes (which may be written or unwritten, gleaned from practice and tacitly accepted and observed as normative). Because political organizations are occasionally somewhat amorphous, the functions of their various organs are not clear and binding and change with changing circumstances and needs, *actual practice* is often more reliable than written rules when judging their degree of democracy.

The content of the will of a political organization is relatively stable because those who harbor radically different opinions and objectives join other political organizations or form new ones. The inertia of a political organization brings it into conflict with changes caused by the development of society which necessitate changes in its existing program and traditional behavior. This tension produces in many political organizations various tendencies, and sundry components of the organization pursue goals not identical with the purpose established by the organization as a whole. Groups that pursue diverging opinions within the same political organization, are called *factions.*

Such disunity does not necessarily endanger the cohesion of a political organization insofar as it does not affect principles and overall political postulates on which the organization is based. It may be formalized by a *federal structure* of a political organization. Various tendencies and interests within the organization have their own organization, remain within the common organization and are represented in its organs entrusted by formulating its will, with the provision that they will submit to the decision of the pertinent organs in their actions outside the organization. Another feature of a federal structure of a political organization is that it allows collective membership of non-political organizations which, in pursuing their own specific goals, nevertheless have demands on the government, demands that are identical with the program of a given political organization. Such organizations may be granted representation in the will-forming organs of the political organization proportional to their contribution to the common goal, (an arrangement which enables the political organization to adjust more flexibly to a changing political environment and extends its influence beyond the limits of its own members and/or movement. (The presence of trade unions in the British Labor Party is an example.)

If the divergence of elements within a political organization is such that it cannot be reconciled within a common framework or if a faction, part, or member of a political organization takes action against the stated program of the organization, it leaves the political organization or is expelled.

Propaganda

Propagating its program is an indispensable component of the activity of a political organization. It serves to gain adherents to its political movement and to enlist members into its organs.

Propaganda is aimed primarily at the factors which it considers as decisive and which the political organization expects to open to it access to public power; these factors can be individuals or groups. In a military dictatorship, the political organization tries to gain supporters for its goals among key military personnel, in a democracy, among voters. Its propaganda either tries to convince its targets that the implementation of its program will aid them in attaining their own goals, or it tries to change the targets' opinions and objectives (the contents of their purpose of happiness) so that they will find the implementation of its political program as useful. The common denominator of propaganda is the *creation or utilization of a dissatisfaction with the present or impending (future) situation of society.* This process of fomenting dissatisfaction is called "raising the awareness" of the targets; subjects of will that do not share the intended dissatisfaction and the political program to its termination, are dubbed "lacking awareness"; those who share it, are "aware" or "concerned," terms which in themselves have propaganda value.

Spreading a political movement and propagandizing a political organization is done in two forms: political and non—political.

The *political* way of propaganda consists of open promotion of the political organization; the organization openly proclaims its political nature, publicizes its program, exalts its leaders and demands a share in the state power.

In the *non-political way,* the organization does not act in its own name, it acts through the intermediary of its members and strives to influence others by their actions; its members or adherents represent and defend the objectives of its program on the basis of scientific, moral, religious, economic and/or other arguments and postulates.

The most impotent means of spreading a political movement are the spoken word, print and electronic media (TV and broadcasting) which put at the disposal of a political organization a new method of influencing the public combining the collective approach with individuality (see Appendix 1).

A part of the manipulation of public opinion is the use of slogans, symbols and terminology with a value laden content that appeal more to the sentimental, rather than the rational, side of human psychology, endeavor to change the relationship between the message and its recipient from freedom and reasoning to cause and effect, from thought to reflex. This "bending" of the human mind has lately resulted in a systematic and scientific invention of terminology which introduces new words for existing thought contents so that their traditional positive connotations are changed into negative ones and vice versa, and intentional provocation of opponents introduces formerly unacceptable concepts into the public discourse.

Financing

An indispensable part of actions of a political organization is economic activity which provides material means for its functioning, especially finances. Various possible sources of financing a political organization are membership contributions and contributions of supporters, profit from its own enterprises, assistance from public funds, means extorted from subjects who are not members of the organization nor of its movement.

The first source comprises all goods donated to the political party to defray the expenses of its political activities, such as regular membership fees, admission fees to political and entertainment events organized by the political organization, and occasional gifts. Income from membership fees is significant only if the organization has mass membership so that the total is significant even if the individual fees are low. Deserving of special attention is financing through donations by members and supporters, because they may deeply influence the policies of the organization, as its organs deciding on the organization's program and operations, take into account if this or that decision would not bring about a withholding of further financial support, and thus weaken the organization.

The second source of financing is return of business enterprises owned by the organization. Business enterprises owned by the political organization decrease its dependence on outside influences and represent a strong support in times of political reversals because they are able to provide jobs and income for members, and thus preserve cadres necessary for new expansion.

Financing of political organizations from public funds has a twofold, radically different character. On one hand, its purpose can be to eliminate or limit the influence of money on the formation of political will by prohibiting or limiting contributions from private sources and substituting for them contributions from public funds granted according to an objective standard, for instance according to the number of votes received or number of members. On the other hand, the purpose of financing from public treasury may be used as a means to grant advantages to political organizations which share in the government, against those that are excluded (the opposition). The transfer of public funds to political organizations is done either openly (for instance contributions for political campaigns based on law), or indirectly (in the form of grants from various budget appropriations for cultural, security and other purposes).

Finally, a political organization may obtain funds for its activities by pressuring vulnerable subject by threats of harm or by harming the attainment of their objectives. Among its methods are intimidation, blackmail, hostage taking, theft, robberies and other violent acts.

Managing Legislators

The penultimate purpose of a political organization is to transform its will into the will of the state, i.e., into laws. Because legislative power belongs to the state, organs of a political organization cannot make laws. It is possible, however, and from the political organization's view desirable, that legislators create laws with a content that implements the program and demands of a political organization. Therefore, the political organization must make sure that they do so.

In order to ensure the identity of acts of legislators with its program, a political organization creates special bodies which prepare the material and proposals for legal norms (study groups) and joint committees or commissions of its representatives in the legislative or self-governing organs of the state and of the leading members of its own (territorially, materially or functionally) corresponding organs. These bodies discuss goals to be pursued by the state or its autonomous units and formulate their implementation through legislation in ways that conform with the program of the organization. The solution of public problems is thus not left to the legislators alone and pertinent organs of the political organization charged with the implementation of its will watch that the actions of its representatives do not deviate from its political program and that their position is united and consistent, i.e., a political organization assures that, in their performance of their legislative function, its representatives and adherents act as its subordinate organs. This dependence of legislators on their political organization is frequently resented by them and their groupings (clubs, caucuses) strive to reverse their relationships: from being instruments of a political organization to the organization being their own instrument.

Political organizations have seldom legal means by which to force their representatives into obedience. On the contrary, the law often guarantees and orders legislators to act independently. Political organizations are therefore limited to rely on factual power. The most frequent reason why legislators follow instructions of their political organization is that an organization which caused or helped them to gain their position can also cause or help them to lose it (if not immediately, then later), and expelling a member will mostly achieve this goal. Other non-legal or illegal means are economic, psychological and physical pressure which, in terrorist organizations, includes killing the disobedient member and/or members of his family.

Some political organizations create a specific organ to settle disputes between members, between a member and the organization or between its factions. This organ has a judicial function: it examines whether the objects of a complaint or dispute have violated certain norms, especially acted against the program or interest of the organization by infringing law or decency.

Political Organizations and Personalities

Political personalities are individuals who achieved outstanding results in politics.

A political movement arises from a reaction to an unsatisfactory situation and aims at its correction, i.e., betterment. The translation of such a mood or movement in a clear political program and the choice of means of its implementation, and its transformation into a political organization require the intervention of human reason of which only an exceptional individual is capable. During this evolution of a diffuse mood to a defined political purpose, its initiator impresses on it certain personal marks, his individual contribution towards the expression of commonly felt and objectively existing needs. However, his true function is that of a catalyst, a "spokesman for the times" who expresses their atmosphere, gives voice to their ambience. Such a personality rises to the top of a political party or creates his own, and his rise is the faster the better he articulates the needs of his time. He becomes a political leader.

The other type of a political personality differs from the spokesman of his times by not articulating the needs of his era, but by anticipating a coming era; he is ahead of his time, predicts, anticipates or prepares the future. Such a "prophetic personality" exerts a long term impact which depends on the celerity and accuracy with which the development of society corresponds with his analyses.The fate of such individuals, political and non-political, is usually a tragic one— they pay for their uniqueness by crucifixion, execution, incarceration or rejection. In political parties, they are usually the voice of reform, innovation, and often in opposition. This type of political personality becomes a political leader only, if and when events confirm his anticipation, if and when the means recommended by him are accepted, and if a personality of the preceding type does not arise to assume leadership by appropriating his ideas and implementing them when the times are ripe for them, possibly in an amended form.

There is no inevitable, necessary relationship between personalities and politics or political organizations. When such a relationship exists, it is not due to the fact that an individual qualifies as a personality, but it is created by a *free decision* of a personality to get involved in politics, to influence the direction of public affairs.

This decision is of two kinds. It can be evoked by the concern that those who direct public affairs, do not pay enough attention to knowledge and convictions the personality has, for instance certain scientific discoveries. Ecologists arrive to certain conclusions on which activities are permissible if life or nature on the planet can survive; eugenicist determine what health and mental qualities people should have to be allowed to live; environmentalists pressure for measures to prevent the imminent arrival of an ice age or greenhouse effect, nuclear scientists wish to direct military strategy, and so on. Likewise do economists, sociologists, educationists, behavioral scientist and experts in other sciences. Such personalities surround themselves with people of the same opinion and originate or join movements of identical or similar convictions. These are breeding grounds for pressure groups which enter politics to promote their conclusions and to apply or enforce them through sharing in the directing of public affairs. Such an interaction is not limited to personalities of science, although it is the most frequent one in modern times; it applies also to personalities of other spheres of culture: arts, religion, sports. This type of a relationship of a personality with political organizations, mainly political parties, can be classified as *parasitic* because he uses political organizations to attain goals which by their origin and character have nothing in common with its existing program. An extreme case of this approach is the creation of a political organization or party whose program centers on the implementation of such personality's demands (e.g., the secret societies of the Enlightenment era).

A different type of relations between a personality and a political organization arises, if the personality decides to support a political program for its contents to such an extent that he is willing to assist it by lending his authority to its efforts. Such cooperation takes on many forms: behind the scenes or participation in public appearances, in fund raising, in demonstrations and protests, signing petitions. (Film stars march in demonstrations, top performers in sports join financial drives, prominent scientists write articles or appear on TV programs to advocate the party of their choice.) The assumption here is that the public will extend the respect for a personality's authority gained in his special field also to the field of politics. This opinion is erroneous, but nevertheless widespread; many citizens who respect the authority of a person, for instance, in sports or in film, assume that a political program cannot be bad if such an authority supports it. This relationship between a personality and a political organization can be described as *symbiotic*.

Elitism is an attitude of personalities aiming at implementing a program of a transformation of society mainly through bypassing the political process as well as direct involvement in political organizations. This is the latest non-democratic approach to governing (see Chapter 7 and 22).

CHAPTER 4

POLITICAL PROGRAM

Its Nature

A political organization is a phenomenon whose parts are formed into a whole by its purpose which must be generally understandable, because it is on the basis of this purpose that a political organization attracts supporters, enlists members and acts, i.e., acquires means and utilizes them. This common purpose is expressed in its program and this program is the *source of the cohesion* of its parts; therefore the program of a political organization must contain the basic elements of the definition of politics, i.e., at least:

the purpose of the organization's politics, i.e., the description of the situation it aims to achieve;

its *object*, i.e., its object of care which is identical with the group of people whose betterment the political organization pursues;

its *means*, i.e., an overview of measures the state should take in order to achieve the desired goal.

The political program is frequently accompanied by enumeration of principles of a normative moralizing nature which are supposed to justify and explain the demands of the program. If the political movement whose product the political organization is, originated from an ideological movement (religious, philosophical, scientific), the political organization underpins its program by the reasoning that preceded its formation and which it accepts as its *ideology* or, if it is sufficiently systematic and extensive, as its *world view* which again, according to its character, may be religious, philosophical, scientific.

In addition to this *ideological* program, a political organization must also state the means by which it intends to obtain (or extend or maintain, which means the same thing in the context of political struggle) participation in the government. The sum of these means constitutes its *practical* program which also determines the political organization's structure.

The ideological as well as the practical programs frequently include postulates which are impossible to achieve or are mutually incompatible, either because of insufficient and uncritical reasoning or intentionally in order to attract supporters — they are only slogans. Therefore actions of a political organization are not infrequently inconsistent with its proclaimed goals.

Political programs are not always formulated exactly and at one time — amendments, additions and interpretations, sometimes contradictory, may be presented in various speeches or publications. Moreover, they are affected by the evolution of the ideological movement in which they are rooted. Notwithstanding these uncertainties the program is the reason for the existence of a political organization and the process of formulating its program is identical with the process of the organization's forming its political will.

Its Goal

The purpose of politics is the betterment of the situation of a certain group of people.

In order to be able to recognize "betterment," it is necessary to know not only the present situation but also to know what is the ideal, the goal pursued by the subject of volition, in the given case by the political organization. Only then is it possible to qualify as "betterment" any change which brings closer the willed ideal or goal, and a change in the opposite direction as deterioration.

The term "betterment" does not indicate what are the concrete contents of the objective, how does the pursued ideal look. The usage of such a term in the definition indicates that views about the situation to be achieved vary. Politically active subjects harbor different, even contradictory ideas about the arrangement of the society which is their object of care; nevertheless, their actions are politics insofar as they pursue the attainment of their sundry ideals through participation in government. They may go in different directions, but they all go "forward," all pursue "progress," they all agree in pursuance of a better future, a better society, a better world, but this agreement is meaningless unless they fail to agree also in the concrete contents of their respective visions.

Nevertheless, there are certain elements of the "betterment" common to all political organizations because all their programs are, in the last instance, derived from the common goal of all people, namely the goal of happiness: man wants to be satisfied as much as possible. And man will not be satisfied until he adjusts to his ideas also society with its elements: culture and civilization, and extends them to other societies or at least does secure his own society from changes caused by some other society.

Society's ability to impose one's own arrangement on the environment, i.e., on its own members and on members of other societies, is its *power*. The sum of material conditions securing the growth, the expansion of its nature, is its *wealth*. There is an interrelationship between power and wealth: power is the expression of a society's ability to organize its own material conditions, i.e., to ensure its own wealth; wealth as the sum of material conditions supporting the development of a society, contributes to its ability to impose on other societies its own goals, i.e., to an increase of power. In this sense, the increase of power and wealth is included in every primary political goal. There is, however a difference in a political goal which aims at the increase of power and wealth of the *society as such*, or the increase of wealth and power of its *individual members*. These two versions of the term "betterment of the situation of a group of people" are not mutually exclusive, but they are not identical and could be contradictory.

Its Object of Care

Purpose of politics is the betterment of the situation of a *certain group of people*. The targeted "group of people" is the object of care of politically active subjects and must be identified in the program of political organizations.

Individuals form groups on the basis of most varied sources of cohesion: causal (territory, origin), intentional (interests) and normative (religion) and such groups and individuals form other groups which sometimes overlap, sometimes are mutually exclusive. Because there is a presumption of free will of political subjects, any group of people can be their object of care. In practice, only groups that have considerable importance for a larger number of politically active subjects (individuals or organizations) become the object of care of politics. As the situations of societies change, the interests of their components shift, and therefore also politics' objects of care change. As a general rule, however, it can be stated that objects of care of political actions are those groups to which politically active subjects belong.

Empirically, the following groups of people have been or are objects of care in the recent past and present:

A *class* is a plurality of people who have the same relationship towards the means of production. In modern society, the following classes are objects of care: The working class (proletariat) are people who do not own means of production and are constrained to making a living by working with them for wages, and *bureaucracy* whose members work with them indirectly in administration and organization for salaries. The name of *bourgeoisie* was given to those who own the means of production. They are subdivided into two groups: those who own so many means of production that it frees them from the need to work with them personally, the *capitalists*, and those who must work with them personally (*small entrepreneurs*). People who control factually the means of production without owning them are the *managerial class*. This class exists in all economic systems. An intangible means of production is expertise; those who possess it, form the knowledge class. Identical relationship towards means of production is the basis of identical interests which clash with those of other groups. Political terminology accepted for this clash is the term "class struggle."

Nations arose historically through suppression of weaker biological groups and their intermixing. Biological groups are those whose source of cohesion are common inherited qualities (genes) — tribes, clans, families. The molding of these groups into a nation took place under strong pressure of the state power used by or created by the dominant group, through which it assimilated the subdued groups. The permanence and stability of this new formation grew by suppression of societal organs of the subdued groups and their replacement by social organs of the new common society. Because this process progressed with strong participation of incipient state power, there arose a connection between state and nation, statehood and nationhood. In some cultural areas, this connection became so strong that the concept of nationality merged with the concept of citizenship; in other areas, these two concepts are strictly separated, even mutually hostile. During years of togetherness biological groups, originally bound together only by the rule of one of them, developed common cultural qualities (primarily common language, common religion, common traditions, common history), and this common cultural environment gradually became the main source of cohesion of its various parts and overshadowed the primary roots, namely the belonging to the constituent biological groups. A nation endures as long as the influx of new biological and cultural elements does not change substantially its spiritual environment. In view of their biological foundations, nations have endured as the most indestructible among all human groups.

Humanity is a biological group whose source of cohesion is its members' belonging to genus Homo sapiens. It has increasingly become the object of care in modern politics.

The *state* in this connection (in its sociological meaning) is a group of persons having rights and duties stemming from the same legal system. There is some uncertainty whether this definition includes citizens of a state living in the territory of another state.

A *church* is a community of people believing into same norms of behavior proceeding from a transcendental normgiver, and practicing their organized observance.

The group whose betterment is the purpose of the subject of will may, but does not have to, be the group to which he belongs; the reason of dissatisfaction of an American can be, for instance, the existence of slavery in the Sudan or suppression of human rights in China.

One result of the maximizing nature of the purpose of happiness ("as much as possible") is also that the behavior or existence of another group can be and often is an obstacle to the betterment of the situation of the the group which is the object of care; therefore the objective of betterment of its situation may include and often includes deterioration of the situation of another group; this, however, is not the main purpose of the subject of will, it is a means towards its achievement.

Relatively new are political movements whose object of care are *non-human* — some types of animals, plants or all of nature. As long as their demands are included in programs of political organizations, they may be subsumed under the general term of "betterment of the conditions of a certain group of people" in the sense that they are a part of the ideal how human society should behave.

State as General Means of Politics

The behavior of subjects endowed with freedom is directed by norms which belong to various normative systems: by religious, moral, legal norms, traditions, customs, social conventions and other. Among them, law (in the sense of the entirety of legal norms) differs from the others by its consistency and enforceability; therefore it is the general means chosen by political organizations for the realization of their vision of a better society.

The law is a consistent, complete, objective, understandable, codified and logically arranged system of duties. The term "right" in the legal sense denotes only either someone's duty to act in favor the holder of the right (entitlement) or a duty of others to abstain from interfering with certain actions of the holder of a right — a "right" without a corresponding duty is an empty symbol.

Constitution

All legal norms derive their validity from a *constitution*. The constitution is the highest legal norm which does not derive its validity from any higher legal norm; this does not exclude its claim to derive from a norm of another normative system: morals, religion or custom, nor a possibility to be judged (as good or bad) from the viewpoint of such norms. By the act of creating a constitution, its authors create at the same time the first organ of a state — the constitutional body (assembly, convention).

Since the constitution and its origin are not the fulfillment of another, higher legal obligation, they must be understood as an act of will of the state, i.e., a purpose attributed to the state. In this sense, the term "state" covers a number of political organizations which agreed among themselves (or one political organization which decided) how to impose their will on the inhabitants of a certain territory by means of a legal system, and what form the legal system should have in order to accomplish their political purpose, i.e. their concept of a "good" society. By creating a constitution they simultaneously create the state; the precondition of this action is of course that they posses a power sufficient to enforce the norms of the constitution at least until the state creates its own executive organs which will enforce its will, its legal system beginning with the provisions of the constitution through the various layers of norms (laws, regulations) down to an individual judgment of a duly constituted court or a fine imposed by a policeman for a traffic violation. *A constitution is the expression of a sovereign (i.e., not subject to a law) and enforceable will of a political organization or organizations in what way they will create legal duties binding the population of a territory.* According to international custom, a government of such a territory is considered as legitimate as and when it succeeds in enforcing its will on a firmly determined territory for a longer period of time.

If a constitution is created by several political organizations it is necessary to ascertain to what extent their individual programs will be expressed by the constitution. The outcome depends mainly on two determinants: *the comparative power relationship between the politi-*

cal organizations authoring the constitution, and the *extent of resistance* to be expected from non-participating political organizations and the population. Within this framework, the programs for the maximum betterment of a certain group of people of the various political organizations will be implemented by law in proportions whose relationship will form the material solidarity of the new primary optimal (complex) purpose ascribed to the state.

The constitution expresses the existing power relationships, but also contains provisions how their changes can (or cannot) be reflected in the creation of the state's will. As soon as this agreement, i.e., the constitution, is concluded, the political organizations that authored it become immediately subject to its provisions and must submit to them.

Constitution's provisions on what should be (within the limits of its validity) considered as legal, are of two types: material and formal. *Material* provisions list the contents which legislation must or must not have and the contents of duties the state may or may not impose. *Formal* provisions determine procedures that must be observed for legal norms to be valid; among them the most important are those regulating valid ways of changing the constitution. Each legal system contains rules according to which it may be changed, and describes the organs authorized to do so as well as the related procedures. Norms not issued according to the provisions of formal law are legally invalid; norms issued according to the provisions of formal law, are legally valid and protected by the entire force of the state.

It is mainly the type of constitution which determines the type of the state, whether it be democratic or autocratic, federalist or centralistic, based on free enterprise and market economy or on central planning and public ownership, as well as the proportions in which these various options are combined. As long as the constitution and the law are observed, the state is a *lawful* state. An entirely different situation arises if any political organization or their combination attains so much power that it is able to enforce its will even against the state's will as expressed in its constitution and law — this is an *unlawful* state which has lost its sovereignty in favor of the dominant political organization(s). In such a state, law has only a secondary, supplemental validity — where the organs of the ruling political organization do not impose directly their own will. In the present, also other actors than political organizations manage to share or outstrip the state's sovereignty (see Chapters 7 and 11).

As the foundation of the state and source of its legal system, it is desirable that its constitution be stable. Formal law underpins the stability of the constitution by provisions which make its changes more difficult than changes of other legal provisions, and surround them by stricter demands. Although important, such provisions in themselves cannot cloth the constitution with the moral authority it needs as the keystone of the entire system; such authority is gained by tradition (long duration of the constitution), and where tradition is lacking, legal continuity, which means a uninterrupted legally valid derivation from the original constitution of the state.

The Law

One characteristic of law is its consistency. A legal system evolves by imposition of new duties and obliteration of old duties.. This takes place by creation of norms which derive their validity from immediately superior, higher norms. The validity of legal norms is equal; there are no legal norms more or less valid than others, but (like purposive systems they reflect) they are hierarchically ordered. *Higher norms* have a wider scope, i.e., they create duties for a larger number of subjects (individual or corporate subjects) and their contents are of a more general nature; *lower norms* have a narrower scope (fewer subjects of duty), and their contents are more specific. The lowest norms are *concrete norms*: creation of a duty with concrete specifications imposed on a concrete subject. Usage has created specific designations for the various levels of the legal pyramid; using them produces the following picture:

constitution
constitutional laws
laws
government regulations
regulations of lower self-governing bodies
court findings and administrative decisions.

A legal system thus formulates logical chains derived from the highest norm (constitution) all the way to the lowest norm. Because all legal norms have the same validity, even the lowest norms are enforced by the full power of the state.

Organized enforceability is the second characteristic of law. Almost all legal norms, and especially concrete norms are sanctioned, i.e., their violation produces punishment. Punishment is a harm inflicted on the punished subject. Law imposes on state and other public organs the duty to inflict on those who fail to fulfill their duty, a harm on otherwise protected goods, such as life, health, freedom and property. Only exceptionally are certain norms unprotected by sanctions; their violation has only the consequence that acts so performed are legally invalid. The special position of legal norms among other norms ordering the life of societies (moral, religious, tradition, custom) and the key role of the legislative power in creating laws is substantially different from other means to better the situation of groups of people, and its use therefore distinguishes politics from other endeavors pursuing the same objective.

A political victory is not safe unless it is consolidated by the imposition of a legal system which corresponds to the ideals (objectives) of the victorious political organization(s).

The territory on which a state's legal system is valid, is the territory belonging to the state, its borders are determined by the validity of the applicable law. The inhabitants of the territory are the state's subjects. ([4]) In general, states enforce the validity of their laws on all persons, citizens or not, during a stay on their respective territories (the one exception being the duty to serve in their military), but deny them the same rights as those granted to their own citizens; however, by the ascendance of supranational organizations, the right of states to do so is being eroded together with some other aspects of their sovereignty (see Chapter 25).

CHAPTER 5

STATE AS A POLITICAL ORGANIZATION

Sovereignty

The definition of politics as actions whose purpose is the betterment of the situation of a certain group of people through sharing in the directing of public affairs includes also the state as a kind of political organization. The state differs in two respects from other political organizations. It does not have to strive to attain a share of state power because it is, within the sphere of its power, sovereign, implements its objective by its own organs and can impose duties on all physical and corporate subjects of volition so that they, too, become its instruments or organs. It does not select its object of care, it is given: it is the people under its sovereignty, and the goal how the objective of care should look is determined by the legislators. Only after this objective is defined, can the state perceive and implement "betterment" which then equals a movement towards the realization of the objective given by law.

In modern times, the state is the only institution legitimized to use physical coercion to enforce obedience. In this respect, a part of the state is also the bureaucratic apparatus which enforces the will of the state (enforces laws) and the judiciary which applies it (determines if a violation occurred and the related punishment).

The evolution of the state resulted in various types of use of supreme power: states autocratic and democratic, pluralistic and monistic, centralized and decentralized, presidential and parliamentary, elective and hereditary, unitary and self-governing ([4]). In all these types there appeared similar necessary organs which are divided into three great groups: legislative, executive and judiciary (*"the separation of powers"*) Their actions form the government in the wider sense of the word regardless of whether they are divided among a legislative body, administration (government in the narrower sense of the word) and a supreme court, or concentrated in one person — a king or a president.

Because each norm has its normgiver, a hierarchy of normgivers exists side by side with the hierarchy of norms. The entire legal system is the expression of the state's will and the actions of secondary normgivers express this will, but there are important differences in the viewpoint from which secondary norms are created. It is necessary to distinguish organs that create norms because it is their duty, from those that, in the creation of legal norms, look at the law as a means of implementing their aims that are derived from the political purposes of their creators and through the normative process become a part of the purpose, of the objective of the state. Organs that in this manner *create* the will of the state according to their political objectives hold the *legislative* power.

In order to implement its will (expressed by law), the state has organs whose purpose is to execute it — the organs of *executive* power. The purpose of executive power is to transform law into reality either by the state's own organs or by forcing the subjects of the state to do so through fulfillment of their (legal) duties. Enforceability is a crucial quality of law and is the basis of the state's internal sovereignty as well as external independence.

Enforceability requires, in certain situations, application of physical force in a measure sufficient to overcome resistance. This presupposes availability of suitable and sufficient executive and enforcement means. Among them, the decisive one is the possession and use of arms. Arms destined for the enforcement of the will of the state against its own subjects are usually entrusted to security organs: police (private, local, state), prison guards, militias; arms destined against outside threats to the sovereignty and integrity of the state are entrusted to the army. Only in exceptional circumstances is the army used to protect the state's sovereignty against its own citizens.

Existence and occasional utilization of physical means enables the state to circumscribe and limit its subjects' liberties: personal (imprisonment, traffic regulations, military or labor service) and material (taxes, fines, confiscation, expropriation, building codes, environmental regulations). By their use, the state acquires control of additional means for implementing its will — buildings, means of production, transportation and communications. Among them, state organs which conduct economic activities form a special group. Their purpose is to provide goods serving the fulfillment of subjective goals of the state's subjects, or needed for the attainment of purposes of the state.

No matter how the possession of coercive means is arranged, it requires that organs of the executive power be organized hierarchically; their highest instance is the *government* (administration) of the state. The government (in the narrowest sense of the word) is the group of persons responsible for and directing important sectors of the executive power — internal security, army, industry, commerce, agriculture, education, relations with other states — customarily called "ministers"— with their presiding officer (prime minister or premier). In the presidential type of government, it is the president who holds the position of the head of the executive power.

No matter how extensive its powers, the government is usually responsible to the institution which is the real source of the state's will. This source can be the citizenry (in the form of direct election of the president or in the form of representative democracy), or a monopolistic political organization, a coalition of political organizations, but also a military junta, a monarch or a dictator.

Organs of the executive power act on the basis of purposive thinking, i.e., trying to achieve their objectives according to the rule of maximum benefits at minimum costs, but this objective is not determined by them, it is given to them, ordered by a legal norm in a lawful state, by instructions from the organs of the ruling political entity in a lawless state.

Purposive thinking is inadmissible in the judiciary. The duty of organs of *judicial* power is to determine whether this or that fact is consistent or inconsistent with valid legal norms, and what punishment applies; theirs is normative thinking: determination of legal validity. These organs *apply* the will of the state by applying its abstract expressions in the law to the immensely variegated concrete actions of individuals or other subjects of volition (and legal duties).

The combination of judicial and executive powers is the foundation of the enforceability of the will of the state through the enforcement of law. When judging it useful for its purpose, the state increases legal penalties and strengthens its executive power to an extent necessary to have its will prevail, i.e., to bring its subjects to submit to its legal order. Its consistency and enforceability means that the right to make laws, i.e. the legislative power, is the most effective means of transformation of the society subject to a given legal system. *The directing of public affairs is identical with the legislative power.*

Divided Sovereignty

A state whose legal system is uniform, is a *unitary* state; a state whose legal system is so varied that it cannot be logically attributed to one norm-giving subject, is a *composite* state in which sovereignty is divided. Because power has a tendency to expand, there is always a tension between common organs of a composite state and its constituent parts; the common organs have a tendency to centralize and increase the scope of their powers, and this contest is one of the sources of political dynamics in a composite state.

Federation

The division of sovereignty can have several degrees. Its most successful form has been the *federation*. The main characteristic of a federation is that its components (members) are equally sovereign among themselves as well as in their relationship to the federation in all matters which they have not transferred or reserved for the common organs. Federated members retain sovereignty in all areas which they have not transferred to the federation; *in areas they have transferred to the common authority, the federation assumes sovereignty and its members are subordinated.* Without this relationship it is impossible to consider a grouping to be a federation or a common state because sovereignty at least in relations with other states is the essence of statehood

In order to attain or secure common interests, a federation is formed either when (a) a unitary state transfers a defined part of its sovereignty to lower entities and keeps the rest, or (b) sovereign entities transfer a defined part of their sovereignty to a joint organ and keep the rest. In either case, one of the parties must give up something. Therefore, the basis of the federative process is a clear idea of the extent and importance of common interests of the federating entities because this extent determines the extent of the sovereignty transferred (or left) to the federal organs. Within the scope of their jurisdiction, federal organs have the authority to implement their objectives through their own legislative, executive and judicial organs over the entire territory of the federation; outside the scope of their jurisdiction, they have no right to interfere. This results in a parallel structure of legislatures, governments and courts existing side by side, whose jurisdictions do not overlap or contradict each other.

Other composite states

A confederation is a grouping of states which create, by common agreement, common organs for joint performance of certain activities while retaining their separate sovereignties. Their common organs do not have their own legislative, executive or judicial powers and their decisions are subject to approval or rejection of member states. A unique case of a confederation is a personal union — a confederation of sovereign states that have the same person as their head of state. The head of state with his personal advisors and bureaucracy is their only common organ. (The most successful of personal unions was the Hapsburg empire; it fell apart when its central organs tried to transform it into a unitary state.)

States that retain their full sovereignty and band together to pursue common interests, are *alliances*. To pursue such common interests, especially long term interests, a common executive (bureaucracy) is created. In order to arrive at a decision, unanimity of all members is required. Any other common organs have only an advisory role. In the recent past, alliances began changing into more stable and permanent supranational organizations by limiting the rule of unanimity and thus the individual members' sovereignty. The centralizing tendencies usually start with military or economic coordination, and the bureaucracies entrusted with the execution thereof gradually assume increased independence and enlarge the scope of their activities. The development of UN, NATO and the European Union are contemporary examples of such a process.

Allocation of Sovereignty

The extent of jurisdiction and mutual relations of state organs can be arranged in various ways.

Centralization

is the form of government where a central legislative power is the only source of the state's will, where the state's will (expressed by legislation) is executed by a central government (through a centralized bureaucracy) and where the judicial power is invested in one system of courts enforcing one hierarchical, i.e., derived from one highest legal norm, system reaching from the Supreme Court down to the individual policeman imposing a fine for violation of traffic regulations.

Decentralization

is the form of government in which the creation of the state's will is centralized in one legislative body, but its implementation (executive power) is placed under the authority of local organs (elected in democracies, appointed in autocracies). The supervision of executive organs on the lower levels is entrusted to local organs only or, most often, to local organs in which are included representatives of the central government to guarantee a degree of uniformity in the implementation of the central legislation. The central legislative power decides *what* will be done, fully or partly independent lower organs decide *how* it will be done. The instruments of enforcement and execution belong to the state and the cost of their activities is defrayed by the central government from its state-wide budget.

Self-government

is the form of government in which the state's legislative power delegates a part of its jurisdiction to lower organs (elected in democracies, appointed in autocracies) which create legislation within the framework of the laws, i.e., self-governing bodies which have within the limits of the law the right to create norms according to their own political will. Self-governing (autonomous) bodies determine both *what* will be done as well as *how* it will be done. The instruments of enforcement and execution belong to them and the cost of their activities is defrayed from their own resources, i.e., they have the right to impose taxes, fees and duties. (Feudalism was a typical example of this system.)

The line separating decentralization from self-government is not quite clear especially where the legislature of a decentralized state issues norms with a small content, i.e., it leaves to the object of duty a wide scope of ways of implementation so that the lower organs have an opportunity to interject their political objectives during the concretization of the higher norm. Decentralization then phases over into self-government.

In a decentralized state or a state with self-government, the sovereignty remains centered in the highest organs of the state (legislature, government, judiciary) and the norms originated with lower organs possess the same validity (are binding on the subjects of the state) to the same extent as the norms created by the highest organs of the state. Therefore norms of autonomous bodies are often enforced by central organs of the state (courts, police) although the autonomous bodies have their own executive organs.

Self-government is the most important among the arrangements of a state's administration. It is the simplest and most natural way of directing public affairs: those affected by them (1) decide to what purpose public affairs are to be conducted, (2) execute their decisions, and (3) defray related expenses. Self-government rests on the following preconditions:

1. the authority of self-governing (autonomous) institutions is based on the constitution or other laws,

2. they issue legally binding norms in matters falling under their jurisdiction inclusive of taxes and fees necessary to defray their expenses,
3. norms issued by autonomous institutions must not deviate from the law or any other higher norm, and being a part of the legal order they are enforceable by the state power,
4. self-governing institutions must not impose duties or cause harm to those not subject to their jurisdiction,
5. their decisions are implemented by organs which are subordinated and responsible to them, i.e., they possess their own executive and judicial power and own appropriate means of enforcing and implementing their valid decision.

The scope of self-government, i.e., its jurisdiction, is defined by the superior legal norm(s) and limited to those who belong to the self-governing unit.

This principle seems to be clear, but in practice, it can lead to conflicts ([5]). If these conflicts cannot be prevented by more accurate definition of the pertinent legal norms or solved by other means (financial incentives or disincentives), the decision is made by the judiciary, eventually the Supreme Court or Constitutional Court.

Grants from budgets of higher level bodies are a frequent method of settling such conflicts. The are a welcome source of funds and also a way of curtailing the independence of autonomous bodies. There are three types of grants:

— unconditional grants, for instance the distribution of budget surpluses of a higher body to its subordinate bodies;

— conditional grants which can be used only for certain purposes determined by the grantor such as following certain programs of education in schools under jurisdiction of communities or counties, amelioration of infrastructure (roads, bridges), environmental protection, etc.; mostly projects which the self-governing units would not undertake on their own (the latest and most grandiose program of this kind is the Goal 2000 program streamlining education at the expense of local autonomy and advocated by the federal executive in the United States);

— matching grants which are similar to conditional grants except that the higher body matches funds spent by a lower body for a certain purpose the higher body considers desirable.

All such grants result in influencing the grantee in favor of decisions made by the grantor and are used for this purpose when the grantor does not have the jurisdiction over the decisions of the grantee nor does it have the obligations to contribute to grantee financially or otherwise. The threat that such contribution will be missed while other self-governing units will accept it and thus gain economic advantages forfeited by the refusal of a grant, finally induces all potential grantees "voluntarily" to submit to the grantor. Considered under the purpose desired by the grantor, offer of grants is an effective means to achieve uniformity in the area of its jurisdiction and to equalize social disparities between its parts, which is important.

Another means serving the same purpose is to rearrange the territories of lower autonomous administrative units or to establish new units encompassing economically, racially or culturally different people in order to initiate or strengthen amalgamating processes. Therefore constitution or legal provisions subjecting re-districting to the approval of the affected autonomous units are an important safeguard of self-government.

What was said above about grants applies n the same measure to bureaucracies. It is essential for self-government to have its own bureaucracy paid by it and responsible only to its normgiving organs. A bureaucrat is loyal primarily to the source of his compensation, and it is impossible to serve two masters. The establishment and maintenance of its own bureaucratic apparatus might seem uneconomical and possibly an unnecessary duplication, but it is a price self-government must pay for its autonomy; moreover, it can control the expenses of its own bureaucracy, but the cost of a bureaucracy subordinated to a higher level of administration must ultimately also be defrayed by the same people, without the same level of control.

Self-government is either functional or territorial.

Functional self-government.

The purpose of the state is optimal, i.e., a composite of maximum objectives mutually competing for limited resources. Certain technical secondary objectives can be separated out of the primary purpose and their implementation in the relative area entrusted by the state to autonomous institutions whose decisions (norms) are legally valid and enforceable. The state may also allocate to them funds to be utilized in the pursuit of their respective objective. Examples of such institutions are the National Endowment of Arts, National Endowment for Democracy, the Federal Reserve Board; in lower units they are called Authorities of Boards, such as a Park Authority, School Board etc.

A state organized along the lines of functional autonomy is a *corporate state.* Its principle is to entrust decisions about a certain sector of life to representatives of groups that share it or are interested in it: for instance in automobile industry to representatives of factory owners, unions, consumers and the government (the latter having possibly a veto power). The idea is that the common interest will overcome or at least mitigate opposite interests within the given area and thus enhance social peace.

The widest application of this principle was made by the fascist state in Italy (which does not mean that each corporate state must be a fascist state).

Territorial self-government.

This embraces citizens living in a given territory authorized to issue legally valid norms by which they are subsequently bound. Territorial self-government is usually (but not always) arranged so that smaller units are parts of and subordinated to larger units.

In a democracy, the selection of representatives of the inhabitants of an autonomous unit is governed by a universal norm (constitution or law), or each unit has the right to create its own election procedures; there is room for various forms of territorial self-government which coexist and can be changed by the decision of their subjects to correspond to local conditions (size of territory or population, complexity of needs, and other). In the United States, the types of local government are: council, council — strong mayor, commissioners, council — manager. There exist a number of combinations of these types.

In autocracies, representatives of autonomous units are either appointed or otherwise selected without participation of the subjects of duty.

Representatives of self-governing units decide and act in the scope and manner granted them by nationwide or local legal provisions. In order to control their activities, central institutions frequently create their own parallel bureaucracy without whose agreement or approval the norms issued by self-governing units have no legal validity.

Local Self-government

For most people, the most important autonomous body is *local* self-government, i.e., a self-governing unit whose inhabitants have the power and the knowledge — or access to the knowledge — to make intelligent and informed decisions about its norms, their implementation, the persons making them as well as the background against which they are made.

The prevailing norms of local self-government are the community (municipality, village, township, city) and the county. Within their framework, various forms of direct democracy are possible — votes at township meetings or by referendum — reinforced by sundry regulations: the obligation of self-governing bodies to hold meetings open to or with participation of the public, the obligation to issue regular reports on the management, especially financial management, of the self-governing unit, the obligation to issue regulations or other decisions only after consideration of comments by the public or by directly involved persons, and other forms of participation. The American experience has proven that an important part of the citizens' control of their local government is the principle that communities or counties are allowed to assume financial obligations exceeding the duration of the office of present office holders only after approval by a referendum..

Local self-governments determine most peoples' day-to-day life by the *services* they provide and the typical *obligations* they impose.

Traditionally, and in many countries, communities have the authority of limiting voting rights to persons who have resided in their territory for a certain period of time and having fulfilled certain conditions (for instance, no criminal records) were granted the right of residence; non-residents do not have the same rights (6).

In general, the autonomy of local political bodies is losing its importance under the influence of standardizing pressures exerted by the industrial society.

Consolidation of Autonomous Bodies

The fact that higher and larger autonomous units than local governments are common indicates that there are causes or reasons for the formers' creation. They may be summed up as follows: technology, economy, military power, social needs, protection of *common* interests, standardization. A certain amount of centralization becomes necessary when smaller units do not show willingness to solve the above listed tasks by voluntary normalization. Examples of such voluntary normalization are the acceptance of human rights by the Conference on Security and Cooperation in Europe, acceptance of an identical commercial code by the states of the Union, formulation of Uniform Customs and Practice for international banking.

The post-World War II period brought about a significant *global strengthening of centralization*. *Extra-political* centralization takes place especially in two key areas: economy and culture (including entertainment). International (multinational) economic organizations centralize global economy through introduction (occasionally introduction imposed by the International Monetary Fund and the World Bank) of market economy, private enterprise and abolition of duties. Global mass media centralize the distribution and explanation of information and steer culture towards uniformity by creating its components (TV plays, film, videos, songs, electronic networks).

Politically, international centralization progresses through the growing power of supra-national institutions, i.e., their bureaucracies, forming and enforcing a "new world order." The main obstacle to these global centralizing tendencies is the existence of nation-states; therefore their independence is continuously whittled down and portions of their sovereignty transferred voluntarily or not so voluntarily to the extra-political and political centers of worldwide power.

Reduced Sovereignty

The sovereign power of the state is never absolute in practice, and in the recent past certain organizations were able to carve out enclaves in which the state is powerless; within such enclaves their will is supreme, but they are not recognized as sovereign legally although they are not subject to the will of the state practically.

Their precursors were the war lords in China and Japan and the robber barons in Europe, more recently the control of Sicily by the Mafia. They are at present the great international crime organizations which hold as their base certain territories in a semblance of the double government scheme of Trotsky: their existence is made possible by tolerance and support of the local population. The two most powerful examples are the drug cartels of Colombia and crime mafias in Chechnya. In Colombia, in spite of armed assistance the state obtained from abroad (the United States), the drug cartel fought to a standstill efforts of the government to eradicate or at least limit its activities. The Chechnya mafia even managed to elect one of its chieftains as president who then declared independence from the Russian commonwealth and by combining the crime lords' case with local nationalism, managed to stymie Russian efforts to reassert sovereignty over that area.

Similar tendencies exist in other states in locally adjusted and reduced forms which resulted in a sort of modus vivendi with the state through a combination of violence and corruption. Such is the case of Mexico and Japan; in Japan, the crime syndicates police areas where their interest (gambling, drugs, whorehouses, porno, child prostitution) are located; and maintain brutally the safety of their "customers" against random robberies, muggings and attacks.

It appears that no single democratic state, no matter how powerful, is capable of extirpating the international networks of these huge, wealthy and powerful organizations with their own tribal government structure, armed terrorist groups, enforcers, airplanes, flotillas of ships, lawyers and political connections. Only dictatorships or totalitarian states occasionally managed to do so, at the price of a brutal suppression of basic human rights and civil liberties. In view of this impotence, this form of coexistence of states with organized lawlessness must be included among the enumeration of existing systems of government.

CHAPTER 6

DOMESTIC POLICY I — DEMOCRACY: RULE OF THE CITIZEN

People Know Best

Democracy is the form of government in which those on whom the law imposes duties decide about the use of the legislative power, i.e., the formation of the will of the state is arranged according to the principle of *autonomy*. Members of a democratic state are *citizens* and are guaranteed by the constitution the right to share in the formation of the will of the state provided they comply with pertinent legal norms.

Democracy is commonly justified by the assertion that people know best what is good *for them*. This justification while true, is incomplete. Democracy rests on the assumption that people know best what *is* good — good not only for themselves as individuals or members of a certain group, but good also for society as a whole and good absolutely. The community of citizens who reason on the basis of the diversity of their lives' experience using their common sense and with assistance of tradition and religion arrives by its majority conclusions at a more correct recognition of what is absolutely good and just than minorities distinguished from others by this or that ontological property: origin, race, class, education, wealth, power or some other characteristic.

In modern society, this means assigning to experts a supportive and *advisory* role. It means rejection of a system, in which experts would *decide*: eugenicists who may marry and have children and what strains of genes may continue and which ones must be eliminated, demographic experts how many people may be born and where, who may live and who may not; nutritionists what food is to be grown, prepared and consumed; sexologists the relation between sexes and the use of sex; ecologists when and where and how people use nature; educationists what and how children must be taught, a national endowment for arts would decide what art is to be promoted, a national endowment of sciences would determine which sciences and which scientific theories or discoveries are to be pursued, a medical board would allocate resources according to its conclusions as to which type of citizen is to be cured and which type is to be provided only with palliatives or "death with dignity," and so on wherever a group of specialists or experts brings their specialty to bear on the lives of others- a system of total lack of freedom. Democracy is based on the premise that those who would have to obey the experts' precepts have the final word whether they want to accept such duties or not or to what extent.

According to a commonly accepted assertion, in a democracy all power proceeds from *the people*, not from individuals. This means that the decisions on the formation of the state's will are made by the citizenry as a whole, not by each inhabitant of the state as an individual. The individual's freedom is limited in two respects: under specific circumstances he is subject to the will of others even if he disagrees with it, and his own will has a legal effect only if expressed in a manner defined by the law. Laws issued without the prescribed participation of citizens are not legally binding; this, however, does not entitle each and every citizen to decide which legal norms he will consider as valid and which not; a system in which everyone would decide if he is or is not bound to observe this or that law would be *anarchy*. In democracy, the population of the state is the object of the state's care and individual citizens while empowered to share in the formulation of the state's will according to their goals of happiness, have the duty to obey the law whether their agree or disagree with this or that particular legal norm. (As subjects of will, i.e. of freedom, they have the ability to refuse to comply with the law, which is not the same thing as denying its validity.) For those who do not have the right to vote, and whose votes did not comply with legal provisions delineating the way of participation in the formulation of the state's will, or whose representatives were legally excluded from norm-giving, the norms issued by the state are not autonomous, but heterogeneous, imposed from the outside, an expression of someone else's will.

The Road from the Will of the Citizen to the Will of the State

Citizens entitled to share in the formulation of the will of the state are *voters*. The constitution determines the way in which they exercise their empowerment.

A voter who will become a subject of duty under a new law, shares in its issuance in three possible ways:

1. voters themselves issue laws — direct democracy,
2. voters decide on proposals (drafts) of laws — referendum,
3. voters decide on who will have legislative power — representative democracy.

In a representative democracy, by casting his vote the voter shares in the decision who will be a legislator as well as what the contents of the laws will be, because he votes for *persons* as well as for *programs* they propose.

Voters have the right to assemble in groups on the basis of their opinions on the best arrangement of society, i.e., on the basis of political programs, and strive to influence the legislation. Democracy is characterized by institutions which protect this free formation of the political will of the people. The constitution allocates to citizens a certain sphere in which they are free, i.e., in which the state is prevented from imposing any duties, and should a norm interfering with this sphere be issued, it is legally invalid. This sphere of citizen's freedom is commonly called "fundamental liberties." Recent developments of international law tend to extend the protection of certain rights to every inhabitant of the state, citizen or not, on the basis of the theory that certain rights are innate to every human being, are "inalienable human rights" and therefore must be granted to every human being everywhere regardless of citizenship. The extent of such "inalienable human rights" is not firmly established and has the tendency to expand.

The rights of a citizen may become illusory unless his person and livelihood are protected. Therefore the first and main civil liberties are personal liberty which protects him from coercion by power, and material independence which protects him from economic coercion. Joined to these two basic liberties are liberties that secure his participation in public affairs by protecting the emergence of new opinions: freedom of thought, religion, scientific research; the dissemination of opinions: freedom of talk, press and expression; and the pursuit of opinions: freedom of assembly, of association and of petition.

Democracy secures the observance of civil liberties through law. *Democracies are lawful states*, i.e., punishment (harm of otherwise protected values: life, health, freedom and property) may be inflicted only on a person who violated a legal provision. Such violation as well as the pertinent punishment must be clearly stated in the respective law: this is the requirement of *specificity* of law. A law stating "Everyone who commits a wrong will be punished" is not sufficient, because such a law permits arbitrary interpretation, thus ceases to be an instrument of justice and may become a convenient instrument of political persecution.

Civil liberties are secured by legal *certainty*:

— the commands of the governing political organization or organizations must be issued in a specific manner, normally by way of a law, otherwise they are not binding and are legally invalid;
— punishment may be inflicted only if the bearer of a legal duty violated it in a way described in the law: *it is prohibited to inflict punishment without a violation of the law* (the principle '"nulla poena sine lege");
— only a punishment specified in the law may be imposed so that the violator knows beforehand what harm to expect for the violation; this principle invalidates retroactive laws;
— punishment can be imposed only after a court of law has determined or confirmed that *the punished violation did truly take place*; this determination takes place before independent judges and/or juries; in instances of minor violations the law may entrust the imposition of punishment to organs of the executive branch, always subject to judicial review;
— retroactive laws cannot be enacted; no one can be punished for actions that represent the infraction of a law that did not exist at the time of the action.

Elections

The legally binding expression of the will of the voter in the legislative process is his *vote*, the legally binding and according to legal provisions exercised expression of the will of citizens is *voting*, the right to express relevantly one's will is the *right to vote*. All voters have the same (equal) right to vote and the right to vote is the rule, i.e., it belongs to everyone who is considered by the law as mentally mature and morally responsible and meets special requirements established by the state (registration, a certain duration of residence, citizenship). Mental maturity is commonly determined by age, in certain legal systems also the ability to read and write, as prerequisite for inclusion in voters' registers. Moral integrity is determined from the standpoint of the law, i.e., by absence of certain criminal acts and a deprivation of the right to vote by a decision of the court or some other legally valid norm; otherwise, personal morality of the voter is irrelevant to his right to vote.

Because of the equality of votes, the *number of votes* is the determining factor in the formation of the state's will. This does not necessarily mean that a majority of the population or even a majority of voters has a decisive share in the direction of public affairs. The will of persons authorized to vote who failed to vote does not count; nor do invalid votes. The equality of votes is vouchsafed and enforced by the executive power of the state, a power exceeding the power potential (economic, social, intellectual, organizational) of other subjects to such an extent that they are unable to use it legally to influence voting. Democracy excludes from the decision making process, at least theoretically, any component of power except *numerical relationships*; political organizations whose purpose is to win votes are called *political parties*. Actually, other elements of power also make their impact felt: political parties representing the interest of well organized groups, especially those ready to use force or violence, as well as political parties representing groups yielding great economic power have in practice a greater share in the management of public affairs than warranted by the number of their votes and elected legislators.

Electoral Systems

An electoral system is the total of regulations determining the manner in which voting becomes a legally valid and binding part of the legislative process.

Modern technology makes possible and more frequent the use of *direct* democracy in the form of *referendums* especially in smaller (autonomous) territorial units, and laws mandate that state organs hold public hearings (personal) or invite comments (in writing) prior to issuance of legal norms. Comments and hearings increase the participation of citizens in the management of public affairs; yet they are not the same as democracy. In the first place, legislative organs are not bound by the opinions so expressed; in the second place, these procedures increase disproportionally the influence of well organized opinion and interest groups which arrange an avalanche of comments in favor of their positions, thus distort public opinion and one-sidedly impress or even intimidate the legislators.

Because modern states are large, the number of voters great and state activities complex, *representative* democracy is the prevailing form of democracy. The voting performed according to legal provisions takes the form of elections, persons entitled to vote — the electorate — elect, i.e., choose (the possibility of choice is the substance of electing) the person they entrust with the legislative power and/or other functions (judicial or executive) in public life. The right to elect is active electoral right, the right to be elected is passive electoral right. Electoral systems usually prescribe more stringent conditions for the right to be elected than for the right to participate in elections; the strictness of the conditions is usually commensurate with the importance of the office to be filled.

For practical reasons, the national territory is divided into *electoral districts*. Such districts are independent entities for the purpose of nominating candidates and counting votes. Electoral systems that emphasize the personal character of candidates and their relationship with the voters provide for election of persons, voters choose between *individual* candidates; electoral systems emphasizing programs provide for election of ballots listing candidates of identical opinions and program, voters choose between *lists* of candidates. Elected candidates are said to have received the *mandate* to represent the electorate and to create the state's will on its behalf.

Electoral systems are evaluated on the basis of two criteria: *how accurately they reflect the opinions of the electorate* and *how they create conditions for a firm and efficient governing* of the state. At first glance, these two criteria are mutually exclusive: the more accurately the composition of a legislature reflects public opinion, and the more accurately the activities of the legislature correspond to the various trends of the citizenry, the more complicated, difficult and volatile is the formulation of the state's will; firm, effective and steady directing of public affairs demands that the legislative body be composed so as to produce a state's will which is consistent and steady.

Electoral systems belong to two general groups according to the provision as to what type of majority they require for the election of a candidate.

Majority electoral system

The system of majority representation is, in its pure form, a system in which a *relative* majority is sufficient for the election of a candidate: the candidate who or the list of candidates which received the greatest number of votes, is/are elected; the other candidates are not and the voters who voted for them have no representation (their votes are forfeited). As a mechanical consequence of this system, the voting power of the victors is increased and that of the losers is decreased (actually: lost): the proportion of the representation of the victors in the legislative bodies is greater than the proportion of their voters in the electorate; for the losers, the effects are the opposite.

The majority system has the tendency to provide the political organization that gained the most votes (relative majority) with an absolute majority in the legislature, which meets the requirement for a firm, consistent and steady governing of the state. This, however, is not always the case. If three or more political organizations present candidates or lists, there is the possibility that none of them prevails in the majority of electoral districts, and the need for a coalition government arises. Also in the event that only two political organizations present their candidates or lists, in a certain distribution of voters, the less numerous votes can elect a majority of candidates ([7]).

The overvaluation of the votes of the victorious party underscores *the direction* in which public opinion is changing; this keeps democracy vital; the voter realizes that he can affect the outcome of elections exactly because a relatively small shift in votes is magnified by the overvaluation and undervaluation respectively of the winning and losing votes, and causes significant shifts in the relationship of the mandates.

Because of the importance of the overvaluation of votes in favor of the victorious party it is relevant to determine whose votes are overvalued. *Overvalued are the votes of voters who switched to the victorious party.* The votes of party faithfuls and of extremes tend to offset each other; victory is decided by the fluctuating center. This fact affects the character of the entire political process: political parties orient themselves in action and propaganda towards gaining the votes of the center. Consequently the majority system is *centripetal,* it does not divide the citizenry into diametrally opposed blocks; the overvaluing of the center has a calming effect and the center, albeit not having its own political organization, influences the policies of all parties. Political parties must pay attention to all streams of public opinion because the omission of any one of them could, by gain or loss of one single vote, cause the victory or defeat of a candidate or list. Therefore, political organizations submit to the electorate a clear program in currently important matters, but in other questions they represent a conglomerate of an entire scale of opinions whose supporters seek accommodation *within* the political organization. The result is an election program of generalities and compromises with the exception of what is perceived as the crucial question or questions of the day. ("It's the economy, stupid!") If such compromises and accommodations of various trends within the political organization cannot be reached, the factions enter the elections separately with the risk that none of the splinter groups will be represented in the legislation even if together they have the majority of votes.On the other hand, under certain circumstances the majority system gives a key role to a well organized ideologically uncompromising minority which even if unable to switch to the adversary political party, may still, by threatening to withhold the votes of its adherents and thus to cause it to lose the elections, impose its demands on the ideologically closer party.

The principle of overvaluing the votes for the victor and undervaluing the votes for the loser gives the mandate to the relative majority in each electoral district. Because adherents of ideologically close political movements prefer to concentrate their votes on an acceptable candidate rather than to split them among several candidates of a similar attitude, and thus to contribute to the election of a candidate of an ideologically opposite political party, the *polarization of voters* leads gradually to the survival of only two relevant political parties in each district. The pressure towards consolidation of political organizations into two is effective nationwide in each electoral district, but not necessarily in favor of the same two political parties. Where the electorate is homogeneous to such an extent that its needs find expression in nationwide (state-wide) political movements, the two resulting political parties are also state-wide, nationwide. If the electorate is diverse, the system results in forming *territorial* parties according to the special needs of local electorates, and the overall result is a system of entrenched particularist political parties, rather than a two-party system.

Proportional electoral system

The system of pure proportional representation reflects most accurately the actual opinion of the electorate. In its pure form, votes delivered nationwide in favor of individual political parties are totalled up and mandates for the legislative assembly are allocated according to the percentage of the total of valid votes cast. The mechanical sensitivity of this system results in the *multiplication of political parties* because it preserves the existing ones and facilitates and encourages creation of new ones. In a large political body such as the electorate of a state, almost any political program can find enough adherents to obtain representation in the legislature. (In a legislature of 300 members, a party has to obtain only one third of one percent of the electorate in order to qualify for a mandate. To gain one third of one percent of a large group of people for almost any opinion is practically certain.) The tendency to create new parties is reinforced by the *rigidity of existing parties* whose inertia funnels innovative ideological or political movements towards the organization of new parties even for small ideological or personal differences.

The system of proportional representation is based on the principle that the outcome of elections, i.e., number of elected candidates should correspond to the numbers of votes cast for them. Because it is impossible to divide physical persons according to the percentages of votes cast, this system is constrained to *use party lists*; from each party ballot is elected the number of candidates corresponding to the percentage of votes cast for it. Because this system prevents the loss of almost any single vote, it encourages psychologically the *emphasis on differences* of secondary importance and their elevation to important issues, thus to the atomization of the electorate; its effects are *centrifugal*. Proportional representation reflects properly the distribution of votes, but it also *distorts the true picture of public opinion* by obscuring its fundamental division on substantive issues, emphasizes real as well as artificially provoked differences, fractures the political expression of an articulate public opinion into intolerant splinters.

In the system of majority representation, the decisive element in elections is the fluid center of the voters; in proportional representation it is just the opposite: the *decisive role lays with the steady cadres* of party faithful — members and voters; the impact of the fluctuating votes is minimal. Voters who switch party allegiance are usually relatively few, and when divided among a large number of political parties, their action achieves at best the shift of a few mandates, which has hardly any influence on the overall direction of politics. The proportional system takes no cognizance of trends and dynamics of the population's thinking.

Combination electoral systems

In order to overcome the shortcomings of the two basic systems, there exist various combinations of them. The most important ones are:

a. the majority principle is applied in each electoral district only if a candidate or a list of candidates receive the absolute majority; if not, there takes place a *second round of voting* in which the voters can choose only between the two leading candidates (or lists):
b. the electoral district is assigned more than one mandate. The available mandates are allocated to candidates in order of the highest numbers of votes;
c. each voter has *more than one vote* which he may give to one candidate or split among several candidates;

d. voters have the right to *write in* candidates, cross them out or change their order on lists;
e. political organizations must obtain a certain percentage of votes nationwide and/or in a number of districts in order to qualify for a mandate; if this *qualification threshold* is not reached, its candidates are not given a mandate and votes cast in their favor are forfeited or rather accrue to the qualifying parties according to the relationship of votes cast for them; the requirement of such a qualifying minimum can result in a situation where a minority of qualified voters attains the right to form the state's will to the exclusion of the (splintered) majority, and *reinforces the tendency towards a two-party system* by eliminating chances of survival of small and new parties.

Selection of Candidates

Provisions regulating the selection of candidates are no less important than those regulating the exercise of the right to vote.

The fullest empowerment is granted to the voter by systems which allow write-in of names on the ballot. By writing in a name of his preference, the voter performs both the act of nominating and selecting (voting for) his nominee.

Close to this alternative is the right to set up so-called independent candidates, i.e., candidates who do not belong to or at least do not represent any established political party. To qualify as an independent candidate, the nominee for candidacy must submit to the authorities a certain minimum number of voters' signatures supporting the candidacy either nationwide, in an electoral district or in a certain territory (in local elections).

In most instances, candidates are presented by political parties according to their internal selection procedures. The most populist form are so-called open primaries. Primaries consist in selecting candidates for elections by the membership of the party from ballots showing the names of persons who qualified as candidates. In open primaries, any one who declares himself to be a party member, is empowered to vote; no additional identification and/or condition is required. If such primaries permit also write-in of nominees, they approach closely the system allowing write-ins on the election ballots. It allows voting in party primaries to members of no party or even members of another political party ("cross-over" voting).

While this approach is the rule in the United States, in other countries the participation in primaries is contingent upon proof of party membership by a membership card and depends frequently on membership dues having been paid, and the list of nominees is composed by certain organs of the pertinent political party enlarged by those who have obtained the support of a number of members or some important part of the party's organization. A strong voice in selection of candidates is granted to members also if local or county party organizations have the right to nominate candidates.

In order to safeguard a party's coherence, its statutes may guarantee to its leadership the right to "filter" or screen nominees proposed for primaries or for candidacy, or to reserve to the leadership the right to compose the list of candidates either directly or in cooperation with high-level territorial or national meetings of delegates. Another method to preserve the traditions and continuity of a party is automatic candidature of certain party functionaries, for instance members of the presidium or chairman of its larger segments, former elected representatives (incumbents) and members of the government.

The method of selecting candidates is related to the type of electoral system in that the majority system favors more influence of local membership while the proportional system tends to strengthen the power of higher organs of a party. In general, the mode of nominating candidates for election reflect the degree of internal democracy of a political party.

Governing a Democracy through Separated Powers

The preservation of civil liberties is protected in a democracy also organizationally by a system of mutual checks and balances of the state powers and by the obligation of their holders to preserve the legality of their actions.

Legislature

In a representative democracy, the sovereignty of the state resides with the highest representative organ (parliament, national assembly, congress) which in principle possesses the exclusive right to issue laws as the only norms hierarchically immediately subordinated to (immediately derived from) the constitution, and further legal norms (regulations and provisions of the executive power as well as court decisions and judgements) derive their validity from laws. The power of the state, this greatest existing concentration of power, may be directed only against those who violate the law, and laws must not violate the constitution and the civil liberties and human rights there incorporated.

Legal transfer of the power to issue laws to some other organ of the state (to the president or the government) or granting other norms the same legal status as to laws (presidential decrees, government resolutions, regulations issued by bureaucracies) indicates that autocratic elements are intruding in the democratic system. The same effect have laws that leave a wide power to interpret and specify resulting duties to organs not constitutionally entrusted with norm-giving, i.e., organs of the administration or the judiciary.

The primary originator of the state's will in a democracy is the *legislature*. The constitution of the state determines whether the state gives preference to its stability, its efficiency or prefers sensitivity to changes in public opinion, i.e., mainly to the results of the most recent elections.

The *stability* of the state is enhanced by a bicameral system provided that the composition of each of the legislature's two bodies is based on different election criteria, such as different requirements for passive and active right of vote (usually different age limits), different terms of office, and/or a different voting system. The effect of this arrangement is to prevent sudden and transitory changes in public opinion from becoming equally sudden and transitory changes in the policies of the state. This is important especially in societies where the media exert great influence on the population, can whip up a transitory, but strong, emotional wave of criticism or enthusiasm, and thus destabilize the state.

Another variation of enhancing the stability of the state is the division of jurisdictions between the two legislative bodies. Some constitutions reserve legislative initiative to one body, the one most responsive to public opinion, and give to the other body the power to disapprove (delay, return) it. The most frequent is the requirement that a legislative proposal becomes law only if approved by both chambers; if one of the chambers fails to approve the draft voted by the other chamber, the draft does not become law or its validity is postponed until additional procedural steps are taken (referral to a reconciliation committee and a vote on the reconciled version, in the United States).

The main justification for a unicameral legislature is the recourse to the principle that the legislature should reflect as closely as possible the composition of the electorate and its will and opinions, otherwise it will alienate those whose will it is supposed to represent, express and implement. The stability of the state's will in a unicameral system is strengthened by a provision that elections to it are staggered so that only a portion, like a third, of its members, is elected at the same time. Radical and abrupt fluctuations of state policies are thus moderated and the next elections confirm whether previous changes in the attitude of the electorate were transitory or enduring.

The stability of the state can be protected by provisions which give the head of the state (president, monarch, in some cases the military) the right to postpone or deny validity to a law, sometimes combined with the authorization to dissolve the legislature and to initiate new elections under certain constitutionally specified circumstances, especially the legislature's inability to form a governing majority or to overcome a gridlock between the legislature and the executive power.

The Executive

The *efficiency* (and *accountability*) of the government (in the widest sense of the word) depends in a democracy on the voting system: whether it ensures or at least promotes the formation of a legislative majority necessary for the formation and formulation of the state's will. In this regard, the most incisive impact is exerted by the influence voting systems have on the number of political parties.

Majority government.

The majority electoral system increases the *accountability* of the parties. Achieving absolute majority in the legislature in a proportionate electoral system is practically impossible; but a majority system usually brings about such result. In the interest of its election victory a party must satisfy a scale of political movements; therefore the debate about a program of their potential government takes place inside political parties and precedes the elections. If a party achieves absolute majority of the norm-giving body, its responsibility for the success (or failure) to implement its election program and for concrete and visible achievements of its rule is clear. The tendency to credit or blame the party for all results mean that the next election voters will decide clearly about the direction of the state's will in the following term and about the persons who will govern it: the leaders of contending parties are known and the voters take them into consideration when casting their ballots; this limits and/or makes superfluous behind-the-scenes deals between political parties and pressure groups regarding the government program or personal composition of the government; the outcome of the elections determines it directly.

Coalition government

A coalition government becomes necessary if no political party has, in the legislature, a majority to implement its program (and, in a parliamentary system, to form a government). Such a situation is exceptional in a state with a majority electoral system and the rule in states with a proportional electoral system. Then the program and personal composition of the government must be decided by a compromise between several political parties and their goals. This struggle which in a majority system takes place within the parties prior to elections, takes place under a proportional system in the legislature after elections and creates a crisis of the state. Because the proportional system favors creation of political parties representing material interests, the necessary compromises are formed mainly on the basis of mutual concessions of an economic nature: each party must give up a part of its program in exchange for the support of other parts of its program by other parties, and vice versa.

The whole of political parties associated for the purpose of implementing identical or complementary portions of their respective programs is called a *coalition* of parties. The coalition parties articulate a common program as a joint purpose whose unity is given by the material solidarity of its secondary purposes furnished by the programs of the participating parties. The relationship in which their programs are included is based on the power relationship of individual coalition parties and influenced by the power relationship between the individual groups ("objects of care") represented by the coalition and the opposition parties, in which calculation the power of the state apparatus is mostly to the credit of the parties representing the majority.

There is one exception. The necessity to find a majority for the creation of a program and the establishment of a government deforms the formulation of the will of the state by giving small parties needed for attaining the majority an influence exceeding their numerical strength among the voters, and grants the power of veto to each coalition party willing to leave the coalition and thus to reduce its representation in the legislature to a minority. Under such circumstances, small coalition parties can have a disproportional influence and can dictate their conditions to much larger parties, because they hold the key to the survival or fall of the government and the stability of the state. Governments of states with a proportional electoral system are thus paralyzed in their formulation of programs and in their actions, incapable of pursuing systematically long term measures to solve problems, and unstable, because the governing majority breaks apart each time when any one of the governing coalition parties reaches the conclusion that a switch to the opposition would permit the opposition to become the new majority in the legislature and would grant the switching party more influence in the new coalition than it had in the previous one.

The instability of coalition governments is enhanced by the fact each political party enters elections on its own and competes implicitly or explicitly also with its coalition partners. This cleavage between the election campaign and the necessity of a post-election coalition causes insincerity of cooperation, difficulty in forming a coalition and its instability. The jealousy of coalition partners and leaving the coalition for propaganda purposes are consequences of this cleavage. Rather than concentrating on the implementation of its program, each coalition party is intent more in preventing others from implementing their program. This policy is possible as long as its departure from the coalition would mean, for other partners, a loss of the necessary majority, and such loss would cause them a greater harm than the sabotage of the implementation of parts of their programs.

As a result, states governed by the practice of coalition building are seldom capable of effecting deep changes of society no matter how urgent and critical they might be. This applies especially to social problems and to such matters which would demand significant sacrifices from all citizens. It is the reason why such democracies are at a disadvantage when faced by non-democratic political actors, domestic or foreign. A large part of citizens loses interest in the defense of a state whose system consistently proves it incapable to act because each of its governing political organizations watches jealously that none of them achieves a significant progress. This dissatisfaction is augmented by the fact that in the system of coalition government, a citizen is unable to distinguish which of the coalition parties is really responsible for successes or failures of the state's policies. Each of them claims all credit for progress, each blames other partners for failures and justifies its participation in the coalition by claims of preventing even greater failures. Because the society drifts or stagnates, voters cannot make a judgement whether this or that program is good or bad, remain faithful to their respective parties and ascribe its incompetence to other parties because only the implementation of a program can bring proof of its value. If a political party has no opportunity to implement its program, the public has no way of judging the quality of an individual party's programs and representatives.

The coalition system promotes irresponsibility both among the governing parties and in the opposition. Because no party is able to implement fully its program and be held responsible for its consequences, programs of all parties acquire the nature of propaganda and demagoguery: the parties know in advance they will able to realize them only in part, at best. This reinforces the negative attitude of citizens towards politics in general and undermines their faith into the democratic political system.

The legislative power creates the will of the state; it is the task of the executive to implement it. This means that, conceptually, the executive power is subordinated to the legislative power. If this relationship is reflected in the organization of the state, the state is a parliamentary democracy; if not, it is a presidential democracy.

The substance of *parliamentary* democracy is the organizational dependence of the highest organ of executive power — the government (in the narrower sense of the word, in the United States the "administration") — on the parliament which means that the government must not be in disagreement with the parliament. When such a disagreement occurs and is identified by the legally provided manner (usually by loss of majority support of the government in the legislature, vote of nonconfidence), the government must resign and be replaced by one that has the confidence of the parliament expressed by a majority vote. According to some constitutions, the harmony between the legislature and the government is renewed by a recourse to the electorate, i.e., by new elections. The newly elected parliament is superior to the government like the dissolved parliament was. The superiority is expressed either by the fact that the composition of an existing government is subject to the parliament's approval or by the fact that a new government is selected by the legislature. Consequently, legislature has a decisive say also about the personal composition of the government. In parliamentary democracies, the parliament frequently also elects the head of the state (president).

The substance of *presidential* democracy is organizational equality of the executive headed by the president (often elected by popular vote or a body of electors, not by the legislature) with the legislative body. The executive must execute the state's will as expressed by laws, and to that extent it is subordinated to the legislature, but its composition and existence does not depend on the agreement of the parliament. The legislative power can enforce its will or oppose the will of the executive by controlling the funding of the administration's activities through denying or allocating funds for certain purposes, but cannot overrule it: the result is a gridlock. The mutual relationship of the legislative and executive powers is determined by the constitution, and the judicial power, independent of the legislature as well as of the executive, decides whether either of the other branches (legislative or executive) violated its provisions.

The Judiciary

In view of the importance of by whom and how it is established whether a violation of the law took place and which penalty is attached to it, a certain arrangement of the judiciary is inseparable from a democracy. The judiciary has a final word in the question if, how and against whom the the machinery of the state is to be activated. Therefore, the institution of the judiciary in a democracy generally observes several principles:

— Independence of judges. In the performance of his office, a judge is bound by the wording of the law, but *only* by the wording of the law. Special organs composed of judges (disciplinary commissions) determine whether a judge violated the law in the performance of his office, and the impeachment and/or removal of judges for malfeasance in office is often reserved to the highest organs of the legislature or the administration. A party to a litigation has the right of appeal and the decision belongs only to a higher court (appellate court, supreme court or constitutional court), not to the legislature or the administration.

— Customary jurisdiction. Everyone must be judged by the court of his jurisdiction, i.e., everyone must be judged only by those courts under whose jurisdiction they belong according to the law. The state is prohibited from selecting, for political reasons, a court which it expects to condemn an innocent person, or a court which would free a guilty person. This principle includes the prohibition of establishing exceptional courts which could be used for encroachment of civil liberties or human rights, as well as the prohibition of transferring judicial power to other organs of the state, especially to organs of the executive power.

— "No plaintiff — no judge." Courts may act only on the basis of an accusation or complaint. This principle is the opposite of the principle of inquisition when a court may initiate proceedings (investigation and sentencing) without an accusation or complaint by an authorized person, but it does not prevent an organ of the executive power from having a right and/or duty to prosecute certain violations of the law they have become cognizant of, i.e., to submit an accusation or complaint to a court.

— Courts have the duty *ex officio* to handle every matter brought before them by a proper party in a proper way and to treat all parties equally in investigating the subject matter and in sentencing. It is a duty of the judiciary to prosecute very violation of the law, no matter by whom committed.

— The court may pass judgment only on the basis of material truth as ascertained by it during its own proceedings. It must not take for granted results of investigation by other organs, nor a confession of the accused; even if there is a confession, the court must determine that such confession corresponds to reality, is materially true. The principle of material truth is the opposite of the principle of formal truth when the court decides on the basis of compliance with or violation of some procedural rules by the parties to the dispute. If formalities are violated, the violator is subject to punishment, but the violation must not protect a guilty party from punishment .

— The principle of immediacy and oral presentation prohibits sentencing on the basis of only written documents. A court may decide only on the basis of its own, immediate and direct experience gained during the court proceedings from examination of witnesses, of the plaintiff and of the defendant and/or their legal representatives. The defendant (the accused) must be given full opportunity to defend himself personally and through his attorney.

— Generally, the court must conduct hearings and pronounce its findings publicly to facilitate control and criticism of any violation of the law or favoritism towards either contending party.. This principle is the opposite of sentencing *in camera,* secretly and with the exclusion of the public.

Exceptions to the above enumerated principles must be based on law which, in turn, must respect the constitutionally guaranteed civil liberties and human rights. While the independence of the judiciary protects democracy from the violation by the legislature and the government, it leaves it open to the undermining by arbitrariness of the judiciary.

The decisions of the courts consist in transformation of *abstract* legal norms of the laws, rules, regulations and decrees into *concrete* norms; a court determines in given concrete circumstances what the concretely identified subject of duty must concretely do (or suffer). The jurisdiction of courts includes also the right to instruct organs of the state to perform a punishment of concrete person or persons. Therefore, the performance of the judicial power is a link of the chain of normgiving; it differs from legislating in that the court acts and decides not on the basis of what a judge or judges believe should be, but on the basis of what the legislature has determined that should be. Between these two opinions there can be and in practice sometimes is a difference which produces a tension and can lead the court to observe the formal requirements of the law while replacing, in concrete decisions and pronouncements, the intent of the law by the court's or judges' own opinion. In this way, the judiciary can arrogate to itself the role of the legislative and/or executive power and substitute the will of judges for the will of the state as duly expressed by the processes of elections and norm-giving.

This tendency is reinforced by three circumstances. First, there is the principle of independence of the judiciary which guarantees that court decision may be changed only by other organs of the judiciary. If these higher organs have a concept of justice different from that of the legislators, it is very difficult to prevent the judiciary from intruding in the sphere of the legislative or executive powers. Second, the judiciary has usually the authority to decide about the constitutionality of legal norms. This means that a court can pronounce any legal norm including laws as not in accordance with the constitution, and therefore as invalid. The decision on such a pronouncement lies normally with a higher instance of the judiciary, and if its highest instance (Supreme Court or Constitutional Court) confirms it, there may be no further appeal from such a decision, no matter how arbitrary is the Court's interpretation of the constitution (the principle expressed by a U.S. Supreme Court Justice then applies: the Constitution is what the Court pronounces the Constitution to be). Third, if the legal system is built less on the letter of the law than on precedent, any such pronouncement of a court, unless successfully challenged, creates a precedent which permeates the decisions of the entire judiciary and thus has the power to transform the entire society. The principle of precedence deviates from the principle that the judiciary is empowered only to issue concrete norms, i.e., norms dealing with one particular case, and circumvents such restriction: the judiciary has then the power to create abstract norms which have the validity not only of law, but even of the constitution itself.

This process is defended in legal theory by the so-called activist understanding of the role of the judiciary, namely, that it is not the role of the judiciary to apply the "dead letter" of the law, but to "promote justice" whenever the legislature fails to do so. Because "justice" is in this connection only a different designation for the "betterment of the situation of a certain group of people", the activist concept of the judiciary transfers in fact the power of legislation and of imposing a constitution to the judiciary which can by its decisions and the preferences of independent judges expand, restrict, change or render ineffective even fundamental civil rights. Since the judiciary is exempt from controls by the citizenry, this development is detrimental to democracy: elected organs are reduced to deciding trivia while fundamental changes are made via judicial pronouncements.

In order to prevent the expansion of the judiciary at the expense of the legislative power, constitutions include various provisions: judges are elected by the citizens in the same way as legislators, their tenure is limited, legislatures have the power to exempt certain issues from the jurisdiction of courts and reserve them to central or local normgivers, to impeach and recall judges under certain circumstances.

Dividing the State

A political organization in power usually tries to fill positions within the executive and judicial branches with its own members, authorized to do it by the law or via facti. The organs of the executive implement purposes whose contents are determined by legal norms, and organs of the judiciary evaluate certain facts according to the appropriate legal norm; nevertheless, the decisions of both are influenced to some extent by the opinions and the purposes of happiness of the persons performing these tasks. A political party (or parties) dominating the legislative branch and formulating the will of the state in accordance with its ideology and program, assumes correctly that the organs of the executive and judicial powers will perform their functions in its intent more faithfully if they are occupied by its own members and adherents of the same political or ideological movement. The same applies to the opposition: if it manages to keep the possession of important positions in the administration and the judiciary in the hands of its adherents and to prevent the victorious political organization from replacing them with its own people, it may be able not only to sabotage the will of the majority party, but even to implement the minority's objectives.

The occupation of positions of the non-legislative powers by adherents of the governing party (parties) or the opposition party (parties) does not in itself change the nature of the state as long as adherents of political parties observe the legal norms governing their duties. The lawfulness of the state, however, is diminished if the personnel of these branches implement the will of their favorite political parties or movements rather than the will of the state. Such is the case especially in democracies with a proportional electoral system and the practice of coalition government. Because the mechanics of coalition government impede the implementation of their respective political programs political parties endeavor to dominate normgiving not only in the legislature (where they are paralyzed by other parties), but to substitute, in the non-legislative portions of the state structure under their control, their respective programs for the purpose of the state.

The responsibility of the government (administration) to the legislature, i.e., representatives of political parties, is a means by which political parties can and do widely influence the personal composition of the judicial and executive apparatus. In a parliamentary democracy, this influence is apparent already in the composition of the government which is completely or prevailingly constituted from representatives of the governing political party or governing coalition according to agreements reached during preceding negotiations. In the same manner, the entire bureaucracy of the state is then modified: each party fills positions and promotions with its adherents in the sector of the state administration assigned to its ministers. Because in this process, loyalty to a political party plays a stronger role than professional qualifications, the efficiency of the state administration suffers and its growth and cost flourish.

Bureaucrats who owe their positions to a certain political party, follow in the performance of their duties the party's objectives rather than the objectives of the state. This undermines in reality the equality of citizens because political appointees in the state administration favor members of their political party in comparison to non-members. Various sections of the state administration become a domain of various political parties especially if certain ministries are in the hands of the same party for a long period of time. This disrupts the unity (material solidarity) of the state's purpose, the will of the state loses consistency, activities of the state's organs cannot be deduced from the primary purpose (legislated program) of the state, the state's organs act at cross-purposes with each other and with the state's will expressed by its legal order. From the actions of its organs it is no more possible to determine the state's primary purpose, because it would have to be logically concluded that the state promotes and opposes at the same time identical objectives. The state splinters. ([8])

CHAPTER 7

DOMESTIC POLICY II: RULE AND OBEDIENCE (AUTOCRACY)

After half a century during which the world was safe for democracy, it would seem outdated and superfluous to pay much attention to its conquered enemy. Not so. A careful analysis of autocratic systems, especially their modern versions, and its careful comparison with the present situation will disclose, how much of non-democratic thinking and practices has survived and is waiting for those who consider themselves capable or called to rule over others without their consent. This justifies the extent given to this system of government against which, after all, democracy is a shortlived newcomer in human history.

Autocracy

Autocracy is the form of government in which the formation of the state's will takes place according to the principle of *heteronomy*, i.e., that those who are subjects of duty of the legal order do not share in the normgiving, legislative power; their will is legally irrelevant in the creation of the state's will, they are subjected to an outside will whose manifestation is declared as valid and binding by the state's constitution. Legal (political) heteronomy determines the nature of the society and the structure of the state. Members of such a state are not its citizens, but its subjects. This does not mean that the subjects have no influence on the constitution. They exert it by their mere existence, because in an autocracy, too, it is true that the constitution is, ultimately, the outcome of the interplay of power relationships in the society, and autocracy, too, must beware of provoking such a resistance of its subjects that would surpass its means of enforcement or weaken it in relation to other states to such an extent that the independence of the state would be lost.

Each autocracy is based on the principle that power belongs to those who possess a certain ontological quality lacking in the rest of the members of society. The types of autocracy are described by designation of the group possessing the legislative power: the hereditary ruler (absolutism), the nobles (aristocracy), the wealthy (plutocracy), the powerful (oligarchy), the priesthood (theocracy), the knowledge class (technocracy).

The legal system is the means through which the state implements its will by imposing duties on its subjects, but on the other hand — provided it is a lawful state — by defining their duties it defines also a sphere in which they are "free" (the term "freedom" means in this connection "absence of legal duty"; e.g., "religious freedom" means that the state does not impose any duties on its subjects in the sphere of religion) to pursue their individual purposes of happiness. The autocratic lawful state tolerates a certain scope of freedom either because it expects that its subjects will act in furtherance of its purpose on their own also in the area of freedom because their purposes and the state's purpose are parallel, or else because it realizes that the cost of creation and maintenance of a system of enforcement would from the view of the state's purpose cause more harm than gain. In an autocratic lawful state its subjects may utilize their sphere of freedom no matter how limited to act in a way the state considers harmful, possibly also for efforts to gain a share in the legislative power, i.e., for political purposes. Therefore, only certain lawless forms of autocracy deserve detailed attention.

A Lawless State

The designation "lawless state" is actually a *contradictio in adiecto*, because the state is the reference point of a legal system, and therefore a state cannot exist in the absence of a legal system. The term "lawless state" is used to designate a status of society where a legal system exists (therefore a state also exists), but does not apply to all: there exists a political organization or group which stands above the law, and therefore also above the state. The state is not sovereign, sovereign is only the ruling political organization: because the state's will expressed by law is systematically violated by the ruling political organization, the state loses, within its territory, its sovereignty and retains it only externally, in its relation to other states.

One typical sign of a lawless state is the abandonment of the requirement of legislative specificity. When imposing duties, i.e., when issuing laws, the state uses expressions allowing for wide interpretations, in order to narrow the sphere of citizens' freedom. For a lawless state it is symptomatic that its executive power punishes not only violations of the law, but also a mere *infringement on or threat to the interests of the power holders* who, themselves, decide by whom and how their interests have been, could have been or were intended to be violated, and that violation of law is not punished if observance of law would affect the interest of the ruling political organization or of some of its members. The criminalization of "anti-state attitude" is a typical example of such a legal provision which is sometimes called a "rubber paragraph" due to its flexibility and malleability.

The vagueness of legal formulations is complemented by the arrangement of the judicial power. The attainment of the state's purpose would not be secure if courts, as organs called to determine whether such or such action is or is not in agreement with the law, were to apply laws in a way which follows the letter of the law, but simultaneously interpret legal provision in a manner protecting the legally defined sphere of freedom of the subjects even against the interests of the ruling political organization. A lawless state prefers over the judiciary, organs of the executive power which act in the interest of the legislator and do not examine whether or not certain actions remain outside the law. Therefore, courts are transformed into parts of the executive power or are replaced by the executive outright. In especially important instances, the legislature reserves for itself the performance of judicial responsibilities or transfers it to specially created judicial organs whose compliance it considers as guaranteed (martial law courts, military courts, people's tribunals). The proceedings of such courts are usually inquisitorial, i.e., the accuser's and judge's functions are merged; the same organ investigates the matter and passes sentence, possibly even without a hearing of the accused; occasionally, it also executes the sentence. Another way of insuring compliance of the judiciary with the wishes of the ruling political organizations, are the so-called proceedings *in camera:* the proceedings are secret, with the exception of direct participants no one is informed about the process or its outcome. In a lawful state, everything not prohibited is permitted; in a lawless state, everything not specifically permitted, is prohibited, and also things permitted may be punished if considered as against "the interest of the state" or "interest of society."

When the will of the ruling political organization is stronger than the will of the state, the state's constitution is irrelevant. A lawless state may be — according to its constitution — democratic, constitutional or autocratic, it can guarantee legally on paper human rights and fundamental freedoms; when constitutional provisions clash with the will of the ruling political organization, they are disregarded.

Types of lawless states are absolutism, dictatorship, managerial state, totalitarianism and decentralized totalitarianism.

Absolutism

In the past, lawless autocracy was represented by absolutism — an autocratic state in which the legislative, executive and judicial powers were concentrated in the function of the monarch; in this sense, his power was absolute. The nature of absolutism was succintly expressed by French king Louis XIV by the sentence "L"Etat — c'est moi" (I am the state).

This state form perished because of the divergence between its normative status (all power concentrated in the person of the monarch) and its ontological status — in reality the ruler's power was not absolute, because the preventive and repressive means at his disposal were incapable of preventing the formation of independent ideological movements and corresponding political movements, nor to inhibit the resulting political organizations from attaining means sufficient to force their way into sharing the management of public affairs.

Dictatorship

The system of lawless autocracy was more recently perfected by dictatorship. An unsurpassed definition of dictatorship was coined by Lenin: ". . .a dictatorship is an authority based directly on force, an authority which is absolutely unrestricted by any laws or regulations. . . The dictatorship means . . . power, unlimited power, based on force and not on law. . ." ([9]). Dictatorship means the subordination of the state to the will of the ruling political organization. The law becomes a subsidiary means of implementing the political organization's will; the main means is direct power, force.

Although dictatorship is a factual, not legal, situation, the ruling political organizations uses also the legal system for its purposes. Because it has absolute control of the legislative, judicial and executive powers, it utilizes this control for the creation of legal norms which impose a modicum of order in those spheres of the life of society, which are politically neutral, such as traffic regulations, contractual law, or which free the political organization from the necessity to interfere continuously through its own organs with the functioning of society. Force is exerted either by certain parts of the executive power of the state, which are under direct control of the political organization, such as secret security services of the police and/or the army, or by elements of the political organization directly, such as its militia, storm troupers, or organized mass violence directed against politically undesirable targets.

The duality of enforcement organs — the state's and the ruling organization's — introduces a new element in the power equation of a dictatorship: in the state's organization arises a power player capable of challenging the ruling political organization. Here not only the power relationship of the governing political organization to the dominated social complex is important, but also the relationship of that organization to the state apparatus. If the political organization does not wield sufficient power of its own with which to enforce obedience towards its will independent of the state's machinery, the rule over the society and the state shifts to the most powerful part of the state's apparatus — usually the army or to the secret police, or to some of their units.

Compared with the complexity and sensitivity of industrialized societies absolutism as well as dictatorship are rather crude and primitive ways of governing and not viable as means of ruling large populations. Only in politically and economically underdeveloped societies survives dictatorship and is yielding to democracy or exists as a transitory stage to more sophisticated forms of autocracy.

Updated Autocracy — Managerism

The first stage in using modern technology for the creation of a lawless autocratic state is called here a *managerial state*. Under the term "manager" or "political manager" is understood a person holding a position formally under the control of a superior organizational level and *in reality* independent and not responsible to anybody. This new system's control over society is a concentration of factual power in the hands of a permanent power center independent of the state power and superior to it. This center is a non-recallable and noncontrollable group of political managers and is not subordinated to any norms, not even its own. *A managerial state is the dictatorship of an internally undemocratic political party, (further simply "the Party") realized by ideological corruption of the masses and scientific utilization of means of social control furnished by contemporary sociological and technological progress.*

A. Preconditions

A managerial state can arise only under certain conditions of which the most relevant are:

— democracy

— masses living in want, who feel they have nothing to lose (except formal freedom which in practice they can exert only to a limited extent, or not at all) concentrated in large numbers in the key centers of the state, mostly possessing the right to vote, who, due to their lack of education and political knowledge, are malleable in the hands of trained expert agitators from their own milieu, who appeal to their emotions and immediate needs,

— a mass movement of dissatisfaction with existing conditions, combined with a strong desire for a fast and thorough change of the social order, whether resulting from direct observation or from propaganda,

— confusion and impotence of political parties in solving long standing social problems and in effecting radical changes that would bring about quick improvement,

— possibility of perfect centralization of the state through technical means and sociological and psychological techniques.

Dormant in these and related conditions are forces which, once centrally mobilized for the purpose of achieving and securing the management of public affairs, have explosive power . For their release and utilization there is needed only a relatively small autocratically organized group — a managerial political party ("the Party").

The structure of a managerial political party corresponds to its central purpose: attaining power. Because of the scope of its final aims, it must be permeated by a uniform will. Its central group uses the following techniques to maintain unity of the party: selectivity in acceptance of members, verticalization of communication processes, complete subordination of lower organizational levels to those immediately above them, and exclusion of factions. In such a party, there can be only one managerial group and changes in its composition can occur only from within it; the Party's members do not influence them. Once achieved, such centralization bolstered by creation of an bureaucratic apparatus, guarantees unity and efficiency of the entire organization.

Attached to this set-up is a *propaganda apparatus* using a wide variety of means, which acts directly in the name of the Party, or indirectly, without disclosing affiliation with the Party, spreads the ideological movement in which the Party is rooted, by expert, scientific, ethical, philosophical, religious, etc., opinions and demands, always according to directions emanating from the managerial center combining the political and non-political ways of propaganda. Great emphasis is put on publications, among them dailies and weeklies. In addition to its own press, the Party pursues the influencing of the independent, the trade and special interests press by camouflaged ownership or infiltration. Complementing the periodical publications are brochures, leaflets, books. Part of the propaganda apparatus are mass speakers and individual agitators, and when indicated, mass demonstrations and marches. The general tone of all propaganda is assertive, authoritative, admitting no doubts; the Party's movement and its goals are presented with enthusiasm, opponents are ridiculed and discredited.

Another arm of the managerial center is the Party's *intelligence network* which collects information on the movement itself (numbers and names of active members, activity and achievements of lower organizational units) and on its opponents, with special attention given to their economic position, connections and personal indiscretions. Obtained information is correlated by special small groups which use also infiltrators and spies in other political parties and in the state's apparatus.

Attached to the Party are organizations pursuing aims attractive to members of the movement the Party endeavors to use: trade unions, women and youth organizations, peace organizations, organizations of minorities, and so forth, called by the Party *"mass organizations."* Some of them are founded by the Party and are openly its parts, some of them are infiltrated so that Party members rise to leadership positions where they pursue the purposes of the managerial center rather than those of the organization's members. This arrangement allows the managerial center to isolate itself from the influence of these mass organizations while at the same time influencing them and including them in its power sphere.

B. Building its own sphere of power

During this stage, when the Party does not yet possess a share in the government, its primary goal is to build its own power base. It is not engaged in securing conditions for normgiving within the framework of the current legal order. Though the Party organs may temporarily respect the law, they do so only for opportunity's sake. The managerial center's real aim is to effect a shift in the power relationships in the society by evolving systematically a power sphere in which the state has no authority and in which the only recognized authority is the will of the center of the Party, until this sphere of power is sufficiently strong to challenge the power of the state. (Trotsky called this process "creation of a dual government.")

The managerial center therefore targets primarily the group which, in spite of being in minority, has the greatest power potential: numbers, concentration, and militancy (the "progressive forces" of society). In an industrialized state, such a group are the workers: they are daily concentrated in large numbers in key cities of the country, working in the hierarchical organization of enterprises, it is used to discipline, it is relatively easy to organize, and it has the potential to paralyze the life of the entire society by simply stopping work. For this last feature especially, the power of workers approaches or equals the power of the state, and if the Party succeeds in uniting them under its leadership, the main condition for seizing power of the state is achieved. In developed countries, students are next to workers on the ladder of power; what they lack in discipline and impact on economy, they make up by a greater readiness to take risks and by their long term potential to ascend to important positions in the life of society. Dissatisfied and radical minorities are another welcome pool of supporters. In countries in the first stages of industrialization, the mass of workers is joined by the destitute masses concentrated in the proximity of large cities, especially the capital. In pre-industrial countries, the potentially most powerful element are peasants and agricultural workers, due to their numbers and importance for the economy; by their dispersion, they are an unfit object of organization, but a fit object of terror; if the state is unable to protect them, they can be cowed into submission by acts of violence, brutality and cruelty.

For a successful progress towards power, the division of society into two antagonistic groups is necessary and the more militant and resolute part (the progressive forces) must be on the side or under the direction of the managerial center. In the already divided and uneasy society such a split is either already existing or easy to provoke. The revolutionary party starts by promoting dissent, i.e., a radical rejection of the existing order, and a fundamental division between the supporters and critics of the state. Its propaganda, in the political as well as non-political form, steadily increases dissatisfaction with the existing situation and assigns the guilt to the state without regard to the truth or untruth of its assertions (demagoguery) by appealing to feelings and instincts; it justifies its arguments ideologically by theories which demonstrate (or appear to demonstrate) the inevitable collapse of the existing order and the emergence of a new, perfect one in which the revolutionaries and their adherents will attain the fulfillment of their ideals. Once such a split has started, it is deepened: the managerial center aggravates the tensions and increases the dissatisfaction of the militant side by stressing, magnifying and dissecting its wants. The excited and impassioned masses are presented with a simple (i.e., something everyone can understand) and seductive (i.e., something everybody wants) program of immediate and radical change derived from one central idea of the Party's program, a "loaded" idea which responds to the mass movement of discontent and appeals to the needs this movement expresses — *the inflammatory idea*. The inflammatory idea conforms with a strong impulse or emotion (envy, chauvinism, xenophobia, hunger, sex) calculated to make critical thought more difficult and to inspire its adherents to extraordinary effort in its realization and in destructions of its true or alleged opponents, and promises to fulfill their purposes of happiness by its realization. Disguised as its byproduct, the program brings with it also measures undermining democracy. Inherent as well as incidental shortcomings of democratic institutions are used to justify open demands to abolish democratic institutions or to insist on reforms which would destroy significant areas of the democratic structure of the state. (Because the Party presents its revolutionary program with no intention of carrying it out, but merely as a means of capturing the allegiance of the masses, this process is hereafter referred to as the *ideological corruption* of the masses.)

Such a conviction is necessary to motivate people to accept the hardships and risks which a fight with the state entails. This degree of devotion brings to the resistance exceptionally self-sacrificing and courageous elements disinclined to accept any solution of existing dissatisfaction by a compromise; in their minds, only a revolution — and seizure of power by its leaders — can bring about the promised paradise. Therefore the political organization which plans the revolution, must maintain and increase the dissatisfaction motivating its members and adherents, by rejecting all compromising proposals, increasing its demands past the limit of possibility, denouncing the government's attempts to better the situation as fraud, sign of weakness, and concessions to be followed by additional concessions provided the revolutionary movement is not deceived and stands firm.

If changes in accordance with the Party's program are attempted by the state, they are denounced as insufficient or insincere and/or sabotaged by the power sphere under the managerial center's control, until they fail. Then, or if they are not attempted by the government, the masses, after the past preparation, definitely join the camp of the managers breaking with the rest of society in a storm of strikes, accusations and persecutions and when finally they culminate in a bloody clash between the organs of the state and the movement led by the Party, the door to mutual accommodation is definitely closed. Polarization of the population is accelerated and consolidated by intentional provocation. An intentional creation of a clash between both sides is a *provocation*. This happens as a part of the development of the conflict which typically starts with individual terror, attacks on police stations, grows into mass anti-government and illegal protests, demonstrations, marches, strikes (often combined with occupation of important buildings, vandalism of stores, overturning of vehicles) which make violent confrontation inevitable. Members of the revolutionary movement part ways with the rest of the society in a storm of strikes, blood-letting, mutual incriminations and persecution; the drawing of a bloody line between the two camps closes definitely any road towards mutual understanding and agreement. Because the backbone of the revolutionary movement is its political organization, defeats suffered in such clashes are from its standpoint profitable according to Lenin's slogan "The worse — the better," providing, of course, that the state does not use its temporary defeat to rectify the sources of discontent. Even if the state wins in a particular conflict, the power base of the managerial center has become strengthened and consolidated, and permits it to continue and renew the struggle from a more favorable position.

The rallying point of the Party is the inflammatory idea. The counterpoint to it is *a contradictory idea* which is imputed to the opponents and blamed for all life's troubles, including failures of the movement itself. If the opponents have no such contradictory idea, they are even worse off since then the managers are free to impute them anything. The contradictory idea is also an important preparatory psychological step for future policies of the Party: it demonizes its opponents and dehumanizes its adherents.

C. Entering the government

Once it has sufficiently widened its sphere of power, the managerial political party is able to force its way into government. In order to do so it allies itself with reform political parties which, too, endeavor to solve the extant crisis of society. Democratic political parties which, engaged in efforts to ameliorate the situation and unable to achieve it, are ultimately induced by a combination of the pressure of their own membership, public opinion and partisan egoism to make a deal with the Party in the hope that participation in government will change its character of the latter or that the managerial center can be prevented from destroying democracy. Such an inclusion of the Party into democratic government represents, in itself, a deep fracture in the established system: by sharing in the government, the Party does not change its basic strategy: the only, and decisive, change is that now it begins to incorporate into its own sphere of power also sections of the state apparatus.

In pursuing this aim, it must consider all other parties, allied or opposed, as competitors and ultimately enemies. To weaken these competitors, it first of all divides them into two groups. Those of the weaker group are not only discredited and excluded from participation in the government, but destroyed as organized units. As a rule, this is done by using those parts of the state apparatus entrusted to the Party's representatives in the government, preferably by the instrumentality of secret security services and/or special laws for the protection of State security and special courts (so-called "people's courts," in practice often lynching by a mob) whose institution and/or direction it obtained as a precondition of enabling its coalition partners to form the government. This destruction of the opposition is important for the future progress of the Party because it definitely gives the Party a superiority over its temporary allies. When the Party decides that the time for seizing all power of the state has come, they will no longer have the support they would otherwise have found in the — now destroyed — opposition.

Within the coalition, the Party creates a narrower block which forces gradually the outsiders out of the government into opposition, and continues this process until it possesses all power alone, and the remaining coalition partners, if any, are deprived of autonomy and share in formulating the will of the state and are also incorporated into the power sphere of the managerial center. For this purpose the Party must retain the leading position in any block in which it participates so that it can impose its will upon its partners and carry on the process of elimination. Its power base independent of its share in the government, and a sharp awareness of its ultimate goals makes it easier.

Outwardly, this process assumes the appearance of normal democratic horse-trading practices between political parties, with one difference: while the Party willingly grants its partners advantages of narrow personal and partisan character and of economic nature, it obtains concessions of a state-political nature in exchange. By these concessions it gradually accumulates the control of most important sectors of the state apparatus which then cease functioning as organs of the state and act as organs of the Party. By control of the armed units of the executive branch (the military and the police) and organs influencing public opinion (the media and educational institutions) the managerial center controls the physical space and the channels through which new members are introduced in both the physical and sociological "spaces."

Sooner or later, a conflict between the Party and its coalition partners is unavoidable, and usually arises, or rather is provoked, at a time set by the managerial center when it feels strong enough to absorb the remaining parts of the state administration into its sphere of power and to impose such political changes which are equivalent of depriving all other political organizations of their capability of independent volition. To achieve this aim, the Party must prevent a consolidation of the situation prior to its seizure of power; therefore, it keeps the political process boiling, society guessing and its partners and opponents on the defensive. Because the Party utilizes for the seizure of power its dominion over (parts of) the state apparatus, it implements the overthrow of the system by a putsch rather than a revolution. The conflict provoked at a time when the power superiority is clearly on the Party's side and in which the Party is supported by mass organizations and by its part of the State administration usually ends with a quick liquidation of the opposition. Democracy is pushed aside. The birthday of dictatorship has arrived.

D. In power

Even after usurpation of state power, the managerial power sphere is still a foreign body in a democratically organized society, and the Party must struggle with its resistance. Having reached the stage of dictatorship, the Party uses the combined power of its own and of the State to absorb the entire society in its power sphere whose form is wholly different from a democratic society with its decentralization, diffused communication processes and numerous autonomous subjects of volition. A managerial center creates a hierarchical society with vertical communication processes, in which it aims to be the sole source of will, not only of the state, but also of organizations, groups, and individuals viewed not as subjects of freedom, but rather as means of realization of abstract plans and concepts.

The main tool of such an uprooting of the entire society is the completion of the ideological corruption of the masses still represented as a conflict between the Party's inflammatory (and corrupting) idea and the contradictory idea whose basic characteristics are stressed and made absolute. The Party constantly paints a vivid picture of the state of bliss to be reached through the achievement of the program presented by the managerial center. Regular reports on positive results are to mark the gradual implementation of the inflammatory idea and prove the achievability of its goals. Material advantages rewarding supporters are represented to them as well as to the rest of the society as anticipation of the well-being in which everybody will gradually participate.

The inflammatory idea is complemented by the contradictory idea whose true importance becomes fully evident only at this stage. The uprooting and moulding of society by the managerial center demands so many sacrifices and so much cruelty that it would be impossible to achieve without a cold and merciless conviction (not hate, because even hate is too human a sentiment for the managers' needs) of its adherents that it is necessary to destroy its opponents regardless of their individual guilt or innocence and personal motivation. This conviction is built up in the movement already from its very inception during the period of oppression and conflict with the state power by propaganda dehumanizing the Party's adherents and demonizing the movement's enemies. Their alleged baseness justifies even the most inhuman measures against them, especially against those who are losers in internal conflicts in the managerial center.

The contradictory idea fulfills also another need. The discrepancy between the aims of an autocracy and the objectives of its subjects grows with the degree of centralization of power. In the managerial state which represents the ultimate in centralization, the dissatisfaction of its subjects is correspondingly intense. The state is capable of thwarting its crystallization and organization, but not its existence. It can attempt to canalize and vent it by the use of the contradictory idea which acquires thus a new dimension: it not only centers dissatisfaction on opponents, it also diverts it from the rulers by presenting to the public a target whose responsibility for every failure is absolute. Such a diversion would not be convincing enough in the abstract; the managers must present to the dissatisfied people concrete persons as bearers and agents of the contradictory idea and to destroy them without mercy. In such a way, the mentality of a besieged camp is created and the existence of an enemy becomes a necessity and a permanent institution of a managerial state; if no enemy exists, it must be invented and produced. And it must be an enemy proportionate, by its magnitude, to the size of the existing discontent. Therefore a foreign state or group of states is promoted to the role of the main bearer of the contradictory idea; terror against potentially inimical groups is combined with purges of the Party apparatus and liquidations of losers in the intramural political and personal infighting in the managerial center, and such an artificially created united front is presented to the public as an instrument of foreign promoters of the contradictory idea.

At this stage of the development of a managerial state, the monopoly of creating, executing and applying political will, i.e., formulation, proclamation and implementation of a political program, is located in the managerial center and secured by the effectiveness of the ideological corruption of the masses. To overcome inertia or resistance of its subjects, the managerial center proceeds simultaneously in two ways:

1. The will of the subjects is changed so as to become identical with that of the Party. This is done by (a) persuasion: the managerial center communicates to everyone its ideology, systematically elaborated and psychologically ironed out; (b) suppressing and distorting facts which would cast doubts on its ideology or evoke desires conflicting with its will, (c) creating artificial conflicts between the ideals of its subjects by counter-positioning individual secondary purposes of their goals of happiness and by realizing some of them at the expense of others (for instance, the ideal of material security at the expense of political freedom, or of national independence at the expense of human rights, or a typical example: securing the education of children in exchange for denouncing colleagues — the so-called breaking of characters). In this way a part of the opposition can be won over, another part paralyzed in its efforts to strive uncompromisingly for the attainment of *all* the secondary purposes of their goal of happiness.

2. Those whose will cannot be changed, are forced to act in conformity with the will of the Party and in conflict with their own will, because they are threatened by or subjected to harm exceeding the harm caused by subordination of one's own will to the will of the managerial center. Such harm can affect their property, health or life or other values (property, health or life of family, friends, community).

Because the change of actualized qualities is more difficult than the molding of persons whose qualities are still only potentialities, the Party concentrates efforts at ideological corruption on those whose opinions and will are still undeveloped: youth, especially children, and social strata with a lower education level, especially workers. Groups which cannot be won over or whose convincing is unlikely, are intimidated, suppressed or liquidated on the basis of their profiles without investigating individual attitudes of their members.

The process of shaping the will of society's members would be undermined if it were carried out or interfered with by a subject of volition other than the managerial center. It must be therefore implemented *exclusively*, by a *system of monopolies* which serve to protect the power of the Party and to transform society. They are:

1. Monopoly of communications. The possession and use of mass communications media is reserved to the Party directly or indirectly (through the state or subordinated organizations); means of communication of private nature (typewriters, computers, printers, mimeographs) are either controlled (registered) or inaccessible. By the use of this monopoly, the Party intrudes in the minds of each subject with its ideology and by its assertions and interpretations and prevents other subjects from spreading different information or opinions. This monopoly insures also that distortion or suppression of facts will not be discovered and that members of the targeted society obtain only such information which is apt to form their will in accordance with the will of the power center.

2. Monopoly of intellectual leadership. The ruling political organization occupies by its devoted member all positions requiring theoretical knowledge. This is true especially with regard to positions in education. The contents of education are dictated by Party ideology (the inflammatory and contradictory ideas). Higher education is accessible only to those whose loyalty to the ruling political organization and its ideology appears certain. The Party ideology is represented as the official ideology, as the very idea of the *state*. As a consequence, criticism or doubt of the Party ideology and its interpretation are criminalized as enmity towards the state, possibly treason, and legally punishable.

   Such "state ideology" is proclaimed everywhere and decisions are made in its spirit and intentions, because they are in the hands of people who do not know any other way of thinking. The monopoly of intellectual leadership also guarantees that the state ideology will not be confronted by an intellectually comparable or superior criticism and/or the rise of a new ideology growing out of the reality created by the dictatorship. In conjunction with the monopoly of public communications, the monopoly of intellectual leadership allows the Party to manipulate language. Current (traditional) meanings of terms replaced with new meanings more suitable for the needs of the power holders not only prevent exact and critical thinking, but moreover deprive the subjects of terms as instruments by which they could formulate independent ideas.

3. Monopoly of organization. The position of the managerial center is endangered and its monopolies disrupted by the existence of any kind of independent organization even within the framework of the Party. Any economic, cultural, youth, religious, labor, or political organization can become a breeding ground of political ideas, produce a political movement and become, in time, a competitor or an opponent. The power center counters these dangers by the following steps:

   — It dissolves organizations whose purpose is achieving a share in the direction of public affairs, i.e., primarily other political organizations, and those left it deprives of any autonomy — their programs, activities, leadership and representatives are directly and constantly determined by the power center and/or its organs.

   — It unifies organizations difficult to dissolve due to their nature. It creates united labor unions, a united youth organization, a united physical education and sports organization, a united organization of writers, and so forth; associations which do not merge with any of these mammoth organizations, are dissolved. Only the united organizations are officially recognized. Most members of the leadership of these official organizations are members of the Party; a personal union exists between these leaders and functionaries of the Party, the most important ones are members of the power center.

By creating this structure, the managerial center obtains an instrument of domination of society because almost every person is induced or compelled to be a member of one or more of these "transmission belts and levers" (Lenin's terminology) of the dictatorship. At the same time, the monopoly of organization prevents opponents of the regime to gather in some of the official organizations and to form there a nucleus of resistance, and membership in one of the official organizations functions as a means of control of the behavior and attitude of almost every citizen of the subjugated state.

The monopoly of organization is not completed by incorporation of all legal organizations. To secure it, the Party must also prevent the formation of illegal organizations. In addition to the control function of the "belts and transmissions," this purpose is served by ubiquitous secret services equipped by the best up-to-date technology. Their networks of undercover agents, denunciators, confidants and provocateurs infiltrate the society and also control each other (to prevent any of them from becoming rivals to the managerial center). With their assistance, illegal organizations with a potential considered dangerous to the managerial center, are liquidated under the pretext that they endanger the state (which is untrue because the managerial center is a subject of volition separate from the state). Intelligence services moreover infiltrate, observe, influence or create illegal organizations they do not consider as immediately dangerous for the regime; these illegal organizations serve to identify and channel discontent and are liquidated when becoming dangerous or unnecessary. (On the other hand, they can take advantage of this temporary tolerance in order to effect maximum damage to the ruling regime prior to their liquidation.)

By the very existence of secret service networks, the monopoly of organization is insured indirectly; the fear of their agents and confidants deters the dissatisfied from organizing, and unorganized dissatisfaction is not (immediately) dangerous (although in the long run, it is fatal to the best organized autocratic system). Fear and distrust are augmented by mass terror striking groups of probable or potential enemies of the system. If some of their members are really illegally organized, their organizations are damaged, if not destroyed by these measures.

The monopoly of organization is not really a monopoly of the Party; it is a monopoly of the managerial center. It therefore guards also, and mainly, against the rise of other power centers within the Party. Intelligence services observe connections and actions of its leaders and members of the managerial center and prepare dossiers for use during purges of a losing faction.

4. Monopoly of means of production. The Party achieves its control of means of production in two ways. It either organizes their owners into groups to which it assigns obligatory production targets and all other economic relations as well because, as a part of this monopoly, it assumes control and/or ownership of financial institutions, transportation and distribution organizations. Or the ownership and/or disposition of means of production is transferred to the state or to organizations immediately subordinated to the Party. Either way assures the Party the utilization of all resources of the nation's economy and puts it at the service of implementa-

tion of its goals. Among others, this monopoly provides it with a means of materially rewarding its followers and materially destroying its enemies, which is of extraordinary importance for the transformation of society. The resistance which the Party evokes by imposing its will against the purposes of the majority is too strong and too complex to be overcome by penal measures. The control over the means of production is an instrument flexible, informal and generally available by which to mete out rewards and punishments: promotions and advancement on one side motivate obedience and productivity, on the others side threats or fear of demotion, transfer to a worse job or loss of employment (there is no other employer than the government run by the Party) will compel almost anyone to submit "voluntarily" to the will of the Party without the necessity of overt punishment.

5. Monopoly of arms. The control of production, possession and use of weapons, exclusive allocation of the latest and most destructive weaponry to units composed by the most reliable Party members, combined with controls of means of conveyance of information, persons and material, enables an excellently equipped minority to dominate a defenseless majority and to concentrate its resources promptly on any break-out of open resistance with an overwhelming force to isolate it and destroy it before it can spread.

To maintain these monopolies requires that all key positions, also minor one, be occupied by proven followers of the ideology, the program and the policies of the managerial center. It is the Party where they are organized. The creation of the Party's will is concentrated in the managerial center; the Party is an instrument of its implementation and of control and rule over its members. Already in the preparatory stage, the influence of members on the creation of the Party's will is limited; after the seizure of power it is completely eliminated so that no element of the Party can become the spokesman of the opinions and demands of the population. The managerial center which holds the state apparatus in check by the Party and the mass organizations controls the Party by its bureaucratic apparatus, by an internal Party intelligence network and by the state organs of the state, mainly army and police.

Because all key positions of the society are held by Party members, only Party members can seriously threaten the position of the managerial center. They are therefore subject to the greatest demands; they are carefully observed and cruelly punished if they fail to meet assigned tasks, show insubordination or independence. A preventive measure against the rise of a competing power center in the Party is the purge — periodical transfer and removal of persons who held an important position for a long time and had an opportunity to build their own cadre of followers and supporters.

Since individual persons of the center are identified with the Party program and ideology, differences in interpretation of the program and ideology become personal differences, and personal differences become differences of opinions on matters of policy. Because the complete unity of will of the power center is the pivotal point of the entire system, it must be preserved at all cost. Therefore personal and political differences which threaten such unity, are safely solved only by the liquidation of the power of one faction. Such power liquidation is usually sealed by the physical liquidation of the losers.

Totalitarianism

Once the reorganization of society reaches this stage, society is no longer only dominated, but its life and the life of its members in all its facets are directly shaped by the managerial center. The dictatorship has become total, the system has turned into totalitarianism.

Its development passes through three stages: that of suppression, of repression and of oppression. Suppression takes place prior, during and immediately after seizure of power and consists in eliminating actual individual political adversaries. It is characterized by the so-called revolutionary justice, savagery and brutal application of force.

Repression follows. It is directed against social groups whose members are silent or likely opponents. This stage is characterized by terror and staged monster-processes, concentration camps, confiscations and expropriations. The unrelenting pressure of the totalitarian machinery isolates and destroys opponents, strips them of hope and courage. Horizontal communications are almost destroyed and replaced by vertical communications culminating at the managerial center. Even within the family unit parents do not dare to speak openly in front of their children. Critics of the regime do not know each other, do not know of factors working in their favor, each of them faces the whole concentrated power of the Party and the state alone. The system of monopolies forms and transforms the views of the youth and of the formerly ideologically amorphous part of the population and consolidates the mass foundation of the regime.

Oppression is put into place after the actual as well as potential opponents have been crushed: it eliminates the possibility of the crystallization of any opposition. While the first two stages display violence and use repressive means, the last stage relies primarily on preventive means. Intimidation replaces violence. It functions by dissuading its subjects from even claiming, much less exerting their legal and human rights. This "anticipatory adjustment" with its attendant cynicism and passivity of growing strata of the population makes systematic use of force superfluous; the method changes to "silent oppression." The regime does not find it necessary to go after flies with howitzers; but it keeps the howitzers ready and uses them both as a deterrent and as the means of last resort as soon as stirrings of independence among the population become apparent

In initial stages of totalitarianism, discrimination is directed against actual adversaries and groups of a suspect profile. In a mature totalitarianism discrimination is total and triggered by any nonconformist trait, by deviation from "political correctness"; any subject who deviates from the expected behavior, loses the chance to live a normal (often even a marginal) existence: intellectuals who pursue their profession (science, philosophy, music, literature) in an independent manner, reformers who show concern about social issues (environment, nuclear power, sexual morality, family), persons who choose a different lifestyle, but also persons who attract attention by improving their house, buy new furniture, acquire a luxury car, have unusual supplies of coal and gas, regularly receive the same visitors, belong to a private group practicing music, trips or even regular card games or chess. It applies to individuals who make remarks indicating a nonconformist opinion and to those who become conspicuous by their non-involvement in officially sponsored organizations and/or activities, and finally also those who incurred in their private life the displeasure of some power figure or of an informer. There is less apparent brutality, but the scope of human rights (the sphere of freedom) for the general population is actually narrower that in the two preceding stages of suppression and repression; in fact, it comes close to zero.

The full totalitarian control consists mainly of (1) abolition of privacy, (2) conditioning through education, (3) punishment through social degradation, and (4) administrative harassment.

(1) Nonconformity (deviation from political correctness) is determined primarily on the basis of records kept by the executive branch of the state (mostly some branch of secret police). In a mature totalitarian state it maintains on everyone his personal file which contains general statistical information plus information on anything extraordinary (overachievement, underachievement), political activity or passivity, independent views, doubtful economic activity (hoarding, us-

ing his position for personal gain, diverting public property for personal profit), family life, sexual life, social life (recurring visits by the same circle of people, type of dress, decoration of windows at official celebrations), discrepancy between official income and standard of living. The data are gathered from official sources (court records, police records, employer, local government, Party records), but mainly rely on "unofficial" sources (informers, neighbors, colleagues, anonymous complaints or denunciations) who report matters not accessible to official sources (family quarrels, illicit sexual relations, unusual purchases of goods). The file is used for extortion, discrimination and/or criminal proceedings, as necessary, mostly to pressure for performance of activities which are not obligatory and which the subject is unwilling to perform (most frequently reporting on persons considered politically suspect or unreliable and on instances of politically incorrect attitudes).

(2) Indoctrination by the educational system begins early; it is an important part of the monopoly of intellectual leadership. The totalitarian system shies from bringing up the child in the family; it prefers that both parents be employed and the child be placed in nurseries and later in a state-run child care unit. From there, the child progresses to kindergarten and then to elementary education. Elementary school attendance usually brings into open the conflict of family values and the totalitarian ideology. Elementary schools are used both to inculcate in the children the official values and to check, by questionnaires, questions and discussions, the attitudes of parents. All educators are trained in a variety of "value clarification" techniques used to uncover deviant views (of pupils or of their parents).

At the time of adolescence and the beginnings of independent judgment, the system takes care that the free time available for formation and realization of nonconformist cultural elements is cut back as much as possible. Young people are required to enlist in the united youth organization which is part of the organizational monopoly of the Party and adds another channel of control. Active participation in directed cultural or recreational events is demanded and pupils and students are advised officially that their advancement on the educational ladder and later in their profession depends directly on the intensity and direction of their participation in such organizations. As members, they are under constant supervision by the appointed organization leaders whose observations are entered into their personal file.

Besides serving as a medium of indoctrination, the educational system serves as a medium of informal discrimination. From elementary schools on up to universities, teachers and professors not only impart information, but also investigate their pupils' opinions in study circles and seminars during discussions of public affairs and important events. Pupils and students learn early that certain opinions result in lower grades, denial of higher education, sometimes scolding or ridicule in front of their classmates. They also observe that this occurs mostly when they reproduce opinions they learned at home. As a result, parents avoid disclosing some of their opinions to their children, and vice versa; and children learn to dissimulate their parents' opinions from teachers, counsellors and colleagues. *A schizophrenic division of societal life takes place* since childhood. On one side stands the official culture, the formal public life carried on by the entire educational establishment, by mass media and by the entire propaganda machinery; on the other side exists the alternative (sub)culture of the private life sphere.

At the time of leaving elementary school, children are guided to a career; this "guidance" is as "voluntary" as any other activity in a totalitarian state. The selection depends on a profile of the applicant collected during his elementary school years; it contains not only abilities, it stresses primarily opinions and attitudes. A critical moment in the admission process is the interview in which the applicant tries to convince his interviewer of his positive attitude towards the regime and his sincere belief in the tenets of the inflammatory and contradictory ideas. The split in his personality is thus reinforced, especially if he is required to spy and inform on his colleagues as proof of his sincerity. The need for conformity and submissiveness is forcefully impressed on his character already prior to his adolescence and maturity.

The control function of the educational system extends to the educators as well. Only persons considered to be loyal to the regime are entrusted with the role of educators, and reliable Party members among students report on the contents of their lectures and their general attitude. School administrators examine whether lower grades are assigned to students of politically correct profiles and higher grades to those of nonconformist attitudes; if this is so, the teacher or professor is reprimanded or dismissed. Grading is supposed to be adjusted on basis of political correctness; during individual examinations, easier questions are put to students known for their loyalty to the regime, and more difficult ones to those suspect of a critical or independent attitude. (This leads to grotesque situations in which the examiner goads the student towards the right answers, respectively supplies them himself in form of comments, or tries to confuse the student through interruptions and unfriendly comments — according to the predestined outcome of the exam.) In view of this filtering out very few individuals suspected of nonconformity gain access to higher education and, consequently, to more important positions in society, on the other hand, incompetents graduate successfully and assume leadership positions. The same control applies to leaders of the official youth and other organizations; if they are reported as exhibiting politically incorrect attitudes, the consequences are more harmful for them than they are for nonconformist rank-and-file.

(3) The primary disincentive to nonconformity is the threat of status (job) demotion. Assignment of status is entirely under the Party's control exercised through state organs. Status demotion is the ordinary and most effective way of deterring the population from politically incorrect behavior, because it causes threefold harm. The affected person is deprived of the opportunity to hold a job which he finds interesting, for which he is qualified by his education or his abilities. With the demotion, there is financial loss. In view of the low productivity of this system, wages, salaries and pensions are low, barely covering the necessities of life. Therefore, even a moderate deterioration can push the victim and his family over the poverty level.

Low productivity causes scarcity of goods which in turn creates an entire economic subsystem of a "parallel" or "gray" economy based on bribes, pilfering of public property and a black market in goods and services. The parallel economy, although illegal or extra-legal, is tolerated because it enables the economy to function. By tolerating it, the "mature totalitarian regime" turns it into an additional vehicle of control. In the first place, the widespread participation in the parallel economy absorbs the energy of the subjects and redirects it from questions of politics, economics and ideology to the immediate non-ideological issues of individual and material improvement. In the second place, the participant in the parallel economy must have something to offer: influence, goods or services. The access to any of them is contingent upon the official status of the supplier in the official economic system. Thus the removal from a higher level status position diminishes not only one's legitimate income, but also his possibility to provide favors for which he is able to demand return favors and he often loses quite substantial income from the parallel economy (a doctor who is denied practicing medicine, is unable to bolster his income by obtaining "under the table" payments for better care; a dismissed bureaucrat is unable to provide more favorable treatment, a sales lady who lost her job loses also the option of putting aside scarce goods for her preferred customers, a worker dismissed from a factory is deprived of the possibility of "diverting" materials from the publicly owned factory where he works, and barter it for other, similarly "diverted" goods for use it in his moonlighting job). To be excluded from the networks of mutual services and counter-services is equal to loss of purchasing power in a market economy. Thus, the effects of status demotion are multiplied.

This applies mutatis mutandis also to the better situated strata of society where the loss of social prestige and economic means is psychologically felt stronger and has thus a stronger deterrent impact. The effects are multiplied, if the affected person is officially or unofficially blacklisted. This is tantamount to excommunication from society; the blacklisted person is not allowed to be granted adequate employment, there is a limit to the compensation he or his family may obtain, and he is forced to seek and accept the most unpleasant and least remunerated jobs because unemployment is considered parasitism on society — who does not work and in spite of that eats, is assumed to do so at the expense and to the detriment of society, which is punishable under the law.

In addition, participation in the parallel economy is usually illegal, yet practically everybody is forced to do it by the incompetence of the official economy. But the tolerance by the regime does not apply to nonconformists. While the transgressions are reported and entered into a personal file, they are used only when politically convenient — for demotion or prosecution. Thus every citizen lives under the threat of criminal prosecution for his "underground" economic activities and is well aware that this threat will be activated if he should show signs of nonconformity.

4. Administrative harassment. Under administrative harassment fall actions by authorities, mainly the police, which fall short of identifiable violation of laws, but nevertheless cause discomfort and economic loss to their targets and imply possible more serious measures in the future. Such harassment is applied at random to all citizens to keep them in line, and is intensified when there is indication of nonconformity. There are several common types of harassment: summons to appear at a police station for verification of identity documents (possibly several times in a week); or because of alleged presence at a car accident; searches: police are authorized to enter and search one's apartment for any "due cause," even faked; reviews of income tax reports, demand of proof of legitimate provenience of funds on the occasion of more expensive purchases, interrogation of friends, request for documents proving that purchases were effected on the official market.

Besides being a general means of intimidation, these measures are used more frequently against citizens who behave in a nonconformist way without breaking any law (for instance, failure to display a flag on days of official celebrations, refusal to sign required petitions or to contribute voluntarily to politically correct charities). It is maintained until the deviant behavior is abandoned.

For recalcitrant nonconformists, there are stronger measures. The target may be driven to a faraway location at night and released there to find his way home. He may be followed ostensibly by plainclothes men, persons he meets may be requested to produce identity papers or may be retained. He may be stopped by the police when leaving a grocery store, his purchases checked and stolen merchandise or drugs "found" among them, illegal publications or arms are "discovered" in his home. If he implies the police might have framed him, he may be guilty of "defamation of a public official" which is a punishable violation of the law. "Dissidents" are attacked and beaten by "unknown perpetrators" whom the police cannot uncover, and the victim is advised that his attitude provokes anger and disgust on the part of law abiding citizens against whose manifestations the police is unable to provide protection.

The most serious manner of administrative harassment is submitting the deviants to psychiatric examination and "cure" of their inability to adjust to the environment, fixed illusions of persecution mania (paranoia querulans), harassment of authorities, and other mental illnesses. Such patients are subject to mind changing treatments by drugs, and their official designation as mentally ill undercuts their credibility.

In spite of all efforts to the contrary, information about all inhabitants of the state cannot be complete: they are too many and the maintenance of a perfect system is financially too onerous. The ruling political organization compensates for this shortcoming by *terror*. For invisible oppression to succeed it is necessary not to be limited only to those whose nonconformist thinking or acting became obvious. The methods of administrative harassment must be applied randomly and daily to ordinary citizens who gave no cause for punishment — the Party demonstrates to them and their environment what would be the consequences if they dared to voice demands, no matter how legally justified. Therefore citizens do not complain or protest because they either do not dare to do so or are already conditioned to accept injustice as a part of the daily life. Since everybody violates the law in some way, they are mostly content to have gotten away so cheaply.

The citizen is aware of his helplessness and adjusts his behavior to the demands of political correctness although he considers them senseless and harmful.

The cumulative effect of the infringements on privacy, of the educational system, the economic pressures and administrative harassment and fear from denunciations from private persons ("the thought police") moulds the individual into a subservient being who does not even consider claiming his legal rights; he prefers to resort to lying, cheating, pretending and hypocrisy; his anticipatory adjustment constitutes the goal and success of the "invisible oppression." The population is dissuaded from resisting and yields to the demands and even tacit expectations of the Party. Society reaches the state of anomie — it has not accepted the value system of the rulers and has been prevented from creating or preserving a different one. Practical materialism forms the contents of the purpose of happiness; material well-being of the individual and of his family is equated with "the good." Therefore, open violence is rarely necessary: it suffices to threaten this content of one's primary purpose in order to obtain submission. Oppression exists, but it is invisible.

Regardless of this achievement, the system cannot stop its degeneration. The fastest consequence of the transformation of society into a hierarchical pyramid with the managerial center at its apex, is the loss of control of the rulers by the subjects. Absolute power leads inevitably to abuse if for no other reason than because the power holders lack an objective view of their actions and lose contact with their subjects affected by their decisions. This results in alienation between the normgivers and the subjects of duty — arrogance on the side of the rulers and distrust on the side of the subjects. The necessity to keep the population in a state of continuous enthusiasm causes exaggeration of official optimism to an extent which is counterproductive: its glaring discrepancy with reality destroys its credibility. The need to maintain pressure on the population produces an extensive police apparatus and a strong army and devours society's limited resources.

Lack of control of the rulers by their subjects engenders a high number of faulty decisions and arbitrariness which find expression in corruption, favoritism and rapacity at public expense and intensifies the decline of work ethics and of productivity. In spite of technology allowing instant communications with the entire territory of the state, the centralization inevitable for prevention of the rise of a competing power center, brings with it laggardness, confusion and inefficiency of the apparatus of the Party and of the state. The consequences of bureaucratization appear: the bureaucracy grows numerically and declines qualitatively. Absence of freedom stifles creativity. Unconditional, literally mindless conformity to the power center required from each citizen combined with suspiciousness and brutality towards anything nonconformist creates stagnation of social and technological progress visible primarily in the apparatus of the totalitarian state. Members of the managerial center as well as other holders of key positions turn from support of the power center towards augmenting personal power and wealth. Resulting purges remove from the apparatus potential and actual adversaries, emerged power centers and inefficient elements as bearers of the contradictory idea.

None of these measures can heal the basic weakness of this system of governing: the government's purpose inevitably interferes with the purposes of happiness of its subjects, and the concentration of exclusive power increases this divergence to the level of conflict and incompatibility. The system of power monopolies enables the Party to prevent manifestations of dissatisfaction, and the endeavor to channel it against the bearers of the contradictory idea only depresses further the credibility of the government. The accumulated frustration of the population, because unable to vent itself on its true source: the regime, turns against secondary targets: the immediate surroundings. People become egoistic, suspicious, distrustful, intolerant, envious and contentious, informing on and denouncing their fellow citizens out of envy becomes widespread.

After society has been subjected for a certain period of time to the effects of the system of power monopolies and sees no hope for a change from abroad, the totalitarian regime is *internally* consolidated. It is a society saturated with cynicism, hypocrisy and distrust whose members release their frustration and the nervous tension by irritability and envy towards their neighbors. The repercussions on the productivity of society are tremendous. For the system which violates and deforms them mentally and morally, people have only contempt and subvert it by apathy and reluctance because other, even legally permissible ways of venting disagreement are closed. The dissatisfaction remains, but is no longer dangerous; it cannot change from an amorphous feeling into a political movement with a clear political program which would react to the situation and solve its problems. Dynamism takes place only inside the ruling political organization, and even there it is impotent without the existence of disagreements in the managerial center. No matter how rotten inside, the managerial state is vulnerable only from the outside — through the penetration of its monopolies; but then its vulnerability is extreme, exactly because of its internal weakness. This fact dictates its relations with other states: as long as any state remain outside of its sphere of power, it feels threatened and is threatened.

Totalitarianism prevents differentiation as well as selection, and therefore does not evolve; it stagnates. The maintenance of an enormous preventive and repressive apparatus consumes an ever growing share of its economy which is inefficient, anyway. Therefore, it lags behind societies with a more appropriate structure and the managerial center faces an insoluble dilemma: either to completely isolate the state under its domination from the rest of the world, or to conquer the rest of the world. If it chooses the first opinion, it is vulnerable to technological development of the "free" world it cannot match: radio, television, computers subvert its monopolies of information and intellectual leadership; if it chooses the second option, it finds out that its lagging economy is incapable of producing the resources needed for an undertaking of such size.

The hopelessness of this dilemma induces the managerial center to attempt a revival of the creative forces of society by controlled admission of differentiation and selection. Such attempts undercut the very root of a mature totalitarian system, because its structure has become so fragile that it lacks the strength to keep the evolutionary elements within limits in which they would revive it to the necessary degree and avoid its disruption and collapse.

It is, therefore, safe to assume that like its predecessors, even this form of autocracy is a thing of the past. It has, nevertheless, been subjected here to detailed dissection because numerous of its elements are capable of reappearing in a new connection and under improved forms.

Decentralized Totalitarianism

It can be considered as proven that centralized totalitarianism is not viable. The question remains whether this applies also to a system which would divest itself of the burden of centralization and yet share most of the other features of a managerial and totalitarian state. Such a system is taking and in part already has taken shape distinct enough to be analyzed.

A decentralized totalitarian system is a state in which members of a science-derived ideological movement of an authoritarian minority occupy in society so many key positions that they are able to (1) impose the goals of the movement on society primarily by extra-legal means, and (2) deny access to power to members of any other ideological movement by using elements of a totalitarian state in its mature stage. The similarities of this new form of a lawless state to totalitarianism are such that its complete description would repeat the preceding chapter; it is therefore preferable and shorter to point out the differences.

The main difference is that this system is not anchored in a political managerial center; it is anchored in an ideological movement whose members react to challenges in basically identical ways without directions from a central body. Therefore they have earned, in polemics, the designations of "herd of independent minds" or "the hive" which aim to capture adequately the spontaneous uniformity of these protagonists of an improved humanity.

The other basic difference stems from the recognition that, in order to dominate society, it is not necessary to destroy all opponents or adversaries; it is sufficient to ensure that they remain powerless. In this respect, decentralized totalitarianism resembles the mature stage of totalitarianism where the rulers do not deem it necessary any more to annihilate each samizdat, to punish every ever so small nonconformist trait, to execute or incarcerate each dissident — because they are not dangerous any more. As a consequence, the decentralized totalitarianism's power monopolies are not total — they are near-monopolies limited in their extent by their sufficiency in accordance with the curve of declining utility.

A. Preconditions

A decentralized totalitarian system arises under the following conditions:

— A developed democracy of an industrialized or post-industrialized society with widely established managerism, with a public opinion generally considering science as final arbiter also in matters of social and moral norms so that the most recent scientific discoveries and conclusions are accepted as the highest authority for the arrangement of society, in other words: create the contents of what is a *betterment of the conditions* of society. The object of care of such purposes is usually the entire humanity, if not the whole of nature or the entire planet. The discoveries of scientific research from which such purposes are derived, form the ideology of the movement and they survive even if the scientific conclusions from which they are derived, are controversial, overtaken by research or disproved by experience. (During the latest past, the most influential of such ideologies are: overpopulation of the world, relative value of human life, reduction of the relation between sexes to the genitals, feminism and some ecological theories.)

Expert knowledge of the various sectors of the life of modern society is indispensable for an efficient implementation of technical purposes that arise from its development. The indispensable owners of this expertise can and often do arrive at the certainty that they know better than other members of society how life should be arranged in the area of their particular expertise, and strive to reach ways and means to do so. The proponents of a better society, better humanity or a better world do not derive their authority from the consent of society, but from their objective qualities, their expertise which lifts them above those who lack similar knowledge ("ratiocentrism" in the term of Czech author and president Vaclav Havel).

— A well developed knowledge class in possession of power nuclei of society, some members of which are convinced of their intellectual superiority over less educated strata and derives from this superiority its right/duty to lead them to a better life even against their will. Ideological movements arising within the knowledge class then become autocratic. The logical basis of their action is their self-assurance that the results of their scientific research are certain and true, and therefore cannot be subjected to decisions of those lacking their expertise. Such ideological movements (further on designated as the "Movement" for the sake of brevity) turn autocratic insofar as their adherents are convinced about the correctness of their ideas on the betterment of society to such an extent, that they proceed to their implementation regardless of the opinion of those whom they affect, even if the proposed and implemented changes bring about the disruption of existing morals and institutions (international relations, economic systems, cultures built on non-scientific premises and social, moral, religious and traditional norms), replace them by new ones and entail liquidation of "harmful" (under the objectives of the Movement) parts of society (members of a lower or subhuman race, superfluous children, subnormal individuals: the handicapped, incurables, mentally ill, over-aged). The changes affect deeply almost everybody and are therefore impossible to realize without compulsion and force. The ideological movements advocating such deep changes turn into interest and pressure groups which pursue their maximum objective (pedagogues voice unlimited demands for the improvement of the educational system, ecologists demand arresting industrial development, eugenicist demand the right to control procreation, and so on).

As any nonconformist, hemmed in and yet aggressive minority, the Movement is characterized by an above average solidarity of its members: they know each other and naturally assist each other in attaining authority and power. This process must have reached a certain degree before a Movement endeavors to impose their conclusions on society without its consent. Being a minority, in spite of its power, it does so either by manipulation (managerism) or compulsion (through bureaucracy) to the detriment of democracy.

— A widespread dissatisfaction with the situation of public affairs based on the political and economic corruption of the state apparatus which leads to the demand that decisions should be left to experts rather than "politicians", i.e., political professionals and managers. This attitude strengthens the position of the knowledge class and causes experts to share in all three branches of the government. The result is that the public as well as normgiving organs are excluded from debates among experts and appointed, unelected committees of experts make decision in political questions, decisions considered as improper for the public to question because they were made by qualified experts on a scientific basis.

— A new scientific discovery (in any field: biology, ecology, sociology, anthropology, medicine, technology, even physics and astronomy) made by a prestigious representative or institution (university) of the knowledge class, whose application would have far-reaching (and in the opinion of its author and his adherents) beneficial effects for the life of society and/or whose disregard would have catastrophic consequences. Individuals of this conviction form a scientific movement which shades over into an ideological movement, and demands derived from this discovery represent a program whose implementation would radically improve the situation of the object of care of the movement.

— Dominant position of members of the Movement in mass communications media (see Appendix 1) and other popular channels of forming the society's habits mainly in entertainment.

— Awareness that the application of this vitally important discovery and the implementation of the resulting program will meet with resistance of people who do not belong to the knowledge class (and, in the eyes of its members, disagreement with the Movement disqualifies automatically from membership in the knowledge class), but who are in the majority; this resistance is diagnosed as lack of intelligence or knowledge, influence of ingrained biases and irrational prejudices (especially of religious nature) or corruption by selfish interest groups. From this situation flows the moral obligation (a) to educate or re-educate the unenlightened majority and to "heighten its awareness"; (b) not to wait for the results of this re-education process and apply the discovery and the movement's program immediately in practice before irreversible harm is done, and (c) to impose it on the recalcitrant majority by force if necessary.

B. Building Own Sphere of Power

The creation of a power sphere begins when this conviction is internalized by that part of the knowledge class whose members do make important decisions affecting the life of society thanks to their exclusive ownership of the most important "means of production," i.e., information and expertise, and who are therefore practically beyond control of "the people", cannot be replaced or dismissed. The goal is to replace the existing "civil religion" by a new "civil religion" based on the ideology of the Movement. The innovators and reformers become autocratic and authoritarian. By "civil religion" is understood the system of values which society considers as self-evident and which are beyond any criticism; to criticize them "is not done" and is rejected as lapse of decency and proper manners. A civil religion is thus protected by society through proscribing its detractors and deviants.

Modern applied psychology furnishes knowledge which makes it possible to prepare a systematic plan for the manipulation of public opinion in order to weaken and discredit the existing value system without the manipulated majority becoming aware of the process. Psychologists and sociologists as well as experts in marketing, advertising and propaganda know that people do not act on the basis of rational deliberations, but can be more easily moved and convinced, when their rationality is circumvented.

1. Near-monopoly of information is needed to implement such a process as the Movement's adherents secure their hold on important positions in the mass media: television, radio, videos, newspapers, magazines, books and movies. They are the main source of information and important actors in politics because by selecting news they also determine the sequence, contents and limits of cultural and political discussions and mold public opinion at least to the extent to which they publish or not publish reports on events. The near-monopoly of information includes also the editorship of giant publishing houses; they ensure that politically incorrect books are not accepted for publication, and decide also what kind of books will be accepted for sale by the large distribution networks of booksellers and outlets; they prevent politically incorrect books and

magazines published by small local publishing houses from reaching a wide audience.

2. Near-monopoly of intellectual leadership. The strategy of gaining the monopoly of intellectual leadership in a communist state has been described (by an anti-communist underground organization) as follows: "In the first place, they strive to make Marxist ideology the basis of everyone's thinking. . . . Therefore, Marxism is taught to children as a main subject; therefore the press, radio, literature, theater, movies, art deal only with subjects that relate, positively or negatively, both in proper manner, with Marxism and communism. Other problems are non-existent." By replacing, in this quotation, the word "Marxism" by the ideology of the Movement, the above description very closely mirrors campaigns which create a near-monopoly of information and intellectual leadership for the latest science-derived program in a democratic society. The pattern of such a successful campaign of building a near-monopoly of intellectual leadership is then repeated over and over:

Step 1. For the discussion of the new ideology create a new terminology, usually with a scientific flavor, with a twofold objective. The primary objective is to disguise and de-emphasize the difference between the new thinking and demands and the traditional values.The manipulation of language, the creation of buzzwords that inhibit rational thinking, has reached the level of science (see appendix 2), and although the public has become aware of these manipulations, repeated and consistent use by the media brings the new terms into common usage and replaces the former, more realistic ones. The secondary objective is to dehumanize the victims of measures deduced from the ideological principle of the Movement.

Step 2. Select or manufacture an exceptional, even isolated, hard case and give it wide publicity (see Appendix 3) justifying remedies contrary to the prevailing ethics by recourse to its other values, mostly "compassion." The manipulators are aware of the principle that the greatest vulnerability of democracy lies not in its violation for reprehensible purposes, but for purposes which are morally attractive and good.

Step 3. By using the selected hard case make an unthinkable and unacceptable opinion or recommendation the subject of a public discussion in which its defense is presented as an example of intellectual courage and integrity attacking established unfounded taboos. The debate is dragged out until the terminology shifts as follows: first, the new opinion is presented as innovative, then as controversial, then the majority opinion is also dubbed as controversial, then the majority opinion is represented as outdated, oppressive and insensitive. Sympathy is diverted from those who are victims of the new ideology to those who victimize them by stressing the latters' "hard and painful choice", "difficult decisions," and by branding the defenders of the victims as "lacking compassion."

Step 4. In this climate, defenders of traditional values are excluded from prestigious positions in society prevailingly held by the members of the Movement (in universities, mass communications media), their arguments are either omitted or mentioned only critically or with ridicule. During publicized (televised) panels and discussions they are invited so that they are in a minority and discussions are directed so as to keep them on the defensive. This is true also about the composition of sundry government commission of experts. Because the Movement holds key positions in the institutions of intellectual life, its representatives have the reputation of most prestigious experts and therefore have a majority on commissions of experts; their opponents are included only as window dressing so as to provide a minority report documenting impartiality of the commission, and filed away without any relevance. (See Appendix 4)

Step 5. Shift the controversy from the intellectual to the sentimental by publishing novels, video-cassettes, movies and televised "docudramas" in which defenders of the traditional values are depicted as the bad guys (the greedy entrepreneur, fraudulent evangelical preacher, adulterous priest or nun, cynical member of the CIA) and the protagonists of the new morality as the good guys: unselfish, courageous, intelligent, persecuted and in the end against unbelievable odds victorious. In this process of breaking tradition, songs and music directed at the youth have great impact (see Appendix 1).

The near-monopoly of intellectual leadership includes the power to decide about the contents of education in elementary and higher schools. Although by law and international treaties the final word on education belongs to parents, the Movement shifts the decision making to educational experts and professionals as well as their organizations and eliminates the public's influence to such an extent that pupils and students are forbidden to reveal the contents of lectures or school books to parents; children entrusted to the educators are led to consider their parents' opinions as outdated, if not outright stupid, and parental authority is undermined in many ways (value clarification, questionnaires, encouragement of children's "independence" which is actually disobedience, by school counselors, librarians or health professionals).

3. Near-monopoly of organization. The Movement is not organized as such, it is *not* a conspiracy, but includes formal and informal nuclei in institutions which are occupied or controlled by its adherents: universities, learned societies, clubs, important organizations such as labor unions, associations of industrialists and clubs of financial power brokers, social organizations and social events, visits, receptions, private meetings. A preferred mode of association is the creation of outwardly independent organizations pursuing each its own distinct goals which, nevertheless, complement each other within the ranges of the the movement, support each other and often are linked by the leadership of the same persons ([10]). These groupings exhibit solidarity and participate in politics as pressure groups or act within political parties where their mutual solidarity gives them influence beyond their numbers. *The spontaneous uniformity of their reactions represents an effective parallel of the monopoly of organization.*

   This power of networking is augmented by infringement on or disruption of organized activities of others, especially organs of the state if they defend the traditional values still expressed by the laws. Such methods are: civil disobedience, impeding undesirable activities (logging of forests, building atomic plants) by forming human chains, sit-ins, occupation of buildings or disruption of traffic, marches, manifestations and demonstrations of nonviolent or violent nature, upscaled to the degree of mass vandalism or local uprising. These methods are facilitated by leniency and sympathy of the Movement's members located in important positions of the judicial, legislative and executive powers of the state; attempts to use the same methods in the interest of values contrary to the Movement's ideology are punished much more severely and have no hope of succeeding.

4. Monopoly of the means of production. The centralized type of control over the means of production exercised by totalitarianism is not appropriate for the Movement due to its diffuse structure. Rather than concentrating ownership of means of production in their own hands, members of the Movement use their expertise to manage means of production owned by others, and to direct economy

through financial operations. By gaining control of many other subjects' resources through banking, investment counselling, trusts and stock market operations, they dispose with amounts equalling or exceeding resources of some states and their power.

In securing its superiority, the Movement uses the method of social degradation similar to that of a totalitarian state, with the difference that it is mostly limited to the exclusion of the nonconformist person or institution from power and does not pursue his or its economic ruin, like a totalitarian Party does. By securing a near-monopoly on acquisition and application of knowledge and expertise, the most valuable "means of production" in post-industrialized economies, the Movement realizes an equivalent of the monopoly of material means of production.

5. Monopoly of arms. Because its unity and uniformity is spontaneous and decentralized, the Movement can attain a monopoly on arms only by proxy; such a proxy is the state. It is, therefore, averse to possession of arms by individuals or their organizations and favors their restriction to organs of the executive branch. This leaves the Movement vulnerable to the use of this monopoly for seizure of power by armed elements of the state apparatus either through lawless utilization of authority (by the police) or through institution of a dictatorship (by the military). The Movement is therefore wary also of a monopoly of arms in the hands of the state, especially because its control of the society bypasses the state and the state is not under its legal, official control. Because decentralized totalitarianism is only in the early stages of its development, it is impossible to predict how it will solve this dilemma; there are indications that creation of private security forces protecting their employers or of armed forces outside of the control of the state and under control of supranational organizations could be the way.

C. Penetrating the State

Decentralized totalitarianism relies much more heavily on preventive, rather than repressive means of societal control. An important part of it is the ideological corruption of the masses facilitated by the three above described near-monopolies and based on the antithesis of the inflammatory idea (for instance the vision of a perfect humanity whose carefully selected and numerically limited members live in the midst of unblemished nature in material ease and without pain) and the contradictory idea (nature destroyed by pollution peopled by overcrowded homeless masses dying of famine and thirst and suffering painful illnesses which could have been compassionately terminated).

It is bolstered by social degradation with economic consequences, and enforcement through organs of the state is not preferred. In realization of its aims, the Movement relies primarily on the pervasive managerization of society: on possession of power "knots" in all spheres of society's life, especially in economy, rather than on the organs of the state. The conclusions and values of the Movement are not implemented democratically, i.e., by spreading the movement's ideas, having them incorporated into political programs and then transformed into the will of the state through the legislative process. Rather, adherents of the Movement implement their ideas without the awareness or even against the will of the citizenry. Nevertheless, without sharing in the legitimate means of enforcement the Movement cannot implement the radical changes it plans; the inertia of the majority and deliberate resistance of a minority of the population would not allow it.

Because it is unable to attain a share in the direction of public affairs through democratic political processes (obtain a majority of votes for its program in elections), it acquires a share in the state's coercive power by circumventing democracy. In incorporating parts of the state organs into its sphere of power, the Movement has at its disposal its adherents within the state structure mainly in the non-legislative branches, i.e., in the executive and the judiciary. It utilizes their authority in several ways.

1. Usurpation of norm-giving in the name of expertise, as illustrated by following examples: In the system of obligatory public education, teachers and professors individually or through their organizations deny parents the authority of determining their children's education through changes in the programs, methods and courses by educationists. Librarians refuse to remove from public libraries books offensive to the community (pornography and advocacy of violent behavior), although directed to do so by the relevant authorities which pay their salaries. Doctors in hospitals refuse to comply with regulations restricting the practice of allowing children born with defects to die by withholding medical care. Artists render ineffective a law prohibiting funding of obscene art from public funds, as unacceptable censorship.

2. Usurping legislative power by utilization of the judicial branch. In remolding society and its morals, the judiciary plays a decisive role by redefinition of constitutional provisions and by interpretations of law which expand certain fundamental liberties and restrict others.

Being independent of the legislative branch, the Movement's adherents in the judiciary can transform the part of the culture, which represents the society's civil religion, i.e., values and concepts whose violation is generally considered "unthinkable" and "self-evident", and/or enact by judicial fiat measures rejected by the political process or invalidate laws enacted democratically ("judicial activism"). By accepting and dragging out spurious litigations the judiciary can also obstruct legitimate private or governmental activities contrary to the Movements ideology (production of armaments, construction of atomic power plants, building of dams, cutting lumber in privately or publicly owned forests, drilling for oil in the ocean or in areas inhabited by wildlife, etc.). The judiciary also restricts and punishes use of force by the police when used against segments of the population which are an object of special care of the Movement.

3. Utilization of sectors of the executive branch which are not directly under the control of legislative organs and are in hands of adherents of the Movement. By appropriate wording of regulations or implementing instructions, bureaucracy can obtain results not allowed by or prohibited by the law by enforcing "voluntary" compliance with its provisions contrary to to the intent of the lawgivers (example: racial quotas explicitly prohibited by the law, introduced as "voluntary" under threat of financial discrimination, and subsequently sanctioned by the courts).

   The judiciary can serve the purpose of enrolling parts of the executive branch into obedience of the Movement. Where courts are occupied by judges graduated by the prestigious schools dominated by the Movement's ideology and ideologues, the Movement uses them systematically to circumvent the legislatures in matters in which it could not obtain a legislative majority or succeed only with difficulty. The procedure is as follows: An organization belonging to the Movement or created by its members for that purpose, searches for or manufactures an event fulfilling the requirements of a hard case as described above under the paragraph dealing with the near-monopoly of intellectual leadership, and makes the case an object of litigation before a court or courts whose judges are known in advance to be adherents or sympathizers of the Movement. The litigation accompanied by unisono comments of the media under the Movement's influence is pursued all the way up to the highest appropriate judicial authority which decides in favor of the plaintiff. Laws and regulations of self-governing bodies issued in accordance with the democratic process in defense of the prevailing moral and social values and which are the object of the complaint, are then annulled by the judicial decision and the state's executive power is put in the position of enforcing them against the evident will of the citizenry (see Appendix 5).

D) In Power.

Decentralized totalitarianism can be considered as established, when "political correctness" or "cultural correctness" has become for the population the guiding norm whose violations entails extralegal punishment, i.e., harm of otherwise protected values. The contents of the norm of "correctness" are nowhere defined, much less legalized; nevertheless, everybody knows what "political/cultural correctness" means. Everybody is also aware that violations of that norm entail punishment, even if the law does not prohibit such incorrect behavior or protects it. Indictment can be raised by anyone even on the basis of private conversation or an overheard joke; no protection of privacy applies against this ubiquitous "thought police" nor is there any appeal. Nor is the punishment anywhere specified and subject to any fixed procedure; nevertheless, it is predictable: according to the deviation, for a student it may mean expulsion or postponement of examinations, for a professor refusal of tenure, for a bureaucrat no more promotions, for an employee dismissal, for anybody denial of otherwise available assistance from public or charitable funds, for a press reporter or TV commentator loss of a job, for a cabinet member a resignation.

The methods of a decentralized totalitarian state are similar to the methods of a mature totalitarian state. They consist mainly in unrelenting economic and social pressure whose extent is invisible, but omnipresent. The law may protect freedom of expression, but expressing certain opinions known as politically or culturally incorrect, has disagreeable consequences. A book not using politically correct terminology has problems finding a publisher, and if published, will not be distributed by the large bookselling companies. Articles written in an incorrect style will be published only by newspapers and publishing houses considered as non-prestigious..

The Movement subjects also the past to revision. New editions of books of old authors and translations are adjusted to the new norms of correctness (cf. frequent new translations, actually rewrites, of the bible or of Catholic rituals). Even fairy tales are rewritten. The language, clothing, social conventions are changed. Over custom, language and social habits decentralized totalitarianism achieves a degree of control of which totalitarian regimes could not even dream.

Decentralized totalitarianism has several advantages over other forms of autocracy. One of them is anonymity. Its leaders seek primarily power and affluence, not glory; they often shun publicity and prefer anonymity. The public does not know who makes the decisions of moving entire industries from the United States to Mexico or from Japan to Canada. The public does not know who negotiates the extra-political global concentration of industry, finance, communications. The public does not know who holds the power to ruin currencies and bankrupt national economies. The public does not know who decides which life-styles and value systems the mass media will extol and spread and which ones they will treat with silence or ridicule. The public does not know who sits on the committees of the sundry international, regional and global organizations and prepares action programs subsequently implemented by international bureaucracies although never subjected and/or approved by any democratic process. The public does not know who diverts international institutions from their role of integrating nations and states to the objective of abolishing states' independence and national diversity. Anonymity guarantees immunity, frees from accountability and responsibility.

The appropriation of power by the Movement is not marked by any date, any visible event, revolution or putsch, it is therefore invisible to the majority of the population and protesting groups lack, in the presence of the Movements near-monopoly of information, the means to evoke, spread and crystallize dissatisfaction. Their pathetic attempts at printing and distributing limited edition bulletins, semi-samizdat publications and at sustaining small local radio stations are ignored or ridiculed by the mass media. The fact that the ruling Movement has no identifiable center, means that disagreement and dissatisfaction have no identifiable and vulnerable target. This elusiveness of the responsible subjects of volition deludes critics to suspect conspiracies and secret societies which they cannot prove because they are non-existent. Members and adherents of the Movement are of course in touch with each other and communicate at meetings, conventions and congresses of institutions they control and at private visits and gatherings, and they discuss plans and arrive at decisions. But the assertion of secret and mysterious activities misses the target, damages credibility of its authors and is easily rendered ridiculous. Anonymity protects those who are responsible for the formulation and enforcement of sundry measures advocated by the Movement. But who knows and can generate interest in the names of members of various expert commissions, managers of charitable funds and boards of prestigious universities whose resolutions are put into practice by non-public and extra-legal means whether the state approves them or not?

The choice of not stamping out all opposition brings about a considerable savings of energy of the Movement. In this regard, the law of diminishing returns applies. The last expended means bring the least results and are the most expensive ones. The harm to the objective of the Movement which would be caused by its attempt to eliminate all opposition, would be greater than the harm which can be caused by an impotent opposition. Non-existence of drastic repressive and preventive measures effectively masks the autocratic structure of society.

It is still impossible to gauge the full potential of a better totalitarian system superior to its predecessor in that it does not require sacrifices, but in exchange for freedom pretends to give people candy in the form of "rights."

CHAPTER 8

OBJECT OF CARE

The state's object of care is its entire population, and the state's objective is to bring it (closer) to the implementation of the program defined by its source of will.

Pluralism

The population is not an organized entity, nor is it an amorphous entity. Each of its individuals pursues certain secondary goals similar or identical with other subjects, and in accordance with this similarity (or identity) they form not only movements, but also groups with the same interest. Such common interests may be commercial, labor, agricultural, gender oriented, regional, ideological, religious, ethnic, national, minority and any other of the myriad of purposes derived fom the purpose of happiness, capable of being expressed, communicated and found to be in common with similar derived purposes of others..

Interest groups exist in any type of state, they are expressions of pluralism of its population, an important part of each political system as they express and crystallize particular interests in the form of demands on the system, or in its support, propose solutions to their particular problems and recommend or resist certain measures taken by the public power. By their demands and attitudes, they affect domestic policies and can also influence foreign policy of the state, especially if they maintain contacts and cooperation with groups of similar interests abroad.

For *autocratic* systems, pluralism created by interest groups represents a potential competition to the ruling political organization, because they grant at least some form of support against the state; they give their members an opportunity to be active in areas in which they are interested (for instance chess players in chess or trade unionists in labor organizations) and to participate in public affairs in ways outside of politics; their representatives have an opportunity to voice publicly their opinions and needs. Totalitarian states, therefore, integrate them into their system of monopolies and use them for their own purposes.

In *democracies*, interest groups contribute to create *political* pluralism. Members of society are free to aggregate in groups and to organize, and thus protect and promote their interests and ideas. All groups have a chance to share freely and actively in political life in defense of their members' interest, compete or cooperate with each other, but no group has so much power as to dominate political life; power is widely dispersed. Because interest groups can back certain political programs, parties or politicians, the government is sensitive to their needs and demands.

In a democracy, interest groups have several traits common with political parties: both aggregate and articulate opinions and needs, both express such needs in the form of demands and both act as political subjects demanding that the state include such demands into its purpose of betterment of society.

Minorities

The fact that all people under the state's sovereignty are its object of care, does not mean that the ideal to which its policies (= utilization of its means) lead is the providing of power and wealth for all parts of society. The ideal of society as formulated by the political process (the legislature) usually includes the increase of power and wealth of some groups at the expense of other groups. Some political ideals include a complete removal (liquidation) of certain portions of society; the communist ideal had no place for owners of means of production, the Nazi ideal of society had no place for members of certain racial groups. The successor states of Yugoslavia have no place for members of other than one nationality. The elimination of minorities is the goal of many states especially if said minorities threaten their state's existence or integrity. The elimination of unwanted or undesirable components is, in the value system of a state which pursues the elimination, "betterment" in the sense that it implements the program of governing political organizations transformed legally into the will of the state.

For *autocratic* states, minorities do not represent a separate problem; they are a part of the overall effort to impose the will of the ruling political organization on the entire population. Methods of oppression used against everybody differ in degree, but not in kind, when used against members of minorities. Depending on the political ideal of the state, members of minorities can either escape the intensified persecution by giving up their minority status, like renouncing their ethnic, national or religious allegiance and accepting ethnicity, nationality or religion demanded by the state. In other instances, such option is not left to them: they are considered "enemies of the state" by virtue of their very existence as they are members of an undesirable group and cannot change their appurtenance by an action of will; their source of cohesion with the group is causal and not optional; their discrimination or persecution is permanent.

For a *democratic* state, minorities present a twofold problem: heterogeneity of norms felt by an outvoted minority, and incompatibility of equality of individuals with equality of groups.

The fact that outvoted minorities will be subject to the will of numerical majorities and that the norms issued by the majorities will be imposed upon them without their consent, is integral to democracy. One of the main features of democracy, which permits the outvoted minority to tolerate and respect norms given against its will by a majority, is the possibility that the minority has the chance of becoming a majority and to change the heterogeneous norms. However, when the situation is such that it prevents permanently or for a long tim the outvoted minority from becoming a majority, democracy becomes in the eyes of the minority a "dictatorship of the majority" even if all the rights of the members of the minority are equal to the rights of the majority and are fully respected.

Equality for Individuals

Acceptance of heterogeneous norms by the minority is facilitated by the limitations imposed on the state by the democratic form of government, i.e., laws must not interfere with fundamental liberties and human rights of members of minorities. This delineates for each individual a sphere of freedom inviolable by the state. Such basic rights are embodied in the constitution, and in order that they cannot be affected even by amendments of the constitution, there is the tendency to put certain spheres of life completely beyond the jurisdiction of the state, i.e., place them *above* the constitution. This type of rights is called "*inalienable* human rights."

Because the nature of inalienable rights is not contingent upon the constitution, it has to be considered as a norm superior to the constitution, and be derived from a normgiver superior to the state. As an ordering legal principle, this superiority was adopted by British colonies in North America as justification of their segregation from England: their legal philosophy appealed to the Creator who created people as equal and endowed them with certain inalienable rights whose violation empowered the state's subjects to revolt. The Declaration of Independence mentions only three such rights: life, liberty and pursuit of happiness, and the Constitution left open the question who, if any (except, of course, the Creator) is authorized to create additional inalienable rights. In practice, this power, actually the power to define the will of the Creator, was usurped by the Supreme Court and the arbitrariness by which it was discovering, narrowing and expanding inalienable rights, evoked efforts to subject this normgiving to the political process and equate it with an amendment of the Constitution.

As long as the derivation of inalienable rights from the will of the Creator is accepted as real, their content and extent remains basically a religious question; once this acceptance becomes questionable, the entire concept of inalienability is undermined and different concepts of their normgiver are brought forward. The French Revolution that replaced the rule of God by a rule of Reason, deduced the inalienability of some rights from the very nature of man; man has inalienable rights simply because he is human. This philosophy very quickly became even more vulnerable than the American concept because different people can for different reasons arrive at different rights inherent in man's nature. The relative inalienability of such rights was expressed by the very text of the Declaration des Droits de l'Homme which allowed their limitations by law and led to revolutionary terror, a phenomenon through which the American Revolution never passed.

The philosophy of inalienability of human rights found a new and strong support in international law; the demand for respect of inalienable rights was a very effective means by which democratic states defeated autocratic states in both world wars. (For their present role in international relations see Chapter 24.)

Preferences for Individuals

Observance of human rights and civil liberties creates a formal equality of opportunities and equality of opportunities leads to competition in which some individuals get ahead and others remain behind. If the winners in the competition — in schools, jobs, life — are sorted on the basis of properties which are the source of coherence of minorities (race, gender, nationality, religion) and if numbers of minority members are substantially higher or lower than its share of the population, the question is posed why the results are such as they are. The explanations are of two types: One of them finds the explanation in the properties of the minority members. They may be caused by heredity of genes proper to certain groups (Chinese and Jews dominate on American universities in mathematics and theoretical physics, in chess Russians, in sports Negroes). Another explanation is based on sociological facts (in American schools, the best students are children of immigrants from the Far East, the lowest are Afro-Americans; the cause is said to be the family structure of these minorities: immigrants from the Far East maintain a hierarchical structure of the family with relatively strict discipline and high regard for education; the Negro family has mostly fallen apart during the last two decades — about half of them has no father; in a high percentage of families already the third generation lives on welfare.

The other type of explanations locates the reasons of unequal results outside of the minorities; these explanations come mostly from members or advocates of low performance minorities. The simplest explanation is that the below average achievements are due to hidden, but real prejudices of the rest of the society (racism, religious intolerance). Another explanation is the accusation of the entire culture — patriarchy is responsible for a lower percentage of women in leading positions; industrial civilization overvalues technological and technocratic competence in comparison to other abilities.

Both explanations agree that the principle of formal equality of opportunity is unjust because not all competitors start from the same material point of departure. From this reasoning derive two demands. The principle of equal opportunity must be replaced by the *principle of equal results*. Where results are not equal, this in itself is a proof of discrimination. The principle of equal rights and equal liberties must be replaced by the principle of fairness which is basically a somewhat diluted principle of solidarity: the weaker must be supported at the expense of the stronger, so that the outcome is the same. Translated into practice this means that various groups strive to be legally recognized as victimized minorities (such is in the United States the status of women who are legally a minority while numerically being a majority), and that their leaders carefully follow the statistical composition of all areas of life: what percentage is given in school books to female, Negro, Indian and Hispanic authors, how many pages in history are devoted to non-Christian religions, how many hurricanes are given male or female names, how many faces of this or that group appear on stamps, members of which minority have been promoted in this or that corporation, how many homosexuals were denied renting apartments, how many public projects are assigned to minority owned businesses, what is the percentage of minority members jailed for criminal offenses, and so on *ad infinitum*.

The principles of equal results and subjectively defined fairness can be implemented only by abandoning the principle of equality of all citizens in favor of members of minorities. The size of this abandonment is proportionate to the actual power relationship between the majority and the relative minority and the power relationship of the minority to the state. The state gives priority in allocating material aid, opportunity and positions to members of a minority (minorities) over members of the majority. (A political movement and/or a political party advocating this reverse discrimination is not necessarily composed only of members of the minority which is its object of care; it comprises also other individuals for whom the betterment of the status of a minority is a part of the purpose of happiness. This is true especially when the discrimination of a minority is real and generally recognized as such). If the basis for the allocation of certain goods is a numerical relationship, the allocated proportions represent quotas whose implementation is enforced by the state power. Quotas can decide access to jobs, promotions, education, to housing, number of employees and their hierarchical positions, numbers and functions in public administration and in the highest organs of the state or even in number of convicts on the death row. If access is related to competitive tests and if the outcome is unfavorable for a minority, changes in the scoring of tests are introduced. One of the changes is the socalled race- or gender-norming: prior to comparing test results, a multiplier is applied to scores of minority members; if this practice is challenged, the ratings of various questions or composition of tests are adjusted so as to bring about the desired results ([11]). This type of equalization of results causes resentment of those who are its victims, i.e., members of the majority, and affects adversely mutual individual and group relations between the majority and the favorized minorities.

Equality for groups

The demands of minority groups may not be, and often are not, satisfied by satisfaction of private needs of their individual members. Democracy, civil liberties and human rights, and principles of equality of results and fairness are insufficient in cases, when a minority group pursues also a goal of securing equality for itself *as a whole*. This is true mainly about national and religious minorities and creates a conflict between two concepts of equality; one of them is based on the principle of equal individuals, the other on the principle of equal groups (without regard to the number of members).

In the organization of a democratic state, those two concepts of equality are irreconcilable. Integral application of the principle of equality of individuals means that the numerically stronger group can always outvote the smaller group; integral application of the principle of equality of groups means that a vote of each member of a minority has politically a greater weight than a vote of a member of the majority. Members of the majority consider this as discrimination.

One way of solving this dilemma is to chose one of the principles and enforce it by means of the state's power. This causes constant tension and alienation of a permanent group of citizens to the legal order and necessitates increased outlays for enforcement of the law against the dissatisfied group, especially if it feels morally justified in using illegal means of political struggle — passive resistance (civil disobedience) or violence (terror). Another option is adopting quotas according to which the minority and majority groups are represented equally and not in proportion to their numerical share of the population. This necessitates enforcement against the majority which might resist in the same way.

Another solution to the contention between the two principles is often sought in the bicameral system of the legislature: one house is elected on the principle of equality of citizens, the other house is elected on the basis of equality of groups constituting the state, for instance of national minorities ("House of Nationalities"). Laws do not acquire validity unless approved by a majority of both houses. This arrangement can still create situations, when representatives of the majority allied with a minority of the delegates of the other groups can consistently impose their will on a majority of the representatives of the minority (minorities). An instrument to prevent this from happening is the rule called "prohibition of majorization": for a law to be adopted, a majority of all groups represented in the "chamber of equal representation of minorities" is required. In practice, this method has succeeded nowhere.

Still another option of how to comply with the requests of minorities is *decentralization* of state structure on the territorial basis. It is practical only if members of the minority inhabit a continuous and reasonably compact territory. In this case, the constitution can assign to lower level normgivers a share of the central legislative, executive and judicial powers sufficient to satisfy the minorities' demands. Such a decentralization granted to an area inhabited by one minority and not to other parts of the state, it is called *autonomy* of the territory privileged in this way. States are usually hesitant to grant extensive autonomy because it harbors the potential that the autonomous territory will declare its independence of the state's sovereignty and opt for its own sovereignty or the sovereignty of another state.

All of the above mentioned methods of securing rights of minorities are in practice variously combined, but any arrangement based on equality of numerically unequal groups harbors one danger which grows in proportion to the numerical disparity between majority and minority (minorities), namely that the price paid for elimination of dissatisfaction and alienation of a minority is the creation of dissatisfaction and alienation of the majority . Under certain circumstances, the only peaceful solution is the legal separation of the majority and the minority which preserves the democratic principle of equality of citizens by the division of the state's sovereignty, in extreme situations the cessation of territory to another state or the break-up of the common state.

Anti-Semitism

Anti-Semitism requires a separate analysis because it differs in important ways from other types of discrimination and because the protection against it has its specific features.

In the first place, its designation is inaccurate. By anti-Semitism is not meant discrimination of any Semitic nation or ethnic group, but only of a certain branch of the Semitic race, namely the Jews. Nor is the definition of Jewishness or Jewry quite clear — is it a religious, race, national or ethnic minority? Because the definition of the term is not clear, it is not clear who is affected as a member of the discriminated group, respectively who belongs to it. Here all three, possibly four, characteristics play a role: Jews are a Semitic nation whose cultural source of cohesion is a specific religion. As a nation they are characterized by the fact that a majority of its members for a majority of its history lived among other nations as a minority and that only they survived these conditions as a combination of a national and religious community.

In this connection, it is useful to mention one biological fact: the average weight of a male brain exceeds the average weight of a female brain; the average weigth of a brain of a white male brain of a white female; the average brain of a male of the Negro race equals the average weight of a brain of a white female; the average weight of a brain of a white male equals the average weight of a Mongol female brain and does not reach the average weight of the brain of Mongol males. But the average weight of Jews' brains equals the average weight of the Mongols, i.e., exceeds the average brain of the members of the rest of the white race. The importance of these relationships is a matter of dispute among biologists, anthropologists, sociologists and politicians, but it is a factual datum.

A unique feature of the status of the Jewish minority is that international law and international institutions grant it a special protection not granted to any other minority; for instance the European Union does not grant membership to states where anti-Semitism exists. Nor is the content of this term anywhere specified. It includes, of course, the defamation of Jews as a nation or denial of equal rights to persons considered and/or claiming to be Jewish; sometimes, any criticism of the state of Israel, whether its foreign policy (annexation of conquered territories) or domestic policies (discrimination of Arabs) is pilloried as anti-Semitism; the same applies to collection and/or publication of statistics about the share of Jews in the upper management of certain sectors (finance, business, mass media) or professions (physicians, lawyers).

There exists a certain pattern repeating itself in Jewish history. They arrive in a foreign country under pressure (political, military, economic) as needy immigrants; then, for whatever reason, in a relatively short time they rise to leadership and advantageous positions. This produces, in the aboriginal population, first envy and then hatred. As a minority in strange surroundings, the Jewish minority (which always brings with it its own organizational structure) relies on protection of the ruler or of the government which, in the eyes of underprivileged strata, identifies it with the oppressors and alienates them even more. It is these least educated and most disadvantaged parts of the population which are the first to "avenge" themselves on Jews as a group. (A similar phenomenon are attacks on Asian owned businesses in the Negro neighborhoods of American cities.)

The perceptibility of Jews is increased by their inability to merge with the host nation. This is inevitable. What can German myths, Slav history, Wickliff's and Luther's efforts at reforming Christendom, wars and blood letting about national borders mean to a member of a nation to whom God Himself was personally acting as lawgiver because He selected them as His special nation thousands of years before all these nations and Christianity even existed? How important can empire building of the Habsburgs, the British Empire or the settlement of

America appear to a member of the nation which survived long ago the emergence and disappearance of mightier empires (Babylonians, Assyrians, Persians, Romans)? His perspectives must of necessity be different from the attitude of those who lack them. The limits of Jewish identification with the cultures of the host nations brings with itself a certain distance accompanied with an admixture of condescendence towards the domestic culture, resulting from the excellence of Jewish culture, the tradition of Jews as the elect nation and the unique continuity of their history which precedes and exceeds the very existence of the host nations.

The success of Jewish elements in the host nations is related to their ability to view and understand the world from another, different angle, to discover relationships not perceptible to the surrounding culture. Among the best thinkers of Jewish origin, this ability manifests itself by unique revelations which the domestic culture is sometimes able to assimilate, but sometimes not; if not, they produce a disruptive effect. Jesus had such an influence on the ancient world; Marx on economics and politics; Freud and Jung on morality; Einstein on physics, Gloria Steinem, Bella Abzug and Betty Friedan on marriage and sexual relations. The primitive envy and hatred then acquire a cultural dimension, and because the domestic population cannot equal the Jewish minority in any other way, it reaches for the last resort of those who find themselves in a corner, endangered, helpless to match those of superior mind: violence which takes on the form of formal discrimination, expulsion or even genocide. This was the fate of the Jewry from their settlement in Egypt up to the Third Reich. It is a sign of the intellectual dominance of the Jewish mind that they managed to obtain the condemnation of all their host nations in various eras and various continents while preventing the examination of the common element of their tribulations: the effects of their presence on a foreign environment.

From the superiority of the abilities of members of the Jewish group flows also a basic difference between the prohibition of anti-Semitism from other measures aiming at protection of minorities. Minorities commonly strive to have their own protected sphere of cultural freedom and a numerically proportional share in the wealth and power in the state. These demands result in claims for autonomy and quotas. The prohibition of anti-Semitism does not aim in the same direction: it demands removal of all obstacles to free competition, cultural or economic, it strives to free members of the Jewish community from any limitations and barriers by any kind of application of power. They do not need autonomy or quotas; where their innate abilities are given free play, the strength of their culture and the power of their intellect will secure for them positions and influence exceeding visibly their numbers. Rise of anti-Jewish sentiments among the populace follows. Historically, the Jewish communities relied on the protection of the ruler or the group in power; at present, the indispensable condition of their free growth is individualistic democracy and a new world order whose organs would guarantee them the necessary freedom and security against application of power wherever they feel or are endangered. In the past, the strategy of relying on rulers and governments failed sooner or later because national rulers or governments would be reluctant to use force against their own people in protection of an markedly different community; on the contrary, they often used anti-Semitic passions for their own purposes. Because this motif of national solidarity is lacking in international organizations, there is hope that international organizations could grant them the desired protection; if a latent resentment of the indigenous population can be prevented, remains in doubt.

CHAPTER 9

ECONOMY

The collapse of state planned and/or directed economies marked the triumph of the free economy, and at the same time diverted the attention from the general overview of the types of economic systems. Nevertheless, such an analysis is indispensable for an active academic or practising participant in political theory and practice.

In order to achieve the purpose of happiness, each individual acquires goods and utilizes them. This is his economic activity. The total of the economic activities of individuals as well as that of other subjects of volition pursuing their sundry technical objectives constitutes the economy of the state.

Each individual is a subject of duty of the state under whose sovereignty he lives, as well as a part of the state's object of care that encompasses all persons on the state's territory. Therefore, the state observes and evaluates the economy on its territory from the standpoint of the state's idea of a good (or better) society and interferes with it when it finds economy's results harmful or not useful enough.

According to the basic principle under which an economy functions, economic systems fall into two groups: economic activities are driven by the needs of individuals as perceived by them — economic individualism — or by the needs of society as perceived by the state — socialism.

Individualism

The individualistic economic system is built on the premise that every individual takes care of himself, i.e., procures and utilizes means according to the purposes derived from his primary purpose of happiness. Subjects of volition acting under an objective technical purpose proceed similarly. The main features of such system are as follows:

Each legally recognized subject of will, whether an individual or a collective body (business, corporation, partnership) acts independently in economic matters following singlemindedly his or its purpose. As a consequence, available goods (= useful objects) are divided among the subjects of economic activities to the extent to which he or it is able to obtain by his or its own efforts. Material freedom, i.e., the possibility to act according to one's primary purpose, is secured legally. The possession of appropriate goods, if guaranteed by law, becomes one's *ownership*; without it, one's political freedom and rights are constrained in practice and may become illusory.

The principle of economy (to obtain a maximum usefulness at the cost of minimum harm) generates division of labor and trade: the subject of economic actions swaps (exchanges) his (i.e., owned by him) goods of lesser utility for goods in the possession or ownership of other subjects who, for their own purposes, rate the utility of the owner's goods higher than the usefulness of goods in their own possession (ownership). *Trade (exchange, swapping) takes place when interests of the trading parties are complementary, and ceases as the trade becomes harmful to one of the trading parties.*

The network of exchanges creates a *market* from which the designation of this system as a *market economy* is derived. It assumes that individuals are better qualified to take care of their needs than the state. Its main characteristic is *its productivity*. Consumers (buyers) communicate their needs to distributing organizations (retailers and wholesalers) who in turn place orders of the goods in demand to producers. To serve the needs of consumers becomes the pivotal point of the economy, because each entrepreneur follows the objective of maximum profit whose size depends on ability to satisfy customers' demands.

Exchanges of goods and services are radically facilitated by the existence of a good which is acceptable to all economic subjects as a common denominator in which they can express the degree of usefulness by which they value the traded goods. Such a good, originally having its own intrinsic value, i.e., mostly rare metals, has been gradually replaced by an imaginary claim on a portion of the goods produced by society: paper money (supplemented by the use of checks and more recently so-called plastic money and electronic transfers). The system of exchange changed to a *monetary economy*. On the market, economic subjects offer goods demanded by other economic subjects for a number of units of the exchange medium, i.e., money, according to the grade of usefulness perceived by them with regard of their respective goals; they place a *price* on the the goods they offer. The existence of a market generates production of goods their owners do not need for themselves, but produce only to place them on the market; such goods are *merchandise*. If demand increases, prices rise, if supply increases, prices fall; similarly, falling prices increase demand, increased demand lowers the amount of available goods, and prices rise . Buyers compete with each other, and so do sellers. Individualist economy is a *competitive* economy. Competition is in prices as well as quality of the goods offered and conditions (terms) of payment. Those who sell below the cost of producing or acquiring their merchandise and those for whose merchandise there is no demand, are eliminated from the market. Competition is the dynamic force of a market economy: it lowers prices and increases the variety and quality of goods.

In order to fill its role as common denominator of various goods, money must be stable, the monetary unit must have the same value in time, must buy the same quantity of merchandise or its equivalent also in the future. Fluctuation of the purchasing power of the monetary unit impedes forward planning and favors certain economic subjects while harming others. When the purchasing power of a monetary unit rises (deflation), existing borrowers must spent a higher than expected quantity of goods in order to pay off the same amount of their borrowings. If the purchasing power declines (inflation), the lenders are able to obtain only a lesser quantity of goods for the amount of the loan than they would have at the time of lending. Deflation favors lenders, inflation favors borrowers. Both distort and disrupt the equilibrium of the economy created by the markets, and thus subvert the market economy.

Market economy oscillates between economic growth and recession. During the period of prosperity, the income of consumers rises and enables them to increase their purchases. In order to satisfy their demand, producers increase the supply of goods to the market. Increased demand of goods and services by consumers and their suppliers creates a pressure on prices and forces prices of goods, labor and money upward. When the prices, especially the price of money (interest rates) reaches a certain point, they become prohibitive for consumers as well as suppliers (producers), and they stop buying. Due to diminished demand, enterprises overburdened by interest or producing unsalable merchandise are forced to stop or restrict production and start to dismiss employees. If those who lost jobs are also overburdened by borrowings, they are unable to keep up their payments for houses, cars, furniture. etc., and must give them up at a loss. With the decline of prices the consumers and suppliers who avoided overextension during the previous period of an economic boom, start buying again; production picks up, jobs open, the unemployed begin to share again in the economic processes, and the recession turns into a new economic upswing, into recovery. (The period between recession and recovery varies according to circumstances. During World War Two, Germany and Japan were so heavily affected by the war that the accumulated demand provided a long period of prosperity.)

Goods are produced by *work*, but work alone is not sufficient. To be effective, the worker needs tools as means of production. With the progress of technology, means of production become more complicated and more expensive. In order to produce, the entrepreneur must have available the goods needed to obtain in exchange the means of production. In a monetary economy, this means he must accumulate the necessary amount of money, the necessary capital. Because the individualistic economy is based on the principle that everybody takes care of himself, the natural law of the survival of the fittest applies. In a monetary economy, fitness does not reside in physical qualities; nor are mental qualities the most important; fitness — strength — belongs to those who have at their disposal the largest amounts of money, who are owners of capital, capitalists; an individualistic economic system is also a capitalist system, *capitalism*.

Owners of capital exchange it for means of production, and if they themselves do not work with them, they hire others who perform the work for a compensation, usually monetary; the size of the compensation is determined on the market (labor market) by demand and supply similarly to the price of goods. The utilization of means of production and labor requires efficiency and efficiency requires organization; this can be handled by the owners themselves or by experts (managers) hired for this purpose. Thus is born a subject different from its constituent parts with a separate primary purpose that is objective and can be communicated. This purpose is maximum monetary profit, the subject of will thus created is an enterprise. *An enterprise is an organization of capital and labor for the purpose of monetary profit*. Because the utilization of means of production is controlled by their owners and because owners are private individuals, the system is also called the *private* or *free enterprise system*.

Ownership of means of production is important because economic fluctuation affects primarily those who do not own them, i.e., those who are constrained to procure their livelihood on the market of labor. The individualist economic system results in the division of society into two groups. The source of coherence of one of them is that its members *do own means of production*, of the other the fact that they *do not own means of production*. On the basis of their interests, each group creates economic and political organizations. The main point of contention between them is how to divide the results of their joint economic undertakings, i.e., the profit of their enterprise, because ultimately the share of one of the participants in the enterprise — capital (owners), labor (wage earners) and organization (managers) inevitably diminishes the share devolving to the other participants. For dealing with the others, mainly the owners, labor organizes into unions which create a sort of monopolies on the labor market. Politically, labor attempts to secure legislation which would involve the powers of the state in matters of the division of the joint result of the workers' and their employers' efforts, by legislating minimum wages, pension funds, working hours, work environment, hiring and firing, profit sharing and labor participation in the management of the enterprise (i.e., utilization of the means of production owned by others) or even in a change of the entire economic system.

Rather than be entrepreneurs, owners of capital may consider it to be to their advantage to lend, for a price, the money to other subjects of economic activities. This price is called *interest* and is determined on the market of capital on the basis of supply and demand for various types of loans (long term, short term, secured, unsecured) in the same way as the price of goods and of labor. These three markets are interconnected and influence each other. Demand for goods creates a demand for capital and labor so that interest rates and wages rise; a lower interest rate facilitates lower prices which in turn stimulates demand. The movement in the price of labor has a similar effect. This interrelationship increases the efficiency of this economic system. Through its price mechanism, the market of goods dampens the production of certain goods and encourages others. A change in preference for certain goods is accompanied by a corresponding shift in demand for types of labor and wage levels. The resulting relocation of workers cannot be handled administratively. In a market economy, the market of goods is inseparably connected with the labor market; both are affected by and affect the market of capital. Competition forces every enterprise to produce well and economically. In the system of private enterprise, competition and the interest of the entrepreneur in profit is a permanent guarantee of productivity.

The market economy balances supply and demand, but it also *creates demand artificially*. Artificial creation of demand is called *market-*

ing. Demand is created by causing potential customers to feel dissatisfaction with their situation, a dissatisfaction that can be overcome only by purchasing certain goods or services. To produce dissatisfaction, entrepreneurs and their hired specialists (also entrepreneurs) utilize modern means of social control from opinion research and demographic studies to psychological manipulation and subliminal stimulation. Joining pleasing impressions (pleasant music, pictures — especially of seductive females and virile males) with offers of certain goods alternates with attempts at creating feelings of inferiority which can be overcome only by acquisition of the advertised products; without them the objects of advertising would be unacceptable to members of the opposite sex or avoided by their peers. A frequent device of marketing is to represent the purchase of the promoted articles or services as a duty towards self ("you owe it to yourself") or others (to protect your family by insurance or alarm installations, to secure children's education by opening a savings account or purchasing a share in a mutual fund). Constant reinforcing of concern about one's own or one's family health (blood pressure, arthritis, cholesterol, depression, impotence, heart failure, stroke, loss of hair, bad breath, body odors and so forth) generates sales of exercise equipment, dieting programs, frequent medical examinations, unnecessary surgical and chemical interventions, toiletries and medications, fear of radiations and of chemical pollution of food, building materials, paints, air, water.

Long term effects of these influences affect the mental equilibrium of the targeted population — on one side the constant evoking of the feeling of dissatisfaction, inferiority, anxiety, fear for life, on the other hand, the constant effort to acquire additional means (money) to purchase new goods or services which would heal the negative feelings. This influence on individuals affects the entire culture because the marketing addresses the widest audience and appeals to the widest, most common motivations and most basic instincts at the expense of good taste, reason and sensitivity. The unceasing search for the "latest" type of merchandise results in exaggeration of minute improvements or changes and triggers purchases of new goods even if the previous items are still usable and useful. Artificial creation of demand thus increases the dynamism of the market economy: constant research, constant improvement, constant rise of the standard of living, phenomena summed up under the concepts of "consumerism" and "instant gratification" result in a culture where everyone is convinced that he is entitled to everything, immediately, and at the same time lives in a state of anxiety, dissatisfaction and tension. The steep increase in the standard of living is paid for by increased consumption of energy and material resources and rising indebtedness, private and public.

Competition gradually causes concentration of enterprises and capital as less efficient enterprises are forced out of the market and extensive sources of capital enable financially strong enterprises to undertake expensive innovations and rationalizations which are beyond the means of smaller entrepreneurs. This tendency is reinforced by the bureaucratization of public administration — compliance with rules, regulations and paperwork burdens small enterprises relatively more than large ones. In order to secure the greatest profits, large enterprises substitute agreements for competition and form consortia, cartels, syndicates and trusts which monopolize production of a certain merchandise and manage it so as to achieve a maximum of profit. Such management is not simple, because their pricing and production policies must take into consideration the status of the entire national economy, political circumstances and foreign relations, and requires extensive planning. Competition between enterprises changes into conflicts between syndicates until it reaches certain equilibrium and ultimately agreements between syndicates and conglomerates on the basis of their maximum profits. The equilibrium between syndicates is accompanied by artificial restriction of production and consumption at higher prices. The suppression of competition weakens the influence of the market and undercuts the dynamism of this economic system. In their own interest, large companies slow down technical progress also by purchases of inventions, patents or of smaller enterprises which could introduce innovations that would devalue extensive investments in existing production methods or products. The same tendencies are followed by labor unions which consider technological improvements as threat to jobs or wage levels of their members. New technology sometimes remains unutilized at all or at least until the investments in old methods or products have profitably paid for themselves.

Connected with the existence of huge enterprises is a phenomenon to which only recently appropriate attention began to be given, although already half a century ago James Burnham called attention to it in the path breaking book *The Managerial Society*, namely the role of the third player in the functioning of enterprises, namely professional managers. If a class is constituted by the relationship of its members to the means of production, then managers are a class consisting of those who dispose with means of production belonging to others. The interests of managers are often identified with the interests of capitalists, because managers were alleged to be compensated according to their success in increasing the profitability of an enterprise. This concept is erroneous. Because the return of an enterprise is divided between labor represented by workers, capital represented by owners, and organizational skills represented by professional managers and the bureaucracy, the interest of managers is not always identical with the interest of the owners or of labor. In big enterprises where professional managers make most of the decisions, they manage the enterprise for their own benefits even at the price of causing it damage or collapse. They increase their salaries and compensation regardless of the financial situation of the enterprise and leave it as soon as its future appears questionable. In view of the demand for good managers, their future is less dependent on the fate of an enterprise than the future of workers and owners. The education of the members of this class reinforces this tendency and recommends that a specialist in management plan to change several times his employer during his career. It is in his interest to show fast and impressive results, obtain an appropriate compensation and reputation, and then leave for another enterprise before long-term unfavorable consequences of his management become apparent. When this occurs, he is already active in a different enterprise and problems caused by him are "inherited" by his successor, a new manager who requests and obtains an even higher compensation than his predecessor. He, too, uses effective short term measures, and the process repeats itself. Long term consequences, if unfavorable, are born by the owners and employees. (This type of management is prevalent in American enterprises and Japanese critics cite it as one of the main reasons for a relative decline of American proficiency.)

State and the Economy

The state whose object of care is society, assigns value to capitalism according to the degree this economic system advances society towards the state's idea of what represents a betterment of society. If the state's purpose includes increase of national wealth, the state considers on one hand the increase of national product and on the other hand its distribution. National product is the total of goods (including services) which society — the "nation" — produces. National wealth increases with increase of capital invested in means of production which causes higher production. But its distribution is also important; a nation prospers most if the national product is divided so that society as a whole evolves towards the ideal of life, health and culture of society as it is established by the political process. The state is interested in distributing the national product according to the objective needs of society as a whole.

The growth of production, which means ultimately the volume of goods available for distribution, is in inverse relationship to their allocation according to the objective need and its consequence — an egalitarian development of society. The highest productivity is not achieved when goods are allocated according to the objective needs of society (as perceived by the state). In this regard, pure capitalism results in the worst distribution of goods and the most unequal development of society simultaneously with maximum productivity and technical progress accompanied by the highest creation of capital necessary to sustain the related expansion of and improvement of the means of production. The principle of individual responsibility and competition are here the driving force. On the other hand, for political reasons (stability of society and social peace) the state may be interested and mostly is interested in such a distribution of income that the gap between highest and lowest incomes is not as large as pure capitalism would produce. It therefore seeks a *more egalitarian distribution* of income. Capitalism as a play of free forces brings, in a certain sense and in certain regards, society closer to the state's ideal than other economic systems, due to its higher productivity and faster pace of technical progress.

The state intervenes in the spontaneity of capitalist economy in the interest of the *growth* of GNP (gross national product) whenever the principle of maximum profit results in restriction of productivity and slowdown of technical progress. Such intervention takes the form of protection of competition, prohibition of price fixing, of monopolies and near-monopolies, syndicates. In the interest of objective values of society such as health and life of its members, the state interferes with the freedom of economic activities by regulations concerning the quality of products, truth in advertising, controls of production and imports, protection of environment, testing of medical drugs and procedures, obligatory responsibility for the safety of merchandise and — as a special group of laws and regulations — protection and safety of workers. It influences the composition of merchandise by taxing those types of goods and services it considers as objectively harmful, and by tax advantages or outright subsidies supports production and activities it considers as objectively beneficial. Progressive taxation is the most effective means by which the state affects high incomes or large properties and transfers them to groups which, according to its standards, need it. In certain areas, the state implements its objectives by producing desirable goods or services by its own means of production organized in publicly owned enterprises which do not pursue the goal of maximizing profits, but of producing goods of the best technical quality at minimum cost.

When these and other ways of influencing the size, composition and distribution of the national product are applied and combined to such an extent that the results of the national economy are not any more decided by the dynamics of a market economy and private enterprise, but by the objective defined by the state, the free economy changes into *directed economy*. The most frequent examples of directed economy are economies directed towards increase of the military strength of the state.

The combined effects of the markets of goods, labor and capital constantly seek and establish an equilibrium between demand and supply. Free economy can establish an equilibrium in which demand and supply are in balance at the cost of leaving out of the economy a group of persons who do not own any means of production and whose work society does not need — economy stabilizes in a situation of permanent unemployment which it does not need to overcome in order to maintain its automatic functioning, or would overcome only very slowly. In such a situation, the unemployed represent a group excluded from the economic process as if exiled to an empty island. In order to live, such group needs to create on its island an economy, and for this end, it needs tools, machinery, materials — generally speaking: capital. If unemployment reaches a certain extent, such capital cannot be procured by taxation because its scope would cause the breakdown of the entire system. Under such circumstances, the state creates the necessary capital for those whom the system excluded, by manipulating the currency — by inflation. The states adopts a budgetary deficit to cover the expenses of products not required by the market, but socially useful: programs of public works, production of armaments, subsidies for education, research, arts, improving infrastructure, cleaning up environment. The result is the same as if the state had given to those exiled on the island capital for the establishment of their own economy in practice interconnected with the free enterprise system. The state thus disturbs the existing equilibrium of the market and forces it to seek a new balance which includes those previously excluded. The same method can be used to revive the dynamism of a stagnant economy which does not perform in a way satisfactory to the state; this is known as "priming" an economic recovery.

Socialism

A state can conclude (and in some instances historically did conclude) that influencing a free economy does not suffice for the implementation of its objective of a better (or good) society. It decides that it is necessary to plan the implementation and to guarantee the performance of the plan by taking over the control of the means of production: It can either acquire their ownership (through investment, expropriation or confiscation) or it can leave them formally in the ownership of capitalists while substituting their owners' right of disposing with them by the obligation to execute the imperatives of the state's plan. In this way, the state seeks to replace the spontaneity of the market by a rationally conceived plan to be realized by means of production concentrated in its hands, whether openly or factually. These two properties characterize *socialism*.

When production is concentrated in the hands of the state, the entire structure of economy is fundamentally changed, because the profit motif disappears: the state has no need to make money — in reality, it already owns everything. Success is not measured by financial return: it is measured by achieved progress of society towards the ideal pursued by the state or rather the political program pursued by the ruling political organization(s) through the instrumentality of the state. True competition disappears, its place is taken by the *plan*. A plan is the core of socialist economy, and the principle on which the plan is constructed, determines the type of socialism. It can be cooperative or solidarist depending on the moral maxim it pursues: justice or equality, merit or need.

The Cooperative System

The cooperative economic system is organized on the principle that the only reason for compensation is work and that work is to be compensated according to merit. It is basically a technocratic system which presupposes the existence of a quantitative measuring unit, a common denominator to which all kinds of work can be reduced and compared. The conflict between the three components of a capitalist enterprise disappears: capital is in the hands of the state, organization (management) is considered as work.

The plan is composed on the basis of the wants of the members of society, i.e. on the basis of demand. The state does not limit its subjects in their choices of goods, i.e., it does not allocate goods; on the contrary, it follows the demands of its subjects and produces goods they demand according to their purposes of happiness, in the quantities they demand. This presupposes constant identification of the composition and volume of demand, central direction, expansion of production, if the demand of certain sort increases, and reduction where it declines. *Workers must be reallocated* from one sector to another according to the shifts in demand, the reallocation to be effected administratively. In this system, everyone has the *right to work* and must work in the job to which he is assigned on the basis of the plan. Work is allocated, the cost of goods and the compensation for work is proportional to the amount of work performed.

In practice, this system encounters several fundamental problems. The key one is that the technical measuring unit of work, the work's common denominator, does not exist. Therefore, the basic presupposition of the cooperative system is limited to measuring performance of identical kind of work: the principle "same compensation for the same performance" in practice means the introduction of piecework combined with graduated work tables, bonuses for technical innovations, improvement of work organization or simplification of production, profit sharing, punishments for poor performance and forced labor camps.

As soon as the principle of "same compensation for the same performance" is applied to different types of work, its evaluation becomes largely arbitrary and depends on the purposes wanted by the evaluator. It is called compensation according to the worker's contribution to society. In autocratic states, the highest valuation is given to the work of members of various security organs protecting the system, and the arbitrariness appears in many other areas. There exist various systems of points which replace by points the missing common unit for measuring work, but the number of points granted for various types of work changes according to the interests of the active and passive participants in the process. An enterprise needing theoretical expertise allocates a higher number of points to higher education than to practical experience; an enterprise needing experienced employees, will do the opposite. The situation is similar on the side of those whose work is being evaluated: nurses assert that a higher number of points should be allocated for responsibility for life and health; miners demand that exhausting and dangerous work deserves a higher number of points. The result is that members of different professions compare their numbers of points with the evaluation of members of other professions, naturally find their own work undervalued and unappreciated, and insist on adjustments. This generates a steady pressure on increase of wages not corresponding to increased performance.

Another problem lies in the planning of production. Because the composition of production depends in this system on the purposes of happiness of members of society, it is constantly changing. No technology has been discovered, and probably cannot be discovered, which could capture these changes currently and transform the plan on their basis. The composition of production always limps behind the composition of demand, and the gap between goods society (people) demands, and goods the state is able to supply, increases.

The third problem is the allocation of work. It is true that no economic system allows that everyone work on what he would like to do and where and when he would like to do it, but it is equally true that everyone attempts to do so. In an economic system where workers must be transferred in accordance with the plan by administrative fiat, the question inevitably arises which one among the workers will be transferred, and what will his new assignment be, and each of them generates every possible effort to influence the selection in accordance with his purpose of happiness, not in accordance with the purpose followed by the state (as expressed by the plan). This produces protectionism, bribes, influence peddling and other forms of corruption, subterfuges, excuses and appeals of those who are dissatisfied or have been wronged; all this slows down and inhibits the necessary shifts of labor, and when the reallocation is completed, the demand has changed again, and the entire process is repeated.

The fourth problem consists in the bureaucratization of economy. The executive power of the state swallows the entire economy. The application of this power must be directed by norms which translate abstract norms into more concrete ones. If the norms are not specific enough, each bureaucrat passes on the decision to his superior, because he is expected to comply exactly with regulations, not show flexibility and risk taking. Although the purpose of bureaucracy is to act in accordance with the will of the state, the interest of bureaucrats as a profession are not identical with the interests of the state. The position of a bureaucrat in the bureaucratic hierarchy depends on the extent of his jurisdiction which concretely means on the number of his subordinates. If the state orders this number to be reduced, it acts against the bureaucrat's interest, and this conflict of interest joined to the resistance of the workers selected for transfer, is an effective brake on the performance of the state's instructions.

Similar resistance meets introduction of new methods of work, new inventions and new organization, which all require additional expenditure of effort to learn new approaches, changes in existing regulations and established procedures, amendments to the plan, seeking new suppliers of materials and outlets for new products, reassignment or restrictions of the work force and more administrative work (accounting, new forms, additional reports).

Due to these problems, a cooperative economic system evidences steady pressure on wages without corresponding increase of productivity, i.e., has a built-in inflationary tendency; is incapable of satisfying demand, is not able to adjust the composition of the labor force to the demands on production, and loses efficiency due to the growth of bureaucracy. As long as its functioning is enforced by an autocratic state, resp. a dictatorship, and isolated from other states, this system is capable of consolidation, or rather: stagnation, on a lower standard of living; but when exposed to competition with a state whose economy is more efficient and more flexible, it cannot survive because it is not capable of producing enough goods needed both for the normal functioning of society, and at the same time for maintaining a military power needed to meet or remove competition with other states.

Solidarism

applies as an absolute a principle which always existed in the family, namely that the weakest members of the group are given the most of care by the strongest family members at the expense of the latters' own interest: members of a family are solidary. Because it absolutizes the principle of support of the weak by the (or at the expense of) the strong, such an economic system is called solidarism.

In solidarism, the state does not create a plan according to the demands of its citizens; it formulates the plan as a means to bring, through directing consumption and supply, society as a whole to the implementation of an ideal whose concrete contents (type of life, health and culture) are determined politically. A citizen is no longer a subject taking care of himself, he is an object of care by the state. The state creates a link between strong and weak members of society so that the strong ones must assist those who are farthest from its ideal. The production and utilization of goods are directed by the state according of the principle of *personal solidarity*. The citizen has not only the right, but also the duty to work to the best of his ability in such capacity and on such a job as assigned to him by the state; the strong ones must bear the heaviest burden, the weak ones only as much as they are able to. Work is not rewarded according to the amount of work produced, but according to each individual's objective needs as projected onto him by the state's purpose. Because the needs of weak and ill members of society are the greatest, they receive proportionally most of produced goods although their productivity is lowest.

In solidarism, everybody's existence is assured, i.e., food, clothing, shelter, education, culture and recreation, and everybody has the duty to work on his assigned task. He can not chose what he would like to have, do or be; the state allocates to him goods in the quantity and assortment needed to bring the society as a whole closer to the state's ideal. Rationing and distribution by vouchers is the creation and expression of solidarism: those with the greatest needs: children, ill persons, those holding exhausting jobs obtain more and different goods than the rest. Complete solidarism appears to be the most ideal economic system because it seems to guarantee that society as a whole will progress most rapidly and surely to the ideal situation of equality of all and that the state will not permit anyone to suffer lack of necessary goods.

Solidarism assumes that the state knows better how to take care of its citizens, than those citizens themselves. Therefore, it is appropriately described as *command economy*. Its main problem is that it simply cannot take care of the needs of each individual so that its objective purpose and the individual purposes of its subjects frequently differ or are contradictory. Because the purpose of the state in time becomes distorted to suit the interests of those who wield power, in its final stage its purpose and the purposes of its members clash at every step. The result is inefficiency and ultimately collapse of its centrally directed economy: food rots in warehouses and is missing in shops; grandiose enterprises are conceived and begun, but never finished, goods can be obtained only on a black market.

What was said above about the role of bureaucracy in a cooperative economy, applies to a much greater degree also to solidarism. Solidarism's distribution of goods is almost the opposite of the share individuals have in the goods' production. This undermines productivity which must be maintained by an all pervading system of controls and enforcement which alienates the population. Its principle "contribute as much as you can and consume as much as you need" changes in practice to "contribute as little as you can and consume as much as you can," because the ideal to whose likeness the states transforms (in the view of its members: deforms) its individual members, *is not the ideal of these individuals*, but its own.

The conclusions concerning the viability of the cooperative are valid even for solidarism, only more so.

Reverse Solidarism

Gradually there arose the philosophical foundation and piecemeal application of a different system which has a similar ideal like solidarism: a society of individuals physically and mentally healthy and provided with all means necessary to the full actualization of their potential. The difference is in the process how to achieve this ideal: where solidarism endeavors to attain such an ideal by supporting the weak at the expense of the strong, this new solidarism tries to achieve the same goal by concentrating the resources in favor of the strong members of society and denying them to the deficient ones. In view of this new economic system, public *as well as private* resources spent on nourishing, clothing, housing and caring for those incapable of caring for themselves are wasted. They would be "better" (from the standpoint of the state's ideal) utilized to develop the potential of individuals gifted and productive.

There are two guiding principles of this economic system.

First: In an ideal society, *no individual should be economically dependent on another individual;* each should be able to provide for himself. There are individuals incapable of doing so: children, the aged, the handicapped, mentally retarded, incurably ill, or otherwise unproductive. The state, not individuals, must take care of those; sometimes, they "are better off" dead and are provided with euthanasia or assisted suicide. The capitalist system reinforces this tendency by its inherent pressure to increase the standard of living; the effort to reach and/or maintain such a standard leads all adult members of a family, especially the husband and wife, to seek and accept gainful employment and to stow away the family's unprofitable members in institutions fully or partly financed from the public treasury: the children to nurseries, kindergartens, schools and fraternities, the ill members to hospitals, the aged ones to old age homes or nursing care.

The second principle unavoidably flows from the first one. Society, concretely, the state, has only limited resources, and must therefore decide how to use them "best", and the "best" use is to spend them on those who can be somehow useful from the standpoint of the ideal of society as pursued by the state. To spend or to tolerate spending resources on individuals incapable of doing so, is unjustifiable waste.

A very clear explanation of the principles of reverse solidarism was spelled out in the preparation of a "new paradigm" of health care ethics by the leaders of the World Health Organization. Under the slogan of "integration of ethics into overall health policy," WHO opposes individual health care to "public health care measures that would benefit the entire community." While it claims that it integrates health care to individuals to health care needs of whole populations, it actually gives priority to the latter over the former. (This is especially visible in its criticism of the Hippocratic Oath and in weighing the advantages and disadvantages of euthanasia: among positive elements of euthanasia it encloses eliminating *financial suffering* of the family and implicitly of the community.) The reform of health care in the United States proposed by the President's commission in 1995 was based on this principle: allocation of resources for various types of patients was to be decided by an independent Board excluded from the control of legislature, which emphasized so-called family planning and reproductive health over care and cure of those whose lives are deemed to be meaningless and not worth living, and, therefore, most need medical attention. For those, palliatives and a death with dignity would be preferable to cure and an extension of life.

Prevention rather than cure is the main guideline of this approach, i.e., an eugenic approach to reproduction. By legislating conditions for marriage: investigating genetic history of applicants and prescribing the number of children permitted per marriage (cf. population policy in China) the pool of genetic material of society would be purged of undesirable strains.

The origin of reverse solidarism is threefold. The primary one is the advance of medical knowledge which has extended dramatically the average life span and is capable of significantly prolonging life by artificial — and expensive — means. The second source is the demographic development in industrialized nations. Cost of medical care must be born ultimately by the productive generation. The numerical relation of its members to the members of the departing generations is continuing to decrease in consequence of diminishing reproduction. (In Germany, one of the most advanced cases, it will be 5:1 at the beginning of the next century.) If the cost of having and raising children is added to the cost of taking care of the aged, the burden on the productive generation is evidently heavy. The third root of reverse solidarism is the shift of the responsibility for the unproductive members of society to the state. This means that the size of savings which people accumulated during their productive life for their unproductive years, plays a steadily diminishing role in the extent and quality of care they receive. In the United States, cost of surgical interventions and nursing care exhausts very rapidly even considerable lifetime savings.

The shift of empowerment and responsibility for its members from family to public institutions plays an additional role: their scale of values is different from that of family members. In the purpose of happiness can be and in general actually are included also the secondary objectives of mutual love, compassion, gratefulness, mutual obligations or religious norms, for whose implementation the individual is willing to spend certain, and often considerable, means at the expense of other secondary purposes whose material solidarity (cf. p.7) constitutes his primary purpose. Such secondary purposes are non-existent in the decision of the state, hospitals or insurance companies; institutions evaluate the utilization of means mainly from the standpoint of financial cost — the state expenditures, hospitals and insurance companies profit, because institutions lack human motivations such as enumerated above. For the decisions of institutions it is a very convincing argument that performing an abortion of a weak or sickly preborn child is less expensive than pre- and post-natal care or cure, and such calculations scientifically prepared, are decisive for the type of medical care, medical recommendations and institutional pressure received by the patient. (Moral coercion has here a significant role: as Governor Lamm stated in a speech to recipients of Medicare: it is a duty of those over a certain age to " make room" for the new generation and not burden it by a "selfish" desire to live.) The same applies to persons considered incurable, too old, and generally all those whose health care would generate expenses significantly exceeding those of their painless demise. This is the reason why the properties of reverse solidarism appeared first in the sphere of health care; there is no reason why they should not be extended to other areas substantially financed from public means such as education or social security.

Reverse solidarism is necessarily unfriendly to family and other mediating institutions between the individual and the state whose role and jurisdiction is radically expanded. After the obvious failure of socialism, reverse solidarism is superimposed on economic individualism so that it strives to monopolize the obtaining and allocation of means in areas of key importance for the achievement of its primary purpose. In order to achieve such monopolies, it is necessary to use the state's power; after such monopoly is created, the allocation of means is separated from the control of legislators by the creation of independent commissions or boards of experts not responsible to the normgivers nor to the public. Such bodies then assign the means received from public treasury, in accordance with principles of rationing in solidarism, but in reverse: those closest to the ideal of a society composed of individuals physically vigorous, highly intelligent and productive, receive the greatest share of entrusted means, those who are most remote from such an ideal, are excluded or eliminated in one way or another.

Links between Economic and Political Systems

Economic systems influence political systems and vice versa.

Capitalism grants citizens the greatest extent of personal freedom. In theory, each participant is free to work or not; even he who relinquishes it by contracting to do a job, retains the option to utilize his property to undertake his own enterprise and to utilize his possibilities and abilities in a way most profitable for him. Therefore, this economic system is compatible with democracy, or rather: presupposes democracy. In practice, this freedom is limited by material circumstances. French author Proudhon commented that the majesty of law prohibits equally the rich and the beggar to sleep under bridges. Individualistic economy is a system where everyone seeks to make a living as well as he can, and suffers poverty if he does not own any means of production and cannot find work. The separation of labor from ownership of the means of production renders workers most vulnerable to economic cycles. Free competition in the markets of goods, money and labor can result in an equilibrium in which some workers are not included, are not needed and are condemned by the system to poverty from which they are unable to escape by their own efforts.

This is the main reason why, in certain societies, a part of the people find attractive a system which offers economic certainty, i.e., work, in exchange for a part of their freedom — the cooperative system. There, all means of production are concentrated in the hands of the state and production is planned in response to demand. Inevitably, the plan requires the forfeiture of the freedom to chose one's work and assignment of labor to jobs according to the needs of the plan. The sole entrepreneur ruling the entire production, offering jobs and assigning work is the state. From the standpoint of democracy as a system of individual freedom, a complete cooperative system is deficient in that it *denies people the right to free enterprise, choice of work and utilization of individual personal qualities;* it limits people to the choice of either working at an assigned job or suffering hunger. Therefore, the pure cooperative system is incompatible with democracy; for its functioning, a strongly autocratic form of government, preferably a dictatorship, is needed. A total cooperative system removes the existential and economic uncertainty of all who work or are able to work, but does not take care of those who are unable to work, and has no place for those who are unwilling to work at all or at the assigned job. It guarantees a "just" compensation to those who work, but does not provide for those who work not.

Solidarism, even under the assumption it could function economically, *deprives the individual of all freedom.* Total solidarism is incompatible with democracy because it considers the individual as an object of the state's care, whom it provides with life, health, culture and recreation according to its ideal. Solidarism of either form requires a totalitarian system; solidarism of the classical form requires a centralized totality, a reverse solidarism a decentralized totalitarian system.

In reality, pure economic systems do not exist; *all economies are mixtures* of their types and are characterized only by the scope of preponderance of this or that principle. After the experience with the so-called real socialism as well as the experience of democratic states with strong elements of socialism, there exists a consensus that the flexibility and productivity of the *market economy* with preponderance of private ownership of means of production, is the best instrument to achieve a democratically created ideal of society. Under the impact of the collapse of planned economy, existing shortcomings of the free market economy are overlooked to the same extent as shortcomings of socialism tended to be overlooked after World War Two. In order to survive in a democratic system, i.e., in a system of free competition of ideologies and free elections, the free economic system is forced to incorporate strong elements of the socialist systems. In areas where free economy does not result in a society live, healthy and cultural, it is complemented by *elements of solidarism*. The freedom of enterprise, consumption and work of each individual is in principle preserved, but every one, individual or enterprise, has the duty to contribute a portion of income or profit to defray the expenses of measures the state designates as necessary for progress to its politically defined ideal: education, health care, military, and social security. The contribution is assessed on the basis of solidarist principles: the state's subjects of duty contribute according to their ability, according to the size of income, and the state uses these contributions where it needs them: education, illness, recreation, and so forth. According to the abilities and inclinations of the population, the mixed economy includes also *elements of the cooperative system* such as public ownership of enterprises and management of certain sections of the economy, production as well as services: such as communications, mass media, insurance, financing, production of arms, research. Lately, elements of *reverse solidarism* have become apparent and side by side with elements of solidarism, measures to improve society by elimination of its weak members are increasingly being applied.

CHAPTER 10

BUREAUCRACY

Means of Coercion and Implementation

The ownership alone of means of coercion and implementation does not ensure that they will in fact be utilized in accordance with the state's will, i.e., in accordance with the will of the state's normgiving organs. In addition to ownership it is necessary to ensure that those who have them in their actual possession will use them for implementation or enforcement of the will of the legislators, because legislative organs themselves are not suitable to do so — this is the role of the executive and judicial powers. The creation of bureaucracy is the way that modern society evolved to ensure that the instruments of power will be used by their possessors according to the will of their owners.

Purpose and Structure of Bureaucracy

Bureaucracy is an institution whose purpose is the transmission of the will of an individual or a small group of people to larger groups through administrative activities of persons who for financial and other compensation during a fixed time implement the purposes of their employer rather than their own. The nature of a bureaucracy is determined by the nature of its employer and/or its normgiver: state, party, corporation, church. In his relationship to the employer, a bureaucrat is a subject of duty, i.e., subordinated, and the expression of the employer's will are for the bureaucrat a norm. In order to ensure the implementation of these norms, bureaucracy is organized hierarchically according to the demands of division of labor, centralization of control, requirement of expertise and other rational principles. Bureaucrats in lower positions are subordinates not only of their employer, but also of their superiors in the bureaucratic hierarchy. The uniformity of the acts of the bureaucracy is ensured by rules and regulations whose volume, specialization and complexity grow at least in proportion to the size and complexity of the institutions administered by the bureaucracy; usually they grow faster. As a consequence, individual segments of the bureaucracy lose the perspective of the employer's objective, and follow exactly ("blindly") the letter of the rules and regulations which describe their duties and competence. This gap between the normgiver and his executive power is wider as the position of an individual bureaucrat on the bureaucratic ladder is lower.

To belong to a bureaucracy induces a certain split in the bureaucrat's personality: during the time on the job, he strives to implement an extraneous, assigned (heterodox) purpose, and his own (autonomous) purposes derived from the goal of happiness are pushed aside or possibly suffer harm; a bureaucrat must, on his job, sometimes fulfil duties whose implementation he feels is unpleasant not only because it is burdensome, but also because he disagrees with its contents ("it is against his conscience"). The bureaucrat's employer therefore ensures his subordinates' loyalty in two ways. (1) he tries to align to the greatest possible extent the personal objectives of the employees with his own. A state appeals to patriotism, others, i.e., private employers such as organizations, associations or corporations endeavor to create a feeling of solidarity in their bureaucrats by introducing common emblems, colors, slogans and songs, outings, meals, publications about the progress, growth and perspectives of the employer. (2) The employer strives to gain the loyalty of the bureaucrats by granting or offering them a larger amount of means for the achievement of their private interests, such as steeply increasing wages for the highest levels of the bureaucracy, combined (especially in enterprises) with special compensations for efficiency (sharing in profits and/or ownership of the enterprise), security, often dependent on the length of service, against illness, old age and death, and ways of meeting psychological demands of bureaucrats: prestige (size, location and equipment of the work place), comfort (utilization of the employer's cars or airplanes, dining and recreation facilities), power (expansion of jurisdiction, increase in number of subordinates, especially immediate subordinates such as secretaries, assistants, experts).

Because of the tension existing between the objectives a bureaucrat implements as an executive organ of his employer, and his goal of happiness, bureaucracy is vulnerable to bribes, corruption and protectionism; individual bureaucrats can be induced by an offer of individual advantages to put the interest of the bribing party before the interest of its employer they have the duty to pursue.

State Bureaucracy

Because of the concentration of power in the hands of the state, its bureaucracy is the most important one. It is the most convenient, indeed indispensable, instrument of administering the state, and because it confers much of its power to whomever controls it or its part, states take measures to isolate it from particular political or personal interests and confine it to implementing the will of the state. These measures include life-long security (job security and pensions) and prohibition of arbitrary transfers or demotions. In countries where bureaucrats identify with the state's ideology and interest, these measures contributed to the creation of a professional, impartial and efficient class of civil servants (England, Switzerland, Germany prior to the arrival of dictatorship). In other countries, on the contrary, the same measures became in the hands of bureaucracy, an instrument to oppose, modify and circumvent the will of the state when it contradicts the bureaucrats' convictions or interests.

A ramified and entrenched bureaucracy needed at present by all modern states, is the most powerful among all interest groups in society. By its inertia, solidarity and detailed network of rules and regulations it is able to survive, withstand and overcome deep changes in society, discoveries of science and advances in technology. Attempts to subdue and control bureaucracy have sofar failed in autocratic states (Stalin, Mao-tse-Tung) as well as in democratic states (deregulation and decentralization efforts of American presidents beginning with Nixon and ending with Reagan). In its functioning, bureaucracy has the tendency to deal with people not as persons, but as units, as numbers, to identify equality with uniformity and sameness, and to ignore and suppress differences between members of groups it administers: age, wealth, sex, religion, nationality, language, and other. In modern mass society, such simplification is often necessary, but is also often caused by bureaucracy for its convenience. Up-to-date technology — computers and electronics — combined with progress in biological sciences and concentration of welfare in its hands gives state bureaucracy the potential to mold human groups according to technocratic objectives even in disregard of the will of the legislative power.

CHAPTER 11

MASS COMMUNICATIONS MEDIA

Among institutions that form and transform contemporary culture the first place belongs to mass communications media.

Their exceptional position is anchored primarily in their legal status. Media are commonly protected under the basic civil liberty of the right to free expression. This right is interpreted, especially in the United States, so widely as to include the secrecy of sources, even of criminal ones, publication of absconded secret government documents, interference with military operations, disregard of customary standards of decency. At the same time, they are among the few institutions protected by international treaties where the freedom of press means the freedom of all communications media and is one of the most important freedoms.

Also, mass communications media operate under the form of commercial enterprises; this brings them additional advantages in a world where the introduction of the free enterprise or market system is put on the same footing with democracy, or even above it — business considerations frequently take precedence over human rights considerations. The combination of freedom of expression and freedom of economic activities guarantees that media are able to operate largely outside of state and public control, are often even without civil responsibility for their information and are free to use evermore sophisticated techniques to influence human motivations on an instinctive and subliminal level.

This basis gives them enormous power in politics. One of the most difficult tasks of a political movement is to convince people that they have a reason to be strongly dissatisfied with specific circumstances or personalities.. This task is greatly facilitated by the technological progress of the means of mass communications: television, broadcasts, dailies, magazines, books, movies. Experts in psychology and sociology as well as experts in marketing and propaganda are well aware of and exploit the fact that people do not follow their reason if they are influenced on the instinctive and subconscious levels, if their rationality is circumvented by subliminal triggers of automatic responses.

A part of the manipulation of public opinion is the use of slogans, symbols and even single words with a value laden content that appeal more to the sentimental, rather than the rational, side of human psychology, endeavors to change the relationship between the message and its recipient from freedom and reasoning to cause and effect, from thinking to reflex. This "bending" of the human mind has resulted in a systematic and scientific invention of terminology which introduces new words for existing thought contents so that their traditional positive connotations are changed into negative ones and vice versa, and intentionally provocation of opponents introduces formerly unacceptable concepts into the public discourse. This manipulation of the vocabulary has become especially intense in the questions concerning human life ([12]). Introduction of these biased terms would be impossible without the control of the media.

Spreading political ideology and propaganda of political demands by a combination of spoken word, print, visual image and music results in a manipulation of public opinion. Media entrusted to members of a political organization and a political movement who own or manage them, give them the possibility of spreading their message in ways that hide their political nature and act on their targets' subconscious using all the tools of commercial advertising. Because of its effectiveness, television has become the most powerful and widespread manner of political propaganda.

Politics is based on the acting subject's possession of reason and volition, but the techniques of influencing human reason and volition by activating feelings, instincts and the subconscious of human mind are being constantly perfected in order to narrow the sphere of human freedom during his deciding among choices, in favor of those who are able to apply such technics, i.e., those who manage modern mass communications media. Open and critical communications media are indispensable for free choice. When their possessors distort the selection and mediation of information by assigning them biased priorities, by utilizing manipulative techniques in their interpretation and explanation ("spin"), by prejudging values and attitudes, by representing opinions as facts, by redefining problems and pushing certain solutions, then they diminish in reality the freedom of those to whom their messages are directed. "Hidden persuaders" replace information and arguments. The constant improvements of appealing to the irrational elements of human mentality promise to open the way to a psychological manipulation of such dimensions that the manipulated man becomes participant in the destruction of his own freedom.

In the application of these discoveries, the most apt instrument is television. It is best for fast, short term influencing of the greatest number of people. Its combination of a live picture with spoken word projected on a background of color and music combined with psychological manipulation creates in the public a consensus which can be hardly shaken by rational arguments. This effect was in the past the exclusive domain of rare charismatic speakers born with exceptional personal magnetism, like Hitler, Mussolini or Lenin; modern television can produce it mechanically. It combines the advantages of intimacy (the viewer perceives the commentator personally in his private surroundings) and sharing in a crowd psychology (he is drawn into identification with pictures of mass sufferings, demonstrations, battles, meetings).

Because television is connected with reporting, it determines the contents and timing of public debate already by deciding the sequence and selection of its subjects freely and with no responsibility. If the screens display pictures or discussions of some matter covering religion or its representatives, spokesmen for churches and religious communities are forced to take a stand; their stand becomes the matter for discussions by commentators, sociologists, university professors, philosophers and finally also politicians. By selecting certain such reactions on shows and panels, television predetermines the outcome of public opinion. The same is true in questions of scientific and sociological research whether they concern the weather, environment, the homeless, health insurance, or famine in Somalia, civil war in Yugoslavia and genocide in Burundi. The same applies to the molding of public opinion concerning individuals: television can remake a barely known individual into a national celebrity (in the good and bad sense) within a very short time or consign a personage to oblivion.

The production of mass dissatisfaction in the public has political consequences: it creates a political movement, gives impetus to the rise of a pressure group and influences political decisions. (See Appendix 1a.) The power of television derives not only from what they cover, but also from what they do not cover. (See Appendix 1b.) The impact of television and of the other media is great, when they oppose the government, and still greater, when they act in its support. (See Appendix 1c.)

The items dealt with on television are followed up by other forms of molding the habits and customs of society. Advocacy by television is followed, expanded and pushed through advocacy by articles in the press, scientific or pseudo-scientific discussions and analyses, novels, movies, theater and variety productions, videos, songs and legislative proposals. An especially effective form of molding public opinion are so-called docudramas — novels or plays in which fictitious events and personages are superimposed on actual events and persons so closely that the reader or spectator is unable to distinguish where reality ends and fiction begins, and is deceived into confusing fiction with the truth. If this art form is used to discredit persons and ideas displeased by the media, its commentators write enthusiastic reviews and recommend it to the public. Even if the fictitious nature of certain parts of the story is later clarified and revealed or innocuously admitted, certain irrational and subconscious traces remain, and if continuously reinforced, prevail. (See Appendix 1d.) The media deal similarly with accusations and investigations of their unloved public figures: the accusations are big news and reported prominently; the accused individual is forced out of political life, and when cleared after several years of legal defense, the result is reported as a non-event — and a political career is already destroyed.

The most influential mass communications media are strong business corporations whose primary purpose is and must be profit. As such they are protected by the freedom of the press and expression as well as the freedoms inherent in private enterprise and the principles of a market economy, those who dominate the media are free to invade local cultures, mold them and standardize them in world-wide dimensions. (See Appendix 1e.)

CHAPTER 12

FOREIGN POLICY

Basic Concepts

Foreign policy is the sum of actions of a state which arrange its relationship to other states. In foreign policy, the state acts as a subject of volition and reason rationally implementing its supreme (primary) objective to achieve betterment of the situation of its population and is guided by the rules of purposive thinking, especially by the principle of economy.

This includes, as the precondition to any other action of the state, the preservation of sovereignty over its subjects, respectively citizens: to protect them from becoming subjects of duty of another state, to come under the rule of a foreign legal system, of a foreign sovereignty. Translated into relationship to other states it means that the indispensable derived purpose of each state is to maintain its *independence* vis-à-vis other states.

Joined to this goal is the state's purpose of promoting the interests of its object of care even outside of its own territory. A necessary means to attain these twin purposes is to limit the sovereignty of other states. Such a limitation can be defensive or offensive. A defensive limitation of the sovereignty of other states is achieved, if and when it prevents them from expanding their sovereignty on (parts of) the territory or population of the defending state. It is offensive if it includes infringing upon sovereignty of another state over (parts of) that state's territory or population.

As long as means needed for the betterment of the situation of its population (goods, natural resources, territory, population) are under the sovereignty of another state, a state endeavors to obtain them in one of two possible ways: by exchange or by coercion.

The condition for an exchange (trade) are mutually complementary interests. In this case an exchange takes place, i.e., the parties trade one good for the other, and both realize a gain.

Coercion takes place when one subject (i.e., state) needs a good under the sovereignty of another state to whom it cannot offer anything useful in exchange. In this case, the acquiring state must coerce the possessing state to give up the good in question, by causing the latter a harm exceeding the harm caused by giving up the good. The acquiring state must also take into consideration the cost of coercion — if they do not exceed the gain derived from obtaining the desired object. It is the task of diplomacy to obtain the object by a threat of coercion rather than its execution. The means of diplomacy are secret negotiations, quiet diplomacy, public declarations, diplomatic notes expressing concern, official protests, threatening actions (naval maneuvers, concentration of military forces on the target's borders, mobilization, various degrees of readiness of long range delivery vehicles of arms of mass destruction).

Coercion can be indirect or direct. The indirect way consists in denying to the resisting state means it needs; the direct form consist in application of violence — attack on persons or goods of the resisting state. Indirect coercion consists in preventing the resisting state from obtaining needed goods by commerce (boycott, blockade, sanctions) or psychological pressure on its population; often both methods are combined. Direct coercion takes form of terrorism or war. (Examples of direct coercion were World War I and II, example of indirect coercion was the Cold War.)

Coercion results in a decrease of the affected state's sovereignty in one of two forms: as to extent or as to content.

A state's sovereignty is decreased as to its *content* if the state is forced to abstain from actions which would be in the interest of its object of care, or if it is forced to act in a way in which it would not act if its sovereignty were not limited. Such a limitation of sovereignty can be a commitment not to enter into agreements with other states directed against the interest of the coercing state, to limit its armed forces or the type of their equipment, to abstain from supporting domestic opposition of the coercing state. It can also be the opposite: the affected state can be forced to enter into alliances or international groupings even if it is not in its interest, or to participate in another state's military actions, to undertake economic measures which are against its interest or to grant on its territory to the coercing state the permission or the exclusive right to conduct certain types of economic activities (f.i., exploration, mining, port privileges). The highest form of the loss of sovereignty is when the affected state must change its system, constitution or legal order according to the will of another state or a group of other states.

A state's sovereignty is decreased as to its *extent* if the state is forced to transfer the sovereignty over a part of its territory to another state. The most frequent reasons are: the transfer of a territory is done to enable a part of the affected state's population (for instance, an ethnic or religious minority) to join a state where it possesses majority, or to cede an area representing its military advantage over another state. Other forms of such limitation of sovereignty are the ceding or leasing of military bases to another state or extraterritorial privileges ("concessions") of an economic nature.

A relatively new form of limiting a state's sovereignty consists of enforcing the implementation of international treaties or transferring a part of a state's sovereignty to international organizations dominated or decisively influenced by a state or states whose policy harms the interests of the affected state.

The outcome of foreign policy depends directly on the power relationship between the states. The power of a state consists of its domestic strength and of its foreign relations. Of the two, domestic strength is more important; it determines the scope of actions in the field of foreign relations.

Elements of Power — Domestic Strength

Domestic strength of the state is the result of material as well as spiritual factors. Among the material factors, the most important ones are numerical strength, wealth and military potential. Among the spiritual factors are unity and spirit of sacrifice (willingness to fight) of the population.

Material Factors

Numerical strength of the population is the basis of the economic and military strength of a state. Its importance is growing in the time when military components of power are becoming secondary vis-á-vis democratic principles which attach to numbers more relevance than to other factors. There is a numerical limit below which states cannot preserve their real (as opposed to formal) independence, because the size of their population is not sufficient to bear the costs of maintenance of modern military equipment: the cost of modern intercontinental missiles, airplane carriers, modern aircraft are such that the national product of numerically weak states is unable to cover them. Similarly, interplanetary exploration and its utilization exceeds their possibilities. Small states can participate in similar projects only at the price of giving up a portion of their sovereignty.

Military occupation of numerically strong states and the perpetuation of control over them exceeds even the possibilities of modern means of social control, exhausts the economy of the occupying state. If the occupying state incorporates the occupied state's more numerous population, the numerically stronger population will gradually absorb the occupants and wrestle control of the normgiving power from the hands of the conquerors. This does not apply to short-term economic exploitation; only to long-term exploitation which must be maintained through military means.

The population is the mainstay of the state and the state is the guarantor of the security of its population. The state provides such a measure of security, as the strength of its population permits. A total war makes this relationship even more obvious. The struggle of the states is conducted until complete exhaustion, physical annihilation and destruction of one of the contenders. Victory belongs to the more numerous and more tenacious party. In this type of conflict, the size of the population has a twofold role: to blunt (or execute) the first sudden onslaught, and to overcome numerical losses. ([13]) This function of population strength does not apply in a war fought by arms of mass destruction: nuclear weapons are capable of annihilating equally both large and small populations.

In a confrontation with other states, military or not, chances of a state depend on the pressure coefficient. A pressure coefficient is the relation of the total population of one state compared to the sum total of the populations of all its neighboring states (because conflicts of interest arise mostly among neighboring states, with a concurrent tendency to escalate into military confrontation). In the measure in which the population of neighboring states exceeds the population of one state, the higher is the pressure coefficient and the more insecure is its international situation. Numerical weakness of a state attracts the appetites of stronger neighbors and encourages them to form alliances whose purpose is to acquire parts of the territory of their weak common neighbor or to dismember it completely (example: repeated divisions of Poland among its German and Russian neighbors, division of

Czechoslovakia by its neighbors by and after the Munich agreement). The pressure coefficient is a reliable indicator of the international situation. Where it reaches the highest numbers, the danger of armed conflicts is the greatest; the weakness of small and middle sized states is a permanent source of unrest. (14) The instability in the areas of high pressure coefficients is one of the reasons why the great powers conclude agreements about their "spheres of interest" which include the responsibility for keeping conflicts among their clients to the minimum.

Certain features of nature (oceans, mountains, rivers) form geographically circumscribed units which place some states in a position conducive to attempts to organize this area to its advantage and under its leadership (*geopolitics*). Geopolitical influences are seldom dominant in the short term, but geopolitical factors are permanent and do prevail in the long run. They determine the character of the great powers as maritime or continental, with the U.S.A. the prominent case of the former, and Russia the prominent case of the latter. A maritime power usually aims at controlling the opposite shores of the surrounding oceans, a continental power aims at domination over the continental mass surrounding it. Typical examples of geopolitical units are the North American plain and the North European plain from the Rhine to the Urals, the Danube basin, the Indian peninsula — they all exhibit tendencies to be organized by one state.

Another geopolitical element is the fact that two (or more states) neighboring with a third state have common interests harmful to the state located between them. The result are treaties between the neighbors of a state countered by its treaties with the neighbors of its own neighbors.

The above components of material power of a state determine two other elements: military might and economic might. Military might confers on its possessor short term advantages, economic power is stronger in the long run. If military power does not bring about complete defeat of an economically strong state, economic power will ultimately prevail. Since the Thirty Years war in Europe, there has not been one conflict in which military power prevailed against economic power. The cycle of great empires follows basically a pattern. First, an economically powerful state enlarges its sphere of interest so that it becomes vulnerable. This necessitates military protection; the state must build a strong army. The army uses up means which could be devoted to economic growth, and weakens it in the relationship of upstart states not burdened by such wide interests — and responsibilities. The relative loss of economic strength increases the threat to the superpower's worldwide interests and generates a vicious circle: to protect them it must increase its military power which further undermines it economic strength until new rivals overtake it economically and are victorious in the next military conflict which follows. (Per Paul M. Kennedy, *The Rise and Fall of Great Empires*, Random House, New York, N.Y. — This pattern appeared also in the Cold War except that in lieu of a war the contest took place in the form of an arms race.)

This does not mean that military readiness and the population's willingness to fight can be underestimated. Small states like Switzerland and Israel owe their independence to the fact that they can, in case of need, enlist practically their entire population to increase promptly their military power.

Economic power depends not only on the size of the population, but also on its composition, especially the numerical relationship between old and young generations. As a general rule, it can be said that a society with a diminishing number of members of the younger (productive) generations tends to decline economically and militarily. In the short run, population decline produces rising costs of social programs (pensions, social security, health care, medical needs). The needs of those who have become unproductive or were forced out of the process of production (for any reason, mostly because of age) must be born by the productive strata. If the numerical relationship between the unproductive (old) generations and the productive generations reaches a certain level, the standard of living of the productive generations is under such pressure that it discourages reproduction, so that the presently active generation when aged will overburden their numerically smaller offspring, and the process repeats itself. The long term effects are still more serious; the economy has to adjust repeatedly to the declining purchasing power of the population, fixed investments (buildings, infrastructure, industrial capacity) exceed the needs of a declining population thus obviating the need for inventiveness, initiative and productivity.

Spiritual Factors

The population's unity and spirit of sacrifice can be cultivated by the state by means negative and positive. The negative measures are immediate: the use of the state force against centrifugal movements. They are effective only if such movements are completely liquidated; if they are only suppressed, they will emerge again exactly at the time of international crises when the state is weakened, and they can contribute even to its destruction. The most serious threat to the unity of a state's society are groups that are parts of political, national or religious movements governing a neighboring state, work for the latter's interests and receive support from it. It is impossible to liquidate such movements without weakening the power of the state which keeps them alive.

Positive measures aimed at strengthening the unity and spirit of sacrifice of a population are slower and more indirect because they try to influence the culture and prevailing values of society to make them acceptable and accepted by all its parts. This requires the formulation of an idea, a mission of the state which will be so attractive that all subjects of the state will incorporate it into their purpose of happiness to an extent outweighing other objectives which compete with it within the material solidarity of the primary objective. In a state divided ethnically and socially, but unified in matters of religion, such a unifying idea can be the service to the common faith; in a state divided religiously and socially, the unifying mission can be nationalism; in a state divided religiously, ethnically and socially, such a uniting idea has to consist of service for all of humanity to which each component of society subordinates its particular interests.

State's positive and negative measures aiming at the improvement of the spiritual components of its strength can be combined to be mutually supportive.

Elements of Power — Foreign Relations

The international status of a state depends not on its absolute power, but on the relation of its strength to other states. States whose interests coincide with those of a state, are considered as friendly, those with contrary interest as unfriendly; those whose interest do not affect the state are considered as neutral. Therefore a state seeks to improve its power stature also by seeking and strengthening friendly states and weakening the unfriendly states and their allies. In addition, it acts to transform unfriendly states into either neutral states or friendly states.

Measures which are apt to limit the sovereignty of a state, i.e., actions aimed at *unfriendly* states, may be nonviolent (indirect struggle) and violent (direct clash).

Nonviolent Means — Indirect Struggle

In nature, indirect struggle for survival means that its living environment denies to an organism elements it needs for the development of its potentialities into actualities: light, soil, air, water, food. This indirect struggle can be and often is as deadly as direct clash between organisms. The same applies to struggle between states. The main instrument of an indirect struggle between states is economic power; its forms range from mild ones (introducing import duties, denying access to markets by limiting mutual imports and exports, currency manipulations, denial of loans) to grave ones: interrupting access to sources of raw materials and products including a blockade and culminating in an internationally organized general economic boycott. A peculiar form of economic contest is the arms race; the antagonists strive to build an army which could either secure a military victory or exhaust the opponent economically.

The contest of ideas is another form of the indirect struggle if it intensifies into a propaganda war. Its purpose is to weaken the spiritual elements of the opponent: break up the unity of its population and undermine its willingness to defend its state. A decisive victory in this war is reached when one state replaces its own will (value system) with an opponent's will (value system). This struggle of ideas takes place not only as part of a preparation for a direct clash (when its success can be decisive: the undermining of the will to fight of the opponent's population is tantamount to victory — USA loss in Vietnam), but continues after the termination of the clash, because the loser (or its population) will tenaciously endeavor to reverse the outcome of the lost conflict, until or unless its culture does not internalize the values of the victorious contender.

In every state, there are movements or organizations which disagree with the government. If the state is an unfriendly state, the acting state uses economic means and propaganda to support the opposition because of the probability that its influence or victory will realign the interests of both states in favor of the state from which the opposition received support.

A state does not have to limit itself to supporting an existing opposition; it can endeavor to create it, i.e., to destabilize an unfriendly state. This can be done by personal relationships, but mostly by activities of secret services. Efforts to destabilize an unfriendly state can be combined with economic pressure which affects the standard of living of the unfriendly state's population, and thus creates dissatisfaction to be exploited by the burgeoning opposition. This development can be hastened and intensified also by the propaganda war which connects the economic difficulties with the existing government and its enmity to the acting state. Creating of difficulties for an unfriendly government is not necessarily limited to indirect measures; it can be combined with direct measures such as terrorism and insurgency.

Violent Means

Overt Warfare

The classical form of a violent clash between mutually unfriendly states is *war*, an attempt to impose a state's will upon another state by actual or foreseeable military occupation of a part or the whole of its territory. War is a clash of military forces of two or several states for the purpose of forcing a state (or several states) against its (their) will to comply with demands of another state or states. The means towards achieving this goal is to weaken the military forces of the adversary so that the victorious party can impose its will on the loser. An aggressive war aims at imposing new demands on another state; a defensive war aims at preventing the aggressor to achieve its aim. A defensive war can in time change into an offensive one, and vice versa.

In a war, the state has the choice of one of two strategies: an overwhelming attack ("blitzkrieg") or attrition. The overwhelming attack's purpose is to win victory before its target can mobilize its own resources; it is therefore favored by states which are militarily strong, but weaker economically and/or in other regards. The purpose of the strategy of attrition is to prolong the war, by denying the enemy a decision in order to increase one's own strength and by constant pressure to exploit enemy's weaknesses until its defeat. This is a strategy of economically strong states, and experience proves that it is a winning strategy. It is at the same time a long term strategy because it includes the destruction and exhaustion of the enemy's economic and production potential and disruption of its communications with lasting effects on its economic and military potential for eventual revenge. Overwhelming attacks usually engage only military forces; attrition strategy engages entire populations of both sides.

Except for nuclear arms, the outcome of war is decided by land units of the army (infantry); its other elements have only a supportive role, no matter how important or impressive. The two basic tactics in territorial war are breakthrough and encirclement. The breakthrough is the penetration of the enemy's formations all the way to its rear echelons, interruption of its communications, encirclement of isolated parts of its army and their destruction. Encirclement is the penetration or bypassing of enemy's forces on their wings, interruption of its communications with the rear; the two arms of the attacking army join in a pincer movement and destroy the captive army. Encirclement can be effective especially in a situation created by the adversary's breakthrough whose success stretched its supply roads and communications so that it can be cut off from its bases by a pincer movement against its wings.

The complexity of modern armed conflicts involves not only armies, but the entire population of the warring states during the preparation and the course of the conflict: obligatory military service, arms production, support elements; an armed conflict becomes a total war. In aggressive states, this transformation takes place before the war; attacked states usually mobilize their resources only during the war. If the enemies expect a war to break out, they prepare the means needed for the defeat of the adversary in advance — these preparations lead to an arms race which can discourage the aggressor or exhaust one of the contenders so that it submits to the demands of the stronger state without war. (In this way, Czechoslovakia was defeated in 1938 and the USSR in the Eighties.)

The involvement of civilian population into a war includes (voluntary, but often also involuntary) support of irregular armed groups fighting the possessor of sovereignty over a certain territory — guerillas. In conjunction with a total war, guerilla groups are a part of the resistance against the enemy's government or the occupying power and as such it is, together with sabotage and passive resistance, an element of military operations of allied powers who provide them with supplies and sometimes even leaders of guerilla units.This method was used during World War II on the eastern front by the Soviets and by the western allies in France especially before the invasion. Such cooperation is a part of the war effort and also of foreign policy because at the time of the collapse of the occupation, the control of liberated territory passes to armed, i.e., guerilla groups, and their political preferences are important for future development of international relations.

In a war started to annex a portion of another state's territory the parties at war may anticipate and prejudge the final outcome by destroying the population of the enemy — the war becomes a war of extermination (lately also called "ethnic cleansing"): each state eliminates on the contested territory minorities belonging to the nationality or religion of the enemy, or simply destroys the enemy's population to weaken it in the final phase of the war or even in a possible future conflict. This development led to the conclusion of international treaties regulating the conduct of war with regard to civilian population and prisoners of war, and an extermination war violates such treaties knowingly and intentionally.

The development of military technology is such that war is usually damaging to both parties, the victor as well as the loser, and possibly also to third states not directly involved in the conflict. It remains an alternative to other choices if one side is willing to suffer such damage in the hope of forcing the enemy to forego the acquisition of its desired objective, offensive or defensive. War still is the ultima ratio regum.

Covert Warfare

The awareness of the damage threatening both sides of a war is such that new violent means of struggle were sought and found, means which would skirt open warfare. Such means of covert warfare are, in the order of intensity, terrorism, insurgency (guerilla warfare), revolt, civil war and infiltration.

Terrorism is destruction of the targeted state's important economic objects or members of its population even though they are not involved in any actions against the terrorists. In its simpler form, it derives from the recognition that the effects of a terrorist act exceed disproportionaly its cost. Repeated terrorist acts weaken the targeted population's resolve to deny to the terrorists their demands, and as means of blackmail they are often successful. Blackmail also protects members of the terrorist groups, for instance, by demands to spare or free apprehended terrorists in exchange for sparing or freeing important victims of kidnapping. Because of its elusiveness, even a small terrorist group can inflict serious damage to states incomparatively more powerful. While support of terrorist organizations by a state is an effective means of exerting pressure on an enemy state, it remains unofficial; support of terrorism is always limited to secret services and there is no connection between the terrorists and official representatives of the supporting state. Deniability gives to the state supporting terrorism the flexibility to withdraw it at any time when the cost or danger of support appears to exceed its gains. It also deprives the targeted state of an internationally recognized reason to declare war and, moreover, the potential damage of a war, even if victorious, is much higher than the damage caused by terrorist acts.

This might be a fallacy if terrorism is not aimed at occasional victims, no matter how important, but is part of a continuous campaign of destroying the state's and the society's structure, if it is directed systematically against all kinds and levels of local organs of the state and against politically and socially leading personalities, combined with the use of gruesome forms of violence. Simultaneously, terrorists attack the material structure of the state: communications, sources of energy and supplies of food for the population. In South Vietnam, repeated public torture and executions of representatives of the government (village chairmen and elders, teachers, policemen) and of opinion leaders (doctors, lawyers) by the opposition intimidated the population to such an extent that the sovereignty of the state was held up only during the day by presence of the army while at night, the terrorists took over. This campaign was a successful prelude to the escalation to guerilla warfare and subsequently civil war.

Terrorism can damage and destabilize a state, but not replace it or destroy its sovereignty; it can obtain concessions in individual cases, but is not aimed at acquiring the power to formulate the will of the state. To enter politics, it must be upgraded to an *insurrection* in the form of destroying the state's power locally or guerilla warfare, with visible leaders and a publicized political program. If an unfriendly state aims at weakening its opponent, support of guerillas opens possibilities to influence political processes in the targeted state. It is far more expensive; terrorists need mainly counterfeited documents, small arms and bombs, insurgency needs systematic deliveries of arms, and arms of a more sophisticated type: anti-tank and anti-aircraft missiles, communication equipment, transport, often bases and camps on their sponsor's territory and specialized military training by the sponsor's army, security forces or secret services. As the support of the insurgents grows, so does their dependence on the supporting state; its unofficial representatives (secret agents) co-determine the strategy, tactics, targets and political demands of the insurgents.

The aim of insurgency is to upgrade the conflict into a *civil war*. Civil war is a conflict between armed members of two or more groups of the population or between armed members of the opposition with the armed forces of the state. Revolutionary theory has defined two main strategies of achieving victory. One of them is to concentrate on usurping power in the capital of the country and its main centers. To achieve it, the revolution must obtain sufficient preponderance of power in these targets, and having seized them, it spreads its power to the rest of the country. This preponderance of power was based on factory workers and rebelling units of the army in St.Petersburg, and it led to the communist dictatorship; a similar preponderance in Prague was based on students joined by the capital's population; it led to the overthrow of the communist dictatorship. This strategy is similar to the military strategy of penetrating the opponent's center. The other strategy is similar to encirclement: it consist of gaining control over the countryside and a gradual isolation of the state's power in economic and political centers which then are lost to the government one after another until the entire country is under the rebels' control except the capital which ultimately falls. This is the method used by communists in China. It is prolonged and more difficult, the areas of control change, the government is in control as long as its armed forces are present; they lose it as soon as they have to evacuate the territory because they are needed elsewhere. and the initiative of deciding the pressure points is in the hands of the revolutionaries.

The sponsor state escalates its support to the revolutionaries because failure at this stage would mean the loss of all advantages it has gained until then by its previous support. Its intervention takes the form of infiltration of its regular armed units which pretend to be volunteers and fight on the side of the revolutionaries. They are not acknowledged by the sponsoring state as parts of its own military, but are in reality trained, maintained and commanded by it and have their bases on the intervening state's territory. The infiltration can either function as a provocation which will create a pretext for open military intervention by its regular armed forces, or to help the rebels in setting up a rival government.

At this phase of the struggle, the revolutionary political organization must secure permanent control of a part of the state's territory in which its will replaces the will of the state, and transform it into an impenetrable basis from which the revolution can inflict further damage to the state in order to gain concessions. Under no circumstances will the revolutionary political organization exchange its rule over this power base for the state's concessions, but use it for further enlargement of its power until it absorbs or destroys the target state or replaces it in the conquered territory. It is constrained to do so because of the involvement with its sponsor state without whose assistance it could not survive. To bolster this process, the sponsoring state might recognize representatives of the revolution as the legitimate government of the territory under their control — or as the legitimate government of the entire targeted state.

As such situation develops, the threatened state seeks also assistance abroad. If it is granted, the state becomes materially dependent on it and its sovereignty is diminished, because such assistance is granted in the interest of the helping state. This dependency may force the targeted state to undertake steps which are harmful to its interests, but profitable for the helping state. Such steps can be an escalation of the civil war or its settlement; in the last resort, the conditions of the outcome are negotiated between the sponsors of each side and the contesting parties have no other option but to accept them. In this way, the Vietnam war, originally begun as a conflict between the South Vietnamese government and a North Vietnam sponsored terrorist campaign, was settled by arrangements between the Soviet Union and the United States.

During the application of these violent means of foreign policy, no restraints imposed on conducting a war are observed. Public executions and torture of enemies, expulsion of communities, genocide, are committed by both sides as retaliation, preventive measures or deterrent. A government which fights or expects an outbreak of terrorism or of civil strife might condone or initiate murders of actual or suspected leaders and sympathizers of the opposition and destruction of communities or groups considered as supporters of a dangerous violent-prone opposition as the only method to subdue terrorist conspiracies or guerilla organizations. If successful, after the danger has passed and a normal situation has been reinstated, the perpetrators of such human rights violations are identified, arrested, condemned and punished.

Since the end of World War II, a classical war occurred only exceptionally. Conclusions gained from the experience with the various forms of covert warfare are that, in an open clash of armed irregular groups with regular armed forces, the military is usually victorious; on the other hand, no way has been found for regular military forces to be victorious against terrorism, insurgency or a guerilla war, especially if such groups are supported by a neighboring state or have bases on its territory which a regular army is not permitted to invade. (15)

In view of the interconnection of interests and relations between states, every utilization of violent means harbors the danger of the escalation of a conflict resulting in war. Therefore, the international community observes the principle to deny legitimacy to advantages obtained by violent means, and by applying the methods of indirect, nonviolent measures it tries to pressure the victorious aggressive state to renounce its gains.

If it is a government of a *friendly* state, the acting state supports it against domestic opposition by "foreign aid." Foreign aid includes economic means (loans, grants, free trade) and ideological propaganda which includes cultural exchanges, scholarships and opportunities to publish. In addition, aid takes the form of military aid in funds and equipment, training of police practices and systems up to sending own personnel ("advisors") to aid the friendly government against domestic and foreign enemies. In all these actions, the aiding government may pursue also its specific interests, especially business opportunities and financial advantages.

On a foreign policy plane, a state may support its allies by concluding a treaty of mutual assistance and even placing its own troops on their territory to act as a "trip wire" against military action of enemies: any such action would involve immediately its own army and thus represent an act of war. An ultimate act of protection of friendly governments is formation of alliances or international organizations which guarantee to their members military assistance not only against foreign enemies, but also against attempts to subvert them or their form of government through covert warfare methods described above. In preparation for violent methods of foreign policy, such treaties often include provision for a joint military command structure, joint military exercises, standardization of armaments, facilities and stocks of war material.

CHAPTER 13

INTERNATIONAL ORDER

International Relations

Relations between sovereign states are arranged by treaties which form a complex network of mutual obligations whose observation depends on the will of the contracting parties and on the traditionally recognized principle "pacta sunt servanda rebus sic stantibus" (treaties are to be observed as long as circumstances have remained the same). The assumption is that at the time of concluding treaties, states are equals as to their sovereignty and that this relationship of equality remains unchanged during the treaties' duration, implementation, repudiation or violation.

Reality does not correspond to this theory; international relations are not an unstructured network of treaties woven by equals; actually, they have a structure, an order determined by the strong states, the great powers or superpowers, around whom are grouped the small states. Treaties between superpowers and their contracting partners, especially alliances, have very frequently the nature of norms imposed by the superpower on its weaker allies, and the relationships between the superpowers determine the character to the entire international order. According to the relations between superpowers, the international order has the nature of a balance of power, allocation of spheres of influence, hegemony, subsystem integration or international legal order.

Balance of power is an order in which the great powers, using domestic and foreign policy, diplomacy, threat of war or war prevent other great powers or their groups from acquiring such a preponderance of power that they can force one of the strong states to act against its own interest. This type of international relations is by its very nature unstable and requires unceasing equalizing of power capabilities, because their relationships and exertion of influence are in constant flux and change as individual power centers gain or lose strength as consequence of domestic policy, economic development and other factors.

Allocation of *spheres of influence* is an order in which one or several great powers renounce explicitly or tacitly interference in areas claimed as exclusively reserved for influence by another great power. This order represents a consolidation of the system of balance of power, and its change presupposes a radical shift in the power relationships between the participating great states.

Hegemony is an order in which one of the great powers is so strong that it imposes foreign policy, economic relations and often even domestic policy on other states. Such a system is relatively stable as long the predominant power has the economic strength to fund military forces and a bureaucracy capable of holding its empire together. As the empire expands and as competing new power centers appear within or outside the hegemony, costs of preserving the growing empire increase until they exhaust the hegemon's strength to a degree which permits its breakup by centrifugal inner forces or an attack from outside.

Subsystemic integration is an order in which, for reasons of economy or security, states create voluntarily a joint super-state and on the basis of shared values seek in an integrated whole a greater measure of security than they can provide separately, or a higher standard of economic well-being for their citizens than they can attain from their own resources. A subsystemic integration is mostly part of one of the preceding orders, and therefore its extent and nature is limited by a friendly or unfriendly attitude of any of their dominant great powers.

International legal order is a system which stabilizes international relations and secures the preponderance of a superpower or a group of powers by the creation of generally applicable norms for behavior between states, norms which are generally binding and enforceable. This entails the creation of a normgiver with a jurisdiction superior to the sovereignty of states and attributable to a normgiver able to enforce its observance. In such organizations, formal equality of states is expressed traditionally by the principle of unanimity which can have two degrees: either by the right of veto, i.e., the resolutions of the organization are not binding unless adopted by all members, or by restricting their validity to those members which voted for them.

International Legal Order

From International Organizations to Supranational Organizations

Often, international law or international legal order is identified with the system of treaties between states or with principles regulating such treaties. This identification is incorrect, because that system lacks two constitutive principles of law and legal order: a lawgiver superior to the subjects of duty, and enforceability of laws promulgated by him. As long as states remain sovereign, they are entitled to renounce concluded treaties and/or can be induced to observe them only by applications of power described in the preceding section. This system, in the best case comparable to binding custom, became the target of growing criticism and since the end of World War I attempts were made to transform it into a true legal order, i.e., to create a lawgiver equipped with means of enforcement.

The threat of a nuclear war and the Cold War changed the nature of international relations. The keystone of foreign policy of states is no more the arrangement of relationships with other states, but takes place mainly within the framework and through the intermediary of supranational regional and world organizations. The possibility of a war whose instruments are capable of destroying not only the contending states, but all other states, too, proved that the differentiation of humanity expressed by sovereign nation states exceeded dangerously its integration and reinforced the movements towards increased integration. It made obvious the desirability of a genuine international legal order and rendered acceptable some embryonic forms of institutions which create the supranational will (the legislative function), which control its observance (judicial power) and which enforce it (executive power). International (i.e.,interstate) organizations are thus undergoing a transformation into supranational entities, i.e., entities superior to states, into super-states.

The nature of the legal order of a state is at its beginning shaped by the power relations between competing political organizations. Likewise, the international legal order and its institutions bear evident characteristics of the political alliances which were victorious in both world wars and in the Cold War: of the Western Powers and among them of the United States of America in the first place. The decisive role of the victors is reflected by international organizations ideologically in their principles and organizationally in their constitutions which prescribe that their members abide, in their domestic as well as foreign policies, by principles in harmony with the ideology of the founding states. The power relationship is even more obvious in the enforcement of international norms: without the participation of the strongest members no boycott nor any other forms of economic pressure, and no military might exists which would be capable of an effective intervention again violators.

Worldwide Integration

The creation of an international legal order parallels the development of the domestic legal order. The stronger group of political organizations, in the given case of states, endeavored after World War I to transform its common political objectives into an internationally binding norm. Its content was self-determination of nations, preservation of peace and collective security, its source of will was the League of Nations constituted by and anchored in peace treaties. The weakness of this endeavor laid in the inner contradiction of its concept: the victorious Allies attempted to create an institution superior to states and on the other hand preserved the principle of state sovereignty. The judicial function was performed by the General Assembly through majority decisions in which all states, strong and weak had the same voice. The enforcement medium was sanctions. The power of the League of Nations was undermined by the absence of the United States and experience showed that sanctions were ineffective. Even small states, if summoning sufficient determination, could withstand them, and the discord among the great powers made stronger sanctions impossible. Therefore, this first attempt at creating a universal, binding and enforceable international law failed.

More realistic was the organization of the United Nations created by the victorious coalition at the conclusion of World War II. It was founded on the recognition that it needs a common purpose, and this purpose was decreed by the winners in the form of a Charter whose function paralleled that of a constitution in a state. The founders recognized also that the United Nations organization must take into consideration real circumstances and not to rely simply on the formal principle of equality of all sovereign states without regard to their power; this recognition was expressed by the creation of the Security Council and its permanent members not subject to majority decisions of the General Assembly. The need of a way to enforce the organization's decisions was embodied in the provision of unanimity of the five permanent members of the Security Council whose combined power was (at the time of the creation of UN) such that no state or combination of states could successfully oppose it. UNO did not jettison the principle of sovereignty of nations, but in its structure, it applied the recognition that there are degrees of sovereignty among its members — fully sovereign were only the five states which had the veto power, i.e., the five permanent members of the Security Council.

The United Nations failed for two reasons. Right at the beginning, some members professed the principles of the Charter only by words and contradicted them by deeds. Originally, these were only the states of the Soviet bloc, later their numbers were increased by states newly formed on the ruins of colonial empires; these new states had no tradition of democratic self-government and changed very quickly into various dictatorships imitating the Soviet model of economy. The combination of these two groups gradually attained the majority in the General Assembly. Simultaneously, there developed a lasting split among the permanent members of the Security Council. By using its sovereignty, i.e., its right of veto, the Soviet Union systematically sabotaged the creation of an international legal order based on the principles of the UN Charter, and continued to construct a sphere governed by an order based on the principles of Marx-Leninism in the belief that its philosophical, social and power system would become the international legal system which the Soviet Union would protect and enforce (cf. the Brezhnev doctrine). In the conflict of the western and Soviet ideas of an international legal order, the original concept of the Charter finally prevailed, but resolutions and decisions of the UN have not the character of a norm hierarchically higher than the sovereignty of member states.

Regional Integration

A more promising attempt at the creation of a true international law was the establishment of the Conference on Security and Cooperation in Europe (CSCE). Under American leadership, it began to differentiate its functions in the direction of a state's division of powers. Its regular follow-up conferences served as embryonic judicial and legislative organs which investigated and made judgments on violations of the Helsinki Agreements, especially its "Third Basket" (human rights and civil liberties), by member states, and on the basis of such findings issued (legislated) norms (the Final Acts) completing and enlarging the initial provisions of the Agreement. Both decisions were based on the principle of unanimity, but this unanimity was to a large extent founded on actual power relationships and lately by acceptance of a rule which invalidated the vote of the state whose violations of the Helsinki Agreement provisions were being discussed. For a long time, the effectiveness of this organization was undermined by the existence of two conflicting blocs: NATO and the Warsaw Pact countries, but the demise of the eastern bloc resulted in the acceptance of the ideology of the western bloc (individualism, practical materialism, human rights, democracy, market economy). Thus arose an ideologically quite homogeneous concentration of power which had the potential to establish a world order according to its principles and enforce its validity even against non-member states during a period of a power vacuum in the rest of the world.

The evolution went in another direction by the growing integration of the European Community (EC). This formation arose from the Marshall Plan which made economic assistance of the United States contingent upon the creation by recipient states of a common plan and a common organ for its utilization. Thus each participant had to relinquish a part of its sovereignty in favor of such common organs which were created pragmatically, first to coordinate production of coal and steel. The resulting international bureaucracy became the nucleus of efforts to dismantle additional areas of national sovereignty and transfer them to the supranational institutions. This process culminated in the Maastrich Treaty whose acceptance created a European Union (EU) and abolished national sovereignty over such fundamental issues like citizenship, immigration, penetration by foreign capital, taxes and custom duties, definition of human rights and civil liberties, minority rights and domestic legislation on use of national languages. The Maastrich Treaty is an equivalent of a constitution in a national legal order, various organs (the Council of Foreign Ministers, the European Parliament and various EC and EU Commissions) resemble legislature, the International Court in the Hague performs like a Supreme Court and the emerging European army is reminiscent of the enforcement branch of an executive power.

The movement towards a world legal order (and a world lawgiver) takes place on several levels: globally through the United Nations, regionally through NATO which, widened to the Partnership for Peace by participation of industrialized countries of the Pacific, represents basically the association of (industrially developed) states of the North against the so-called South (underdeveloped countries with reserves of raw materials). Inside the "North" there are several centers: the United States, Western Europe aiming at exclusion of the United States on one side and of Russia on the other side and organized around a Franco-German nucleus, and the Commonwealth of Independent Nations around Russia which resists the merger of its former sphere of influence with the super-state of Western Europe.

Dismantling of National (State) Independence

The integration of Europe initiated the entry into international relations of a new factor: of individuals. Until the elections to the European Parliament, the creation of the will of international organizations was the exclusive domain of states, i.e., their governments. Although the European Parliament has still only a consultative power, the monopoly of international normgiving reserved to states as subjects of political will, has been disrupted and the direct influence of individuals as "citizens" of superstates is bound to grow. The issues of formal and material equality, of individual and group equality, of elimination of power elements except numbers is bound to complicate and slow down the creation of a legal world order.

An important intrusion on state sovereignty is the right of citizens of EU member states to appeal decision of state organs to corresponding international organs via judiciary process. The first breach of state sovereignty in this regard was the admission to CSCE (Conference on Security and Cooperation in Europe) follow-up conferences of representatives of private organizations (called "non-governmental organizations") whose function was to observe violation of human rights provisions by their own states and to bring them to the attention of the conferences. Originally this process respected the principle of state's exclusive international subjectivity by reserving to states only the right to put such complaints on the conference's agenda, but any state, not the state whose citizens the complainants were, could and did do so. Since then the right of individuals to appeal to international organs was formally accepted by EU as well as CSCE. In the opposite direction, a precedent was created by the Nuremberg court which proceeded against citizens of defeated states because they obeyed the laws of their respective states and orders of their superiors. By acting thus, an international entity arrogated to itself the right to violate (the defeated) state's sovereignty by judging their citizens by norms not existing in their respective constitutions, i.e., placed its own norms above the laws of the affected states. The same principle was revived in the prosecution of war criminals guilty of atrocities during the war in Bosnia.

Traditional political theory and constitutional theory are founded on the assumption of the sovereignty of states. A state is sovereign internally, i.e., with regard to its citizens and its population, and externally, i.e., with regard to other states. In the second half of the 20th century, political practice in the sphere of western culture has increasingly deviated from this concept. The starting point of this shift is the theory of inalienable human rights which erodes state sovereignty so-to-speak from below: inalienable human rights are a sphere on which the state must not infringe and in which he must not give preference to its subjects who belong to groups whose source of cohesion is one of the proscribed characteristics: race, nationality, religion, gender. The loss of sovereignty in this direction does not cause the state power over its subjects to decrease, on the contrary. The expansion of the sphere of human rights (16) subverts the sovereignty of states, but expands their jurisdiction by protecting such rights against the majority whose members find themselves being coerced in areas where they used to be free. The selection of rights is moreover arbitrary and irrational; for instance, homosexual behavior is protected, smoking is prosecuted. Expansion of rights of specific minorities causes inevitably the shrinkage of rights of the majority, expands the power of the state and its bureaucracy, and at the same time diminishes the state's sovereignty.

Inalienable rights are also the basis of limiting the sovereignty of the state so-to-say from above, by international organizations which change gradually into organizations superior to states.

So far, the movement towards a global legal order tends to weaken all institutions mediating between the individual and the emerging super-state, and its prime target is the sovereign nation state which has the potential of being its main opponent. Most effective in that respect used to be CSCE (Conference on Security and Cooperation in Europe) building gradually its legislative, judicial and executive power over member states. It was overtaken in this regard by EC, respectively EU. The Maastricht treaty transfers considerable areas of the jurisdiction of states to supranational European institutions and subjects them to majority, rather than unanimous, decisions. Foreign policy, defense, currency, European citizenship and European army, economic planning including adjustment of production to structural changes produced by such planning, coordination of production, creation of a special fund for states to offset harmful effects of adjustments decreed by European institutions, in practice by their bureaucracies, all replace member states' independence. Nor does this limitation of states' sovereignty add to the freedom of their citizens: the state's jurisdiction is only transferred to another, higher bureaucratic level less accessible and less controllable than the bureaucracies of individual states. States are becoming simply territorial administrative units of a European super-state.

The progress towards a world legal order does not take place only in the area of formal law. It is propelled by international bureaucracies and prepared, supported and utilized by extra-political centralizing tendencies which precede legal integration, stabilize it and aid the shrinkage of state's sovereignty. So far, it is obvious mainly in economy: introduction of the market and free enterprise, removal of custom barriers and prohibition of discrimination against foreign investors enable financially strong multinational corporations to penetrate anywhere without regard for borders. Other antidiscrimination rules inhibit measures protecting the native population from a massive invasion of members of other nationalities which threaten to deform the national, religious and cultural character of the respective country.

The accumulation of these influences diminish the usefulness of the state as an instrument for protection of national identity and defender of national interests. For powerful European nations, namely France and Germany — or rather: Germany and France — it means removal of obstacles erected by small nations against their domination, while they shift to the European super-state the defense of their own interests against mightier states, at present primarily against the United States, through customs duties, directing and planning overall European economy, common currency, common foreign policy, army, preferences for member states, and so forth. The small nations are in a different situation: they will miss the protection afforded to them by national independence and state sovereignty.

To be viable, the legal order of a state as the result of power relations between competing political organizations must allow for their shifts. The same applies to the viability of an international legal order and its source — the super-state. A state can become a source of heteronomy and thus an instrument of oppression; the same can happen in a global or regional super-state. Here, the opportunity for oppression of individuals and small nations is even greater; due to the super-states' size the tendency towards centralization, managerization and bureaucratization is stronger than in national states. In such a case, an international, or rather supranational organization could become an instrument of domination of certain states or international ideological movements and organizations over large parts or the whole of humanity.

CHAPTER 14

ABOUT POWER

The state is the locus of several political organizations with different ideas how to better the situation of some group of people, and all of them strive to gain the maximum share of the one and same means — of the direction of public affairs. In following this goal, each organization's goal is in competition or conflict with the same goal of other organizations — a political contest or conflict takes place. The determining factor for actions of a political organization is its relationship to the power of the state and not the relationship towards other political organizations; the relation to the state is primary and the relations to other political organizations are secondary, contingent upon the primary relationship. The main type of political struggle is indirect, for two reasons: in the way of a direct struggle stands the power of the state, and also, the destruction of competing political organizations is easier after gaining the possession of state power rather than before it. Nevertheless, sometimes it assumes the form of a direct physical confrontation, when a political organization attacks physically other organizations: invades or disrupts their meetings, terrorizes its supporters, destroys their means (premises, print shops, displays), liquidates their leaders.

For the political struggle it is important whether the political organizations elects to influence the state through the intermediary of its adherents as individuals, or to share in its management as a subject of will. A political organization can select the former option which can be described as *not truly political*: it does not approach the state as a subject of will, but influences it through personal contacts with individuals who are public officials, to proceed in the performance of their function in accordance with its program. This method pursues the achievement of a political goal, but without possessing a share of the state's power as its means. The *truly political* way to power of a political organization is to strive for a share in the legislative power. Both ways are not mutually exclusive; a political organization may try, and often tries, to implement its ultimate goal by both ways simultaneously.

To the basic features of a political organization described in Chapter 3 additional organs and elements are added, as needed in the effort to obtain a share in the direction of public affairs: a political organization creates its organs and adjusts its structure to its primary objective of gaining a share in the state's power. The various forms of the political struggle as described systematically in this Chapter are in reality variously combined and related as required by efficiency and utility.

A political organization striving to attain or increase its share in the directing of the state, has two options: to strive to attain this goal within the framework of the legal order, i.e., *legally*, or *illegally* by violating or uprooting it. After evaluation of opportunities and/or obstacles represented by the form of government, the nature of its own program, abilities of members and sympathizers, character of the rulers and of competitors, and of distribution of power in society, a political organization opts for the legal or illegal way or their combination according to principles of economy. Among these elements, the structure of the state has the decisive influence on the operations and thus also on the structure of a political organization.

The Legal Way To Power

In an Autocracy

The only legal way of influencing an autocratic state open to a political organization is to convince the holders of state power that the implementation of the political organization's program will serve their own interest and/or the interest of their object of care.

Under an autocratic regime, organizational forms of a political organization must remain rudimental. Its political movement lives and grows under the guise of a non-political (philosophical, religious, labor, etc.) movement and is organized in non-political organizations (universities, learned societies, churches, trade unions). Members of the political movement use such existing institutions or create organizations appropriate for the situation: clubs, associations, circles and organizations which perform, to a limited extent, the basic functions of a political organizations: there they debate and create the political program, spread its ideology, organize adherents and influence lawgivers.

In an autocracy, the non-political way of strengthening the movement takes precedence over openly political activities. Such an approach enables political life and political thinking to outlive even long unsuccessful periods because they are nourished intellectually from these outwardly nonpolitical organizations. Nevertheless, a prolonged period of vain efforts results in abandonment of the legal way to power in favor of illegal struggle.

When a lawless state is in a pressing need of obtaining some concessions from its competitors who are interested in weakening it internally, this may create a favorable situation for its internal opposition to step, under the protection of the foreign powers, openly into the political arena by utilizing the inner contradiction of the regime: the contradiction of the will of the state expressed by the constitution, law and international obligations, and the factual, normatively illegal, situation and the behavior of the agents of the rulers. While professing devotion to the state, opponents or dissidents appeal to the courts to obtain the justice and protection due them under the law. The situation of such individuals is extremely precarious; nevertheless, if their rights are protected by international treaties and if the state(s) contracting and dealing with the lawless state, make the observance of such treaties a condition for concluding any further (especially economic or security) agreements, the lawless state may be forced to observe or restore the legal status over the factual prevailing illegality. Such concession represents a compromising of its basic premise: the superiority of the will of the ruling political organization over its state. Ultimately, such a state must either revert to the era of repression which would weaken it further, or to engage in a retreat which must end in the victory of the will of the state over all its subjects, i.e., also the ruling political organization, and to provide legal security also for its opposition.

In a Democracy — Political Parties

In a democratic state where citizens share in the decisions concerning the legislative power, a political organization that decided in favor of a legal way, has to strive for gaining the maximum possible number of voters because the size of its share of the state's power depends on votes cast for its program and its candidates. The necessity to obtain as many votes as possible gave rise to a special type of political organization: political organizations structured for attracting publicly sympathizers are *political parties*. The political party which receives in elections enough votes so that its representatives, alone or in conjunction with those of other parties, can enact laws and take over the direction of the executive power, implements its program through the power of the state, i.e., it *governs*, while the other political parties which also have their representatives in legislative organs, but not all the attributes (especially the number of elected candidates) to share in the formation of the state's will, criticize its governing, constitute the *opposition*. After a time determined by the law, the governing and opposition parties undergo again elections which ascertain whom the voters entrust to implement their right to co-determine the creation of the state's will for the next period.

Political parties are well developed organizations, with specialized organs for each of their functions. The highest organ of volition of a party is usually the party convention, the highest organ for its will's execution is its central committee headed by a presidium; organs for channeling its will are usually formed by its representatives in legislative organs of the state (parliamentary clubs or caucuses) and by special commissions which deal with the various sectors of the state's administration and prepare the papers and instructions for the Party's public activities.

Party members are usually so numerous that the party needs to be articulated according to their sundry sources of coherence; it creates territorial organization (local, district, state) according to members' residence; women's, youth, students', agricultural, workers', enterprise organizations according to other characteristics enabling the party to gain and influence members and fellow travellers. Their role is to represent within the party specific interest groups and find additional members and voters among these groups. Around political parties cluster organizations pursuing technical goals: economic (trade unions, cooperatives, enterprises, mutual insurance companies) or cultural (educational, social, gymnastic, publishing). Associated organizations too have in addition to pursuing their technical objectives the task of widening the political movement and the membership basis of the party and are sometimes represented in its territorial and central organs by delegates whose number corresponds to the importance of each such group.

The acquisition of adherents is done through evoking among citizens the feelings of dissatisfaction with the existing situation and a desire to correct it, i.e., through modifying the contents of their purpose of happiness so as to insert or preserve in it demands that are in accordance with the party's program. Because among the most powerful human feelings are anger, fear, hate and envy, the party's propaganda appeals primarily to them. Its contents and character depend on whether the political party in question shared successfully in the legislation and government or not. Government parties try to maintain or extend their share in the direction of public affairs by warning against the harm which would be wrought by the victory of the opposition parties, and point to the benefits which their participation in the government brought for the groups in their care as well as for the entire society. The failures of the government are attributed to invincible external obstacles or interference by the opposition and, if there was a coalition government, to non-cooperation of some coalition partners, and the government parties promise to continue in their beneficial policies provided the voters entrust them again with the management of public affairs. Opposition parties, to the contrary, strive for a share in the government by calling attention to the harm caused by the governing parties, be it a real harm or a harm only from the viewpoint of their party programs, they stress mistakes of the government and they attribute to the government parties all failures for which they are responsible as well that for which they have no responsibility, simultaneously assuring the voters that they would take better care of their needs and interests if the legislative and executive powers were given to the opposition. Personal criticism (attacks) on competing parties' leaders form a part of each party's propaganda. The intensity of a party's propaganda is contingent on its program: whether it is committed to the preservation or displacement of the democratic regime. In the latter case, the party is free to use much sharper, mendacious and irresponsible criticism as well as much wide-ranging promises, because, once democracy is destroyed, the party cannot be held responsible by the voters anymore.

A part of political life in the democratic regime is that various political parties submit their programs and candidates to the voters who make their choices and according to their choices cast their votes giving their mandates to those whom they consider best and whom they trust the most as to the fulfillment of their pre-election promises. Political parties, also those representing pressure groups, must justify their political programs as thoroughly as possible, because a program supported by good, convincing arguments has a better chance to be accepted than a program lacking a rationale. They also must expand their program so as to appear beneficial to the greatest number of citizens. Political parties compete not only to cause their demands to prevail, but also to inculcate their ideology to the widest possible number of citizens. In consequence each political party tends to *monopolize the intellectual life* of the entire polity. Ideologies of political parties turn into an intellectual system encompassing, explaining and directing all facets of life, and in the interest of their power position parties obstruct the spreading and application of ideas differing from their ideology.

Politics as Profession — Politicians and the Apparat.

Political parties' extent, complexity and multitude of tasks make a far-reaching division of labor unavoidable. In every political organization, certain functions must be performed by people who devote their time either outright for a salary or for some other economic benefit provided by the political organization. In a political organization appear two groups of persons whose common characteristic is the performance of a political function as profession: some are paid directly by the political party — political secretaries and other employees, here all summed up by the term "*apparat*" (to distinguish them from the apparatus of other institutions), some are paid from the public treasury for performance of functions they hold thanks to a political party — *professional politicians*.

The *apparat* performs mostly work of a mechanical nature, and because political parties seldom have enough means to reward them adequately, the group of secretaries is frequently recruited from those who have manifested extraordinary zeal in voluntary work for the party and who consider even a secretary's paycheck an improvement of their social and economic situation. The apparat of a political party thus becomes a gathering point of persons dynamic, practical and devoted to the political party as an institution, not as a bearer of its particular program. Secretaries are the party's employees, but their position is ordinarily so important that the function of secretary is commonly linked with the membership in a party organ which creates the will of the party and is the starting point for acquiring a legislative function or an economically advantageous position in institutions under the party's influence. For political secretaries, their party's well-being becomes the primary objective which separates them from those who see the party as a instrument for the betterment of society; they put their party above all other institutions and its success above all other values. Therefore, they identify themselves with the political party and their interests with the party's interests and vice versa and arrogate to themselves decisions concerning the party's actions — which in view of the concentration of factual power in the hands of the party apparat is not difficult.

Of key importance for the evolution of a political party is the position assumed by the group of *professional politicians*. The emergence of political professionalism represents a significant milestone in the development of a political organization: a group of people for whom the participation in the directing of public affairs has become a profession, i.e., the main source of income. In the life of politicians, political activities absorb a greater part of their purpose of happiness than in the life of other subjects of volition who participate in politics to the extent that increases their happiness. For politicians, political activities are also their only or main way to provide, for themselves and their families, means for the implementation of all other objectives derived from the purpose of happiness. In practice, this signifies that their private interests (family relationships, need of recreation and entertainment, wealth and personal power, affluence and comfort) conflict constantly with the one and only interest of their political organization, namely to attain or keep a share in the direction of public affairs as a means of betterment of the circumstances of its object of care. The psychological escape from this conflict is the identification of the group of professional politicians with their party: they identify their interests with the interest of their political party. Professional politicians who, out of their innermost motivation and to the detriment of their own and their family's private interests strive for the betterment of their party's object of care, are an exception. (Max Weber distinguishes between politicians who live for politics and those who make a living out of politics.)

Managerization of Political Parties.

The fusion of their private interests with the interest of their political party induces the professional politicians to concentrate, by more or less organized action, the decision making process within the party de facto in their own hands. The group of professional politicians transforms itself in a group of people who are *factually* beyond the control, responsibility and recall by the membership — a group of political managers. The power of this group is not based on the statutes nor mandate of members; they hold functions determining the preparation and execution of important activities (in a political party with a democratic constitution, they are informing the membership, directing the party's press, nominating committees and election committees). Professional politicians have one important interest in common with the apparat: their financial and personal success depends on the success of the party; this makes them allies in the managerization process especially where the ranks of professional politics are filled from the ranks of the apparat. (Cf. also Chapter 7 on managerism.)

In the struggle for votes, political parties which exhibit ideological and action unity of members have an advantage over parties internally disunited and those whose membership is inactive. Competition between parties forces all of them to gradually tighten party discipline, i.e., they require from their membership greater obedience to the highest organs of the party. This brings about the curtailing of the freedom of action of lower organs and centralization of power in the hands of its highest organ. The rights of members, of the convention and of the central committee members become increasingly empty formalities and the party leadership imposes its will not through elected organs which could display their own and different opinions, but directly through the hierarchically organized system of party secretaries and apparat answering directly to the presidium disbursing their salaries. The financial dependence cements the obedience of the secretaries to the presidium, usually through the party's general secretary, and makes the apparat on all levels largely independent from the corresponding elected organs. Rather than serving the territorial elective committee, its secretary actually instructs it as to what to do and to believe on the basis of directives received from the general secretary. The office of general secretary becomes the most powerful office in the party.

The authority to accept or expel members is one way through which the leadership of a political party controls it. Persons who are actually or potentially dangerous to the extant leaders are refused membership or, as happens more often, expelled. The leadership takes care that the right of accepting and expelling members be reserved, in the last instance, to higher organs of the party, the reasons for stripping of membership are formulated so widely as to be almost arbitrary: acting against the interest of the party, violation of party discipline, harming the good name of the party, betraying party principles or the program.

Another way of controlling the party is choosing of candidates for elections. If left to the parties, it becomes usually the domain of the apparat and of professional politicians who, by using various electoral, nominating, recommending and propaganda committees and provisions of automatic candidacy of incumbents and other high party functionaries determine the selection of candidates for positions in the state's legislative, executive and judicial bodies.

The interests of professional politicians and the party apparat diverge in one important point: the source of their income is different. Income of professional politicians depends on their positions in the organs of the state, the income of party bureaucrats depends on their position within the party. Although both groups contribute to the process of managerization, under different circumstances they have a different level of influence. In a situation that requires emphasis on the program and ideology of the party, i.e., in a system of proportional representation, the decisive role falls to the apparat; in a situation that emphasizes the importance of personality, i.e., in a system of majority representation, the decisive role falls to professional politicians. Their role is enhanced up to such a level that the politicians are able to replace the apparat by hired experts in managing elections whose links with the political party are temporary, pecuniary and occasional; their goal is not to implement the party's program, but to elect the candidate or candidates who hired them, and the pre-election program is fully subordinated to this goal. In this instance, the importance of the party's members is even smaller than in political parties with a permanent organization and bureaucracy, because structures through which the membership could express its will, do not exist during the periods between elections. Between elections, the political party subsists actually only in its elected representatives and has no inner life involving members.

Economic enterprises owned by a political party contribute to its managerization. They provide a basis of economic security to the party managerial groups and also limit the membership's importance for the financing of the party — membership fees and contributions become less important and the ownership of economic enterprises enables the party's leadership to offer financial rewards to supporters and thus strengthen their dependence.

Managerization has far-reaching consequences for a political organization. Thanks to its accumulation of power, the dominant managerial group alone exchanges and supplements its members. Because the personal and private interests of its members merged, in their minds, with the interests of the political organization — and vice versa — and because they perceive any menace to their persons as a menace to the political organization, the managerial group exhibits distrust and resistance towards independent party members who evidence a potential to exceed the level of the managers and endanger their position. This, in turn, lowers the personal and intellectual quality of the managerial group — and of the entire organization they dominate. The objective of the party is degraded to a means of holding on to their power; this causes ideological opportunism: obstinacy combined with ideological somersaults. The leadership of the party increases its independence from the party delegates, members and voters, its election becomes a formality orchestrated by the apparat and the membership's influence on its outcome is minimal.

The growing role of ideology in the political struggle, the centralization of political parties and the tightening of party discipline under the guidance of professional politicians and party bureaucrats results in an intellectual stagnation of political life. The introduction of new political ideas inside of established political parties runs into two hurdles:

1. The position of the political party among the public is based on a certain cadre of members and voters gained by its program and ideology. Any change in its program represents a danger that the party could lose a part of proven adherents of its old program in an exchange for an uncertain hope that at least the same number of new voters will be gained from the ranks of sympathizers with the program's innovations. Adherents of the old ideology can be considered safe because the ideology of a modern political party represents a more or less complete world view or attitude, and people change that only rarely. Political parties also fear their opponents could take advantage of any significant changes to describe them as proof that the party's program and/or ideology was wrong and changes are a sign of vacillation and uncertainty. Therefore party leaders try to avoid them and prefer to reduce inevitable changes to secondary additions or minor adjustments of the old program .

2. A more important obstacle to the introduction of innovations in a party's program are its managerial groups. Their members acquired power as bearers and representatives of certain principles and resulting demands. Acknowledgement and recognition of new ideas would be accompanied by ceding power at least partly to the bearers of new ideas. Because the political managers identify the party with themselves and because they consider the program as a means to electoral success and not the goal of the party, it degenerates, in their minds and expressions, into slogans and is understood as slogans aimed at gaining voters. They therefore consider it superfluous, if not harmful, to exchange the well established slogans for new ones, if they cannot expect that the change will bring quick and substantive profit to their interests which, in their eyes, are the same as the interest of the party.

Impact of Electoral Systems

The development of the character of political parties depends to a large extent on legal provisions regulating political parties, especially on the electoral system.

The system of *majority representation* is not favorable to the ideologization of political life (for reasons listed in the section on electoral systems, Chapter 13). The forfeiture of votes cast in favor of the losing party underscores the need for party discipline: the splintering of votes of adherents of the same political movement results in electoral loss for the movement and in victory of its most radical opponents. Therefore candidates as well as voters of the same general orientation overlook less important differences in the interest of their most important demands. Such strengthening of party discipline resulting from the majority system represents education in political maturity and growth of self-discipline rather than strengthening of centralizing tendencies inside the party and opportunity for its managerization and the growth of its apparat. This system which renders a candidate dependent ultimately on the voters of his district, has on the contrary rather decentralizing tendencies and weakens the influence of the party 's central organs. Their support (especially financial support) is of course not insignificant, but the local influences are more important. The candidate's persona and his direct contacts with local party organs and members and the voters' local organizations (cultural, ethnic, religious, sports) delays or obstructs the centralization of professional politicians: their opponents have too great an opportunity to appeal to their constituencies (local party functionaries, members or voters). This does not mean that centralizing tendencies and emergence of political professionalism are non-existent; only that they cannot easily prevail. Competition among politicians of the same party is moderated by their common interests which are reducible to one denominator: they wish to be re-elected. Such common interests include increase of their financial remuneration, increase of the number of employees paid from public monies, postage privileges, restaurants, recreation facilities, paid trips abroad, immunity and a number of minor fringe benefits and privileges.

The majority electoral system diminishes the role of party bureaucracy, but not of parties themselves; candidates of established political parties enjoying their parties' financial, organizational and publicity support have a decisive advantage over independent candidates and over candidates of new parties; experience shows that electoral victories of the latter are indeed exceptional. Therefore, the system favors emergence of a few large political parties of which a mere two are usually represented in the legislature. Only the emergence of radically new problems requiring new responses brings success to a new, third party which is rooted in a new ideological, religious, national etc. movement. In that case, the third party has a chance to survive the pressure of the system, and once it obtains victory in some election districts and if it truly reacts to deeply felt needs of society, the mechanism of the majority electoral system begins to work to its advantage to replace speedily one of the traditional parties; thus the situation reverts to the two-party system. The majority system inhibits the quick success of transitional political movements, but accelerates the success of movements which express lasting needs of the electorate.

The *proportional* electoral system exhibits many opposite tendencies. It does not admit the forfeiture of any votes so that the decisive role belongs to stable blocks of party members and voters and the fluctuating votes have a small effect on the outcome of elections. Political parties therefore concentrate on securing reliable cadres of voters who will cast votes for their party regardless of circumstances, rather than trying to gain the votes of independents. To achieve this reliability, they must produce marked material advantages for voters as members of a certain group, and this group egoism must be morally justified by the program of the party to cement the loyalty of members and voters. This brings to the forefront ideologies explaining the program as a way toward the betterment of the situation for the society as a whole. Because no vote for a party is lost, no matter in which part of the state it is cast, political parties have a tendency to become state-wide, i.e., to formulate their programs exclusively so that it gains for the party the votes of all members of its object of care regardless of their territorial distribution. The result is the creation of parties representing economic interest groups whose group egoism is translated into generally beneficial ideologies, but in actual practice is not moderated by solidarity with other interest groups which are similarly organized.

The interest group it represents fights for its material advantages against other similarly organized groups, and this means on the political scene a shift towards centralization and towards a key role for the party apparat. In order to gain members state-wide, a permanent bureaucracy is needed to which the elected candidates are obligated and without whose support they have no chance to succeed. The creation of the will of the state passes from elected representatives to political secretaries and local organizations are of limited importance in the party.

The proportional electoral system results in the formation of a great number of small, disciplined, economically oriented political parties dominated by the party apparat.

The necessity of forming coalition governments further enhances the power of the political managers. The decisions under what conditions and with which partners a party will join a coalition, what its legislative program will be and which team will represent it in the government is completely in the hands of professional politicians and of the apparat and beyond the reach of party members or voters. Proportional representation not only fails to impede the transformation of political parties into centralized, ideologically monolithic managerial structures, it facilitates the process (while the majority representation includes a number of elements which counteract it). It lacks the necessary incubation and crystallization period imposed by the majority representation on new political parties, and therefore opens the door to radical and autocratic political parties and their progress by recording their electoral successes, no matter how ephemeral, and transforming them into political power.

Summary

By their extensive organizational, propaganda and power structures, political parties dominate largely the contents of public life; new ideas can survive this preponderance only with great difficulty. The result: political programs, arguments and actions lag, to an astonishing extent, behind the development of society and of ideas. The lagging of politics behind the life of society is an obvious indication that a layer of political managers inserted itself between the state and the people who, in a democracy, is the source of the state's will. This layer is the reason why the actions of the state, in spite of its democratic system, do not reflect the political will of its citizens. This gap between politics and the people grows in proportion to the growth of the power of the party's professional politicians and of its apparat.

Political managerism not only impedes the will of the voters, but discredits democracy itself, because it is unable to fulfill its main mission: that those who are subject to laws, share in their formulation. Democracy no longer bridges the gulf between those who rule and those who are ruled. The citizen is forced to conclude that he cannot influence the conduct of public affairs and through elections to change their direction. In times of crisis, the public increasingly believes that by losing democracy it does not, after all, lose too much because in the public's experience democracy does not guarantee the directing of public affairs according to the will of the people. Political apathy of citizens facilitates, by feedback, the consolidation and expansion of the power of the sundry managerial centers and prepares the way towards the acceptance and support of the public for radical and antidemocratic ideas, ideologies and political parties. Democracy is reduced to noisy and hectic pre-election campaigns for which attractive programs are being invented by the same parties and politicians who have had the opportunity and ability to perform them in the past period and failed. The perception of democracy as the "government by the people" is lost and the situation is ready for its liquidation (cf. subsections Managerism, Totalitarianism and Decentralized Totalitarianism in Chapter 7). Therefore, the development of political parties is, for democracy, a question of life and death.

The Illegal Way To Power

The principle of an illegal way to power is the effort to change the existing legal order or its part (usually its highest norm, i.e., the constitution) in a manner contrary to valid legal provisions. A political organization chooses this way if convinced it cannot attain the wanted share on the state's power within the framework of the law either by convincing the ruling political organization or penetrating it in an autocratic system or by obtaining the desired participation through elections in a democratic system, or else if it concludes that it achieves its goal faster by illegal methods.

Influencing the Rulers

By using the *non-political way* the political organization, without sharing in the directing of public affairs, endeavors to influence individuals who perform the tasks of state organs, to act in performance of their functions in accordance with its political program. This is the method usable in an autocracy, but also in a democracy (e.g., Alger Hiss as adviser to President Roosevelt).

These methods can be also illegal. It is illegal if a political organization influences holders of public functions to comply with its goals in exchange for providing them with means of achieving their personal goals of happiness. Such acts constitute *corruption*. Everyone is held to be corruptible; the question is to find the right good he is willing to accept in exchange for pursuing, in his official behavior, the purpose of the corrupting subject rather than the purpose of his function. Most common is the corruption by money followed by corruption of sexual favors. Persons not corruptible by these means can be "bought" by material goods such as a paid travel or vacation, or free use of facilities (cars, air planes, premises). For those who cannot be seduced by these more ordinary bribes, there are goods that have for them a special significance: a stamp collector can be corrupted by the offer of a rare stamp; an art lover by the gift of an exquisite art object; a collector of rare books by the donation of a unique edition. Immaterial goods can be also a medium of corruption: granting of honors and titles, introduction to influential individuals or organizations, profitable insider information, granting favors to the target's family members. These methods of corruption are not an exclusive property of political organizations; they are used also by other subjects of volition: individuals as well as organizations.

A special way of influencing a public official by furthering his goal of happiness is the promise that the political organization will refrain from harming values dear to him (life, health, reputation, property, family members), or threatening to harm them if he does not submit to its demands — *extortion*. An execution of such threats constitutes *terror*; terror can be used also as a deterrence from actions damaging the goals of the illegally acting organization. Terror can be applied discriminately, i.e., against the property of a specific person and his family (bombing, arson), against health or life or indiscriminately against persons and properties which the illegally acting organization considers as values dear to the state: life and health of any citizen, parts of the state's infrastructure or economic and administrative structure (airports, bridges, communication networks, police stations or other public buildings, banks, malls, hotels).

Fighting the System

While these methods harm the state and may possibly force some concessions to the illegal organization's program (but more likely achieve the opposite: application of more violence against the opposition — see below), they are incapable to wrestle the (legislative, executive and judicial) power from the state. But such transfer of power is necessary if the opposition rejects the entire system and/or the structure of society even in the absence of its own ideal of a better system or society. Such a radical rejection is termed *dissent* and the actions resulting from it are *resistance*. This political manner of illegally achieving a political goal requires that the resistance must confront the state power directly, in defiance of the valid legal order, and overcome, by nonviolent or violent means, the power of the state's apparatus which protects the law, and the power of the ruling political organization or organizations which, by supporting the legal order, protect their position. This method's aim is to *overthrow* the state by force, and the above mentioned nonpolitical illegal activities make sense only if they merge into such a confrontation.

Nonviolent confrontations with the government consist of civil disobedience: the refusal to obey the state. It can assume the form of passive disobedience when the movement of resistance ignores the state's normgiving power and its members refuse to comply with their duties. The best known form of passive disobedience is the refusal to perform the military service, but there may be others: the refusal to pay taxes, to perform certain religious rituals, to speak the official language of the state. Active disobedience consists of acts violating the norms of the state without utilizing force. Such are sit-ins in private (restaurants, businesses, abortion clinics) and public locations (school buildings, court houses), blocking traffic or access to certain locations (military installations, nuclear power plants) or interfering with legal activities (logging operations, fishing operations, urban development, industrialization, mining in ecologically sensitive areas), manifestations, demonstrations and protests without required permits. The basic idea of these methods is to overwhelm the executive and/or judicial branches of the government by sheer numbers of violators so that the punishment becomes technically impossible or too onerous for the state and evokes wider and wider sympathy of the public.

The success of nonviolent resistance depends on four conditions: (1) the movement must be massive, (2) a large part of the public must support its aims or condemn the reaction of the government, (3) the state apparatus must include powerful sympathizers with the movement, and (4) the state must refrain from utilizing all of its means against the resistance. If any of these conditions is lacking, the nonviolent resistance fails ([17]). Chances that nonviolent resistance will attain its goal are much better in a democracy than in a modern autocratic state.

Violent resistance demands that the resistance organization acquire organs which are capable of fighting successfully the government (which is the legal embodiment of the state), i.e., the executive branch of the state, possibly reinforced by semi-military organs of the ruling political organization(s).

The resistance which decides to seize power by overthrowing the existing government, acquires its own fighting force either by taking it over ready-made or by building it from its members and fellow-travellers.

The most suitable instrument for seizing power in a state is that part of the state's executive power which is intended and equipped to apply force, especially the military. From the state's standpoint, such an attempt to seize power constitutes insurrection. This way to seize power is facilitated if a political organization already has a share in the government, a share which authorizes its adherents to give orders to the relevant parts of the state apparatus, especially if its adherents hold the ministry of defense (the military and its intelligence services) or the ministry of the interior (police, especially secret police). If a legitimate superior uses the state's executive power for an illegal overthrow of the government, he is performing a putsch. (This method is the preferred way to power of managerial and totalitarian political movements — see above Chapter 7.)

In a similar approach, the political organization substitutes its own objective of seizing power for objectives of organizations structured so that they are capable of changing quickly into a fighting mode, i.e., are organized like the army or police on the basis of discipline and obedience: trade unions, militias, para-military organizations, nationwide physical education associations, hunting and rifle associations. The political organization concentrates on influencing their leadership which, by using its position of authority, maneuvers the membership into a fight with the forces of the government. Negotiations between the leadership of the illegally acting political organization with the leadership of the pertinent parts of the state apparatus or other organizations constitutes conspiracy.

For the overthrow of an existing government, a political organization may solicit and/or obtain the support of another state which supplements by its own means whatever is lacking in the fighting force of the insurgent organization (in this connection see Chapter 12, section on covert war). A domestic overthrow of government is then connected with foreign interference. From the standpoint of the affected state, such negotiations of a political organization with a foreign power constitute *treason.*

If a political organization attempts to seize power by a violent action of its own members, it engages in a *revolution.* (For a detailed description of this strategy of gradual intensification through the steps of dissention, provocation, confrontation and uprising in a democracy see Chapter 7, section on Managerism). Because the state can organize its executive branch better than any other, and especially an illegal, political organization, an uprising or a revolution will succeed only during periods when the state's power is weakened by war, foreign intervention, economic collapse, weakness of the ruling political organizations, or political apathy of the population.

Confrontations strengthen the revolution. The intervention of the state's coercive organs, in view of their (actual or alleged) brutality increase the disgust with politics existing anyway in a large part of the population, and this weakens the state, because, in the final conflict only the forces pro and con count; the others are without significance. Moreover, brutality committed by state organs evokes sympathies with its victims abroad and can even lead to international pressure on the government to cease violations of human rights of the insurgents. Because no such restraints apply to them, their position is strengthened. (About the influence of foreign policy on domestic conflicts see Chapter 12, subsection on covert war.)

The ultimate goal of the revolutionary organization is to transform local clashes into a general conflict with the state's power, i.e., an uprising, an insurrection which escalates into a civil war and, if successful, results in a violent and unconstitutional seizure of power. A violent seizure of power results in a dictatorship whose oppressiveness increases in proportion to the intensity of the defense of the fallen order, even if the revolution intends to install democracy. One reason is the need to offset the damage to the state's legitimacy and authority inflicted by the revolution, another reason is the impossibility to demand from those who brought great sacrifices for the installation of the new order, that they share power with others, and especially with their enemies. The goal of the period of dictatorship is to replace the defeated legal order by a new legal order, because otherwise the revolution's victory is not consolidated and protected.

Measures and countermeasures

Measures of the resistance

Until the resistance movement is ready to confront the state openly, it is constrained to conduct its activities in hiding: secrecy is the best protection against discovery and liquidation. Secrecy depends on the responsibility and discipline of members; it means that each person involved in illegal actions does not disclose his membership, participation or knowledge of the illegal organization to *anyone* not equally involved. This principle allows for no exception, and in view of possible consequences of indiscretion it would appear that this requirement is so obvious that its violation would be only an exception. Experience shows that the opposite is the rule. A member of the resistance very often feels empowered to share his membership, participation or knowledge of various aspects of the resistance with a person or persons who can, in his opinion, be absolutely relied upon not to pass on the secret to anybody: a member of his family, a close friend or, mostly, a sentimental relation of the opposite sex. This expectation is unreasonable — the person breaking secrecy expects from the person to whom he divulges a secret, to be more responsible and disciplined that he himself. This assumption is baseless: the recipient of a secret information feels as empowered to divulge it to other "utterly reliable" persons as the sharer of the information. Once a secret is known to more than three persons it ceases to be a secret; the spread of its knowledge is then unstoppable ([18]).

The need to counteract this inclination of human nature to share secrets produces a number of organizational countermeasures of which the most radical is the execution of resistance members guilty or suspected of violating the principle of secrecy. This measure is taken mostly by guerilla groups. Generally used methods are, in the first place, the utilization of cover names and building an organization consisting of separated small groups. In order to create a more extensive network, such small groups are connected only vertically, not horizontally, in a way which prevents members of one group to know members or activities of another group: messages are passed up to and down from the higher levels of organization between persons not knowing each other's identity, through blind drops or radio contact without any individuals meeting (the so-called spider configuration). In order to prevent infiltration, these measures are reinforced by introduction of code words. Communications take place either at prearranged times and places, with alternative locations and times prearranged, in case that the original arrangements cannot be met, or, for events of emergency, by agreed upon signs or signals, such as an object displayed at a certain location, innocuous letters or postcards with coded messages, telephone calls pretending to be a wrong connection, even ordinary phrases pronounced by a passer-by. It is preferable that persons who arranged communications, are excluded from further illegal activities or removed from the jurisdiction of the state, i.e., sent to the exile. Similarly, the command centers of the resistance should be whenever possible located abroad in spite of the difficulties which arise with regard to communications with the domestic resistance.

In all communications, the need-to-know principle is to be observed. For resistance members isolated from each other and from information about progress or misfortunes of the movement it is most tempting to talk about one's or one's group's activities and exploits in meetings with members of another group. Especially dangerous are any written lists of names and addresses of members. They should not be maintained by, nor given to, even higher organs of the resistance. The same principle applies to any written records; frequently, underground organizations succumb to the temptation to preserve for history records of their activities which must be kept secret in the present. ([18])

Illegality calls also for securing the contents of written communications from discovery. The common means towards this goal are ciphers ([19]). Once the language of the message is known, modern deciphering methods (computers) will break any code provided they have sufficient material. Relatively short messages couched in changing codes are still safe. Messages, coded or plain, can be also secured by invisible writing (most common: lemon juice which becomes visible through application of heat by ironing) placed between lines of an innocuous letter or printed matter, or used to point out the letters of the hidden message by marking them invisibly with a dot or underscoring.

An underground organization is safest if its very existence is unknown to the security organs of the government, but this would mean inactivity, because every activity leaves traces. The organization must therefore weigh the benefits from its actions (harm caused to the government) against the increased risk of discovery and obliteration. This applies primarily to underground organizations whose objective is to create a branched-out network of cells for the purpose of creating an underground political party, a skeleton for a massive uprising at a propitious moment, or a network for gathering information exchangeable for support by a foreign government. If discovered in their preparatory stage, their discovery is identical with liquidation. To avoid obvious actions like public demonstrations, terrorist acts, widespread distribution of anti-government pamphlets is a condition of their survival. Such activities are proper for a well established resistance consisting of mutually isolated small groups loosely connected by a communication system which prevents tracing their connection with other groups and, mainly, their coordination through a common central organ. Each group then pursues its own closely limited activities within the overall framework and purpose of the organization so that, if discovered, its connection with a wider undertaking can be hidden, denied or at least not obvious. Such an organization has a chance of surviving partial discovery and destruction and can renew itself after the danger has passed especially if the coordinating body is at least partly located out of reach of the state's organs, i.e., abroad. Once such a structure is established, it needs some way by which its members are encouraged to withstand the effects of the government's propaganda and the pressure of its security organs. The safest way is through regular broadcasts from abroad; if this is impossible, they have to be replaced by an underground publication. While edited centrally, it should be reproduced in a decentralized way; a copy is delivered through the communications system to the leaders of individual sub-groups which then arrange for preparing an appropriate number of copies and distribute them according to local conditions among members only, among sympathizers or anonymously among the public. Once an underground organization reaches this stage, it develops specialized organs: for editing its newspaper, for its printing, for connection with its exponents abroad, for security, for collating and editing information, for enforcement of discipline and for an open and armed confrontation with the government, when the situation is ripe. If the dissident movement is strong enough, it can create a duplicate organization as a "sleeper," inactive until and if the main organization is liquidated which, in a well organized totalitarian state, cannot be averted indefinitely.

Countermeasures of the government.

The countermeasures of the government consist of (1) discovering the existence of an organized resistance, (2) in ascertaining its size, potential and activities, (3) in destroying it. These tasks are entrusted to specialized parts of the government's security apparatus, namely the secret police and counter-intelligence agencies. In all these activities, secret services routinely employ means which are illegal under the national laws and in violation of international agreements on human rights.

Ad 1: To discover undercover activities, the security services rely on receiving information. Autocratic states maintain for this purpose ubiquitous networks of informers prying even into details of private lives of the population (see Chapter 7), democracies rely on awareness of civic duties of their citizens. In addition, security services build their own networks of individuals. They are recruited by means similar to those described above in the subsection on influencing the rulers.

Ad 2: To ascertain size, the potential and activities of an identified or suspected resistance organization, security organs first infiltrate it and then penetrate it. Infiltration is done by placing in the locus of identified non-conforming actions an agent who observes the environment and on occasion expresses opinions assumed to be identical with those of the dissenters; when finding agreement, he finally voices the need to "do something about it" in the hope that his collocutor either is a member of a resistance group and will introduce him to it, or know about a resistance group and will disclose his knowledge. If the target does not report these feelers to the authorities, this is considered as an indication that dissent exists in the suspected locus, and the target which failed to report the (from the point of the government) criminal behavior, can be arrested, interrogated or blackmailed for criminal neglect. This procedure is repeated until the suspicion proves to be groundless or it succeeds: the agent then gets in touch with the resistance and participates in its activities. In order to penetrate the organization further, he exhibits above average, but not excessive zeal supplemented often with offers of facilities the resistance needs and which are put at his disposal by his superiors for the purpose of gaining confidence and progressing on the levels of command. Such facilities can be access to a copier for printing the underground's newspaper, knowledge of ways of crossing the border, contacts with foreign embassies or visitors, procuring official documents or liaison with other resistance groups. The agent's progress is supported by the arsenal of modern technology: listening and observing devices, tracking of contacts with other members of the group or of liaison with other groups. Once the infiltrator is established, he can be changed into a provocateur: he uses the trust and influence gained in the group to push it in the direction of more obvious, more risky and more severely punishable actions. A variation on this theme is the creation, by security agents, of controlled underground groups which subsequently seek contact with genuine resistance organizations with the ultimate goal of finding the centers of the underground and its communications with abroad.

When the agent's possibilities are considered exhausted, the information gathering shifts to a different level: identified members of the resistance are arrested and subjected to interrogation. It is at this stage that the most flagrant violations of law occur. Exceptionally, cruelties and torture are defended by the interrogators with a crisis situation threatening the lives of third parties; such as knowledge of the placing of a bomb to explode shortly in an airplane, a business mall or a building, which a prisoner refuses to divulge. These situations are rare; most illegal activities are a routine part of interrogations. They consist in breaking the prisoner's spirit, in physical exhaustion, in brutalities, by utilization of technology able to produce insufferable and prolonged pain without endangering the prisoner's life, in utilization of conscience altering drugs (such as scopolamin or amytal) which weaken resistance and ability to withhold information, combined with lie detectors, and other psychiatric treatments. When, in addition to these methods the prisoner is confronted face to face with other arrested members of the group including the infiltrator, and their genuine or faked confessions, preserving secrecy or withholding information is impossible. ([20])

Ad 3. To destroy the resistance, the government either executes or incarcerates its members with or without trial and imprisons actual or potential sympathizers in concentration (re-educational, forced labor, rehabilitation) camps. All of them are designed to inoculate their inmates with such a fear and despair, as to dissuade them from any new attempts at resistance, and some of them are simply extermination camps.

Once the resistance reaches the dimensions of planned terror or guerilla warfare, it is almost impossible to eradicate by the means described above, if it has the support of a significant portion of the population. The irregular armed units of the resistance cannot withstand open battle with regular military forces of the government; but military forces cannot extirpate the resistance without first depriving it of the support of the population, and such an operation cannot be executed without state-sponsored or state-performed terrorism on a large scale. ([21]) All such methods are illegal even if adopted by a state's legitimate government, and international human rights organizations can extend some protection to the victims.

Interaction

The interaction between the resistance and the state is by definition hostile: the resistance pursues the aim of destroying the government, the government pursues the aim of destroying the resistance. Nevertheless, there are important variations within the framework of hostility. Because, generally speaking, without significant foreign help from a foreign state resistance cannot prevail, any variation from unmitigated hostility is in the favor of the resistance.

One form of a relaxation of hostility on the part of the government is described under Ad 2 of the preceding section: during the period of infiltration and penetration of an underground organization, government forces permit resistance activities to go on unhindered, and even support them. The underground organization can during this period inflict to the government significant damage not repairable by its subsequent liquidation (escape of important political leaders across the border, dissemination of publications with long term ideological impact on the readers, transfer of unique information on breakthroughs in military technology, transfer of important politically damaging information about the government's illegal measures of persecution to international media).

A relaxation of pressure on resistance organizations pursuing a certain program or tactics can result from a political decision of the government to concentrate on groups pursuing a different program; instructions to concentrate on organizations planning terrorist activities means that less or no attention is temporarily paid to organizations concentrating on the ideological side of the conflict. In a situation when terrorist acts could not dislodge the regime, spreading the ideological movement which feeds the resistance and feeds politically relevant information to states unfriendly to the government, is in its long term consequences more dangerous to the regime than a few terrorist acts. In certain situations, the government collaborates with selected resistance groups for political reasons ([22]).

The survival potential of the resistance is strongly increased if it can infiltrate the security forces of the government by gaining the help of some of its members. The motivation of such a help can be ideological (sympathy with the program of the resistance, revulsion at actions of the government), economic (bribery), or pragmatic (seeking an alibi for the eventuality of a victory of the resistance); also interservice rivalry — desire to deny a resounding success to another service or another sector of the same service. The main contribution of such a collaborator is warning of infiltration or of impending arrests combined possibly with assistance in the escape of contacts from the resistance, sometimes to protect himself from discovery during his contacts' arrest and interrogation. A practical way of protecting such a collaboration is for the secret service collaborator to list his contact as his agent and infiltrator; the weakness of such arrangement is that ultimately the secret service member must show some pay-off from his so-called agent which is done at the expense of some members of the resistance.

A most important contribution to the resistance is to gain the cooperation of a group of dissenters within the security apparatus motivated either ideologically or practically. Such a group can, not only warn the resistance about danger, but utilize the vast means at the disposal of a secret service to provide its counterpart in the resistance with otherwise unattainable facilities — false documents, secure ways for couriers to and from abroad, transportation (official cars), arms, escape routes for endangered key members of the resistance. As the scope of cooperation grows, the dissenters within the security apparatus cover their activities by pretending that the supported underground organization or group of organizations are under their control; this part of the resistance thus becomes a "protected" organization, protected from inroads by other secret service sections or organizations and generally exempt from arrests. The scope of activities of such "protected" organization is much wider and the benefits for the resistance much greater than they would be otherwise. Here, too, the drawback is that the dissenters must produce results from their cooperation with the resistance, such results can be faked to a certain extent, but there is always the danger that the co-conspirators in the security apparatus will, when under suspicion or in difficulties, produce palpable results at the expense of the underground. This drawback is only partly offset by the certainty that the "protected" organization will not be wiped out completely and will be revived again as long as its nucleus is preserved at least abroad.

Summary

Experience has shown that underground organizations, even with foreign support, have failed to overthrow totalitarian regimes; dissidents who at the right international constellation openly challenged the illegal nature of lawless regimes, succeeded provided they acted at a propitious stage of internal development, i.e., the stage of mature totalitarianism in its oppressive phase. This occurred in the Soviet sphere of power; it failed in an earlier phase of totalitarianism when the managerial center still was ready to re-ignite the phase of suppression, like in China and Vietnam, and the regimes were not as critically dependent on Western concessions as was the Soviet Union. However, the process has not yet ended and a final judgement is pending.

PART B.

OBJECTIVE CRITERIA

PRINCIPLES OF POLITICS

CHAPTER 15

ACHIEVING A PURPOSE

Action originates from the discrepancy between the idea of how man would like the world to be, and the reality of how the world is; action is the effort to bring reality in accordance with the vision of how it is willed to be. The vision, the willed objective, the contents of volition is the acting subject's purpose.

The nature of a purpose is to be achieved (attained, implemented), but its implementation is not inevitable; were it inevitable, it would not be an action, but a law of nature. Its achievement consists in the transformation of a phenomenon (phenomenon = what can be observed) being only willed (wanted) into one also being real, existing. Existence, reality is understood to be a necessary sequence of causes and effects. If the subject of volition wants to change reality to conform to his idea of how reality should be, he must first identify the chain or chains of causes and effects which result in the existence of the willed objective, of the purpose, and if there appear to be several such chains, he chooses the one which achieves the purpose in the most economical way; then he must start the selected chain of causes and effects. The purpose does not indicate this chain; therefore the realization of a purpose depends on three factors: (a) such causal chain must exist, (b) the subject of volition must find it, and (c) he must trigger the chain by creating its cause through his action. Therefore, it must be assumed that the subject of volition possesses not only freedom (will) to act or not to act, but also reason (intelligence) to know how to act.

The process of transforming a willed objective into reality consists in the utilization of a suitable means, a means being an objective willed for its ability to achieve a purpose. The realization of a purpose therefore consists in selecting a suitable means and of utilizing it. The property of a means to be suitable of achieving a given purpose is its usefulness; a means is useful if it has among its qualities a set of causes among whose effects is the willed objective, the purpose. The means, however, by itself does not achieve the purpose; it must be utilized, i.e. set in motion, initiated by the subject of will; the subject which originated the purpose must, first, by reason select the means, and, by free will, cause the chain of effects-causes to start. The selection and utilization of means is an action attributable to an intelligent and free agent and is an integral part of the explanation of phenomena by the principle of freedom. It is distinct from activity which is an effect of causes and is attributed to animate and non-animate objects as well as intelligent beings insofar as it is considered to be a necessary sequence of a cause (its effect).

The achievement of a purpose takes place between two poles: the purpose and the means, and depends on the nature of both. The investigation whether a purpose is achievable or whether a means is useful is the investigation whether the contents of a purpose do not violate the nature ("laws") of the universe — in which case it is not achievable — or if means are capable of achieving the desired end — if they initiate the causal sequence whose effect is the realization of a given purpose's contents. This investigation may be based either on a revealed truth and its norms or on the analysis of reality, of existence, its nature and its "laws". Were this study addressed only to believers in revelation, it would be sufficient to judge purposes and means from the tenets of such revelation, revelation being a direct communication from a metaphysical being to man. Because this study is addressed to all readers, not only to believers in revelation, the study will proceed on the basis of examination of "natural laws" whose validity can be proven empirically to rational creatures. To such it can be convincing; to those who do not accept such basis, it is either superfluous (if they claim superior knowledge — some supernatural insight or natural superiority) or irrelevant (if they reject rationality — deny the possibility of discovering objective truth). Its approach has nevertheless one advantage: it at least allows communications between all persons interested in its object also across the gaps of time: with past thinkers and actors.

Achievability of a purpose and usefulness of a means are objective criteria of any purposive action.

The ability of a means to initiate the causal chain resulting in the purpose constitutes its suitability. The acting subject examines the suitability of means, assigns to them accordingly usefulness and selects the most useful. He can be mistaken in his choice — the selected means is unsuitable, it does not result in the desired reality, and is therefore useless. Because causal chains proceed in time, their uselessness must not be immediately evident. The more complicated the causal chains are, the more difficult it is to determine in advance whether they are suitable or not. The changes of human communities which are the purpose of politics, are very complex and are affected by other, not wanted and independent processes whose effects the subject of volition either ignored or underestimated, but which appear sooner or later. (Brezhnev probably died believing that communism is sure to win; in reality, it was beginning to collapse.)

The unsuitability of means is reflected on the purpose. Achievability of a purpose is its quality that the purpose's contents are a link in a causal chain. If a suitable means is unavailable, the purpose is unachievable. The nature of the purpose may be such that it is outside of the scope of effects caused by the utilization of the means; the purpose may be impossible to achieve. This impossibility may be relative or absolute.

The necessary means may not be available because the acting subject does not know of its existence: either his knowledge is limited or the knowledge of mankind has not (yet) discovered the chain of reactions resulting in the desired objective. (Prior to certain discoveries in physics, the purpose of landing a man on the Moon was unachievable. Prior to the discovery of antibiotics, the purpose of curing certain diseases was unachievable.) The other type of of relative unachievability occurs when the means of achieving the purpose are known, but out of the reach of the acting object. (In politics, the most common example is the impossibility of achieving a desired objective because of lack of necessary finances. For a non-industrialized state it is impossible to achieve space flight because it lacks the means to do it as well as the means of obtaining the needed means.)

Instances of absolute unachievability are purposes for which there is no causal chain that would include the desired effect, because the purposes in themselves are against the very nature of reality, against the very fabric of the universe. This creates a seeming paradox: as the knowledge of existence progresses, newly discovered laws of nature narrow down the scope of achievable purposes and grip man between the pincers of necessity, yet simultaneously the growth of knowledge discloses new causal chains available to man, thus increases the scope of achievable purposes and widens human freedom.

There is another aspect important specifically for politics. It is in the nature of a purpose that it should be achieved, i.e., the subject of volition who conceived the purpose, has simultaneously created an autonomous norm whose subject of duty he is himself. However, all that has been said above about the achievability of a purpose and suitability of means applies also, if the goal of a "better world" (= betterment of the conditions of a group of people) has been imposed on him from the outside, i;.e., by a heteronomous norm (in politics by a legal norm — a law, regulation, sentence). If the subject of volition who conceived the purpose as an autonomous norm, imposes its contents on other subjects of volition, he assumes the role of a normgiver and transforms his autonomous norm into duty for others. These other subjects as subjects of duty incorporate the contents of duty into their own purposive systems as a secondary purpose and become thus for the normgiver means towards the achievement of the his purpose. They may be a most suitable means, however, due to the freedom of man, they also are a means that is highly unreliable.

CHAPTER 16

AVAILABLE MEANS

Man uses means to transpose concepts whose "givenness" (Schall) is only teleological, into the sphere of existence (reality) — the "moral laws in myself" into the "starry heavens above me" (Kant) .

Man's universal means suitable and useful for this process is his *brain* which generates impulses causing various *body* organs to initiate, by their activities, the causal chains leading towards the desired effect. Man looks at the body including the brain as a means of achieving his aims.

Where he is dissatisfied with the degree of usefulness of his body, he increases, by rationally willed acts, the capabilities of his body's specialized organs: strength, speed, accuracy of movements, sight, hearing, as well as his mental faculties: memory, intuition, reasoning, creativity.

The (mechanism of the) body expressed by instincts keeps the body in conflict with the demands of "man" identified as the point of origin of reason and will ("spirit", "soul"); where the body resists exertion, pain or self-denial, "man" forces it, more or less successfully, to submit to strain, pain or renouncement. This tension between the mechanism of the body and man as a source of reason and will not limited by the body's mechanism pervades the entire human life. It can be defined as the conflict of wants generated by the body's instincts with volition (will) generated by reason. (Both antiquity and Christianity considered the subordination of wants to will as virtue, as a victory of freedom over slavery to necessity.)

Man is not restricted to the improvement of his body; he transcends its limitation by using inanimate objects as tools, instruments which increase and complement his abilities: they supplement the strength of his muscles, improve his senses (correct vision, refine touch, sharpen hearing), train memory, count and classify notions and assist in forming conclusions. Tools are activated by human power; they become machines when powered by other than human energy. Their sum combined with the knowledge how to produce and use them constitutes technology which generates its own feedback on man. Machinery fulfills its purpose only under certain conditions. To provide and maintain these conditions can be performed by other machinery, but the ultimate impulse must come from man. The owners of machinery — of means of production — lack the ability to provide all the impulse needed; therefore they must induce other people to do so. Technology thus serves man on one hand and on the other hand, men must serve technology. If they want to use technology, they must respect, provide and maintain the conditions necessary for its functioning and adjust themselves to the changes of the environment caused by technology. Man's instruments co-determine the contents of his purpose of happiness by enabling him to pursue some of its derived purposes which are in competition with other derived purposes of his purposive system (for instance, his health against the survival of the community to which he belongs).

Under certain conditions, the most propitious means of accomplishing one's purpose is to subject other live beings to do his will willingly or unwillingly. The way how to induce living entities to behave in ways man requires of them, was discovered first by experience, later by science. Natural sciences discover how genes and environment limit and predestine causal chains which result in live beings' properties. By controlling the environment and selecting genes man changed plants into means serving his purposes. The same approach — control of the environment and genetic manipulation — succeeded with animals in their taming, albeit to a lesser extent: some species proved themselves resistant to taming, in others the reactions of individuals remained unpredictable even after taming.

The most effective means of an acting subject is man who integrates — out of conviction or because of coercion — the purpose of the acting subject into his own purposive system of happiness, i.e., accepts the acting subject as a normgiver, the normgiver's purpose as norm, its fulfillment as duty, and himself as a subject of duty.

A concrete norm, i.e., a norm which has a unique content and is imposed on a unique subject of duty, is extinguished by its fulfillment, its validity ends. An abstract norm remains valid regardless of its fulfillment: it is implemented repeatedly by the same subject or other subjects, and thus keeps transforming reality continuously and again and again. Achievement of purposes by persons who consider their fulfillment as duty, has become the greatest source of changing the world.

Man as Means

A normgiver institutes a norm because he judges as the most useful way of achieving his purpose to induce another subject of freedom to act according the normgiver's will, not according to his own (the normgiver's will may coincide with the subject's of duty will, but this coincidence is not relevant for the normgiver). The normgiver subordinates another's purposive system to his own.

It depends on the subject of duty, if he wills or does not will to obey the norm; obedience is not inevitable — if it were, it would be a law of nature, a causal relationship, not a duty. The fulfillment of the norm depends on the subject's choice to obey. By such a decision, the contents of the duty become his own purpose, or rather: one of the secondary purposes of his purposive system, and the relevant causal chain a means towards its achievement.

In addition to the relative and absolute unachievability of this purpose due to external circumstances, there are internal obstacles imbedded in the nature of the acting subject of duty, i.e., disobedience.

As long as the normgiver admits that subjects of duty are endowed with reason and will, he overcomes disobedience in two ways. One is a promise of a reward. The normgiver links the fulfillment of duty with granting means the subject of duty needs for the attainment of a purpose willed by him. If the subject of duty is identical with a psychophysical individual, such means can consist in a material reward or in psychological satisfaction: promotion, enlargement of authority, honors, titles, assignment of prestigious goods (cars, the proverbial corner office) and so on. For subjects identical with a point of origin of a purposive system (a "corporate" subject) the normgiver promises or grants means serving the former's purpose (for instance, subsidies or tax advantages for an enterprise whose primary purpose is monetary gain). The other way is punishment: sanctioned norms or an undefined threat of harm. Punishments are designed to increase the cost of disobedience to the point that they act as a deterrent: the profit from disobedience does not exceed the harm caused by noncompliance with the norm. If punishment has to act as a deterrent, its severity is increased in proportion to the expectancy that the subordinated subjects will not fulfill their duty; the normgiver imposes a greater penalty in order to induce them to reorder their priorities. The harm inflicted on the culprit can affect his property (fines, confiscation, loss of a source of income — job, license to perform a profession), his freedom (incarceration, internment), his health (hard labor, dangerous assignments, torture) or existence (loss of life in case of individuals, dissolution in case of organizations or enterprises). Where such punishments do not induce obedience, they are extended to other values dear to the disobedient subject. Persecution of the family or exile from the community have been used as deterrents already prior to the birth of civilization.

Natural sciences discover how causal chains limit or determine reason as well as volition of human beings. Hereditary genes and environment as well as unique experiences determine the scope of knowledge and the choices between alternatives. The impossibility of explaining by causality the human ability to freely reason and decide lies in the impossibility of unraveling the "knot," the crossroad of causal chains which allegedly determine the choices. Attempts to do so and to unravel the "knot" completely and without any unexplained residue can only be derived from a dogmatic and doctrinaire belief that causal relationships are the only valid explanatory principle. The explanation by freedom (volition or norm) admits the existence of a more or less limited, but nevertheless irreducible, irrepressible and by causality inexplicable residue of reason and freedom as indispensable for the understanding of the interaction between the givenness of the world "as it is" and the givenness of the world "as it should be." Experience confirms the truth of this admission; it also corresponds to the way man knows himself: not as an animal, a computer or a machine, but as person: thinking, deciding, acting.

Legal, moral as well as religious normative systems acknowledge limitations in human intelligence and will when judging the guilt of a subject of duty, but only as limitations. Guilt is responsibility for a failure of performing one's duty. As long as guilt is attributed to a factor endowed by freedom and will, the punishment is made commensurate to the extent of the damage caused to the respective (moral, legal, religious) order; the punishment is or is not just or fair. In this sense, the punishment is a part of the order whose integrity it restores. A commensurate (just) punishment is the most effective one because the punished subject recognizes it as morally correct. A just punishment educates, an unjust, too strict or too lenient, punishment hardens.

A consistent explanation of actions as effects of causes, a denial of the faculties of reason and free will leads logically to a denial of a subject's responsibility for his actions and invalidates the very concept of guilt: what is, is an inevitable result of inevitable causes; therefore it cannot be attributed to anyone as his guilt — or merit. If human choices (combination of reason and volition) are explained exclusively as the crossing point of causal chains whose effects are inevitable, the concepts of guilt and punishment become nonsensical holdovers of less enlightened ages and a kind of vengeance. The place of duty is then taken by the requirement of conformity . If the cause of nonconformity is located in the nature of the nonconformist person, it is removed by education or medical care. If the cause lies in the environment, it is removed by changing the environment. According to the extent of nonconformity, this change may mean the restructuring of the entire society or its culture. Groups of people whose nonconformity is diagnosed as incorrigible, must be removed; by extermination or expulsion (Jews on the basis of their race, "class enemies" on the basis of their social origin, minorities on the basis of religion or nationality). A willingness of members of the to-be-removed groups to cooperate with the superior will does not change their fate or the fate of their posterity; their behavior is considered as inevitably predetermined by their racial, class or other environment and/or heredity, their free will as nonexistent and a choice contradicting their predetermination as (lastingly) impossible; therefore their removal is inevitable for the sake of the implementation of the betterment of the object of care.

Attempts to "tame" man have been unsuccessful, but not abandoned; after the failure of efforts to mold human souls by "mental engineering" under communism they center on manipulation of human environment and are being extended to include manipulation of genes.

For the understanding of politics, the explanation of human behavior by necessity is insufficient and barren. Understanding politics, law, economy and statecraft requires the recognition of an area of necessity as well as an area of freedom. Man is present in both of them; his freedom influences the sphere of necessity and necessity hems in his freedom. The knowledge of his limitations does not release man from his freedom and responsibility of recognizing or ignoring such limits but it permits a normgiver to respect the limit of the possible (achievable) and impossible (unachievable).

A normgiver can for a long time force a multitude of subjects of duty to try to achieve the fulfillment of a norm which is unachievable, by increasing penalties in proportion to the difficulty of achieving such norms. If the unachievability is only relative, suitable means may be found by the increased efforts of the subjects of duty. If, however, the norm is absolutely unachievable, the intensification of punishment by torture, family persecution and elimination of groups of the population, is of course in vain. The subjects of duty usually recognize sooner than the normgiver the impossibility of achieving his goal, and punishments evoke anger and resistance. If anger and resistance remain ineffective, the accumulated frustration of people as subjects of duty leads to the loss of exactly those properties which qualify men as the best means for the implementation of a normgiver's will: inventiveness, initiative, cooperation and enthusiasm. Society progresses towards collapse.

CHAPTER 17

CRITERIA OF ENDS AND MEANS

Methodology

To politics (a kind of purposive activities) applies the general principle that a purpose is achievable only through causal chains whose abstractions form the "laws of nature" of natural sciences. Thus the investigation into achievability of purposes and suitability (usefulness) of means consists of determination whether certain purposes are not outside the laws of nature, in which case they are unachievable, and whether certain means does not fail to result in the wanted objective, in which case such means is unsuitable and useless. Therefore, the methodology appropriate (most hermeneutic) to this investigation is that of causality. *Selection of aims contrary to nature's laws and of means which according to scientific knowledge do not lead to the desired effect, is to be rejected.* This is the principal and objectively valid standard of measuring politics. In order to identify the limitations of purposes or means, the identification of natural laws must start with those most abstract (with most extent and least content) and proceed to those more concrete (covering less phenomena, but with more specifics).

Nature of nature

The fundamental nature of existence is change. Constant particles of existence postulated as an explanatory necessity and divided by the process of acquiring additional knowledge into ever smaller and less observable phenomena are grouped into more or less stable, respectively unstable patterns. Science endeavors to quantify the relationships of the origin, changes and dissolution of such patterns and to express them by mathematical formulas. Provided it is able to express them as effects (consequences) of certain causes, it describes such necessary, inevitable relationship as a "law of nature". According to the present level of knowledge achieved by natural sciences the changes are the unfolding of a program located in the cosmic egg from whose explosion (the "Big Bang") arose the cosmos: energy, matter, time and space. The principles of this program are natural laws; they are not created by science, only discovered by it.

The changes that occur in nature exhibit certain common traits, certain regularities, on whose basis they can be described by abstract terms. There are two distinct sequences: evolution and entropy.

Evolution (not to be confused with the Darwinian theory of the origin of species) is the process of actualization of reality's potentiality, it is the *transition from an undifferentiated homogeneity to an integration of distinct heterogeneous parts*. In inanimate matter, the process leads from nebulae to formation of planets and suns integrated into planetary systems and galaxies, from hydrogen atoms to formation of distinct elements, from balls of fluid lava to formation of oceans and continents. In life forms, it explains how variability and selection classifies them into distinct species and integrates them into ecological systems seeking new balance each time their environment and composition change; in the spiritual sphere the variability is producing a wealth of thought and art forms of which only some prevail in the selection process peacefully or violently, and integrate into cultures and civilizations.

This unfolding of potential into actuality does not proceed uniformly. When possibilities of attaining integrated heterogeneity are exhausted in one area of reality, nature as a whole continues this process on a different level. Its components which exhibit the fastest transition from a diffused homogeneity to an integrated differentiated heterogeneity are *carriers (or agents) of evolution*. These are the areas most productive in forming new differentiated and integrated phenomena within reality; they represent the main stream of the unfolding of the cosmos. The actualization of its potentialities thus exhibits degrees which form a continuum accelerating and intensifying evolution in the sense that they produce more better defined forms linked into a more complex unity: evolution shifts to a another level.

Entropy is the reversal of evolution. The area which has become a dead end for evolution, keeps changing; it does not stagnate, but devolves: the links between its parts disappear, their complementary differences decrease until they reach a status of undifferentiated diffuse homogeneity from which a regenerated process of evolution may, but is not certain to arise. The whole of reality is subject to entropy which physics describes as a pervasive process of declining of various intensities of energy until they reach the state of absolute equivalency, of absolute rest, in which there will not be any causes for movement, events, life. Physics expects this state to be reached when the entire matter and energy of the cosmos is uniformly dispersed in the space of the cosmos.. Among the processes going on in the cosmos, entropy represents dissolution and annihilation.

Evolution and entropy can be understood as one process in which entropy balances out evolution, or as two opposite processes where evolution, so to speak, represents a revolt of existence against decline into non-existence, a revolt which culminates in the emergence of life; life reverses the decline of energies and increases their intensity; and mind is its best instrument. Man exhibits awareness of self and of the cosmos, has reason and free will, and therefore *can accept the revolt against nothingness as his mission.*

Life

Evolution is uneven; it exhibits various degrees which follow (not replace) each other and it shifts on new levels from which the unfolding of the creation progresses faster and fuller. Such an evolutionary shift resulted, on earth, in a phenomenon which — as far as human knowledge is concerned — is unique: the emergence of life. The nature of life is its expansionism, its interaction with the environment from which life extracts matter and energy and absorbs them into its own energy-matter patterns. Each live being is a like a whirlpool in the fabric of reality, a whirlpool which adjust to its environment and at the same time affects the environment and sucks from it into itself anything suitable. The typical and main examples of this process are photosynthesis of plants and digestion of animals. This character of all live matter — its vitality, its "élan vitale" results from its time-space structure whose physical and chemical properties cause a continuous process of material and energy changes tending towards an equilibrium whose outcome is the preservation and growth of its inherent pattern. The manifestations of this process constitute life. *Life is unfolding of genes into properties through assimilation of elements from its environment*. When a life form achieves a certain dimension, the whirlpool of its pattern produces smaller ones who continue its original impetus: it multiplies. Propelled by its innate dynamics, life covered almost the entire planet within an astonishingly short time — measured by the duration of the cosmos and of earth. Earth boils, bubbles with life which struggles against all limitations and which created, in man, a being equipped with qualities enabling life to overcome them.

The central property of the *élan vital*, the life force, is to secure its growth. Everything alive grows, and when it reaches the limits of the growth of an individual organism, it continues itself under the form of its offspring; reproduction, propagation is the continuance of the growth of an individual beyond the limits of its own body. To this end, life assumed innumerable forms in order to ensure survival under most varied circumstances and to protect itself against all possible disasters. Through division and budding, seeds, spores, specialized cells in roots, tendrils, tumors and bulbs, vines and branches, life secures the continuance of all its forms.

A revolutionary development of the life force divided the reproductive process into two specialized cells — one fertilizing and the other fertilized — and their bearers, thus increasing its variability, choices for selection and resulting differentiation. Asexual and hermaphrodite species retreat before species of two complementary genders. The price for this improvement was the creation of a new obstacle: life had to made sure that the joining of the two life carrying cells takes place. This ranges from wind spreading pollen to waiting stigmas, and insect bringing it directly to opening flowers, all the way to the formation of special (sexual) organs which place the sperm directly into the ova holding body of the female, all with the function of guaranteeing the survival of the species. Scents, colors, shapes, all are put into the service of instinctive attraction between the carriers of the fertilizing and fertilized cells.

A similar ingenuity is evident in the protection by which nature surrounds the developing embryo: chitinous and webbed containers of larvae and grubs, egg shells, and ultimately its growth within the body of the female; protection granted to the young not only by their parents, but by all the members of a herd, flock, hive. In a disturbed ant heap, ants hurry to carry their pupae into safety, not to save themselves. Thus there appeared on earth seeds of qualities seen nowhere else: self-sacrifice, sympathy, love, compassion.

Live ("animate") matter possesses, due to the fluidity of its structure in its constant striving for a given equilibrium of energies and matter, a much greater degree of variability than other types of matter ("inanimate" matter); this property causes it to be the agent of evolution. The transition from homogeneity to integrated heterogeneity of live matter results in creation of specialized organs for the performance of the various functions of life; because of this characteristic, life beings are named "organisms." A live being is such a pattern of live matter which performs all functions required for life to persist and to grow. Matter endowed with life became the agent of evolution also in the creation of a great variety of "life patterns" integrated in a self-regulating system — an ecology.

Life manifests itself in individual entities which exhibit a varied endowment of survival qualities. In spite of the variability, there remains considerable similarity among large groups of organisms caused by their common origin, or heredity. — the various *species*. Evolution does not progress through individuals, but through species. It is necessarily so because, reproduction being growth beyond the limits of an individual's body, all members of one species form a biological unit whose individual identities are but a transitory embodiment of its life and organisms resulting from the same parents evidence the same genetic inheritance and form classes and species. Evolution is consigned to species primarily because fruitful mating beyond the limits of a species is impossible. Therefore, unusual survival qualities of individuals flow back into the stream of the life of their species by mating with its average members, and their extraordinary qualities become widely dispersed within a few generations; therefore, any individual improvement of survival qualities is mediated through the species. Species, not individuals, are agents of evolution; the preservation of the species by reproduction and propagation as well as protection of the progeny is the strongest function of organisms; their organs are centered around it and it regularly overcomes the drive for individual survival.

There are two distinct components in the process of life's evolution: differentiation and selection.

Differentiation is caused by the variability of organisms. Procreation is accompanied by emergence of traits different from those of the parent organism(s) slightly (variations) or significantly (mutations) which they pass on to their progeny. According to some recent theories, this differentiation is "programmed" in the very origin of the universe.

Selection occurs between the results of differentiation. The inertia of the environment, animate as well as inanimate, resists the transforming drive of life forms, and the final form of an organism is the result of the interaction between its vitality and the environment: The driving force of the evolution, of the actualization of potentialities, is not the environment, but the inner force, the expansiveness of life. An organism either overcomes the resistance caused by the inertia of the environment. at least to a minimal extent or it perishes. Where the assimilation of the environment into a living being ceases, life ceases, live matter dies.

Overcoming the resistance of the environment constitutes the struggle for survival. It goes on in a contest of the expansiveness of life with the inertia of inanimate matter, as well as with the live environment. The contest with the live environment is either indirect (when the infinite voracity of live beings forces them into *competition* for limited resources — plants compete for light, soil and water, animals for nourishment, people for jobs, human organizations for markets or raw materials) or direct *conflict* (when individual organisms attack the existence of others — some animals destroy plants, other animals devour other animals or fight them in defense of their territories, people conduct warfare); exceptionally, individuals of the same or of various species cooperate in this struggle (herds, packs, hives, men).

The results of this process is an integrated differentiated variety against the diffused uniformity of lower life forms: organisms develop, their various life functions concentrate in special organs: for movement, digestion, elimination, reproduction, and so forth. In certain species, differentiation and integration proceeds beyond individuals to such an extent that only their community, not individuals, possess all the life's functions. This is true especially among insects: with ants, bees, wasps the reproduction is limited to one or few selected individuals in the community.

Individual cells of less evolved species are still capable of independent life, in more evolved species, they loose this independence, become interdependent, the individual organs are connected and coordinated, their integration exceeds their differentiation and ensures longer and safer life to its component cells. If their integration is impaired, the entire organism sickens or dies. The greater the specialization and the better the coordination of the various organs, the greater is the survival potential of an organism. The integration of various bodily functions and their organs is done by special organs — a network of nerves with its centers in the spine and the brain; this coordinating and directing function, the mental activity increases the potential for survival of organisms which possess it in a greater measure and more perfect form. Mind causes the organs to perform life's basic function, i.e., to secure its duration and growth. Mental activity is a part of life, and to that extent it follows the same "laws" as apply to all organisms, to all living matter. *By the emergence of mind the unrolling of the universe shifted to a new level of development* and to a new species as its carrier — man.

The species whose organs are more perfectly adapted for the performance of life's functions, gain the upper hand over other species which either become extinct or, more frequently, restricted. Together with the inanimate environment, organisms form an ecology whose balance tends to be automatically renewed: species that multiply beyond certain limits, do not find enough nourishment, are susceptible to epidemics, and the balance of the ecosystem recovers unless a new species arises with qualities against which the old members of the ecosystem lack or are too slow to develop defense mechanisms; then a new balance emerges and a new ecosystem arises.

Mind

Man is a nature's undertaking which, as far as science knows, is unique in the cosmos. In the human species, development *shifted from the corporeal to the mental plateau*. In man, mental activity of the organism exceeds by far the function of coordinating his organs to preserve his body; on the contrary, human body came to serve man's mind. As a species, man hardly evolves bodily, it could be argued that he degenerates, what evolves is his mind. Since the appearance of man, there is an ever greater unfolding of his spiritual faculties within the laws governing evolution: differentiation and selection within each *individual* (instincts, feelings, reasoning; wants and will) and (by competition and conflict) between groups (artists, scientists, mystics, etc.). Certain spiritual activities highly priced by humans, have no direct life serving function (entertainment, art), and therefore are beyond explanation by necessity. Human *collectives* exhibit an exceptional combination of individualism and collectivism. Specialization develops in human communities in the form of division of labor, accumulation of capital, rise of a proletariat, separation of the religious order from the legal order, of the state from the person of its ruler, separation of state's powers, the rise of bureaucracy — all these phenomena are special instances of the general law of evolution. At the same time, individuals retain the ability to live independently; this tension between the individual and the community creates an evolutionary dynamism unequalled elsewhere in nature (or at least on earth).

In spite of many similarities with other species the mind, spirit, distinguishes humanity from them to the same extent that live matter is different from inanimate matter. When compared with the inanimate as well as the animate, spirituality develops distinctively faster. Live matter assimilates its environment to its structure; mind does the same to a radically greater extent. The assertion of one's thoughts, the urging of having one's opinions accepted and implemented is best understood as a form of assimilation of the environment to one's acquired properties. Besides direct and indirect contest on the bodily level there exists in the spiritual world still another form of contest made possible by the extraordinary variability of mental properties: the subjects of certain thoughts do not necessarily fight subjects of differing thought, but try to change the latters' spiritual properties in accordance with their own — a sort of "cultural imperialism" between individuals. Contrary to other organisms, man strives primarily to assimilate to the results of his mental activities — his ideas, his taste, his will, his thoughts — the widest possible nonhuman and human environment by his work, persuasion and coercion. The dimensions in which the minds of great religious teachers, poets, writers, artists and thinkers impacted minds of multitudes and changed cultures, exceed incomparably the assimilative power of live matter. The dimensions in which Napoleon, Stalin, Hitler assimilated to their thought and will, through organization, persuasion and violence the lives of millions of individuals (and destroyed millions) is comparable to natural catastrophes. Within mere thousands of years human activities effected on the surface and character of the planet changes for which geological forces needed millions. Man tamed, i.e., assimilated to his needs, practically the entire sphere of life and is close to doing the same things to inanimate matter on his planet and beyond it. With the growth of the spiritual dimension grows also the size and intensity of conflicts between humans: the savagery with which humans of one set of mental properties (religion, ideology, language) fight humans of another set of mental properties has no equal in nature.

In man, evolution shifted its main stream to the unfolding of his spiritual faculties. Some astrophysicists seeking to find a principle explaining the universe, came to the conclusion that the physical properties of the cosmos result in the creation of life, that the universe is aimed at causing its own contemplation by intelligent beings, concretely man (the so-called anthropic principle formulated by Brandon Carter), as the best hypothesis explaining basic qualities of matter. Of all the explanations of the universe, the by far most plausible is the one assuming that cosmos is constructed as it is so that it gives birth to intelligent life. *Man is cosmos contemplating and perfecting itself.*

Certain results of physics and astronomy confirm this logic. Cosmology has come to the conclusion that the universe is the actualization of the potential of a "cosmic egg" — an infinitely small particle which existed for an infinitesimally short period of time and in which all matter, energy, time and space of the universe were contained and their becoming programmed. A program, however, must have a purpose. An answer to this question was summed up by physicist John Wheeler: "no reason has ever been offered why certain of the constants and initial conditions have the values they do except that otherwise anything like observership as we know it would be impossible". There is no better explanation of the reason why the physical facts of the cosmos are those they are, except the assumption that the cosmos aims at the creation of intelligent beings who can comprehend and appreciate it. An explanation that the cosmos itself brought itself into being and created its order, that it, so to say strives to extend its existence and that it created man by itself, ascribes to cosmos reason and will which experience cannot substantiate. A purpose, however, presupposes will and reason, and will and reason presuppose a rational and free Being outside of the cosmos.

Life covered the planet in an astoundingly short period of time; Homo Sapiens spread all across it in a time still incomparably shorter, and not only inhabited it, but deeply transformed it. The population explosion of the human race is the sign of the success of the life force in its experimentation with various life forms, a proof of the superiority of mind over matter and humanity's triumph over all kinds of obstacles. The human species appeared in nature as a new life form which upset the balance of the biosphere, and the seeking of a new balance is still running its course. One sign of this novelty of the situation is that man acts differently from other organisms in his relationship to them. While they do not care about the impact of their existence on other beings, man does: he uses them, changes them, protects them, selects them even at the cost of self-limitation. There is no "right to life" in nature; no right for the mouse to be protected from the cat; only man will feed wild animals, safeguard them from extinction, keep them as pets. The antithesis man-nature is real and determines future development. A part of the emerging bio-balance is that man regulates nature, and not the reverse. Nature produced man as a being equipped with qualities enabling him to be a spearhead of life in the universe — to free life from its confinement to one small world to explode in space in the same way as it exploded on Earth.

Culture

The process of evolution of live matter is carried on by species which are based on reproduction, on genes inherited from common ancestry. In a similar way, human reproduction created collectives whose members inherited the same physical and mental properties: talent, temperament, degree and types of intelligence, and in addition conserved their spiritual heritage, their culture: language, music, dances, rituals, religion, type of organization. Such collectives, originally a band or a family, then grown into clans and tribes, were in certain areas integrated into larger communities through the strong participation of the power of a state created or wielded by a dominating group, usually the ruling clan of the strongest tribe. This process produced *nations*.

In Europe, nations arose from clans or tribes, or in more abstract terms, from complete biological communities. A biological community is a community whose source of cohesion (i.e., the element which characterizes its components as part of a whole) are inherited potentialities and the resulting actualities (properties). A complete society is a community which performs, through its organs, all functions keeping it alive as a whole. Nations arose from biological communities when one of them through the process of selection (usually in mutual conflict) exerted integrating and assimilative pressure on the subordinated entities by suppressing certain independent functions of the collectives forced into the new whole, by centralized organs for formation of common will and of executive organs primarily for war deprived others from performing some of their functions, transformed them into incomplete societies and thus forced them into a new complete society consisting of itself and the subordinated collectives on a higher level of differentiation.

As is the case with all animated creatures, the nature of a nation is the result of mutual influences of genes and environment. A nation's biological heritage consists of hereditary potentialities of its component biological collectives. The environment is inanimate (the geological formation where the nation lives, its weather, richness of its soil, of minerals and other raw materials) and animate (flora, fauna) including humans (neighboring and other human communities). The natural environment of a nation — his "homeland" (patria, heimat) and its features produced by nature or by humans exercise such a permanent influence that the continuance of a nation is bound to this particular territory.

Among the nation's properties, the most defining ones are the mental, spiritual ones: language, tradition, common history, religion, music, art, philosophy). The continuity of the mental manifestations of a nation (its "national character") is the spiritual formation of a nation, i.e., the manner in which it as a whole expresses itself on the basis of its instincts, feelings and intellectual reactions in the progression of its generations related to their biological continuity: its hereditary conscious and subconscious mental mixture like its physical substance is the present manifestation of the members of the biological communities which originally composed the nation in history. *Belonging to a nation is a matter of causality:* one is born into a nation and even if one leaves it by a decision of the will, one cannot escape its biological and cultural baggage. Reproduction being the growth of one's body beyond its individual limits, the living generation is the embodiment of generations past and future.

The common spiritual, cultural environment, the *national culture,* became the main source of cohesion of a nation and relegated to a secondary, but still important place the original source of cohesion, namely the common origin, common ancestry. The culture of all nations consists of identical or similar elements; all nations speak, sing, dance, paint, reproduce, cook, arrange relationships among their members, raise crops and produce goods, think and organize their activities; the differentiation is apparent in those areas of the common functions of life where they exhibit originality and difference. The most important element which established the self-awareness of a nation is language. The web of language goes much deeper than being a mere instrument of communication. Words express concepts and concepts carve out of the unceasingly changing carpet woven by experience certain constants used by man to capture and master reality. The areas of reality carved out by concepts are different in the sundry languages, sometimes fundamentally, sometimes slightly, but in both cases the discrepancy is visible, perceptible and important (as any translator knows very well), and affects the meaning of words. In addition to the difference in meaning of words there are differences in their ordering. A brain used to a language which requires the change of verbs and adjectives with every change of the subject of a sentence (like Latin or Russian) produces a different kind of reasoning than that developed in the use of languages that do not require this types of coordination (English, Chinese). This is the reason why people feel the forced prohibition of using their language as a gross violation of their innermost self.

Once a national culture is established, it surrounds each member of a nation since childhood and molds his spiritual evolution; it favors the development of certain properties and impedes others, and in the flow of generations intensifies its distinctive characteristics. This spiritual environment receives the fruits of the nation's outstanding individuals which are in harmony with its fundamental traits; they become its components, complement and unfold it as permanent influences on contemporaries and future generations. A nation survives as long as its cultural environment is not substantially altered by influx of alien cultural and biological elements.

A nation is an organic collective, not organized in the sense that all its organs would be centrally directed by one source of volition, resp. one normgiver. Closest to this function comes the organization of the state — with the provision that there exist nations which do not have or have lost their own state and that many manifestations of a nation's life are independent of the state even in nations which have their own state. The importance of a state for the life of a nation lies in the fact that its independence protects the nation and its members from limitation or deformation of the national culture by alien subjects of volition who would assume towards a nation a superior position, i.e., the position of a normgiver. This importance of a state for a nation's life was recognized by international law as the right to national self-determination by the outcome of World War One. It became the defining element of the League of Nations.

Although a nation does not have organs which formally create its will, it is possible to distinguish which of its parts is representing a nation at various times and in various situations of its history according to the traces left in the national culture: sometimes it is the government, sometimes writers or poets, artists, religious leaders or movements or revolutionary organizations. Although it never occurs that all members of a nation follow the same purpose, it is legitimate to attribute collective will to the nation as a whole because its actions are determined not only by the character of its parts (individuals and groups) but also by their mutual relationship and because behind the logically perceived purposive system are found, in reality, beings which exhibit reason and volition. Because the nation is a whole, the consequences of its actions affect all its members whether they agreed with them or not. If the actions of a nation are successful (for instance in foreign policy), all its members benefit whether they participated in it or not; if they are unsuccessful (for instance a lost war), all the nation's members suffer for no other reason but that they belong to it.

On the spiritual, cultural level *nations have the function of agents of evolution*, as agents of differentiation caused by variability and selection molded by integration similar to the role of species on the level of life.

CHAPTER 18

EVERYTHING OUT OF NOTHING — A METAPHYSICAL COMMENT

(Notes belonging to this chapter follow it immediately.)

The logical impossibility of an effect without cause ("the prime cause") leads to the conclusion that explanation requires the utilization of another explanatory principle, namely freedom. Reality exists because it is willed by its creator. This answer while logically correct is empirically impossible: it is a physical impossibility to create something out of nothing. Two explanations have been devised to overcome this problem. (1) The Subject of Freedom acted on existing primordial chaos — creation consists of imposing order on the chaos, being is the result of this order. (2) Because creation of something out of nothing is, under the laws of physics, an impossibility, and because reality exists, it is logically necessary to assume that reality is a part of the Creator.

While the dilemma of something arising from nothing is impossible to solve within the framework of physics, it is possible to solve it within the framework of mathematics. Mathematically it is possible to create something out of nothing by dividing nothing (0) into plus and minus infinity, or rather plus and minus of near-infinity (because mathematical manipulations with infinity are impossible). The emergence of existence from nothing can be therefore expressed by two equations (see annotations at the end of this chapter):

Nothing (non-existence, absence of being): 0=0.
Emergence of being: (∞ — 1/∞) = (∞ — 1/∞).

This equation symbolizes the thought that is the act of creation. (1) To conceive such a thought requires logically a Mind able to formulate it, a Mind beyond time and space because they are Its creation, a Mind that is Being (2) and the only being besides whom there is nothing, absence of anything: nothing does not exist, it literally is non-existence, nothing (3). This Mind is omnipotent because only It exists and there is nothing that could oppose It, and by this limitless power calls forth existence and maintains it.

From this basic equation, an almost infinite number of equations can be derived without violating its validity: from a simple 5 = 5 through a more complex 4+1=3+2, to a more diversified 111+2-54+1-45 = (333x4) — (72x18)+9-30 all the way to equations including integers and differentials and other magic of modern mathematics. Insofar and because numbers and symbols of equations represent like music various frequencies of vibrations, it is possible to picture the universe as a gigantic symphony, a harmony of spheres.

Its existence derives from one basic truth: being is better than non-being. Becoming is the actualization of potentialities programmed into this symphony by its originator, and like each symphony it begins, unfolds and ends. Assuming that the unfolding of reality can be conceived as the implementation of laws of the cosmic equation and its gradual solution, then its final form can be derived from its basic principle that being is better than non-being: it would not be return to its beginning — nothingness— by placing all the pluses and minuses in their purity on one side of the cosmic equation: +(∞ — 1/∞) — (∞ — 1/∞) = 0, but by placing them on opposite sides of the equation: [+](∞ — 1/∞) = [-] (∞ — 1/∞). This solution preserves existence beyond time and change by preventing its positive and negative values from combining and collapsing into nothing. (4)

An act of will presupposes a goal, a purpose. The above quoted conclusion of physics, namely the anthropic principle, can be accepted as its description, if expanded by the understanding and appreciation of the creation through inclusion of the knowledge and appreciation of the Creator: There is no better explanation of the reason why the physical facts of the cosmos are those they are, except the assumption that the cosmos aims at the creation of intelligent beings who can comprehend and appreciate it and its Creator. On the other hand, it discloses the nature of Him: the act of creation is a gratuitous gift to beings who would otherwise never existed, to share in His life, perfection and happiness.

In the equations expressing the unfolding of the physical universe there are pluses and minuses: elements that implement the harmony of the universe, those of becoming, and those of entropy. Life and man are a protest, a revolution against this process of backsliding into nothing. But because man is a being endowed with freedom, he can go both ways. He can be likened to a musician who was given the freedom to enrich a symphony by his own improvisations. This leaves him the freedom either to enrich it — or to disturb and disrupt it. It gives him even the freedom to pronounce judgment on his Creator (5).The causality to which he is subjected limits his freedom (6) and ties him to the perishability of matter, but the spark of freedom enhanced by the intention of the Creator (7) helps him to contribute worthily to the symphony of the spheres. However, mankind has used this freedom to accumulate — in the past and in the future — such a monstrous heap of iniquities not only in the sleaziness of private lives of individuals, but by organized mass destruction of lives beginning with the extermination of entire tribes and ethnic communities to the hundreds of thousands of the victims of Nazism, the tens of millions of lives destroyed by Communism, the hundreds of millions of human beings killed by abortion and the billions whose being was artifically prevented, so that God Himself in the person of His Son had to assume on Himself the sins of the world to bring the equation of good and evil in balance and to return the unfolding of the Cosmos to its right path (8).

T.G.Masaryk, a Czech philosopher and statesman, concluded that the first duty of everybody was to seek understanding of the plan of Providence and then to advance it by each action of everyday life. He called this relationship "synergism of man with God". It is an acceptable way to define absolute good and absolute evil: man's cooperation with the Creator's plan of being is the absolute good, man's disrupting it, reverting being towards nothingness, is the absolute evil. Such are, too, the absolute standards for political action.

Notes:

(1) John 1, vs.1-3. In principio erat Verbum et Verbum erat apud Deum, et Deus erat Verbum. Hoc erat in principio apud Deum. Omnia per ipsum facta sunt: et sine ipso factum est nihil quod factum est. (in ipso vita erat, et vita erat lux hominum: et lux in tenebris lucet et tenebrae eum non comprehenderunt.)
(2) "I am who am" — I am the only Being.
(3) John 1, vs.5: lux in tenebris lucet
(4) Coexistence of haven and hell "forever".
(5) John Paul II, Crossing the Threshold of Hope

(6) "original sin" manifesting itself in the darkening of reason and inclination of the will to evil
(7) grace derived from God's decision that being is better than non-being expressed by his will to save everyone, even sinners.
(8) and continues to do so in the sacrament of the eucharistic sacrifice continuously through his Church.

CHAPTER 19

PRINCIPLES OF POLITICS — ACHIEVABILITY OF ENDS

Political purposes whose contents are contrary to the above tendencies (laws) written into reality (by its Creator), are condemned to failure: endeavors to stop change, to inhibit the variability of spiritual activity, to prevent selection among its products and to disrupt their integration result in chaos and breakdown of cultures, civilizations and societies. The achievability of purposes and usefulness of means depends on observing certain principles: their must be in harmony with the unfolding of the cosmos; they must allow for change; they must include variability and selection; they must safeguard differentiation and integration. The evaluation of the basic elements of politics — its purposes and objects of care — are subjected to these criteria in this chapter. (The next chapter is devoted to the evaluation of means both under the principles governing achievability of ends as well as suitability of means to achieve them.)

Purpose

Politics is actions whose purpose is the betterment of the situation of a certain group of people through participation in the directing of public affairs. The term "betterment" indicates that utilization of a means brings reality closer to the contents of an objective or a norm; it fails to indicate what the contents of the objective or norm are, the situation in reality which the subject of volition intends to achieve. The term "betterment" therefore applies to any such contents and the only objective criterion by which the choice of the political purpose can be judged is its achievability.

The analysis of achievability (cf. Chapter 17) shows that the success of a political objective depends on its compatibility with the "laws of nature". This analysis led to the conclusion that a basic "law of nature" is that of evolution (as defined in Chapter 17, section on nature) and that this unfolding of the universe led to spirituality (mind) as its carrier. Therefore, the highest degree of achievability (and permanence) belongs to politics which is in harmony with this evolution, which identifies itself with its trend. (If cosmos is understood as an act of a being endowed by reason and will, then the highest degree of achievability belongs to politics which represents synergy with this being.) It follows that the objective of politics should be the actualization of spiritual potentialities of a given human collective and that "betterment" of any human collective is identical with the unfolding of its members' spiritual qualities. A subject of politics should therefore construct his or its purposive system, i.e., select and evaluate the suitability and usefulness of means and harmfulness of things and activities, according to whether they contribute or impede the spiritual development of its object of care. Spiritual development as an aim also corresponds to life's tendency to grow reflected in man's objective of happiness which is maximum or optimal — spiritual growth has no limits: it not only encompasses the universe, it aspires to transcend it.

Spiritual development as an objective of politics is a term so wide (so abstract) that it does not permit any deduction which concrete shape spiritual evolution will take; the examination of reality does not disclose any clear-cut, definite form it will assume. Various speculations on this question can exist, but none is able to determine with certainty by which spiritual qualities will be endowed the kind of man towards whom the unfolding of the universe progresses. Due to this uncertainty politics can only aspire to clear obstacles from the working of factors which drive evolution and which are known: variability, selection, differentiation and integration. The factor of variability among humans is the individual; this is a consequence of the immense richness of the genetic endowment of the human race. The factor of selection is contest on three levels: between individuals, between the individual and his collective, and between human collectives. The outcome is differentiation which must never reach the level of disintegration; the element of integration is the creation of society: human collectives are always articulate: an outcome of evolution, a sum of individuals which developed specialized organs for the performance of common and community functions.

The freeing and ordering of the factors of evolution for the purpose of inducing the maximum spiritual growth, depends on the choice of the means of politics, and will be treated in this connection.

Object of care

To the subject of volition, the object of care is usually given: parents take care of their children, a farmer takes care of his fields, and so on. If the object of care is not given and has to be selected, the purpose willed by the subject of volition is the only possible criterion for his (its) choice. If the subject of volition selects from a number of possible objects the one on which he intends to concentrate his care, then he will select the one in which his purpose will be achieved most completely, most easily and most speedily. The selection of the object of care becomes, for the subject of volition, a means towards the achievement of his purpose. A child is a given object of care for its parents; if a couple does not have their own child and seeks a baby for adoption, they will select one whose properties correspond to their ideal of a child concerning sex, race, color of eyes and hair, age, health and any other qualities of the purpose they have in mind. The selection of an adoptive baby is a means towards achieving their goal.

As explained, the objective of politics should be the unfolding of the spiritual qualities (= "betterment") of members of a group of humans. Spirituality is a quality of individual human beings, the objective of politics is not an individual, but a group of men. Therefore, when selecting a group (collective) as an object of care, the decisive criterion is the viability of collectives whose source of cohesion is the same or similar combination of spiritual qualities, that articulates, stabilizes and deepens the attained level of differentiation of the human race, and is thus an agent of the spiritual development of the whole of humanity whose integral part it is.

Insofar as the purpose of politics is to bring about the maximum spiritual development, then the choice of its object of care is the choice of a human collective which possesses the greatest potential for the actualization of this purpose. Such selection is not based on hope, faith or sentiment; it is based on the rational conclusion that political purposes are achievable only as long and to the extent that they are in harmony with natural laws governing reality (cf. the preceding section). Among human collectives which are in reality objects of care of politics, the ones that best fulfills these requirements are nations because of their biological foundation and the spiritual (mental, cultural) environment they produce.

The individuality of national culture is expressed in all areas: religion, morals, law, art, science; in state, economic, social and political institutions, in its civilization (material manifestations — buildings, habitat, roads, airfields, ports; fields, forests, parks, gardens). It represents the variability of spiritual evolution. Selection takes place by competition among nations. Spiritual movements arising in mankind pass through the prism of national cultures, undergo alteration, are integrated (or rejected — but rejection also leaves its traces) by national cultures and in their assimilated forms transposed into reality. The viability of these various forms (of philosophy, art, institutions and civilizations) is tested in their direct or indirect contests, and their most viable variation is then accepted by or imposed on all of humanity or its large parts. The rise of nations transformed the former diffuse and disjointed state of culture into distinct integrated wholes whose variability and competition provides the basis for further spiritual development and integration of humanity on a wider level.

The function of nations as agents of evolution of mankind's mental faculties is rooted in causality and therefore a given. The richness of European culture arose from the interaction and competition of nations; a strong unfolding of human creativity follows usually the era in which a nation becomes aware of and articulates its individuality, its uniqueness and its potential to contribute to mankind's common culture. Areas where evolution into nations has not taken place (Africa, Australia) have contributed much less. Nations as products of unfolding of nature's potentialities have a vitality exceeding that of other human collectives.

Summary

Conclusions following from the preceding two chapters represent the basis for the evaluation of means which form the "sharing in the direction of public affairs." This is their summary:

a) What is the purpose of politics, i.e., what is "betterment of the situation" of a group of people?
   Betterment of the situation of a group of people is a situation which permits, supports and induces its maximum spiritual development.
b) Which group of people should be the "object of care" of politics?
   The object of care of politics should be that group which is the natural agent of spiritual development and which has in spiritual development the same function as species have in the development of life, i.e., the nation.
c) What are the constant means of politics, i.e., under what conditions will the object of care attain its maximum spiritual development?

   The conditions of the object of care are to be in harmony with the general conditions of evolution, i.e., its elements — differentiation and selection are to be present to the largest extent and integration is to exceed differentiation.

CHAPTER 20

PRINCIPLES OF POLITICS — USEFULNESS

Methodology

The means subjected to this scrutiny is given by the very definition of politics: it is "sharing in the direction of public affairs," i.e., the power of the state. The state should be ordered so that it is suitable for the implementation of the above defined purpose selected by the criterion of achievability. The outcome of this search is the identification of guidelines applicable to various arrangements of the state which can serve for the evaluation of political programs and their respective implementation.

The Individual and the Collective

Man is a social being, i.e., a being whose natural environment is the presence of other beings of the same kind. Unlike animal communities where the life of their individual members and their mutual relationship (including conflict) is a function of survival and development of the community, in human communities there exist a tension and conflict between individual members and between their groups as well as between an individual and the group whose member he is. In animal communities, the limitations imposed on members are not experienced as oppression, in human communities they often are. The tension between the community and its individuals, respectively the community and their groups, is the dynamic force driving the differentiation and evolution of human collectives (societies); seen as a manifestation of freedom, this tension takes the form of a conflict of interests of individuals pursuing their subjective goals of happiness singly or together with others, and the collective and its objective goal, in other words, a conflict between the freedom of individuals and the needs of the collective. The balancing of this conflict takes place on a scale whose two limiting points are opposite: either the interest of the abstract individual is considered as supreme or the interest of the collective is considered as supreme: individualism or collectivism. From the standpoint of the spiritual development of the community, the question as posed is erroneous: its answer cannot be "either — or." The arrangement of the object of care is to be such that at a maximum differentiation (individualistic elements) integration is preserved and/or prevails (collectivist elements).

The State as Institution

The main actor of balancing individualistic and collectivists elements in society is the state. Its actions take place in two areas: politics and economy. The political area arranges the relations between individuals and their groups, the economic area arranges the procuring and utilization of their material means.

Individualistic State

The classification of states as individualistic and collectivists is different from the classification as autonomous and heteronomous normgivers. An individualistic state puts freedom of individuals above other values; it has to divide the collective which is its object of care, into individuals and to restrain or subdue individuals and their groups who identify their interests with the interests of the collective as a whole and who consequently strive to put limits on individual interests they consider as harmful for the society, in other words to limit individuals' freedom. This interference is more intrusive if the state adopts in the interest of individual happiness a policy aimed at abolishing differences between individuals so that some do not have advantage over others due to inequality of heredity or environment. The main instrument of such endeavors is the redistribution of material goods in the direction of assistance to the weaker individuals or elimination of the weaker ones in favor of the stronger individuals, the creation of an artificial environment for the spiritual evolution of all individual members of the society, and more recently by efforts to suppress imperfect genes by preventive measures and elimination of individuals who, for any reason (heredity, age, infirmity) are lacking the minimum of qualities considered. The standard of equality too often assumes the shape of uniformity. From the viewpoint of such a purpose of the state, institutions mediating between the state and the individual appear as harmful obstacles especially if they reinforce qualities at variance from the standard: primarily the family with its singularity of heredity and cultural environment, then also private schools, private association based on singular characteristics (gender, religion, nationality) and institutions whose purpose is to promote the interest of groups based on such singularities (primarily churches). The same calculation of benefits and harms induces the state to limit the competence of self-governing entities because they express, articulate and promote their constituents' interests which delay or resist the ideal of equality/uniformity. The autonomy in the formation of the will of the state shifts away from competition between opinions on the best arrangement of society as a whole to a struggle of groups harnessing the power of the state to procure the means for the subjective happiness of their individual members. A state of this type is reduced to function as a heterogeneous normgiver.

In order to safeguard the autonomy of all individuals the state winds up in a situation where it itself must define what is in the interest of individuals, at which point their freedom disproportionately violates the freedom of other individuals, and prevent or punish actions which deviate from its perceptions. For instance, it must violate the freedom of religion, of speech and of assembly to protect the right to abortion or to suppress propagation of anti-semitism; it limits the right to privacy to prevent formation of clubs or associations whose members wish to restrict membership to individuals of the same race, religion, sex or nationality; it violates the right of ownership by prohibiting owners to sell their property or hire employees according to the owners' preferences, and so forth. The result is a status of unceasing conflicts of interest between individuals, groups of individuals and the state which the state (usually by its judicial branch) must decide (for examples see Attachment No.8). A state enforcing consistent individualism is marked by a growth of the executive and judicial branches of government and by bloated bureaucracy — at the expense of individual freedom. In the interest of the abstract individual, the state can not only restrict variability, but also eliminate the evolutionary element of competition and replace it by regulations impossible to create and to enforce without an all-pervading network of bureaucracy which is by its very nature an instrument of heterogeneity and a barrier to autonomy even for those individuals in whose name and interest the state intervenes. From the standpoint of spiritual development, individualism elevated to the highest value is regressive because it limits variability and leads to uniformity and mass conformity.

The elevation of the pursuit of subjective happiness of individuals to the highest value affects society also in another dimension. A purely individualistic state considers family and progeny as matters of individual fancy which it limits directly or indirectly whenever they could impinge on the self-fulfillment of other individuals. Its population policies are not neutral: they prefer an ever growing happiness of a diminishing number of individuals to a lesser degree of happiness of a greater number of individuals. It is a fact that the decision of one generation not to have children would bring about the death of such a society. Such an extreme situation will not occur, but the decision of a great part of a society not to reproduce has consequences considered as harmful even from the standpoint of a society prevailingly individualistic; a decline of spiritual development and viability of societies whose states pursued individualism beyond a certain point is clearly observable (see Appendix 6).

Collectivist state

A collectivist state inclines towards heteronomous normgiving except in instances when the object of care of its ruling political organization is identical with the state's population at least to such an extent that other groups are not strong enough to threaten the society's consensus and when the population is culturally and otherwise integrated to such an extent that the cultural integration takes place of the enforcement by the government. (Such was the situation of the American colonies at the time of the establishment of the American federation: their population originated biologically from Great Britain and was culturally integrated by the protestant Christian faith and ethics whose observance was protected by social pressure and local self-government without the interference of the state; other components — atheists, Catholics and Jews as well as violators of the community's ethics — were excluded from the direction of public affairs while empowered citizens enjoyed extensive liberties in matters of public administration.) In general: the scope of autonomy of subjects of a collectivist state is commensurate with the extent of the cohesion and cultural consensus of its population.

Such a situation is exceptional. As a rule, heteronomy in normgiving prevails, the state and its power are the main or only element of integration. Variability is artificially hampered or precluded, the freedom of individuals is limited or removed, selection takes place artificially by suppression of anything (actually or allegedly) harmful to the object of care or threatening the state which is the means protecting it. The power of the state is extended to the economy in the form of direct regulating or planning economic activities or their performance by state organs. The emerging stratum of professional politicians and bureaucracy replaces in practice the original object of care, and because it is not a collective capable of performing alone all functions needed for its survival, it becomes partly a parasitic element which accelerates the decline of a fully collectivists society or, at best, stabilizes it by stagnation. The results of such an arrangement have been demonstrated by the evolution and fate of the communist society based exclusively on collectivist principles.

State as Cultivator of Spiritual Development

A state whose objective is the maximum spiritual development of a certain collective is not located somewhere on a line connecting fully individualistic and fully collectivist state systems, nor is it a compromise of the two. Its characteristic is such a combination of elements of autonomy and of heteronomy which ensure the maximum space for variability and selection within the framework of the nation's integration. The extent and relationship of these elements depend on a number of factors, among them: homogeneity of the population, the kind of culture, level of education, political responsibility and maturity of the citizens. Because of the abundance of human potentialities which are contradictory in every individual (almost every individual has the potential of a criminal as well as of a saint), the full actualization of all genes into qualities is impossible. The state relies on various kinds of environment to develop the potentialities it considers as good, and impede the development of the potentialities it considers as harmful. Cultural consensus, tradition and social custom assume a large portion of the pressure which the state would otherwise have to exert. In this respect, the freedom of lower institutions works in favor of an organic development of society and has an integrative function: the community's values are handed over to its new members by the influence of the prevailing cultural atmosphere, so that deviations from the prevailing value system must overcome the inertia of the environment, are thus tested and their absorption by the existing culture is not disruptive.

Spiritual developments needs the security provided by a legal state. The lack of security renders variability and selection impossible; the potentialities of the population cannot develop into actualities, they are stymied or deformed. The most favorable environment for spiritual growth is democracy. It secures variability by protecting an "inalienable" sphere of freedom (i.e., a social space in which the state does not impose any duties) to individuals as well as their natural (traditional) and artificial (rationally created) institutions and organizations. Democracy is therefore characterized by a system of human rights (defined by absence of duties towards the state), pluralism of institutions and organizations, a strong system of self-government (cf. Chapter 5) in which higher instances perform only those functions which lower instances are unable to perform at all or only ineffectively. This structure ensures not only a diversity of potentialities, but also a diversity of environments in which they develop, i.e., differentiation. On all levels of public administration and in all organizations of a political nature, normgiving is based on the principle of autonomy.

Among the basic institutions of society, an exceptionally important role in the differentiation as well as integration of society belong to the family and the local community.

The family is a permanent personal and economic community of a man and a women for mutual care and support and the generation and raising of progeny to perpetuate the continuity of propagation. A family perpetuates the biological as well as cultural heritage of the spouses, it performs the inculturation of children; therefore the state has a legitimate interest in its protection and support. Here it conflicts with full individualism which condemns ties restricting complete self-fulfillment of the individual in the utilization of financial resources, pursuit of a career and entertainment and especially sexual exploits. The state protects the family legally by rendering difficult the violation of the marital promises at least to the same extent as it would impede and conceivably punish the violation of other contractual obligations, imposes on parents the obligation to care for their children and protects their right to do so, and empowers them to lay down and enforce the rules of family's life.

The economic foundation of the family is the so-called family wage, i.e., a wage policy which renders the income of one of the parents sufficient to cover the essential needs of the entire family. One way in which the state recognizes the role of maternity is the granting of "salaries" to full-time mothers. These positive measures are complemented by negative measures which transfer the standard of living of citizens free of family ties and responsibilities to those who assume them so that the living standards of the former do not exceed those of the latter in a degree which would dissuade people from forming and raising families.

The function of local communities approaches that of families in the sense that they maintain a measure of physical continuity of their members and their own cultural environment. The state supports communities by granting them the widest possible legal autonomy ("self-government") compatible with the democratic character of the state, and by not syphoning away their needed financial resources and allows communities the right to deny residence to non-residents or to get rid of non-residents whose presence is legally defined as harmful to the community.

The principal means of the state to preserve the integration of its society is the majority principle, no matter how arranged in details; but in itself, this principle is too weak to insure integration. Therefore, prerequisites of democracy include a prevailing societal consensus concerning the purpose (the "mission") of the state or the nation and the corresponding "civic religion" maintained by custom, morals and social pressure. When sections of the population have contradictory principles considered by them, for this or that reason, as inviolable (religious, national, philosophical taboos), the majority principle is considered by the minority as tyranny, and such contradictions result either in restriction of democracy or the collapse of the state. The purest form of democratic integration is the validity of the decision of the majority in the system of direct democracy. In extremis, the so-called Madison's paradox is to be resolved in favor of the majority. Additional measures in favor of integration are: the system of indirect (representative) democracy, the limitation of the number of political parties through majority representation, a minimum number of applicants to qualify for nominating candidates in elections, separation and reinforcement of the executive branch by direct election of the head of the state, the right of the head of the state to govern by decree or a constitutionally secured right of some non-political organization (mostly the army) to assume power in case of the state's imminent or actual disintegration.

The Economic Order

In the economy, the element of variability is represented by self-reliance and personal responsibility, individual initiative, private ownership and private enterprise; the element of selection by competition. These elements cause the economy based on private enterprise and the market to be the order most capable of creating economic growth as the material basis for spiritual development. At the same time, some of its features have side effects acting in the opposite way. It creates needs artificially, it concentrates human attention on material goods and away from spiritual goods. The pressure towards expansion of markets leads to appealing to the most common denominators of the greatest number of people, i.e., to their instincts, and results in standardization of taste and habits on an ever declining level of vulgarity and uniformity — it creates the mass consumer society.

The selectivity of the market brings forth a group of people living in luxury and another one living in want. Poverty (misery, i.e., lack of food, habitat, clothing, education and health care) is an environment inhibiting the unfolding of potential, and luxury is an environment which does not require effort and therefore eliminates the element of selection. The spiritual development of society (of a nation) is therefore narrowed down to a stratum which lives above the level of poverty and below the level of luxury; material sufficiency combined with frugality and effort is the economic environment most favorable for the spiritual development of individuals and of society.

By differentiation evolution deepens the division of society into the rich and the poor and the evolution of ownership of means of production proceeds in the same direction. It leads to the concentration of means of production in the ownership of a narrowing number of gigantic enterprises employing an ever growing number of people; persons not owning means of production are the first ones to suffer from a disequilibrium in the economic balance and the last ones to be integrated in the economic process during the forming of a new balance: their status changes from workers to unemployeds. Extra-political concentration of ownership and centralization of means of production as well as agreements limiting competition and restricting production have consequences inhibiting selection.

The market economy possesses its own selectivity — it influences the access to leading economic functions. The emphasis on financial gains generates a mechanism which selects for key positions persons who see in the accumulation of money the central value of life at the expense of cultural and moral values — economic materialism. This ethic affects and dominates other areas of society, especially politics and public affairs. Voltaire rejected Christianity for his personal life, but approved of it for others, because it prevented his taylor from stealing; however, the reality is such that the market and private enterprise systems can function only if its leaders observe moral values. American economy flourished as long as it ran within the parameters of strict Protestant morality; it began its decline in the Sixties which represent the start of the rejection of any objective morality by American elites.

In order to counteract side effects of economic individualism which inhibit spiritual development the state intervenes in various ways and to various extent.

The state counteracts the increasing polarization of society (the rich and the poor) by transferring a part of the highest incomes to those with the lowest incomes, mainly by progressive taxes and welfare payments, also by luxury or "sin" taxes and property taxes. The obstacles to variability and selection are handled by legislation prohibiting trusts, cartels, price fixing and by measures promoting competition. The composition of the national product is influenced by the state through subsidies for production of desirable goods and by taxing or prohibition of goods harmful to the ideal of a better society.

The state can affect the economy also through its ownership of means of production either as a minority shareholder sharing the decision making process of the corporation, or as a majority shareholder it influences the market by producing goods or providing services which would not be provided by the free play of an individualistic economy.

An ultimate form of integrating interference by the state into the economy is its transformation from a market economy into a directed or planned economy in which the elements of competition, initiative and private ownership are integrated into the fulfillment of the centrally conceived plan of production and consumption. The culmination of of the interference of the state in the economy is the transfer of the ownership of means of production to the state or its organs, i.e., socialism.

A justification for socialism is the assertion that it overcomes the separation of means of production from those who work with them, through the legal fiction that the state represents (also or exclusively) the workers and that means of production owned by the state are actually owned by the workers or by all citizens. This fiction failed in practice: the real decisions concerning the utilization of means of production passed inevitably to the managers and the bureaucracy (a similar development took place also in gigantic enterprises of the capitalist system) to the detriment of productivity, efficiency and inventiveness. Experiments with transferring the decision making in state owned enterprises to employees have failed for another reason: people generally prefer immediate concrete gain to an uncertain hope for a larger gain in the far future. With harmful effects on productivity of the enterprise and the economy, they vote for immediate wage increases or perks rather than for the expectation that their increased and improved performance will somehow benefit them later in the form of profit sharing.

For the protection of the moral environment in which the economy functions, the state can use three methods. First, punishment of economic activities violating the cultural traditions of the society. Second, state ownership of certain key sectors of the economy to manage them technocraticly, i.e., by pursuing the goal of technical perfection rather than financial gain. Third, a steep taxation of the portion of income used for "conspicuous consumption" rather than productive investments encourages the selection to leadership positions of persons motivated by the "building instinct" rather than by facile and fast enrichment —"greed."

The proximate purposes whose attainment should be promoted by the state's selective utilization of the above means are:

The principle of plurality is applied also to economy and allows for competition of all types of entrepreneurship within the framework of both evolutionary principles. In the interest of integration, the state interferes with the economic activity in order to produce a univirtual society, a society in which barriers between economic and social strata are fluid and not rigid, where all members of the society have equal rights and equal duties. In a univirtual society, the distance between the wealthiest and most powerful and the poorest and weakest members is minimized. In order to preserve selection, the state promotes a situation of a steadily improving standard of living in which members of society occupy the social space between poverty (i.e., above the existential minimum) and luxury. Poverty is an absolute quality, not a relative one. To be poor is to be hungry, thirsty, to lack shelter, clothing, to be sick without medical help; one who has less than others have is not necessarily poor.

A corollary of political pluralism is a mixed economy in which coexist planning with competition, dirigism and private enterprise and where the disposition of means of production is spread among the population: through democratic control of publicly owned enterprises, through shares in corporations, through participation in cooperatives, through private ownership of individually or family owned enterprises, and in which taxation and other measures of the state promote a univirtual society of the type which the population has chosen through a democratic legislative process.

Each intervention by the state requires additional bureaucracy, with the usual consequences. The structure of the state as described above (democracy, wih strong self-government) is capable to limit and keep fencing them in. With increasing equality, too, productivity slows down, and, as consequence of progressing equality, the loss of productivity results in the fact that the lowest income of an economically more egalitarian society is lower than it would be in a less egalitarian society due to its higher productivity. This is the point in which economic nivelization must stop. It is possible that, together with the protection of a certain moral standard of economic activities, interference by the state slows down economic growth and technical inventiveness; from the standpoint of spiritual growth, the price paid for acquisition of technical innovations from abroad is to be considered as prevailingly profitable.

Foreign Policy

The purpose of the state is to protect the function of a nation as agent of differentiation and selection in the spiritual evolution of humanity, to be the expression of national individuality in law, economy and institualization of the national life.

The ultimate problem of a pure individualistic state is contest — through competition or conflict — with other states. A pure individualism does not include any rational justification why an individual should sacrifice his possessions, health or even life in order that other individuals can pursue their interests; by doing so the individual would negate his highest value: his own interest. Therefore, a survival of an individualistic state depends on those who reject its philosophical underpinning. In order to overcome this weakness, individualistic states must induce other states to accept also the individualistic political philosophy. The way to accomplish it is their membership in supranational organizations which promote individualistic principles. For this reason, states based on individualistic principles are much more willing to renounce portion of their sovereignty than states pursuing primarily the interest of a nation as a whole: they expect that international organizations will impose through their bureaucracies individualistic values to all membership states (for factual information see Chapter 24).

A state whose primary purpose is the unlimited interest of a certain collective, is in its relation to wider communities, regional or global, a disintegrating factor, because its objective is maximum and therefore leads towards expansion and aggression, i.e., to the promotion of interests and spreading cultural, economic and political (including its sovereignty) values by force.

Contest between nations as agents of spiritual evolution is shifting clearly to competition rather than conflict; therefore readying an aggressive war is evidently the wrong policy. The situation is different in the case of a defensive war: there is the danger that nations and states left behind in competition could have recourse to methods of violent conflict as means of self-assertion or survival, and the same way may be chosen by successful states whose purposes are achievable only at the expense of other states or nations. A state should therefore be ready to fight a defensive war in the sense that aggression will not pay, that even success would cost the aggressor unbearable harm.

The military measures are to be usefully combined with the strengthening of the international law and order provided that self-reliance is not replaced by reliance on others' strength to repel a potential aggressor. Only a state whose defensive strength has the potential to transform an aggressor's success in Pyrrhic victory, is a state really independent and sovereign and ensures that its members will not be subjected the sovereignty of a different state against their will.

International Relations

A state is the sovereign agent of integration with regard to the society subjected to it. In its outward relations, it is an agent of differentiation and selection and therefore requires a counterforce of international integration. Such counterforce can be created only at the expense of the sovereignty of states.

A contractual limitation of states' sovereignty with preservation of the principle of states' sovereignty is not binding and not effective, because not enforceable. Enforceability presupposes the creation of a politically acting subject superior to states and endowed, in at least embryonic form, with powers forming the sovereignty of a state: legislative, judicial and executive powers. This is the equivalent of establishing a super-state which is sovereign and defines as well as enforces the limitation of state sovereignty (see Chapter 12).

From the viewpoint of the spiritual development of humanity it is necessary to subordinate the interrelationship of states to an order which excludes forms of interstate contests prevailingly harmful to humanity as a whole and to limit state sovereignty by institutions which guarantee such an order and/or enforce its observance even by non-members, or at least defend members' common values against outside threats. Under no circumstances, however, should such integration interfere with the freedom of individual states to be an independent legal, economic and institutional expression of various national cultures.

Such restriction of the power of supranational (the word supranational is used instead of the more accurate, but not common expression "superstate") institutions requires a legal limitation and definition of their jurisdiction right at the time of their constitution, i.e., in their charter, statutes or other founding document, as well as structural measures. The purpose of both is to render impossible or at least difficult the use of a partial limitation of state sovereignty for the purpose of subjugating some nations by others or by the supranational bureaucracy which will inevitable arise with a tendency to pursue their own agenda rather than to execute the will of its respective normgivers. Such tendencies manifest themselves by limitation of the states' jurisdiction over their own subjects (citizens, other inhabitants, organizations). Limitations of the state's power concerning movement of its population and its composition, freedom of association, economic activities and armed forces can result in the loss of the independence of a nation in spite of the preservation of a formal independence of its state. Parallel and commensurate with the abdication of part of their sovereignties, nations must strengthen and/or create self-governing and non-governmental organizations for the preservation and development of their culture and identity. An exclusive reliance on the power of the state will be impossible in an era of supranational institutions.

The sovereignty of states in supranational organizations is protected by the principle of legal equality of states, but legal equality does not arrest the shifts in actual power relations. Such shifts occur regardless of states' legal equality outside the framework of supranational institutions, but ultimately are reflected even there. Especially important for nations is to conserve the control of their economy, because after the elimination of conflicts, i.e., after securing peace, the changes in power relationships shifted to the area of indirect contest, in the first place to economic competition. The evolution of supranational organizations is abandoning the principle of unanimity in both its forms in favor of informal, ad hoc flexible arrangements which reflect more accurately the power relationship of participants (for example, the role of the United States in the conflict with Iraq, its intervention in Panama and in Granada, or the air strike on Libya).

Attempts to express formally the power relationships of states by their representation in supranational organizations on the basis of the size of their respective populations are successful only when other power factors, especially economic strength, are per capita more or less equal, otherwise the numbers do not reflect the real situation at all. (A state possessing nuclear armaments is superior to a state not capable to produce it even if the latter's population is significantly more numerous.) One of the possibilities of future development of supranational organizations is a bicameral system where one of the chambers is based on the principle of equality of states represented by their governments, the other chamber on populations represented by directly elected representatives. Another, possibly parallel option is a constitution based on a Charter of Inalienable Rights of Nations similar to the Charter of Human Rights and granting to each member state an area outside of jurisdiction of any international organization.

None of these arrangements does resolve the explosive tensions stemming from the fact that borders of states and of nations do not coincide and that a state cannot fulfill integrally its role of expressing the national individuality and protecting the national interest without somehow infringing on the development of national or other minorities. So far the development was in the direction of violent rearrangement of such borders so that both coincide, with accompanying "ethnic cleansing", expulsion of other nationalities or even genocide.

At the same time, the protection of minority rights evidences features reminiscent of sovereignty based on personality rather than on territory, when a national state arrogates itself the right of protection or interference over members of the same nationality on the territory under the sovereignty of other states.

From the standpoint of national interests, the territorial principle is defensive while the personality principle opens the door to penetration of states protecting the interests of nations already settled on a territory. Experience of recent history has demonstrated that granting equal personal rights to all citizens regardless of nationality does not solve this problem and that ignoring the vitality and reality of nations in the building of an international order is dysfunctional. Therefore, for the foreseeable future, peaceful transfers of population and adjustments of borders seem to be the only alternative to drawn out tensions erupting repeatedly in violent conflicts of civil, guerilla, and genocidal wars with the potential of destroying peace between states drawn into such conflicts.

The progress of international relations from national states, i.e., states whose primary purpose is formed by the culture of one nation, to supranational and/or international entities by renouncing a part of national sovereignties to supranational authorities can be based on mutual accommodations or, like the emergence of domestic law, by imposition of an order by force. From the standpoint of spiritual growth of humanity, the former way is more useful, but the latter way is more practical and feasible. Their mutual interpenetration and combination is, of course, possible and probable starting with sanctions against a certain state or group of states in the interest of peace or for international humanitarian interventions and progressing towards defense of common interests of humanity such as prohibition of chemical, bacteriological or nuclear armaments or protection of environment or common resources to undertaking common global projects like regulation of weather and space exploration or colonization. The technical means are available, but politics has not yet found the proper organizational forms to actualize all technology's potentialities.

CHAPTER 21

CRITERIA OF CRITERIA

Man being a free agent has the option of deciding to endeavor to achieve the unachievable and may deceive himself temporarily into thinking he is succeeding, especially since the ultimate effects are not immediately recognizable (even if predictable) and can be postponed by escalation of pressure on subjects of duty. In reality, he is then contributing to a cosmic regression, to universe's entropy which is the opposite of the unfolding of the full potential of creation. Preventing change, inhibiting variability of thought and/or competition of ideas, breaking up integration of culture, civilization, institutions causes chaos and breakdown of society, and thus failure of intended political objectives — because they were unachievable from their inception and thus doomed to fail.

Limitations of Science

Science is the main instrument used by man to seek out and verify causal chains and their effects. The authority of science derives from the successes of natural sciences, which proved them to be an instrument both reliable and fruitful. In the examination of nature, causal chains are relatively easy to isolate and straightforward. The situation is different when science examines the activities of man and the development of society where the causal chains are so complex and intertwined that they can be explained only by recourse to the principle of "freedom," to be understood as activity which cannot be explained by the cause and effect relationship at all or at least not completely. In many instances, insufficiently critical reliance on science produced unsatisfactory results: societies and measures undertaken by politics by application of certain scientific discoveries and theories collapsed with catastrophic consequences. Just recently, humanity freed itself from two systems derived from science: nazism derived from anthropology, communism derived from economics, but there is no shortage of learned professors and their followers who are absolutely certain that the discoveries in their field and especially their own discoveries are a certain way towards a better future of humanity, if only the benighted mases would obey: population control, eugenics, managing the environment, integration of races and/or multiculturalism and other discoveries of biology, medicine, sociology and economics. There is a short way of transforming a scientific discovery into ideology, building a movement around it and imposing its demands by the power of the state, even if the coercive methods are far from the primitive violence used by the former autocratic movements.

The failure of science as an sole criterion of usefulness of selected means is caused by several circumstances:

- Science is an open system; it assumes that its results are not final, that they will be corrected, completed or reversed by the results of further research and discoveries. Therefore actions undertaken always in accordance with the latest scientific fashions will inevitably demand corrections which, when affecting society, cannot fail to produce significant losses of material and cultural assets. The fact that political and sociological changes always limp behind technological progress is common knowledge.

- The scope of knowledge gained and attempted is so vast that research, inquiry and scholarship must by specialized. Specialization leads to professional deformation of the mind: overrating one's own specialty in its application to the problems of society. Each specialist considers as erroneous such division of resources which does not allocate to the full and total implementation of his conclusions all the necessary means, and does therefore consider the inclusion of his recommendations into the material solidarity with other derived objectives, with the ensuing limitation, as faulty.

- Science is a system of theories abstracted from experience. Its accuracy therefore depends on the completeness of the experience and of the inclusion of all pertinent observations in the abstraction. The validity of scientific theories is verified by experience (if artificially induced or isolated, called "experiment"). As long as all observed phenomena agree with a theory, the theory is considered as accurate, as truth; if any one phenomenon fails to correspond with the theory, the theory is considered as invalid, as untrue. The probability of discovering such a disturbing phenomenon decreases in proportion to the extent to which a given theory relates, depends on and mutually confirms theories of a more general nature. The more general such theories are, the safer it is to assume that the scientific findings are correct. Such an agreement, however, still does not guarantee of the truth of a theory, because it is impossible to exclude with absolute certainty the possibility of the discovery of an entirely new factor. This is true primarily to the sphere of human actions — the discovery of producing energy by fusion rather than fission would bring about an era of almost unlimited and free energy, uproot the structure of the entire industrial civilization and render "untrue" many present political, sociological and economic presuppositions and "laws." The same applies also to the knowledge of physics whose known "laws" are held to lose validity in the conditions during the origin and collapse of the universe.

- The opinions of scientists seldom agree; majority opinions, specially those of scientific authorities bolstered by the media, are taken as true, but it can be considered as proven that neglected or minority opinions have at least a part of the truth. This fallibility of scientists is enhanced by the fact that pursuit of knowledge is not the only component of their primary purpose of happiness: other derived (secondary, tertiary etc.) objectives exert influence on their judgement; sometimes unknowingly, sometimes knowingly their conclusions are biased in favor of objectives other than pure truth, or doubts about their accuracy are not voiced. Such were the prognoses of scientists concerning the effect of nuclear weapons, of industrialization on the weather, of population growth on the environment. Added to the individual human frailties of scholars is the impact of the corrupted science subservient to the sources of funding scientific research: in totalitarian regimes to government, in individualist regimes to corporations, industry subsidized endowments, business conglomerates.

- Observation interferes with the activities of the observed object. This is well recognized in subatomic physics; it is less obvious in induced experiments of social sciences: observed samples of individuals act differently when aware of the observation, than without such knowledge; if unaware, however, they do not act in a way which furnishes the desired data.

- The finiteness of the cosmos interferes with the accuracy of mathematics. The equation of the proverbial "one plus one is two" can be expressed in reality also as 1+1 = 1+0.99999. . . or 1+1=1+1/2+1/4+1/8+1/16+1+1/x. . . . infinitely. However, because the universe is finite, these infinite sequences in reality end short by an infinitesimally small fraction of "1"; however, in view of the size of the universe, these missing "infinitely" small fractions create an undefined or undefinable discrepancy between mathematical formulas and reality.

Correctives

Results of science are to be accepted critically; the question then arises, what criteria are to be applied to them.

Common sense

The most common one is common sense: it is the judgment of the average person. Research and scholarly work in a limited field of knowledge are the privilege of a relatively small number of people. An average person is exposed to a wide variety of challenges and therefore reasons on a basis of a greater wealth of life's experiences than specialists do. The variety of experience joined by a variety of ways of mastering it (intuition, art, feeling in addition to reasoning) described also as "horse sense" or "gut feeling" provides a balance to the one-sidedness of specialists. (This is also a the justification of democracy — see Chapter 6, section on "People know best.")

Customs and Traditions

There is also the network of customs and traditions. Tradition is not what happened in the past, it is what has proven its survival value. The origin of custom and tradition can often be traced to prehistoric times and their similarity to the behavior of social animals: division of functions, between sexes and generations, superiority of the preservation of life and interests of the whole (herd, hive, pride) over the life of its individual members, rules of inborn "morality" and "decency" of behavior is remarkable. (See Attachment No. 7.)

Christianity

Finally, there is religion, more specifically Christianity because the dominant civilization of humanity is historically based on Christianity, and the survival of a civilization is not aided by subversion of its own foundations. Theories are verified by experience, and experience indicates that anti-evolutionary phenomena appeared whenever politics contradicted the tenets of Christianity and that postmodern politics are adopting isolated Christian values as remedies to acute ills of the presence. The main examples are:

— renewed emphasis on family values,
— distrust of the power of a centralized state (the theory of "subsidiarity"),
— establishment of a supranational organization integrating sovereign states,

— preservation of "inalienable rights of nations,"
— assistance to the economically disadvantaged ("preference for the poor"),
— international solidarity of the human race (humanitarian aid, development).

There are other reasons than expediency arguing for the recognition of Christianity as one of the correctives of science.

Christianity places being over non-being.

Christianity recognizes the imperfection of human nature: man's reason is flawed and his will is inclined to evil; the need of betterment of the human race is the basis of all political programs and movements.

The universe appears to have order, direction and sense, i.e., a purpose, therefore, it is the act of intelligent will; and it is not unreasonable to assume that such a will entered in communication with its creation and creatures, in order to assure that its purpose will be accomplished.

Christianity shifts the priorities of human life from natural and reasonable purposes — increase of wealth and power — to contrary values — humility and poverty — as the true meaning of human life; this is a shift which transcends human nature and which is of transcendent origin .

Political science poses questions it cannot answer, and it seeks their answers in political philosophy. Political philosophy shifts its unanswerable questions to general philosophy; but philosophy is unable to answer all questions it itself generates. It would be unreasonable to disregard, to deliberately ignore, answers given to these questions by revelation (see James V. Schall, *At the Limits of Political Philosophy*, ed. Catholic University of America Press, 1996)

An explanation that the cosmos alone gave itself its beginning, that it itself on its own strives to prolong its existence and that it created man through its own powers attributes to cosmos intelligence and will which experience does not find. Christianity places the word (the "Word") which produced the equation dividing nothing into plus and minus near-infinity, outside the universe. It attributes it to an actor who, by his own definition "I am Who AM" — is the absolute existence endowed by absolute life subsisting in dynamic relations between three poles whose integration forms one — the trinitarian God. This God omnipotent vis-à-vis the nothingness pronounced his creative word and maintains and develops the harmony of being out of limitless generosity, to enable the product of his creation — man — to share in his absolute being and in his creative act. Such participation is possible only to someone who is a likeness of the Creator in possessing reason and will, possessing freedom. Freedom allows the created being to go against the Creator's plan, to pronounce judgment over God (John Paul II, *On the Threshold of Hope*), to condemn, reject him and to act regardless or in opposition of the plan of Providence, to do "evil" (disturb the symphony of creation pre-programmed by God) rather than "good" (complementing and enriching this symphony).

According to Christianity man used his freedom to accumulate negatives (to pile up evil in the past, present and future) to such an extent that to offset it, God himself became man and through his life in total conformity with God's plan restored the balance of the cosmic equation and regained for humanity the possibility to synchronize its being with its creator.

Christianity asserts that being is better than non-being because the Word has been spoken, God created the universe, He pronounced it good in its original form. Christianity also agrees that the universe will end, that the symphony will play itself out and its equations will be solved. "The Sun will vanish and the World will perish," says an old song; but this will not end by balancing the plusses and minuses on the level of 0=0. On the contrary, all the pluses will accumulate on one side of the equation and all the minuses on the other, and will remain so past the existence of time: the ones in opposition to the Creator, the others in communion with Him.

Summary and Tentative Conclusion

In order to remain on the basis of political science, the three above mentioned correctives can be only what they are: correctives. Science remains the main dynamic force propelling humanity on its way to the preservation of the human spirit, of life in general and of being in the abstract. The correctives cannot replace science in its function of gaining knowledge of being and of application of such knowledge. However, where such application leads to politics which contradicts common sense, destroys tradition and traditional institutions and violates Christian ethics, it is reasonable to assume that such politics either misinterprets scientific knowledge or generalizes scientific findings beyond the limits of their validity. *It is prudent to avoid such ideologies and such policies.*

PART C.

QUO VADIS, HOMO?

ENTROPY VERSUS EVOLUTION

CHAPTER 22

STRUCTURAL SHIFTS IN SOCIETY [(23)]

The source of political action is discontent with the situation of a certain human group. It is discontent with the extent of its power and wealth; but its roots usually go deeper: it is the discontent with the very nature of man and his destiny which are perceived as lacking and needing improvement. The conviction about the essential imperfection of man is common to all religions and underlies also nonreligious ideologies. Historically, the defining of human deficiency and the ways towards its correction originated with visionaries and prophets; in modern times, this role was assumed by intellectual elites.

The term "intellectual" characterizes here not only individuals dealing mainly with theories; it encompasses all those whose occupation is to create, deal with or represent symbols — primarily in science, and also in arts and entertainment as well as politics.

The generalizations of the nature and of the impact of elites in this chapter are derived primarily from the experience in the United States for the simple reason, that it has gone farthest in this direction by attracting and concentrating excellence in most areas of human endeavor reaching from sports, entertainment, performing and other arts to social and exact sciences and has drained the world of its best talent. The greatest aggregations of talent in the world are in New York, Hollywood, and Washington, the centers of cultural, economic and political power, which give the elites the best opportunities for personal advancement and also advancement of their visions for the betterment of humanity. Also the exceptional position of the judiciary and the Supreme Court in the American Constitution has enabled the elites to make their impact felt faster and stronger than it has been in other nations.

Emergence of Elites

An elite is a group of persons whose source of cohesion is excellence in their common specific area of competence. Accordingly, there exist elites in politics, religion, sports, arts, science, economy and finances.

In contemporary society, elites perform two indispensable functions. They facilitate the realization of subjective as well as objective (technical) goals by discoveries of the most useful means, i.e., means that achieve the given goals at the least cost with the greatest profit. At the same time they are the carriers of differentiation, and therefore an evolutionary plus especially in a democracy, because they inject the culture with new elements that can engender and often do engender new political movements and political organizations. The importance of elites increases in the measure in which political processes fail to solve outstanding problems of the society; incompetence of governments results in greater reliance on expertise and this reliance has created a direct entry into the government of experts which leads to the elimination of the citizenry from sharing in the deliberations and decisions of experts and specialists.

Modern society bestows on exceptional individuals the recognition of excellence primarily by material, rather than symbolic rewards; stunning incomes rather than honors, status or respect of peers are the common denominator of members of the elites in the area of western civilization. Their wealth is seldom derived from production of goods; their world is the world of abstractions and symbols. People and their lives are classified by the elite as types and captured as statistics, statistics become equations, equations become models and models are translated into mathematical, scientific and artistic symbols from which other symbols and patterns are derived by deduction and speculation. The elite are experts in the creation and exploitation of abstract concepts and models, whether they are mathematical models for trading in commodities, shares or currencies, for management of currency, models for creating new demands and marketing products, for social engineering, visual models for living promoted by novels, plays, films, videos, songs — or publicized personal behavior of sport or film stars, prominent politicians or entertainers; computer games are used as the basis of political, economic, foreign policy and military decisions. As their areas of influence overlap, their importance grows. Film stars interfere with politics and military strategy and attain political positions (the most spectacular example being Ronald Reagan), television commentators and journalists push proposals on how to reform society, change laws or conduct foreign policy, leading sportsmen assume the role of critics of traditions and institutions. Thus, a world of symbols arises in which words and impressions ("images") have more impact than reality which becomes more and more abstract and transformed in accordance with the elite's models.

The very principles of democracy protect the elites' activities. Professional experts are protected by the freedom of scientific research and the dissemination of their results by the freedom of information. Economic activities are protected by the principles of private property, free enterprise and free market. Art and entertainment are protected by the freedom of press and expression. Their interdependence enhances their invulnerability making possible extrapolitical concentration of power immune from interference by the state and from democratic political processes; on the contrary, economic and intellectual elites determine the nature of culture in global dimensions and thus are able to dominate political processes in various ways and extent.

The elites' "means of production" are seldom material; they are intellectual brilliance and top education (own or purchased) combined with the ability to distinguish and exploit relevant and privileged information to which they have preferential access. Their income is based on manipulation of data and finely honed expertise which is highly appreciated and rewarded by the owners of capital on whose behalf and with whose assets the experts trade on the exchanges of commodities, currencies and financial instruments, buy and sell real estate, direct marketing, develop cybernetics, direct movie studios, manage museums, create and select programs for mass media, teach at universities, direct research and produce literature and songs.

Their power over the lives of other people is immense. Even if they never milked a cow or planted a row of corn, they decide the fate of agriculture in entire areas of the world; through market manipulations they create or destroy whole sectors of a nation's economy. They are mostly independent of society's prosperity; the knowledge of symbols enables them to profit equally from economic boom and from economic slump. Because they think in terms of symbols and models and not in terms of concrete human lives, they isolate themselves mentally from the impact of their actions on the fate of those who bear the brunt of their consequences. For the victims they may feel compassion, but not responsibility. In terms of material goods, they create very little; theirs is rather a parasitic existence.

A Cosmopolitan Community

The opportunities of the elites, especially the economic, technological and scientific ones, are not limited by ties to the place of their residence and loyalty to a country or nation: the space for their opportunities is the world. This causes their mobility: they go to where they find the best financial conditions and their best appreciation, whether at universities, international corporations or international bureaucracies. They often change their employer and moving from one state or continent to another is, for them, normal because the "market" for their abilities is international. Their fates are mostly connected with multinational corporations which span borders of nation states. Their objective is to assure the functioning of their employers' empires as a whole; this prevents them from respecting the interests of the nation of their origin. To be tied down to one place such as a permanent home for having a family and bringing up children is an obstacle on the way towards excellence and success.

International elites form a global community of an extraordinary type of people with specific needs and interests: to perfect the world of symbols and the securing their application planet-wide creates among their members an international solidarity placed, in their value system, way above other ties, be it family, local community, nation or state. "Home" is where employment and entertainment are; home are national and international organizations and professional associations based on specialization in esoteric fields, whose members compete with each other to excel among their peers by their expertise, academic career or publication of scientific papers and tomes. They have more in common with their counterparts anywhere in the world, America, Hong Kong, Tokyo or Brussels, than with the people among whom they live.

This solidarity of outlook and interests is reinforced by the fact, that the members of elites are mostly alumni of a handful of the best schools in the world, especially the universities in the United States (Harvard and Stanford, MIT and UCLA, etc.) which attract the best brains of the world by offering them the best working conditions and highest financial rewards. The contact with teachers and students of many nations and the resulting cosmopolitan environment contributes to their "outgrowing the provincial needs" of their nation, religion, history and culture and forming a unique type of solidarity based on mutual respect, personal ties, friendships and — to a large degree — also the expectation of advantages stemming from their mutual assistance and preferences.

Life-style

In its present stage of development, democratic society whose economy is based on the principles of private ownership of means of production, free enterprise and free market, rewards extravagantly its intellectual elites. Their incomes are not derived from personal wealth, especially ownership and management of means of production; it is derived from manipulation of symbols in demand at the time when technology is forcing an overhaul of the existing system of manufacturing and finance. Their incomes are mostly invested also in symbols: bank accounts, mutual funds, stocks and bonds. Whenever their wealth is invested in fixed objects (land, real estate, factories), elites usually hire others to administer them; nor do they display any great attachment to them; they are objects of speculation (selling, buying, mergers, dismantling, bankruptcies) — with the exception of a pride in their luxurious habitats and "toys" (cars, airplanes, yachts).

Their rapidly increasing incomes (cf. the rising salaries of top game players and their coaches) separate the elites from the rest of the society, and this separation is increased by their mobility and their life-style characterized not only by conspicuous consumption, but also by a physical segregation from the common life and people. Their lives are in many regards similar to the lives of the nomenclatura in Soviet society. They congregate increasingly in exclusive localities, enclaves inaccessible to others, with their own security forces, own regulations, hospitals, best schools, theaters, restaurants, clubs, physical health, sports and games facilities.

They control the influx of new people by zoning regulations and high taxes, and if someone undesired still manages to penetrate, he is not accepted and is finally forced to leave by social ostracism and pressure. They consider themselves and are indeed the aristocracy of the intellect which owns its position only to themselves and their own achievements. This contributes to their self-confidence and their isolationism. They leave their enclaves only to travel to their places of work by protected routes or conveyances, or when they seek relaxation and entertainment. In the work place, they are isolated from outside intrusions by cohorts of company guards, subordinates and secretaries, and with the progress of cybernetics, even this contact with the outside world becomes superfluous: increasingly they can perform their activities from anywhere — their homes, cars, hotel rooms or airplanes. When travelling, they remain within the ambiance of luxurious conveyances, hotels, exclusive resorts.

They can demand and get the best services, as "America is becoming a two-tiered society; an overclass of highly compensated people vs. an underclass of dead-ended, underemployed, dissatisfied, no-chance people." ([24]) A continuous society changes into an hourglass type society: on the top are individuals with very high incomes (in the United States at most 20%), while the incomes of the rest stagnate or decrease. The "overclass" of elites dealing with symbols visibly increases its power and wealth, the remaining 80% lose influence as well as economic security.

Elitism

When, in such a situation, the elites exceed their social functions, they usurp the legislative or executive powers of the government and endanger democracy.

During this century, democracy overcame three great adversaries: theocratic monarchies (in World War I), nationalist dictatorships (in World War II) and communist totalitarianism (in the Cold War). In spite of these victories, democracy is again in danger. It is in danger also after the demise of Communism, because in every society, there are those who are convinced that, by virtue of their outstanding qualities, they know better that ordinary people what is good for the populace, for society and for humanity. Elites become a danger to democracy, when their members are so convinced of their intellectual superiority and the infallibility of their opinions that they consider themselves entitled, called or obliged to override the legitimate source of the state's will whenever their conclusions and demands are not accepted by normal democratic procedures or are not adopted and executed by the power of the state as fast and as extensively as the respective elites deem necessary. The functioning of the elites turns into *elitism*, as and when they strive to transform society according to their speculative models without its consent, and into *scientism* when they disregard the limitations of science and disdain other sources of knowledge. This intellectual arrogance encourages the opinion that only scientists and experts are capable of contributing to the formation of decisions and that "unqualified" people should obey those who consider themselves qualified by their education, theoretical knowledge and approval of their peers. If the backward populace does not accept the wisdom of their betters willingly, they may feel justified in circumventing the democratic norm-giving organs, use managerial methods or bureaucratic power.

From the combination of scientism and elitism can arise an ideology and an ideological movement which, if intolerant, can become an intellectual straightjacket on the entire society. Once non-conforming opinions — past or new ones — are not met by arguments or experiments, but by application of power at the disposal of the elites, through preventing or inhibiting dissenting publications, when non-conforming members of the elites are disadvantaged professionally and financially — excluded from teaching positions, excluded from participation in professional conferences or government's advisory commissions, denied access to media and otherwise silenced — democracy is in danger. If a majority of the "knowledge class" holding the most important "means of production", i.e., expert knowledge and through it key positions in society, applies them in accordance with the same ideology, these are the beginnings of a decentralized totalitarianism. The elites produce "The Movement" managing the society without regard to its political system and institutions..

This is the stage to which the United States and (through its own and other developed countries' activities) the world is headed or has arrived, and the ideology of this elitist movement formulate the plans whose implementation its members pursue. Its importance is increased by two factors: first the fact that the USA is the only superpower, and if it can be manipulated into pursuing the elitist goals, the elites' power is greatly enhanced; and second, the fact that these goals coincide to a great extent with the interests of another powerful group to which democracy is sometimes inconvenient: those who find it to be an obstacle to acquiring more and more wealth. Real power belongs not to the intellectual elites, but to economic elites who own the majority of means of production in the world, i.e., the so-called multinational, actually supra-national corporations. In the year 1995, seven most industrialized nations controlled 18 trillion dollars our of 25 trillion of the global GNP; the remaining 7 trillion was divided among 231 nations out of the total number of 238. Because the adjustment of this imbalance would involve far-going changes in the economic structure of the world, economic elites adopted enthusiastically the elitist ideology, and thanks to the extra-political concentration of the economy and especially of mass communications media are economic elites the main promoter of the elitist culture globally. The control of the majority of the world's means of production and the freedom to pursue extra-political concentration, when wedded to the political and military might of the industrialized nations, creates a power which justifies expectations that the new world order will be shaped in accordance with elitist ideology whose exportation and imposition on nations and cultures represents an ideological imperialism of global dimensions. Therefore the following chapter is devoted to its dissection.

CHAPTER 23

THE IDEOLOGY OF WESTERN ELITES

New Civic Religion

Western elites, or rather: elitists, differ greatly from their anti-democratic predecessors. While the latter misused values of natural human morality for their purposes, present elites oppose and disintegrate them. They value self-fulfillment over self-sacrifice, self-expression over self-discipline, painless liquidation of sufferers over charity and care, the abnormal over the normal, parts over the whole, the individual over society, rights over duties.

Ideological Individualism

Rights without Obligations

Classical totalitarianism professed to achieve the well-being of individuals through the betterment of society, the elitist ideology equates the well-being of individuals with the betterment of society. Groups, biological entities, organizations, institutions — all are reduced to individuals; individuals are reduced to bodies, and bodies to bodily functions. The meaning of "well-being" is redefined accordingly. Freedom is conceived as the ability to fulfill one's wants, not as the ability to implement one's will and its goals. For the first time in history of human culture, self-limitation and fulfillment of duties was declared to be undesirable, and egocentrism, self-fulfillment and moral autonomy of the individual proclaimed to be the virtue which supersedes heteronomous obligations and duties. To be fully oneself is the absolute norm, all other norms are relative; morality becomes an autonomous norm — everyone creates the contents of his own moral system. This philosophical individualism is absolute, and combined with scientific as well as moral relativism it forms the basis of the elitists' ideology. Everyone has his own truth: what is true for one is not true for others. Absolute truth is unknowable or does not exist. Absolute moral norms do not exist; everyone has his own morality, what is good for one is not necessarily good for others. Therefore the elites formulate morality to suit their wants; because, for individualism, the individual is the only reality, they live in the present and the future, and this defines the character of their culture, entertainment and lifestyle: instant gratification and conspicuous consumption.

This attitude has found its philosophical underpinning in two concepts: that of the historical "point zero" and the "irrelevance of facts." According to the former, history is insignificant; a new (postmodern) era has begun which is so different from the previous ones that the past lost all relevance and history is starting again from "point zero." The latter asserts that people can make their decisions only on what they know; therefore facts and "truth" are unimportant, or at least less important than peoples' opinions; because people act on the basis of their opinions, they transform their opinions into reality which obliterates the actual circumstances.. Therefore manipulation of concepts and imaging is the key to power.

Individualism as an ideology creates its own normative system based on *the self;* it is composed of self-confidence; self-determination, self-fulfillment, self-realization. The contents of these wants become parts (derived objectives) of the purpose of happiness of individuals and the general means towards their attainment are economic wealth and political as well as extra-political power. The pursuit of these values (normed and/or willed contents) introduces to society the dynamism of differentiation and selection in the form of competition, but lacks the element of integration. From the standpoint of spiritual development, they have a positive influence (utility) as long as spiritual contents derived from traditional, customary, religious and moral norms acting in the opposite direction, i.e., integrationally (humility, self-criticism, self-discipline, obedience, self-denial, unselfishness) prevail in the composition of individuals' objectives of happiness to such an extent that they represent the consensus, the civic religion of the society. A one-sided prevalence of integration elements which dampens differentiation and selection, undermines the vitality of society. A preponderance of centrifugal factors, i.e., differentiation and competition, causes disintegration of society and has a damaging, counterproductive effect on society's spiritual development and vitality.

The ideology of individualism (which includes economic individualism) begins with treating integrative values as controversial, then denies them and ultimately suppresses them. Among its main targets are feelings of inferiority, self-criticism, self-doubt, guilt — these are never justified, these are "unhealthy." So is born a *culture of shamelessness* (24): there is nothing an individual should be ashamed of, as long as it expresses his "I," his "choice." The process of choice is more important, is superior to the outcome of the choice. Shame is the sign of inner uncertainty, immaturity, a psychological defect. Scruples are to be done away with; there is nothing beyond the pale, nothing too intimate, private, delicate, nothing can be condemned as a deviation or perversity because the principle "if it feels so good, it cannot be wrong" applies. The media dismantle peoples' inclination to distinguish between right and wrong by exposing the public systematically to presentation of activities, especially in the areas of violence and sex, which offend custom, tradition, morals or religion. Feelings of guilt, of incompetence, doubts about one's own value or dignity are presented as the roots of antisocial behavior or criminality. Self-confidence is the medicine for society's ills; once women overcome their feelings of inferiority vis-a-vis men, negroes vis-a-vis whites, homosexuals vis-a-vis persons of normal sex (called "homophobes") , alcoholics vis-a-vis tee-totalers, drop-outs vis-a-vis valedictorians, drug users vis-a-vis those who abstain from drugs, society will be sane and healthy. The responsibility for its problems lies with those who are "judgmental" with regard to individuals of an "alternative life-style" and who attribute failure or criminality to individuals rather than society, upbringing and circumstances.

As a result of these pressures, the sphere of individual freedom, permissiveness and licentiousness constantly grows; the individual is hardly ever ashamed for his behavior; on the contrary, he forces others to "accept him as he is". The individual arrogates to himself the right to impose his individuality on and against all others. Not only do the rights of the majority to make decisions become controversial, the right of the community to live according to its own values is contested and considered as oppression.

Doctrinaire Relativism

As a consequence, objective norms of behavior are resisted; endeavors to defend, formulate or enforce such norms are, in the vocabulary of individualism, attempts to impose one's own opinions on others. Each individual has the right to develop his qualities regardless of their nature because their evaluation and judging by society is interference with the individual's right to self-expression. The individual's will for self-realization ultimately results in the denial of an objective reality and of the possibility to know it. When everybody has his own truth and one's truth is not true for others, then such denial of objective standards makes a *dialog meaningless* and discussion a nonsensical exercise in futility: principled relativism renders it impossible to choose between various opinions: all assertions are equally valid, or invalid, and positive values are attributed to certain processes without regard to their outcome (25).

The relativization of values is reflected in *manipulated language*: some expressions are not acceptable, new terminology is introduced. "Political correctness" language has eliminated expressions such as "deviant", "perverse", "abnormal", they are replaced by words such as "different," ""alternate", "other." Even the term ""normal" is too judgmental when used as a basis for evaluation. This pertains also to physically obvious and measurable properties: for instance persons with disabilities are "differently abled", nations with the lowest standard of living must not be described as undeveloped or underdeveloped, but "developing," and so forth. The tendency to do away with grading in schools (or its various manipulations (11) is aimed in the same direction, because one's own lower grades or someone else's higher grades would induce feelings of inferiority in less successful students, although they are not responsible for such failures: responsible are social circumstances (poverty, discrimination) or their subconscious (parents).

In such a culture, rational discourse must be replaced by *psychological manipulation* and the disappearance of informal controls by an intrusion of *bureaucratic controls* into previously autonomous areas, the requirement of absolute *tolerance*, insistence on multiculturalism, protection of deviant life-styles. Tolerance, however, does not extend to persons and movements which reject this scope of tolerance and the moral relativism; against them, consistent action is taken: their opinions are judged and condemned as reactionary, doctrinaire, imposition of their own opinions on the society, and they are exposed to social and professional discrimination (in access to media, promotion, criticism). In the name of human rights, they become, when needed and when these informal measures do not suffice, a target of the executive power of the state (protection and preference of various minorities and life-styles against the majority (see Appendix No. 7).

The success of elitism is not explicable solely by the techniques of decentralized totalitarianism; it depends largely on the contents of the inflammatory idea presented to the society. Because its philosophy demands that each person be free and able to fulfill his wants, it requires that the manipulators discover what people want, and then convince them they can attain it, and in the process to alienate them to the established civic religion while redefining the concepts of "good" (= what I want) and "bad" (= what is in my way) in the sense of *economic materialism* — pursuit of a career and immediate satisfaction.

The strongest instincts of all higher organisms are self-preservation, need of food, and sex, in this order. Communism derived its strength from the first two instincts — from threats to one's existence (war) and from physical misery (unemployment). In developed societies where the state guarantees protection of life and limb and welfare protects from hunger (in the sense of permanent or prolonged shortage of food), the satisfaction of the sexual instinct acquires a special importance in daily life and permeates entertainment and culture and the demand for limitless sexual permissiveness ("sexual freedom") can be made the instrument of destroying established moral, traditional or religious restrictions (conveniently termed "taboos" to intimate their unscientific nature).

The Social Contract

For politics, the most relevant expression of individualism has become the theory of the social contract, implicitly or explicitly accepted by social sciences in the West. According to this theory, the individual in his original, natural state was entirely free; complete freedom resulted in the struggle of all against all which was damaging to everybody, and therefore individuals concluded, in their own individual interest, a treaty according to which they gave up a part of their freedom in favor of an institution which would enforce such a limitation — this institution is the state. The existence and scope of a state's legitimate power is thus derived from the agreement between individuals, certain areas are entirely excluded from the state's (the government's) interference — the inalienable human rights and civil liberties — and in other areas the state may interfere only with its citizens' consent. The limitation of a citizen's freedom and the limit of the legitimacy of state's interference is expressed by the principle that one individual's freedom to pursue his happiness must not impinge on the same freedom of other individuals. Therefore, if the conditions of such a contract are violated by the state by exceeding its competence, it loses its legitimacy and its members have the right to revolt.

Evaluation

Because democracy has been found (cf. Chapter 20) to be the political system most closely corresponding to the evolutionary principles of being, the relationship to democracy is used as the measuring standard of elitism's qualities.

Polarization

The economic a social polarization inherent in elitism is in itself an impediment to democracy. Still more damaging is the intellectual and ideological polarization which elitism engenders by eroding the middle class. The middle class harbors and protects values which the elites strive to overcome: family, nation, patriotism, religion, local self-government, all opposites of those dear to the elites: cosmopolitism, feminism, sexual permissiveness, unlimited abortion rights. The opinions of "the people" are basically simple: Children benefit if their parents live together, private behavior and private morality have consequences for society and in public affairs, work should be rewarded and workers are entitled to the results of their efforts, public treasury should help those, and only those, who need it and are unable to help themselves, religion is beneficial for society, violations of the law, especially crimes of violence should be punished promptly and strictly. At the same time, the middle class considers some creations of the cultural elites to be ridiculous, senseless or even disgusting .

The elites fail to and don't care to understand the resistance of the middle class to the introduction of the sundry "alternative life-styles" and the social engineering implemented in education, healthcare, environmental protection; they find it incomprehensible how anyone could reject their carefully thought out models and plans for the betterment of society; opposing opinions are due to backwardness ("these people do not understand what all this is about"). They react with contempt, hatred, intolerance and fear to "populism," "right-wing extremists," "reactionaries" and "fundamentalism." The greatest enmity is reserved for religion and especially Christianity. While a certain measure of tolerance is granted to certain protestant denominations, islam, judaism, hinduism, nature worship (goddesses) and also satanism and witchcraft, discrimination against biblical Christianity and against the Catholic Church is implacable and extends from generalities all the way to individuals (see Appendix 8).

The value systems of these two groups, the elites and the middle class, are incompatible, and as the elites ("The Movement"- see Chapter 7) possess key positions and self-assurance, their temptation is great to use methods of managerism and modified totalitarianism. On the other side, the middle class feels that its influence on the direction of the government's policies is small or nil, loses trust in democracy and political debates which center around esoteric political theories of the elites and have very little to do with ordinary peoples' daily worries and interests. Thus the general opinion that politics is dirty business and that all politicians are corrupt, and this disinterest in politics makes the dominance of the elites easier and undermines the hopes for democratically effected changes.

Unequal opportunities.

An important element of democracy is the possibility, or at least the conviction that it guarantees social mobility, i.e., that all citizens have in principle the same opportunity to attain excellence and prominence without any institutional hindrances. In the presence of the elites, this assumption is invalid: their children (provided they have any) have such superior education that their advantages are practically insurmountable. In their suburbs, they attend prestigious colleges which offer special classes or programs for outstanding performers. These schools are equipped with laboratories and interactive computers, students have at their disposal extensive libraries with the latest publications in high-tech, classes are relatively small so that teachers and professors can devote attention to individual students; the wealth of their parents enables them to visit museums, concerts, theaters, foreign travel; at home they have microscopes, telescopes, miniature laboratories, and the newest personal computer hardware and software, connected to international networks. From there, their road takes them directly to elite universities; after graduation they are certain to find employment in jobs whose starting compensation exceeds the average annual income of the population. Technical knowledge is the most profitable "means of production" in a highly industrialized society, and the children of the elites have in this field unbeatable advantage over the rest, provided they show equal interest and intelligence. Because they mostly inherit from their elders a contemptuous attitude towards less capable individuals, the privileges in knowledge and education reinforce the polarization of the society. They belong to The Movement whose consolidation is at present the only serious threat to democracy.

No social contract

The ideology of the social contract and the structure of society derived from it won over states grounded on different principles because it provided for a free play of differentiation and competition. It won as long as its centrifugal elements were offset by integration based on extra-legal origins (custom, tradition, religion) and awareness of a common enemy. When individualism weakened and/or destroyed these elements, the theory of social contract also contributed to the problems of Western civilization for three reasons: it is logically erroneous, normatively incorrect and factually untrue.

Societies do exist.

The logical error of this contractual conception of society derives from a deficient understanding of the relationship of a totality (a whole) and its parts. The social contract's construction reduces society (community, collective) to its parts (individuals) and then assumes that actions of egocentric individuals will result in a collective harmony while each individual has the right to maximum self-determination, self-realization and self-fulfillment insofar as he does not inhibit others in pursuing their own individual purposes to a maximum extent. Translated into exact terminology it assumes that the pursuit of a *maximum* of satisfaction ("happiness") by various individuals in a situation of *limited* means will not result in conflicts of interests. The elimination of certain types of conflict (use of physical violence) means solely that the conflicts will assume different forms (use of checkbook rather than guns). Only if the goals of happiness of all individuals include a significant portion of a common concept of a good or better community, will there be harmony; however, the philosophy of individualism does not provide the basis for such consensus — it must come from other sources to offset individualism's centrifugal tendencies.

Norms are the essence of law

The normative misconception of the Social contract construct is its foundation on rights of individuals understood as civil liberties which normatively represent a void, an absence of duties. This is contrary to the nature of the legal order which is a system of norms, i.e., duties. As a part of a legal system, any right requires the existence of a subject's or subjects' corresponding duty to perform or abstain from performing certain action or actions. When the identity of the subjects of such duty is clear, the law is clear; where the subject of duty is not identified or identified only in general terms (such as "everybody") the clarity of the law is lost and norm-giving passes from the norm-giver to the judiciary or the executive. If the law provides for a "right to work," the question immediately arises: who is the subject whose duty it is to provide work for the holder of the right to work? If the entitled subject has no work, whom can he sue for providing the work? Another example is the "right to life." Its extent itself is unclear: does it include the right to be born, to be provided with medical care (to preserve life), to be provided with nutrition and nursing in the event of disability, and if so, who is the subject of duty?

A legal system based on rights suffers from an additional difficulty. Law defines duties unambiguously; but rights overlap and conflict. Does the right of free exercise of religion give prisoners the right to be provided with special types of meals? or have a special haircut or facial hair? Does the right to property entitle the owner of a building to refuse renting facilities for a bar or tavern? (It does.) Is he also entitled to refuse renting it for an abortion clinic? (No.) Does the right of assembly protect associating on the basis of certain properties with the exclusion of persons not having such properties? In case of nationality, yes; in case of race or gender, no. Does the freedom of expression protect expressions of anti-semitism? No. Expressions of anti-catholic bias? Yes. Conflicts between rights and their enforcement by individuals can lead to bizarre situations when rights of one person can annul the rights of all other members of a whole to which such individual belongs (See Appendix 7.)

Man as *Zoon Politicon*

The factual error of the social contract theory is evident from the nature of man. The theory assumes that society and the state derive from an agreement to form a community by a consent of previously isolated individuals concluded in their subjective interest. In history and prehistory, there is no indication that human communities arose from such an agreement. On the contrary, anthropology as well as similarities with the life of social animals indicate otherwise. If the natural state of man is to be the basis for political theories, they must start with the notion that men in their natural state did not live as isolated individuals, but in communities as social beings. Society therefore did not arise by a transition of naturally isolated individuals from their isolation to a community, a transition based on their rational renouncing of some freedom, men always lived in communities and under conditions limiting their individual behavior which such a type of life involves.

The kind of limitations which existed can be deduced from the behavior of members of primitive human societies as well as the behavior of communities of animals which appear to be physically and mentally closest to homo sapiens. Observation unequivocally shows that their communities are structured so that various members perform various activities (functions) and that their behavior tends mainly to preserve the life and growth of the communities. Repetitive performance of a function by a member of the community creates the supposition and expectation that the same individual will continue to perform it; it becomes his responsibility and a "duty." It is not true that society was put together by individuals, on the contrary, society arose from natural communities and rights and liberties of individuals developed by their gradual shedding of restraints imposed on them by their social nature. Human ability to refuse the performance of functions falling to an individual by virtue of his membership in his community distinguishes human communities from animal ones (Appendix 9). A refusal to perform the expected and natural function usually entails a sanction, mostly expulsion from the community (*aqua et igni interdictio* in old tribal Roman law) . This is the beginning of a system of sanctioned norms backed by the power of the community — rudiments of a legal system.

Summary

In nature the evolutionary elements of differentiation and selection are outweighed by integration; individualism disturbs this natural relationship, therefore it is (by constant enlargement of the sphere of rights and liberties and relativization of all values) ultimately disruptive and anti-evolutionary. Individualism without a counterbalance of duties is unrealizable in the sense that it leads towards the paralysis of society and its disintegration.. A natural integrating element between individuals is their interest in the survival of their biological group, in their posterity, and as long as it is a constituent part of their purpose of happiness, society survives; however, such an interest is, in the light of the philosophy of individualism, illogical and people are conditioned by their elitist cultural environment not to attribute to it too great a value.

Because human life outside of the framework of society is impossible and its survival is in the interest of the presently living generations, integration of an individualist society is provided by a bureaucracy whose growth is in the end counterproductive. To function and exist, the complexity of modern civilization demands from its members interdependence and mutual self-limitation; in a highly evolved society the idea of an individual as a self-willed and self-determining unit is anachronistic.

Individualism as the highest norm of behavior is unrealizable also on the level of individuals. Man is a living being as well as a social being. The properties of self-sacrifice, self-discipline, self-denial are deeply inborn and their roots can be traced to natural laws which regulate the life of each living cell, i.e., also each living cell of every human being. For his complete development, man needs also to develop these fundamental properties which constitute him as a living organism of the "homo sapiens" kind and only in a harmonic development of the potential for unselfish and self-centered properties does a human being acquire personality. The suppression of the self-denying potentialities in favor of the development of self-centered potentialities in the interest of personal happiness can, under the influence of a cultural environment, temporarily stifle and overwhelm the dissatisfaction stemming from the disregard of the altruistic potentialities, but must fail, because man's need of happiness has no limits (is maximum) while the means of achieving it, his own (i.e., physical and spiritual) as well as the acquired ones (power and wealth) are limited. Happiness as an end is, therefore, always an objectively inachievable goal.

In the development of Western civilization, cultural, economic and political disintegrative factors flowing from elitism and its philosophy of individualism, economic materialism and biomaterialism, are increasingly prevailing over integration. This is, basically, the root cause of its difficulties, problems, crises (Appendix 6) and decline.

The situation is a facet of the desintegration of the Western civilization. Many critics and enemies are assiduously working to overthrow it: Moslems who view it as the instrument of Satan, feminists who consider it an oppressive patriarchal structure, blacks who criticize it as a system of domination by the "white devils," environmentalists who charge it with destroying the nature and the planet.

They all have a common adversary: Christianity. And rightly so, because true Christianity is a defender of natural morality, a common sense value system and submission to a will and reason on which existence itself is contingent. These are the principles on which Western civilization was founded. They are all opposed by the elites' ideology, but Western civilization, a development of the Christian civilization, can not survive the steady undermining of its foundations.

Economic Materialism

The fall of Communism represents certainly a victory of the free enterprise system. Its heart is a free market where demand and supply meet; the market maintains their balance through movement of prices, allocates resources in the most effective way, competition lowers prices, increases quality and stimulates unceasing technological progress.

Where are the customers?

This is theory. But the real picture of global economy is different. On one side there is an enormous unsatisfied demand for food and industrial products, on the other side is an enormous capacity to produce food and manufactured goods, and yet, these two do not meet. The reason: the owners of the means of production (this term is to be understood here in its widest sense as all productive assets, all means organized for the purpose of producing goods or services including commerce, finance, communications etc.) in the industrialized nations have no use for items which the masses of prospective buyers in underdeveloped countries can offer in exchange.

The free economic system generates an improvement of efficiency; improvement of efficiency means to produce the same amount of better goods with savings on materials and mainly labor. Work is taken over by machinery, machinery is directed by computers, computers are managed by experts, other labor becomes gradually superfluous: blue collar workers, white collar workers, supervisors and managers. The savings on labor are in reality mass lay-offs of people. Work that consisted of activities which were repetitive and demanded nevertheless a certain level of intelligence, experience and responsibility, such as skilled labor or office workers, are disappearing, and with them decreases the middle class whose main component they are.

Hopes that the information revolution would engender a massive demand for educated experts have failed to realize; the main increase in the demand for labor takes place in personal services. The flood of information made available in technically advanced nations, profits mainly, if not exclusively, those who are familiar with and interested in the global economy and intellectual endeavors — the manipulators of symbols; for the others, technological progress brings principally a more perfect and accessible form of entertainment or new kinds of games and toys. The gap between the knowledge class and the rest of the population is widening rather than closing. The tendency is towards a hourglass society in which only a small fraction will enjoy full benefits of education, money and power.

Islands of Affluence

The gulf of economic imbalance separates developed and underdeveloped nations, but it exists also within the industrialized nations. It is kept under control by social legislation such as unemployment compensation, social security and similar programs. Lately, there are attempts to combine social care with measures of reverse solidarism (Chapter 9) aimed at elimination of unproductive members of society (euthanasia, contraceptives, abortion, assisted suicide). Social programs have so far been able to keep the lid on violence because industrialized nations are wealthy enough to buy themselves social peace. It is doubtful they will be able to do so indefinitely. Already some symptoms of unrest are apparent even in the United States which anticipates the development in the remaining industrialized world: rise of a welfare dependent population, growing national debt, out of control budgets deficits, breakdown of law and order in entire neighborhoods, creation of isolated secure enclaves for the elites, emergence of self-defense militias by citizens expecting a collapse of civilization. The islands of affluence are reaching higher and higher quality of life while becoming smaller and smaller and more and more isolated.

Global Levelling of Wages

The nature of the free enterprise system is to expand and to remove all obstacles hampering its growth. It keeps integrating the world into one global economy. The market has the same levelling effect globally as it has had within individual national economies: free movement of capital and goods, and also of compensation for labor. This assumes two forms: either people from low wage areas move (legally or illegally) to higher wage areas, thus pushing down the wages there; or else the means of production move from higher wage level areas to areas with lower wages, with the same final outcome. This levelling effect is disadvantageous to labor in developed countries and has social and political repercussions.

The Superfluous People

The population of the countries left behind is worse off. Fax machines, cellular telephones and information networks are for their lives totally irrelevant; TV pictures of mass migration, famines and refugee camps are a telling evidence of it. In addition to labor, underdeveloped countries offer raw materials, tourism, and bodies of their citizens (prostitution and sale of children for sex as well as commerce in body parts, especially of aborted fetuses). The compensation for these available "items of commerce" can satisfy only a small fraction of the pent-up demand; most of it remains unsatisfied because owners of the means of production cannot exchange their goods for items for which they have no use. They are limited to dealing with those who can offer useful goods in exchange, i.e., other industrialized countries and the elites of developing nations, and with them they form a balanced economic system. Within it, the advantages of free enterprise are realized: a rising standard of living up to the level of luxury, technological advances, absorbing a growing share in the world's natural resources. Excluded from this circle of affluence are millions of people, indeed the majority of the world's population which — seen from the standpoint of the owners of the means of production — is really superfluous insofar as it has nothing "useful" to offer.

Elitism leads everywhere to a polarization of the society — the "hourglass shape," and this process impacts heavily the middle class of developing countries because it is still in its beginnings and therefore weak. Only the overclass of individuals working with symbols and/or cooperating with the elites of developed countries gains in power and wealth; the rest faces a bleak future or no future whatsoever.

If people cannot secure their livelihood and other desirable goods in exchange for their labor, they might endeavor to obtain them by force. The more numerous such people are, the greater the pressure leading to violence: first domestically (uprisings, collapse of law and order, revolutions, civil war), then to organized violence against other countries (war, terrorism or extortion). Industrialized nations attempt to preclude such development in two ways: by a policy of depopulation through open or hidden coercion, and by a world order on their own terms which would crush in the bud attempts at violent change.

But the situation is ominous. Experts predict shortly a multiplication of mega-cities with populations exceeding eleven million people whose living conditions will be terrible beyond imagination: security, housing, education, water, sewers, all social services unmanageable and unavailable. These perspectives are known, the danger imminent, but few preparations are made to meet them. The only remedy the developed countries are offering and introducing is depopulation.

Evaluation

Because the root of the problem is not numbers of people, but political and economic changes: the degeneration of democracies into elitist societies, extra-political concentration of gigantic multinational corporations, parallel "cultural colonialism" and failure of international institutions to deal effectively with regional and global problems, the attempt at depopulation will either be overtaken by events and fail, or result in a humanity static, stagnant and ultimately declining.

Biomaterialism

The problem of present times is the unequal distribution of material goods between the industrialized and the undeveloped nations, an inequality which has the potential of a violent conflict or a series of violent conflicts. Western elites formulate this problem as a collision of limited natural resources and unlimited human demand, and interpret human demand as a function of the number of people. Their goal: a balance between natural resources and a limited number of physically and mentally perfect people free of want and surrounded with comfort; their means: stopping or reversing population growth, eliminating substandard individuals, eugenic measures aimed at improving the genetic pool of humanity, all this in accordance with the philosophy of biological materialism which is dominant among the elites. It is a combination of neomalthusianism, progress in genetics and techniques of changing genes, eugenics and sexual permissiveness with ecology. Biological materialism proceeds from the assumption that man is an animal whose properties differ in degree, not in essence from other kinds of animals. Man is identical with his bodily processes, these spatio-temporal processes are viewed as consequences of causes which are his genes and his environment. What follows is that *it is possible to improve the human race by the application of the same methods that were already successfully used in breeding (other) animals.* The regulation of human numbers, quality and environment are the center piece of this ideology.

Bioethics

Biomaterialism has its own logic whose conclusions are correctly derived from the above described premises. Their implementation is generally resisted when subjected to evaluation according to the norms of the dominant ethics, whether traditional or Christian. It was correctly anticipated (see Appendix 2) that the utilization of the means proposed by biomaterialism necessitates the creation of a new ethical system which would make them defensible. This task was undertaken by a new branch of philosophy — bioethics.

Bioethics claims to be a new science concentrated in "elite academic centers." Its object is deciding on morality in medical research and practice. Its is a very wide field. Questions taken up by the first congress of bioethicists in October 1994 whose participants virtually declared themselves to be the elite in this new field, were:

Is it moral to produce human embryos in vitro in order to infect them with lethal illnesses for the purpose of experimentation:?

Is it moral, if the owner of a fertility clinic fertilizes his female patients by his own sperm and becomes a biological father of children of dozens of them (an actual case)?

Is it moral to use the tissues or organs of victims of induced abortion to manufacture medicines? to manufacture cosmetics?

Is it moral to kill an unconscious patient at the request of his family?

Is it moral to "terminate the life" of a patient whose care would absorb an disproportionate share of public monies?

Is it moral to cause the death of a comatose patient by dehydration and denial of food?

Is it moral to kill subnormal newborn babies?

It is moral to prescribe if and how many children people may have?

Is it moral to deny unwed mothers welfare unless they submit to "voluntary" sterilization?

Is it moral to refuse assistance to communities with a less than required utilization of contraceptives?

Is cloning of humans moral?

Is it moral to create supplies of embryos and to destroy them if not used?

Is it moral to use frozen embryos also after the death of their parents?

Is it moral to implant an embryo in the body of a women willing to bring it to birth for a monetary compensation? Is it moral to abort such a fetus at the request of its biological parents, if they change their mind after implantation?

Is it moral to implant human embryos in the bodies of animals?

The majority of participants gave a positive answer to all the above questions. The congress then examined the question on what basis were such decisions made, from which moral norm were they deduced. The rationale of the positive answers fell into four groups: (1) The action advances research, and therefore is helpful to all humanity. (2) There is no hope for a cure. (3) The patient suffers pain. (4) The cure is too expensive for the family, insurance company or public treasury and the patient's life is not worth the expense (lacks social usefulness or capacity to live a "meaningful" life, is a living vegetable). As to a general principle on which to base such decisions, the representatives of this new science agreed only on one principle: in arriving at their conclusions, they refuse to take into consideration traditional and especially religious moral principles. As to their own norms, they agreed only that *no general norm exists* and that decisions have to be made on a case to case basis.

Because ethics is a normative system par excellence, it is no wonder that the entire project of bioethics became suspect and bioethicists were described as experts in inventing moral justification for activities which the prevailing morals rejected as immoral or illegal, as experts in inventing reasons why a patient, physician or researcher should or may do something he knows he should not be doing. Does a suffering patient wish to commit suicide? A bioethicist will find reasons for medical assistance. Does a researcher contemplate vivisection on human embryos or freshly aborted babies? A bioethicists will find a moral justification. Does the pharmacological or cosmetic industry utilize tissues or organs of aborts for its production? A bioethicist will prove that it is more moral to use them than to "waste" them. And so forth.

Experts in bioethics find their employment especially in hospitals where they participate in bioethical commissions, convince reluctant patients, their families, physicians and nurses that actions logically derived from the ideology of biomaterialism are justified, even if they contradict generally accepted standards of morality. Even more serious are instances when bioethics is used to support treatments or denial of treatments against the expressed will of the parties involved, i.e., patients or their families. To public knowledge came at least two cases when hospitals refused to treat persons who, in the opinion of the hospital's hired bioethicists, were not capable of meaningful life, although the patient or his family requested treatment and payment from private or public sources was secured. There are no statistics which would record the number of instances when a patient or his family submitted nilly-willy to a decision of a bioethical commission, especially if they were poor, uneducated or dependent on welfare.

It is therefore not surprising when bioethicists are reluctant to submit their opinions to the public and to democratic decision, using the customary justification that an "ordinary" citizen lacks the necessary knowledge to make rational decisions in their field. Attempts of public authorities to regulate some of the most controversial activities meet an indignant resistance as infringement of privacy or the practice of medicine. In the literature of bioethics, "life- or death-giving care" are equivalent. Rather than try to convince the public, A. Kaplan recommended during the above mentioned congress a different approach: to infiltrate panels, commissions and consultative bodies which decide questions of bioethics, and through their intermediary to assert their enlightened and professional opinions. Since then, the legalization of "medicide" by some courts and some states is proof of the effectiveness of such approach.

Regulation of Numbers

In the present situation, biomaterialism equates numerical regulation of population with its reduction or at least zero growth. It is a method based on the axiom that humanity grows geometrically while production of food only arithmetically (malthusianism). The elites especially in the USA (building on the findings of Rockefeller's commission on the family established by president Nixon who subsequently rejected its findings) added the following axiom: not only does the number of people grow, their standard of living also grows and the expectation is that it will continue to grow indefinitely (neomalthusianism). The problem therefore is no longer limited to shortage of food, it includes the exhaustion of irreplaceable natural resources and the contamination of the environment by human actions, mainly industry through which men try to achieve their growing expectations.

The regulation of consumption is left by the elites to the free economy (market). Because free economy constantly fabricates new sources of dissatisfaction and new needs in order to increase profits, this policy of *laissez passer* cannot but create a fast increase of consumption, i.e., utilization of resources. Therefore the elites focus their attention on the second part of the equation of the axiom of economic materialism: not the size of consumption, but the number of consumers which, ultimately, means the number of living human beings. As long as there are societies in which the average consumption equals five, six or more times the consumption per person in other societies, this axiom is wrong, and so are solutions derived from it. Depopulation is then proclaimed as the only means by which the assumed imbalance between human consumption and natural resources is to be redressed.

Sex yes, progeny no

Nature has connected reproduction of the species with the third strongest instinct of living beings, the sex instinct; sexual organs are directly connected with or rather a part of the reproduction organs. In order to stop and reverse the natural growth of humanity unleashed by the progress of medical science and to undo this triumph, it was indispensable to sever the connection between sex and reproduction ([26]).

Providing for the separation of sex from generation required the discovery and introduction of a multitude of mechanical, chemical and surgical contraceptive measures and the replacement of natural and religious norms.

The free market system furnished the first. The most primitive and traditional ways to prevent the birth of another human being have been infanticide and abortion. Surgical procedures of infanticide of handicapped babies and of abortion of unwanted children have been perfected so as to be fast, safe and frequent, and their commercialization gave birth to a most profitable medical practice bringing vast profits to their practitioners while making abortion also financially accessible, government subsidized and/or imposed. Abortion was promptly joined by sterilization (voluntary, under duress or forced).

Mechanical means included an explosion in the production, availability and popularization of condoms and sundry foams, implants and inserts ("femdoms") to prevent the meeting of the sperm and the egg or destroy its consequences. The pharmacological industry subsidized successful research in products to produce infertility in women by pills and implants or to invent abortifacients of conceived embryos.

A new branch of science named sexology undertook the other precondition of depopulation, namely the destruction of norms (traditional, religious and legal designated as "taboos" by the scientists) prohibiting or penalizing artificial means of preventing or destroying the unity of the sexual act with reproduction. The severance of sex from generation got a strong push from the feminist movement whose creators and representatives took the position that women have the same right to enjoy the pleasures of sex as men without having to fear its consequences; this movement became the strongest defender of elective abortion.

Next to mass media, the most effective disseminator of this new ideology is the school system. Education in sexology is for biomaterialism as indispensable as marx-leninism was for the communist ideology. It begins already in grammar school (sometimes even in kindergarten) and continues without interruption for ten to thirteen years — more hours are devoted to it than to reading, writing or any other subject. The approach is clinical and "non-judgmental." This means a graphic description of all sexual activities stressing their equivalency and focusing on two objectives: dismantling any inhibitions and sense of modesty which the sexologues classify as unhealthy and unnatural barriers to full sexual fulfillment ([27]); the other goal is to learn all about the methods of preventing or terminating pregnancy — pregnancy is presented as the only absolute wrong in sexual intercourse, even worse than venereal diseases (renamed as "social diseases" whose sufferers deserve compassion and understanding rather than criticism of their behavior). A schoolbook which recommended sexual abstinence and marriage as the safest methods of preventing infection by venereal diseases had to be withdrawn from California schools; the judiciary decided it was propagating religion and by violating the separation of church and state endangering the free exercise of religion.

In general, this project of inculcating the new civic religion to society has been enormously successful (see Appendix No.11), even if its implementation does not proceed without resistance (see Appendix No. 10).

The severance of sex from procreation has far reaching consequences. Primarily, it fundamentally changed the importance of sex and the relationship between man and woman. Traditionally, the acceptance of a man by a woman meant that she is willing (or at least willing to risk) to offer her body to generate within it his (more exactly their joint) child, that she will feed this child through her own blood and that she will, in spite of discomfort and pain, allow it to grow and bring it in the world.This unique and stunning gift bound the man to provide for her and their child, care for them and protect them and never abandon her — to become "one flesh." This moral obligation was protected by custom and by law in the institution of marriage. Therefore, man and woman approached marriage with serious deliberation and responsibility and its desired foundation was love and not lust. Love was one center around which gravitated a large portion of human culture: songs, dances, poems, dramas, novels.

By substituting barren fornication for love, woman's gift to man lost its uniqueness: it became the equivalent of the opening which homosexuals offer to each other. Actually, it became the equivalent of any moist opening in the human body, and sexual education does not cease to underscore this equivalency: it repeats that there is no clinically substantial difference between copulation, masturbation, anal sex, oral sex and other forms of exciting the genitals; all these forms are a matter of taste, inclination and preference. Love does not have to precede intimacy; casual encounter suffices. Communications media of all types depict extramarital sex as the norm. After months of sexual intimacy, the hero (or heroine) declares to his/her "partner": I think I am beginning to be in love with you. School books on sexology do not speak anymore of men and women, not to mention husband and wife, only about "partners" because anything else would not be clinically objective and could have a judgmental undertone.

In view of the above, it is only logical that marriage loses the justification for its privileged legal position and that live-in partners are obtaining the same status, with special legal protection extended to homosexuals whose life-style is still the object of disapproval of a vast majority. In the United States, a Colorado referendum prohibiting the state from giving homosexuals preferential status was struck down by the Supreme Court in 1997. Open disapproval of cohabitation without marriage and criticism of divorce and of the institution of one-parent families originally common in America's civil religion, has been replaced with indifference and has become considered as bad manners.

The new attitude towards fertility left its mark on the parents-children relationship. From its predominant position having children has been demoted to the same level of importance with other components of happiness; spouses, resp. "partners" evaluate offspring against the career, comfort, pets and entertainment rather than considering all of them as less important than the existence, care and well-being of children. The separation of sex from reproduction resulted also in a widespread "production" of children in other ways, such as artificial insemination, creation of embryos in laboratories, freezing of embryos, their implantation in the uterus of a woman other than their biological mother ("renting a womb"), claim of a right to adopt children by homosexual and lesbian couples, destruction of superfluous or deficient (also "wrong sex") embryos and of frozen unused embryos by the thousands (Great Britain).

The reduction of love to genital stimulation has affected all relationships between people, of different as well as same gender. Sex is assumed to be underlying every action, dress, look and movement. Friendship and camaraderie are assumed to include mutual sexual accommodations. Sexual motivations are attributed to parents embracing and kissing their children or kindergarten personnel patting or stroking their charges (and some of them are sued for molestation decades later on the basis of alleged suppressed memories: the most blatant cases were those of cardinal Bernardin in Chicago and archbishop Groer in Vienna); an eight years old pupil is punished for giving a kiss to a girl of the same age.

Once unleashed, sex became all-pervasive; two observations were proven right. Socrates is right when remarking about sex that "we scratch, because it itches, and it itches because we scratch". An overwhelming part of the culture, from songs to advertisement, is engaged in constantly "scratching" the sex impulse: even in grocery stores, from covers of magazines dozens of beautiful women with partly bared breasts and dentures stare brazenly at shoppers. Nudity sells automobiles as well as recordings of Bach. And the observation of Czechoslovak writer Karel Capek, the creator of the word "robot," was also borne out: that sex requires intensification, requires new and stronger forms of stimulation, until it ends in perversity, use of drugs and ultimately cruelty. Western culture became crude: obscenities invaded the language, spoken, written, sung; pornographic passages and episodes became a must in art and literature: novels, spy and detective stories, science fiction, in dramas, movies, television, on computer networks. All these changes have the same goal and effect: decrease of births and increase in sex. The famous British commentator Malcolm Muggeridge quipped: "Birth control means no births and no control."

Sex became the elites' battering ram shattering the existing civic religion. In the changing of culture, elitism is much more effective than communism. Communism projected the implementation of its promises to the future and demanded sacrifices and self-denial for their achievement. By removing all cultural barriers against utilizing the sexual instinct exclusively for bodily gratification and by supplying the technical means of eliminating its natural consequences, elitism succeeded in offering and delivering to men a wide scale of formerly unattainable or hardly attainable pleasures with no delays, sacrifices and expenses. Delayed consequences and ignored (although predictable and predicted) side effects (epidemics of new venereal diseases, destruction of the institution of marriage, juvenile criminality, overtaxing of social services, failures of public education) are considered by the ideology of biomaterialism as an acceptable price for the achievement of the ultimate goal: control (actually reduction) of births and reversal of the growth of humanity. Viewed from this angle, elitism is a success.

Regulation of Quality

Taming the savages

In the twenties, English philosopher Gilbert Keith Chesterton concluded that the next great heresy will be simply an attack on morality, and especially sexual morality, and that tomorrow's insanity does not reside in Moscow, but breeds much more strongly in the Manhattan.

In 1963, W.H. McNeill, author of the thousand-page long history of the world *The Rise of the West*, concluded, that the next step in perfecting the control of society beyond the level attained by communism in the USSR would be interference with human heredity and manipulation with human genes in order to manufacture conveniently specialized subhuman and superhuman biological species. The resulting increase of efficiency and induced social harmony will give the bureaucracies of the world unforeseeable opportunities to concentrate power. Rationalization and acceleration of human development in the interest of increased productivity and social tranquillity will bring about a social revolution at whose end men will differ from their predecessors as much as modern cattle differ from their wild ancestors. Mankind will be tamed and the population of the post-human kind could become specialized in its functions and differentiated in its properties as insect communities are at present.

Under the impact of biology and biotechniques, humanity made significant progress in the direction of these predictions. In 1970, the famous editorial of the prestigious *California Medicine* (see Appendix 1) called for abandonment of "Christian ethics" of absolute value of human life and its replacement by a more practical ethic of its relative value. Society, primarily physicians, would decide what resources and efforts should be devoted to the curing of those who are to be preserved and who not, whom to feed, shelter, support, educate and give medical assistance, until the control and selectivity of birth is equated by the control and selectivity of dying. The medical profession is to assume the role of veterinarians of the human race.

The eighties saw the first combination of human genes with animal genes, the production of human embryos by in vitro fertilization and experimentation on living embryos.

Since then, progress in that direction accelerated. Since 1992, it became known that remnants of aborted babies were used in the manufacture of cosmetics and drugs, in 1995 it was proven that they are used as food ([28]) under the designation of "uterine material," "product of abortion," "fetal tissue" and similar euphemisms. In 1997, the first transplant of a retina taken from a freshly aborted baby to a patient with fading eyesight was successfully performed. Commerce in human parts, especially kidneys from India and Pakistan to Great Britain, was by then firmly established.

In 1993, the U.S. government spent millions of dollars on showing TV shots exhorting its young citizens to carry contraceptives to dates with their friends. The same year saw the first artificial fertilization of ova taken from the ovaries of freshly aborted babies, their nourishment in laboratories and placing in the uterus of infertile women, the start of experiments to bring to maturity embryos kept in an artificial environment, and attempts to induce a human ovum to grow by stimulation other than by a human sperm. In the same year, a way to sex-less reproduction of a human embryo by cellular multiplication was found — the same way used by the most primitive organisms — except that the division is artificially produced — cloning. According to a discovery in 1997, such cloning can be done from any cell of a body. These methods enable technicians to create series of embryos fed and maintained in laboratories until they develop observable qualities; those with unwanted qualities are then destroyed or used for experimentation with various diseases; the selected ones are imbedded in a human uterus.

The consequences of artificial fertilization, manipulation of genes and cloning of selected embryos are literally fantastic and unforeseeable ([29]). Therefore voices have been raised that further research in this field and its exploitation should be controlled by legislation; equally loud are voices claiming that legislators should not be allowed to make decisions in matters where they lack the necessary expertise and that further development in human biology should be left exclusively to experts and to private enterprise and subsidized from public treasury free of interference.

From the standpoint of scientifically managed breeding of the human race, the contemporary situation is utterly unsatisfactory — it is chaos. People reproduce as they want, they select their breeding partners not according to their own or their partners' genetic heritage, but according looks, wealth, position and irrational feelings such as love, compassion, admiration, desire and passion. This produces an amorphous and unmanageable mass of a variety of ordinary undistinguished beings with the most diverse grades of intelligence and health from which only occasionally and accidentally emerge extraordinary, gifted individuals whose valuable genes become diffused within a few generations. But a field of the most diverse flowers can in no way equal in quality and utility a field of uniformly high yield wheat. From the standpoint of a given technical purpose, it is necessary to eliminate types with undesirable genes and breed special strains with the highest permanent and uniform degree of desirable qualities. Unpredictability and variability must be eliminated by breeding or husbandry.

The introduction of order into the existing chaotic situation and the breeding of humanity in accordance with the demands (ideals) of its breeders, also known as the improvement of the human race, is done in two ways: the cleansing of the genetic inheritance of humanity (eugenics) and the removal of its inferior individuals (euthanasia).

Eugenics

The cleansing of the genetic diversity of the human race consists in measures which prevent bearers of undesirable genes from passing them on to their posterity. As with plants and animals, certain traits must be eliminated, other cultivated. The first step in this direction is the elimination of visibly handicapped people. So far, this takes place by a very primitive method: preborn or newborn babies who evidence obviously undesirable characteristics such as spina bifida, a missing brain or mongolism, are killed or allowed to die. With the progress of biotics, the time of diagnosing a defect is advanced increasingly towards the moment of conception, and so is the moment of aborting fetuses whose genes indicate the tendency towards physical problems: cancer, tuberculosis, high blood pressure, heart diseases, leukemia, but also towards certain mental traits or intellectual deficiencies. The number of genes found to be causing physical and mental deviations is expected to grow in proportion to the improvement of methods of identification. The discoveries of such genes do not serve as basis of seeking their cure as much as the elimination of their bearers to prevent their reproduction.

A perfection of this intervention is the generation of embryos in test tubes. First a number of embryos is conceived with the help of artificial fertilization by (selected, quality) sperm; the embryos are provided with nutrients and kept under observation; at a certain stage a small number is selected and implanted; the others are used for experimentation or destroyed. The development of implanted embryos is followed and only the strongest, i.e., those most corresponding to the standards of biotics, are allowed to mature until birth, others are discarded. This method of improving the human race is still rare, because the mortality of the embryos is too high and the procedure too expensive; but it has a great potential for the future breeding of gifted individuals from the sperm and ova of outstanding (in terms of physical and mental health) individuals.

Another method of eugenics are measures aimed at dissuading adults, supposed to have undesirable genes, from procreation. In certain states applicants for a marriage license must undergo a physical examination during which the pathologies of their ancestors are investigated. If a tendency towards inherited maladies is discovered, applicants are warned that similar problems could appear in their progeny and they are counselled to use contraceptives or sterilization. Eugenic effects might motivate also proposals to subject to forced sterilization criminals guilty of repeated rape, multiple murderers, and single mothers living exclusively on welfare. The same results have also administrative measures intended primarily to reduce the population and which induce or force members of the so-called lowest classes, i.e., practically the poorest members of society, to use contraceptives or undergo sterilization (in India, men who submit to sterilization, get a financial subsidy, in Indonesia villages with less than standard use of contraceptives are refused state's assistance. (30).

Euthanasia

On the other side of the cleansing of the genetic inheritance of the human race are those who are *no longer* healthy: the old, the incurably ill, the "vegetative" ones whose lives are not worth living. For them, euthanasia and assisted suicide are available, with moral suasion and institutional pressure inducing them to make use of such choices to achieve "death with dignity" and not to consume selfishly resources which can be put to better use for those who contribute to society.

In its widest sense, this concept encompasses all methods increasing the quality of life of a society by removing all individuals who have lost the required qualities ("have lost the ability of meaningful life"). Either they are left to die by denial of medical services (passive euthanasia) or are killed (active euthanasia). Both methods are advocated under the label of enlarging the number of inalienable human rights by the addition of another right — the right to a death (with dignity).

In the United States, so far the most common and legalized passive euthanasia is performed on the basis of a formal and legally valid declaration that the signer does not wish his life to be artificially prolonged in case of incurable disease or insufferable pain — the "living will." The courts have not yet decided about the legality of active euthanasia when a physician kills a patient at his request either by prescribing a lethal substance or performs the killing himself (by injection or inhalation of carbon monoxide) — the assisted suicide or medicide. In both instances, the "termination of life" is (in theory) performed according to a decision of the victim.

In practice, the "right to die" shades over into an obligation to die. There is moral and institutional pressure to sign a living will; a refusal is considered to be a sign of a selfish depletion of limited resources, a pressure persons seriously ill and dependent on others find hard to withstand. Some hospitals submit to persons fatally ill or wounded the text of a living will for signature routinely among other documents needed for admission to the hospital (insurance, authorization to perform treatment); some hospitals refuse to admit patients without a living will. If the patient is unconscious or has a guardian, the decision about denial of medical treatment is made by the family, the guardian, the court or the bioethical committee of the hospital.

The replacement of the right to die by an obligation to die was advocated several years ago by a book written by a famous professor of the John Hopkins University. He recommended that patients who exceeded the "natural duration" of life (proposed to be fixed at 72 years of age) should be given palliatives only, no medication. In practice, this principle is already applied by several public health systems (e.g., in Sweden) openly or factually (former Czechoslovakia) where ill persons over a certain age were no longer granted expensive surgeries or other treatments.

The vision of a perfect humanity consisting of a limited number of healthy individuals who do not outlive the time of their productivity is not only a question of ideology, but also a matter of powerful economic interests. The advocacy of euthanasia is based on the use and misuse of especially moving hard cases to manipulate public opinion by evoking compassion, however, the main support for this part of biomaterialism comes from different, palpably economic sources. In the spring of 1996, the media published articles about an extremely difficult kidney transplant on a baby. The surgeon charged (and later waived) a fee of $100,000 and the hospital charged $200,000. It is common knowledge that some doctors prescribe surgery and treatments that are very costly and not always necessary; the justification of the "right to die" was often based on the fact that the life of incurable persons was extended by extraordinary measures even at the price of their pain and suffering — and a catastrophic economic cost.

This situation was aggravated by the shift of responsibility and authority from the family to impersonal institutions — insurance companies and the state — which find a fast performance of the right to die much more economical than protracted cure. The abortion of a mongoloid fetus is much less expensive than its birth and lifelong care, and an institution does not and can not take into consideration the personal ties between family members, which would inspire them to assume a heavier burden than an accountant of an institution aiming at lowering expenses and increasing profitability can afford.

Ecology

The success of medical and technological progress which improved the health and life of humans and resulted in an unprecedented growth of humanity created new circumstances for men, other life forms and the planet. Even the simplest manifestations of life such as breathing, eating, digesting, eliminating, sleeping have a marked impact when performed by six billion individuals. The changes are most dramatic where large numbers of people congregate in small areas (the expected megacities of the next century). Ecology is dealing with these changes in three respects: the exhaustion of natural resources, the destruction of natural environment and the disappearance of certain life forms.

The relative shortage of natural *resources* has been with mankind since its beginnings. It has been handled both by migration accompanied by conquest and by invention of better utilization of given resources. In more recent times, the question has been raised of an absolute limitation of resources — natural resources are finite, and their increased utilization by man could exhaust them with catastrophic consequences. The scope of such resources has been measured and the time until their exhaustion predicted several times, especially as far as oil and certain minerals are concerned; in the recent past, also the exhaustion of resources such as air, water, land and ocean has been announced. ([31]). So far all these predictions have been proven false, some appear ridiculous after past years of experience. The reason is threefold: Reduction and disposal of waste, extraction from waste of usable materials and their recycling, or conversion into energy, energy conservation and environmental restoration and control of pollution practiced by the main sources of contamination, i.e., the industrialized nations, has a growing impact. New deposits of raw materials are being discovered, and methods to mine and refine them are constantly being improved. While the earth's resources are certainly finite, they are flexible: human ingenuity replaces the use of rare and/or expensive materials by transformation of materials which are abundant and inexpensive. The core of the planet is composed of metals; sources of energy from the heat of the earth's core, from the sun and gravitation are practically inexhaustible. The discovery of energy from fusion rather than fission would revolutionize the entire economy — and ecology.

The impact of human multitudes on the *environment* stems mostly from industrialization undertaken to serve human needs increasing both by quantity and by quality. Technology which invented the power to pollute air, water, endanger the ozone layer has also the ability to undo and prevent the damage done by human activities; this pollution is sometimes only a fraction of pollution caused by nature itself, like volcano emissions, impacts of meteors, forest fires.

Ecology attributes special value to species whose survival is threatened by the expansion of mankind; if such *endangered species* is identified, circumstances favorable to its survival and recovery are preserved or created by artificial human intervention. The methods are either transfer of the surviving members of the endangered species to a more favorable area, or reserving for it an area in which its population can recover and grow. This protection of certain species has no grounding in nature; both methods create a pressure on the existing non-human population of the selected area; carnivores destroy other animals; herbivores consume certain plants; the choice which animal life is more valuable than others is largely arbitrary (32).

Summary

The prevailing ideology of the elites approaches ecological problems from two standpoints.

(1) It is preferable to have a small number of people live in an impeccable environment, rather have large numbers of people live in an environments which is less than perfect. This approach ignores the law of decreasing relative utility: the cost of the marginal unit is the greatest, the profit derived from its expenditure is minimal. To expunge the last vestiges of particles from the air is so costly that its impact on society is damaging. If, however, the exclusive goal is to obtain the purest air, then the cost incurred under other society's objectives is irrelevant.

(2) Humans are considered as another type of animal in accordance with the postulate of their breeding; therefore, in certain instances, human interest, livelihoods and sometimes even lives must yield to the interest of (other) animals. (33) A paradox in endangered species protection are measures prohibiting the local population from killing certain animals so that they are available for sportsmen from the rich countries to hunt and kill in order to bring home a rare trophy.

Some extreme environmentalists ("Animal Liberation") claim outright that "people are destroying the planet," find certain animals (like pigs) as more intelligent and therefore more valuable than humans of the same age and in general that endangered species are to be given preference to men because "there are too many people."

The handling of ecological and environmental problems in harmony with the ideology of individualism is inconsistent with adopting a generally valid and applicable objective to be pursued by means capable of being evaluated under such a goal; individualism's relativism does not permit it, but it has one feature in common with the philosophy of biomaterialism: the solutions are sought in the reduction of the human population, at the expense of the human "species." (33)

CHAPTER 24

MANAGING HUMANITY

The implementation and permanence of the achievements of economic and biological materialism can not be secured until it encompasses all of humanity and the entire world, and the power monopolies, especially those of intellectual leadership and of mass communications media, are firmly in the hands of adherents of the elitist ideology and its ideological movement. ([34])

As analyzed in the preceding two chapters, the ideology of the elitist movement and the process of extra-political centralization have the following in common:

(1) the goal of lowering the world's population and eliminating its non-productive members,

(2) universal applicability,

(3) overlapping leadership by elites belonging to the same ideological movement,

(4) the need for an international legal order to protect their activities and pursue their goals.

The window of opportunity of this movement is the present, as long as the United States is the only superpower and its only contemporary rival China pursues the same depopulation policy and remains unable to oppose the creation of a global economy, and as long as no other power centers (Russia, Moslem nations) achieve consolidation. Even at present there appear limits to the possibilities of the new world order imposing its will on very minor, but determined opponents (the intervention in Iraq did not achieve the removal of its aggressive government; in Somalia the resistance of one local tribal leader forced the

United Nations to evacuate the country; the efforts of the international intervention in Bosna will, at best, only disguise the victory of the aggressor; and the resistance of the Palestinians, Syria and Israel to the conclusion of a lasting peace has not been overcome — not to mention the continuous bloodletting in various areas of Africa). To the global implementation of its goals, the elitist movement needs the creation of a true international legal order with legislative, judicial and mainly executive organs superior to its member states.

Taking over U.S. Foreign Policy

The decisive event in elevating the implementation of the elitist movement's ideology to the international and indeed global scene was a study undertaken by the United States National Security Council in 1974 under the chairmanship of Mr.Henry Kissinger. This study about 200 pages long dated December 10, 1974, marked as Memorandum NSSM 200 and entitled "Implications of Worldwide Population Growth for U.S. Security and Overseas Interests" was immediately classified as "secret" and not communicated to the legislative branch of the U.S.Government. By an equally secret decision of President Ford identified as NSDM 314 (National Security Memorandum 314) dated November 26, 1975, it was distributed as a binding political directive to the Secretaries of State, Defense, Agriculture and Treasury, the Department of Health and Human Services, commanders of all three branches of the U.S. military, to the Directors of CIA and AID and the President's economic and environmental councils. (For more details see Appendix 12.)

Since that time, all branches of the U.S. executive have followed, behind the back of the elective organs and without the knowledge of the electorate, in U.S. international relations and activities a radical depopulation policy. NSSM 200 is based on projected growth of humanity as it would be without deliberate interference: 12 billion people in 2075. Due to disparities in the fertility indices of countries, at that time the "developed" countries will represent about 10% of the world population and the "poor" countries about 90% (see Chapter 25, section on application of elitist ideology). Because the United States with 6% of the world population would consume (at that time) about 33% of the world's resources (and expect this share to grow), such a discrepancy would create political and economic disturbances which would endanger the supply of such resources. It is therefore in the U.S.' national and security interest to protect their availability by artificially arresting the growth of the "poor" world's population. The target was set at 8 billion permissible number of people. Because the projected number of the living would, without interference, be 12 billion, the National Security Council decided that the U.S. foreign policy should by intentional and deliberate action prevent or destroy the lives of all people who would otherwise be born over the limit of 8 billion *until the denial of life would reach the amount of 4 billion people in 2075.* Compared with this undertaking, the losses on human life of the two world wars and under the communist and Nazi regimes appear almost puny.

The two documents then propose the methods how to achieve this result. To be effective, this strategy demands the creation of a worldwide commitment of political leaders and of the people in favor of population control. This presupposes two ways: it is necessary to enlist (more accurately: to compel) the support of the governments of the underdeveloped countries and carefully avoid the appearance of a industrialized nations' policy of taking advantage (neocolonialism, exploitation, racial bias) of the underdeveloped countries. The President and the Secretary of State are here charged with the task to convince in person-to-person contacts the leaders of the target nations about the need of braking the growth of their populations and of assuming the "credit" for the introduction and implementation of the necessary measures. It will also be up to these leaders to propose and assert the need of family planning and population stabilization in multinational organizations and in bilateral contacts with other leaders of the targeted nations (Appendix 11).

The argumentation must be couched in terms of individual and family rights to determine the number of their offspring, and the introduction of anti-fertility means and measures is to be portrayed as assistance for the exercise of such rights. The campaign would be conducted on the basis of materials provided by the UN or USIA ([35]). With the carrot came also the stick: "population planning" and its organization had to be integrated in the development plans of underdeveloped countries in order to qualify for assistance. ([36]) The documents also called for the allocation of necessary funds. ([37])

Taking over the United Nations

Rights

For the recommendation that the elitist ideology must be spread in the disguise of implementing individual and family rights the activities of international political institutions are indispensable. The process then follows an identical sequence: (1) universal or widespread wants of individuals are identified; (2) these wants are interpreted as universal "needs," (3) the fulfillment of such needs is translated into "rights" of individuals, (4) the United Nations Organization assumes the responsibility of having these rights implemented through its bureaucracy and its members. The year 1994 was the year in which a super-national organization — the UN through the intermediary of the Office for Population Affairs — arrogated to itself the right to decide population policies of member states as well as their methods including cultural changes imposed from the outside.

A number of such "human rights" with openly depopulating or eugenic purposes have so far failed to be approved as some sort of internationally recognized norms. Such were the right to abortion (failed narrowly at the 1996 Cairo conference), the right to death, the right to homosexual unions or life-styles, the rights of children to sexual activities or information about sexual activities since the beginning of the age of reason (kindergarten), although the legal systems of some (and most of the Western) countries have already legalized them. Also attempts to cloak a right to abortion under the terms of "reproductive rights" or "sexual rights" were repudiated (at the Cairo Conference on Population and Development in September 1994); other "rights" have not made it to the UN level, such as the human right of adultery or of prostitution (mentioned at the Second International Conference on Health and Human Rights at Harvard University in Cambridge, Ma., in October 1996).

More successful are proposed "rights" which respond to real needs of individuals; their approval in principle is intertwined with anti-population measures made possible by intentionally broad wording subject then to interpretation by the executive organs (see Chapter 7, section on the lawless state). The "right to habitation" includes provision that this right is to apply only to small families. The "right to health" includes provisions making assistance conditional on submitting to depopulation measures. This pertains to individuals as well as groups (f.i., cases of India and Indonesia — see Appendix No.11).

The appeal to inalienable human rights served successfully as a battering ram against autocratic states. After this success, various formulations of inalienable rights became a part of international agreements and treaties and became enforceable by joined military, political and mainly economic operations of democratic states and of international organizations. The content and nature of inalienable rights has thus become subject to development; for instance, the last right added to the previous ones are the right to free elections. Each of the inalienable rights newly discovered or invented by international organizations further limits the sovereignty of states and increases the power of international institutions (and bureaucracies) and is used for this purpose.

In the progress towards a superstate, the individualist nature of human rights is used to undermine and whittle down the sovereignty of states. The main instrument to create global uniformity of thinking is the creation of a conflict between the rights of the individual and the national interest and the one-sided assertion of individual rights against the rights of any groups to which he belongs — state, nation, family, church. The target is especially the nation as an organic society which, while subsisting in individuals, has nevertheless its own ontological existence; its existence is nowhere protected under international law, and the protection of national interests is disparaged in domestic law also by international measures limiting states' rights to regulate immigration, to give preference to citizens or members of its founding and sustaining nation, measures protecting minorities to an extent which discriminates against the members of the majority. Other provisions embedded in international treaties open the doors to penetration by extra-political centralizing influences by economic, communication, health and other multinational organizations and their untrammeled activities on the territory of all member states, with the effect of promoting the creation of a homogeneous mass culture on the foundation of common basic instincts and desires of individuals. In 1993, UN's Economic and Social Council (ECOSOC) created a Commission on Human Rights which in turn established a Subcommission on Human Rights composed of appointed experts, and the UN's activities concerning human rights are to be coordinated by a Center for Human Rights and a High Commissioner for Human Rights (position created in 1993) with a program of creating a "universal culture of human rights" in the next century through efforts within the UN system and dialogue with governments. UN Development Fund includes in its program basic education, basic health care and universal family planning as objectives for 2000; sex education is put on the same level of importance as elimination of illiteracy.

The vulnerability of national independence is increased by the centralization of culture in the direction of uniformity based on the lowest common denominator of humans, i.e., their instincts, while their cultural differences are allowed to wither away by neglect and omission. The culture which is at present the bearer of the integration process, emphasizes the autonomy of the individual in his relationship towards national cultures and religions which could generate ideological movements aspiring at an integrated global order of a different kind. This burgeoning conflict can produce effects dangerous to the whole idea of global integration.

The Way: International Bureaucracy

The structure of the United Nations Organization is not conducive to its transformation into a superstate. Its norm-giving power rests in two institutions: the General Assembly and the Security Council. In practice, and largely also according to UN Charter, the Security Council has veto power over resolutions of the General Assembly and each member of the Security Council has a veto power over the resolutions of the Council. Therefore, the norm-giving function of UN is at best cumbersome and the center of activities shifted to an entrenched widespread bureaucracy which endeavors to build up an effective enforcement through military formations created ad hoc from the armed forces of (certain) member states (UNPROFOR, UNOSOM, and others). Plans for the creation of a permanent UN army equipped possibly by nuclear weapons have so far gotten nowhere.

It is of essence that the elitist movement accomplishes its goals through institutions out of reach of the people, i.e., non-elective institutions, of which bureaucracies are the most typical example. The growth of the power and lack of responsibility of bureaucracies has been identified as one of the main threats to democracy. While bureaucracies are hard to keep within bounds even in democracies and were quite out of control in communist countries, the bureaucracies of international organizations are twice removed from the people since international organizations are organizations of governments and not of elected representatives of nations. In the United Nations' organization, the only time when member states can effectively influence its bureaucracy, is at the selection of the Secretary General. Once elected he then appoints the heads of UN Agencies who in turn select, appoint and hire their staff. Only those member states which finance the bulk of the UN expenditures can influence behind the scenes the composition of these international bodies, which means that the United States with a few other Western industrialized states have a key voice in selecting UN staffs. Members of the elitist movement, with a large representation from the Third World countries, dominate the international bureaucracy and use their positions to implement the ideology of economic and biological materialism.

Managing, i.e., at present containing, humanity's procreation by way of coercive population control is the common goal of five specialized agencies of the United Nations Organization: FAO (Food and Agriculture Organization), UNDP (UN Development Program),

UNFPA (UN Population Fund), WHO (World Health Organization), and UNICEF as evidenced by occasional pronouncements of their respective directors and administrators and coordinated succession of world conferences organized according the same pattern.

The bureaucracies of UNO's specialized agencies have practically accepted Kissinger Commission's "World Population Plan of Action" (see Appendix 12) as a plan of breeding the human race to their specifications, have obtained the financial and material means for its implementation and have enforced its execution on the global scale although no such mandate has ever been given to them by the norm-giving bodies of the organization. Moreover, even if the UNO's norm-giving organs wanted to adopt such a plan, it would be against its Charter which does not recognize UNO as a normgiver superior to the individual states and does not relegate them to the role of UNO's subjects of duty. In spite of this, the coercion of nominally sovereign states is routinely practiced through collusion (not conspiracy) of the elites of the United States and certain Western states, agencies of UNO and the World Bank as part of the movement towards reducing to territorial administrative units nation states considered to be the greatest obstacle towards a transformation of the world's nations into a new world order created via facti and not by consensus of states and even less by the decision of their citizens.

The pattern consists of the decision to organize a world conference on a subject which corresponds to the agency's special purpose and touches simultaneously on population control. Such conferences were World Summit for Children (1990), the International Conference on Population and Development in Cairo (1994), World Summit on Social Development in Copenhagen (1995), UN Conference on Women in Beijing (1995), Habitat II Conference in Istanbul (1996), World Food Summit in Rome (1996). A working paper is prepared by the agency's staff, repeatedly discussed and then submitted to the conference. The conference is composed of representatives from governments of member states with the presence and participation of non-government organizations ("NGOs"); procedural technicalities allow the organizers to aid those whose attitude is known to agree with the agency's program. The working paper is then subjected to a discussion of the full session of delegates and its various proposals are, according to the opinions expressed by the governments' representatives, either approved or amended; they are rarely rejected because, if the prepared working paper meets strong opposition, the objectionable portion is amended. The amendment is formulated to gain "consensus" by broadening the wording so that it omits, but does not exclude the controversial provision: If a provision asserting the right to abortion is contested, it is replaced by one guaranteeing reproductive rights; if this is not acceptable, it provides for health care, and if this does not meet with approval, it is replaced with "social services" which, after the conference is ended, is interpreted by the bureaucracy as including, as a matter of course, health care providing also abortion or sterilization which, at the conference, was turned down. If this manipulation fails, the matter is taken up by another conference which will slip them in. This was the case with the Cairo conference whose rejected agenda was subsequently taken up by the Beijing conference; when the FAO Food Summit final preparatory meeting in September 1996 rejected outright the intentions of the prepared working paper, FAO called subsequently a hastily scheduled "intercessionary session" in October during which it managed to introduce some of the rejected proposals into the document. The further step in these tactics is the organizing of implementation sessions and stage-managed follow-up meetings to circumvent the barriers elected by the government delegates during the formal conferences. The results are then submitted to member states for individual ratification, acceptance or implementation.

Importantly, in each of the documents, no matter what the subject is of the respective conference, depopulation measures are dominant ([38]). From the conference cycle, UNDP has composed an integrated plan whose first objective is named "basic social services" interpreted as including reproductive rights and the entire depopulation agenda rejected by the Cairo Conference.

The latest link in this structure was the establishment of a self-appointed Earth Charter Commission pretending to be a creation of "grassroots NGOs" and actually hand picked by high-level UN functionaries whose declarations evidenced the degree of their self-confidence (our emphasis): about the Earth Charter: "This document will stand on its own authority. *It does not need government authority*" (Maurice Strong) and "Development assistance is a key ingredient of successful *global governance*" (James Gustave Speth). The draft of the Charter includes as a key element anti-population measures under the customary guise: "sexual and reproductive health" (Art. 11) joined with "sustainable development" (Art. 10).

The World Bank became an aggressive ally of the population control movement world-wide under the leadership of Mr.McNamara and his elitist followers. In allocation of credit lines and loans, the World Bank insists on inclusion of depopulation measures among its conditions of granting assistance, on many occasions acting as an instrument of U.S. depopulation policy.

Private organizations

If left to the activities of individual governments, the depopulation program could not proceed fast enough to prevent the development its originators and promoters intend to prevent. To achieve this acceleration, cooperation of elitist private organizations is necessary to form the third leg of the depopulation strategy.

The most important and influential among them is the International Planned Parenthood Federation. It was founded as a rather cranky organization by a Mrs. Margaret Sanger with a program of primitive eugenics of preventing the poor and the lower races, i.e., Negroes, Latinos and Jews, from propagating, and having recovered from the bad reputation eugenics suffered due to its Nazi version, it became the main instrument of American upper and upper middle classes to support the strategy of scientific breeding of the entire human race. Its international headquarters are located in Great Britain. Funded generously by public monies ([35]) its network spread throughout the world and became the spearhead of aggressive and sometimes illegal (abortion, sterilization) birth control promoters in most states.

The IPPF is by no means the only important depopulation organization of the United States with international influence; some of the others are: the Population Council, Population Crisis Committee (later Population Action International), the Pathfinder Fund, Association for Voluntary Surgical Contraception, most of them disposing of millions of dollars annually from state budgets, UN's funds and large private foundations. The importance of their support for the "containment" of population consists of coordinating their role as NGOs with the UN bureaucracy at international conferences and is evident also from the share they contribute to birth control activities: (although in many instances, they act only as a conduit of funds obtained from public sources to their utilization in depopulation activities : from 1952 to 1991 it was 1,070,800,000 in constant US dollars ([39]).

The push contributed by the multi- and supranational economic corporations to the depopulation movement worldwide can not be expressed in dollars. The interpretation of human rights and the linkage of democracy with a market economy allows an extra-political concentration of economic activities out of control of individual states. By stifling free exchange of ideas especially in the sphere of mass communications their influence is destructive of national cultures and religious values and creates the universal world culture in the image of elitist values . In September 1996, a "Soap Summit II" of leading producers, directors and writers of "soap operas" took place in New York, with the U.S. Undersecretary of State for Population Affairs outlining the policy of his country: reducing reproduction of humanity was identified as one of the administration's highest priorities and the role of soap operas in the world's re-education was stressed and illustrated by examples and their effectiveness ([40]).

A significant step in the direction of a universal world culture was the 1996 merger of the Time-Warner Corporation with the Turner Broadcasting conglomerate. The resulting structure is the greatest global concentration in the areas of information and culture; at the merger of these two gigantic enterprises among the media the TV commentator on PBS Chicago stated on September 22, 1996, that this joined corporation penetrates into minds of more people than anyone else ("no one not living in the woods is untouched") by its production of movies, publications, music, rapp, television, broadcasts, scientific literature, novels, pornography, video cassettes. It is the principal producer in the fields of reporting and entertainment in the whole world, it owns the most popular English language weeklies (Time, Life, Future, People and others), TV and radio stations all over the world and with the exception of people living in primeval forests every inhabitant of the planet is at least once daily touched by one or another of the products of this mammoth conglomerate.

Other similar mergers followed with the same tendency: to spread into all areas of communications and entertainment. Among them, the most important was the conglomerate founded by the merger of Disney Corp. with ABC television whose aggressivity in programming the elitist ideology overtook in a short time all others.

When internal guidelines of such a giant (issued by managers unknown and not accountable to the people) "suggest" to its employees to substitute, "for accuracy's sake," the term "pro-choice" for "pro-abortion" and the designation "anti-abortion" for "pro-life", then such and similar manipulations of the language have permanent consequences: since men think in concepts expressed by words and the words are furnished to them by the media, they predetermine the boundaries and the outcome of public debates on the issues or prevent thought from forming true conclusions. Attempts of nation states like France or some post-communist countries to isolate their culture from these influences were thwarted in the name of human rights and/or in the interest of compatibility of legal systems of various international bodies and treaties (European Union, NAFTA, BAFFT and others). In this process, NGOs of international dimensions are assuming a growing importance; from their originally consultative status they are changing into pressure groups which homogenize life-styles and cultures of nations in global dimensions.

Results

The implementation of the depopulation plan has progressed very well. Between 1981 and 1991, the population growth of the following nations has dropped significantly: Colombia by 27%, Brazil by 25%, India by 26%, Indonesia by 22%, Mexico by 21%, Turkey by 14%, Nigeria by 10%. As of 1996, below reproduction level, i.e., dying out were all European countries (except Malta) including Russia, in Asia South Korea and Taiwan, in others, the survival is due more to immigration (legal and illegal) than the vitality of the original stock.

These results indicate also that the homogenization of national cultures has made huge progress and that elements of the elitist ideology mainly in the area of sexual permissiveness and promiscuity have taken firm root everywhere. The main obstacle to the spreading of the universal civic religion is the natural inclination of people to have children and thus to extend their lives beyond their death, tradition and religion; such resistance to the emerging universal civic religion is being scientifically undermined. In order to weaken the opposition of religion, AID funded in 1982 the John Hopkins University to conduct research for overcoming Moslem resistance to contraceptive measures in Africa, and in 1986 the University received a grant of 35 million dollars to implement such a program. In the West, traditional churches, with the exception of the Catholic Church, already yielded to the "signs of the times" by relaxing moral norms governing family and sex life and by opening to women participation in the priesthood: women can now be "priests" — they do not care to be priestesses. The United States has admitted women and homosexuals to the military. Due to the papacy the Catholic Church has not changed its doctrine, but the elitist civil religion has made great inroads: most of the Church's theologians rejects doctrinal teaching concerning sexual morals, the clergy generally avoid it and the majority of its believers ignore it. The bulwark of the opposition to the new morality rests with the numerous decentralized small evangelical and biblical churches whose members are impervious to the elitist ideology.

Evaluation

Criticism of biomaterialism and especially its program of quantitative regulation of world population has pointed out the following errors:

1. There is no world-wide food shortage. All Western countries have agricultural surpluses in spite of programs of artificial restraints on production. Africa would be self-sufficient and have food surpluses with introduction of modern technology, especially irrigation. Three countries bordering Lake Malawi — Malawi, Tanzania and Mozambique — each could feed all of Africa with proper use of the abundant resources: fertile soil and fresh water. A joint study of FAO and UNFPA from 1982 concluded that the underdeveloped countries excluding China could sustain 33 billion people; a publication of UNFPA of 1990 asserts that land potentially capable of agricultural production could sustain a world population stabilized at the level of 14 billion people.

2. Famines are seldom occasioned by natural causes; usually they are consequences of an incompetent economic system (in the past mostly socialism/communism) or anarchy (Somalia, Sudan, Mozambique, Rwanda, Burundi, Congo and others). These cases require political solutions; reduction of the number of people can not solve them.

3. Birth control causes progressive aging of the population which puts the burden of sustenance of the growing strata of the aging population on the present productive part of the people; this causes economic hardships and dislocations.

4. The free market system works best under the conditions of expanding markets and demand. Therefore, developed nations strive to expand their markets by penetrating into undeveloped or developing countries through creation of free trade zones (NAFTA and its expansion into South America, the inclusion of Russia into the global economy, expansion of NATO eastward). The effects of depopulation go against this economic expansion and can not be offset by the demand of an increasing standard of living.

5. The use of contraceptives has social and sociological consequences well beyond the control of population: the change of the function or abolition of the institution of the family, disruption of moral norms and their integrating effect, psychological dysfunctions in children and adolescents, epidemics of existing and new venereal diseases.

6. Population cannot be controlled any better than economy; in both cases, the same principles of free market apply; the attempt to control births requires an extension of the power of state bureaucracies to include the most intimate sphere of human life and a totalitarian system exceeding any of its previous incarnations.

7. Depopulation politics can not be arbitrarily arrested or reversed; once the public accepts the elitist civil religion as the normal way of life, it will proceed below the reproductive minimum which will necessitate repleting the population deficit through biotechnology.

It is a fact that a rapidly increasing population creates problems of growth which must be solved by human reason. and that the World Population Plan of Action is an attempt to do so. Based on erroneous philosophy and authoritarian ideology it is bound to fail; but being the only one in existence, it has a monopoly on implementation. Its secretiveness and manipulative ways of implementation prevent its errors from being corrected and its critics who are right in pointing out its mistakes are prevented by the Movement from formulating and presenting alternatives.

CHAPTER 25

AHEAD! — IN THE WRONG DIRECTION

The Movement's ideology and the direction in which it pushes mankind is to be judged against the background of reality.

Life

The so-called population explosion is not an abnormal or unnatural occurrence; on the contrary, it is the result of natural processes of cosmic dimensions which resulted in the emergence of life. (See Chapter 17, sections on life and mind.) Each living being is a whirlpool in the fabric of reality, a whirlpool which adjusts to its environment and at the same time affects the environment and assimilates anything compatible with and suitable for its growth; when it achieves a certain dimension, the whirlpool breaks up into smaller ones which continue the original pattern while their parent(s) might break up and dissolve.

Man

In the human species, this process of perpetuating life, i.e., the reproductive process does not consist in division or budding of an individual, it consists in merging of two specialized cells and their bearers (the male and the female). It is effected by the male organ which places the fertilizing cells prompting life directly into the body of the woman to protect the new member of the human race since the moment of its conception.

Man, equipped with qualities enabling life to overcome its confinement, is the latest outcome of nature's project. In the human species, development shifted from the corporeal to the spiritual plateau. To continue the path of this triumph and to expand it is in harmony with the direction of nature's development, in harmony with life's evident meaning.

Application of Elitist Ideology

Seen from this perspective, the ideology of elitism and most of its derived applications are wrong.

The program of biological materialism and especially the program of blocking human reproduction is anti-nature and contrary to the meaning of the cosmos. It is unthinkable that the life force would erupt in such an abundance only in order to have a carefully regulated number of carefully bred humans live in the midst of carefully maintained "wilderness" spending their time in a careful effort to determine what and how best to eat, drink, fornicate, travel and amuse themselves.

This is closely connected with the role elitism assigns to sex. The role is unnatural and its consequences are deadly — not only in the life of individuals, also in the life of nations. The number of nations which are not reproducing themselves and are on the way of depopulating themselves out of existence, to die out, is a clear proof of it.

No matter how fast the depopulation program proceeds, it inevitably results in a demographic defeat for the nations which are the originators and upholders of Western culture: the nations of Europe and of North America. Their proportion of the world population in 1950: 22.2%, in 1990: 14.6%, in 2050: 8.2%. This demographic basis is too small to protect its own culture, much less can it impose it on the 91.8% of the rest of the world or radiate its own values to it.

This spells failure to the project of imposing a universal elitist culture globally. It may succeed in creating an all-pervasive anomie in large parts of the world, but not gain acceptance of its own values — the same fate which befell the communist attempt to replace national and religious traditions of the people under its rule by its own ideology.

A homogenized universal civic religion is self-defeating also in another respect: by stifling or preventing differentiation and selection, it stops evolving and stagnates, and because change is the basic property of nature, it degenerates. It is perceptibly becoming a mass culture centering on sex and on moronic entertainment

Elitism destroys democracy by removing entire areas of public life from the decision making power of the citizens. The multiplication of "inalienable human rights" through international bodies and their incorporation in national legal systems through international treaties transfers matters connected with such proliferating "human rights" and their interpretation from legislatures to courts — democracy degenerates from the rule of the people, by the people and for the people into government by judges. Reliance on appointed and independent commissions of experts and "experts" funded by the public treasury removes wide areas of social life, from art to medical care, from the purview of elected bodies and from the influence of the people. Democracy withers through apathy of citizens who recognize that their votes have no impact on the way the state and society are going and who realize or suspect that they are not furnished reliable and objective information for their decision-making.

The rise and consolidation of the elitist movement brought about a situation in which very elements of evolution are eliminated and avenues for proper transformation of potentialities into actualities are being closed. This constitutes an abandonment of development and adoption of entropy, an option for nothingness.

Let Future Generations Decide their Destiny

One part of the emerging new bio-balance is that man regulates nature and not the reverse. The question is now how is man to regulate nature. The answer in harmony with nature and the direction of natural development is: in the interest of the survival and growth of his own species and through it of life, but not otherwise — nature does not know destruction of life for comfort or fun. Which brings up the subject of overpopulation and the assertion that natural resources are not sufficient to support a steadily growing number of people with their rising consumption levels and that a resulting expansion of industry destroys nature.

The development of technology proves the fallacy of this assertion. It is estimated that life expectancy until the Middle Ages was between twenty and thirty years. In the last two centuries, Western civilization increased it to 72 years and its advances in agriculture, sanitation and medicine exported to the rest of the world increased the life expectancy of its inhabitants by up to twenty years. This was made possible by a progress of technology whose achievements the elitists are laboring to undo. Yet policies which artificially restrict humanity's growth lead to a society which is at first static, then stagnant and ultimately fallen apart.

Earth contains a practically unlimited quantity of metals; moreover, their recycling and replacement by other materials reduces their usage. As to agriculture, it is impossible to claim shortage of foods while agricultural production is artificially restricted and its "surpluses" in various ways destroyed. The same applies to sources of energy: the heat from the core of the planet and the radiation from its sun are only two among many unused and almost limitless sources of energy. Nor is handling of waste beyond man's capacity to solve it; a being capable of producing chemical damage to the ozone layer is capable also of reversing the process. The problem is rather that the ingenuity of the human race, its technology is directed towards producing more and more luxury for the part of humanity that already lives in affluence and not towards the task of serving mankind as a whole. At present, production is geared towards increasing the standard of living which in turn is understood as an unceasing increase of consumption and comfort even at the cost of depleting accessible natural resources. To continue in this direction is indeed suicidal — because it is contrary to nature and its meaning. It is truly a Civilization of Death. The solution is not to restrict industry, the solution is in changing its direction. A civilization in harmony with nature, i.e., guided by nature's tendencies and laws, will direct its efforts towards the greatest growth of humanity by tapping unused resources, discovery of new materials, utilization and protection of renewable resources, placing environmentally damaging plants on artificial satellites, breaking into interplanetary sources of materials and energy and other options technically feasible but neglected because they do not bring profit, and therefore are neglected in the present state of civilization. Technology is at the threshold of even greater breakthroughs and advances; technology is power, and power can be used for good or detrimental purposes according to the decisions of those who wield it.

Humanity is not too big for Earth — Earth is becoming too small for Man. Visibly, Man is outgrowing the confines of the planet of his origin. To achieve it might be the task for future generations. It will be a difficult task. The present generation's task is to bring them forth, to grant them their life, to give them a chance. If allowed to live, they will find a way. No generation has the right to deprive its progeny of the opportunity to solve their difficulties and to continue the achievements reached by their predecessors, to live and give life.

Meaningful or Meaningless

This evaluation speaks about the meaning of the universe, the purpose of a life force, the aims of nature. More and more, science inclines to the conclusion that the universe originated, by a Big Bang, from a cosmic egg in which the laws of nature were pre-programmed, and that the cosmos plays out this program. But meaning, purpose and aim can originate only from a being possessing intelligence and will outside of the universe and outside of nature, a being which created the cosmos and gave it a purpose and meaning. This "Being" is Life; to deviate from its purposes means the loss of life. In his freedom, man can do it, politics can prefer entropy to evolution and embrace nothingness A sad outcome that would be for the great experiment of the mind which conceived and created the universe. Man can believe he can choose between life and death; he would find out that he can chose only between out of time existing in darkness or in light.

PART D.

PRACTICAL CONCLUSIONS FROM POLITICAL THEORY

CASE STUDY: U.S.A.

CHAPTER 26

NASCENT GLOBAL CIVILIZATION

The most important result of World War II might have been the decomposition of colonialism rather than the destruction of European dictatorships and of Nazi totalitarianism. At the price of protecting traditional social and political structures with their iniquities and inequalities and of preserving primitive economies at the price of abysmal poverty, colonialism prevented bloody national, civil and tribal wars (with its millions of killed and maimed and even more millions of refugees) and the disruption of the poor, but functional economic systems, with catastrophic results (bare survival replaced by mass famine). Its demise created an open field for the competition of the two ramifications of European culture: democracy and totalitarianism.

During this competition, European culture of the one or the other orientation destroyed native original or aboriginal cultures and civilizations of the freed colonial peoples and ended in that sense with a complete victory of European civilization whose Eastern type (communism) finally imploded and the Western stream, that of political democracy and economic free market system, prevailed. This left the United States as the only superpower (with Communist China the only power outside its orbit) capable of creating a new world order by way of international institutions.

Attitudes and ideas of rationalism and scientism which were at the roots of communism were influential also in the West and especially among professors and students of prestigious universities; from their midst came in the United States the opponents of anti-communism and proponents of moral equivalency, unilateral disarmament , nuclear freeze, friendly competition and peaceful co-existence with the Soviet Union. They logically rejected also American patriotism and the important role of Christianity in the American political system. By using the principles of rationalism and scientism, brilliant thinkers among them adopted from Europe and/or created a consistent ideological movement which, by reasoning, trial and error discovered methods how to circumvent the democratic system favoring the less educated masses and how to construct the skeleton of a better, because decentralized, totalitarian system. They have step by step gained the upper hand in American politics, although not full control; having come to a practical alliance with the managers of industry and finance, they gained sufficient leverage to dominate the formulation of world politics (see Chapter 24) and through a kind of feedback reinforced their hold over domestic policies in all Western countries.

As the power of the movement grows and the various facets of its plans of a new world order become more articulated and explicit, it also becomes more evident that the plans must fail:

- The imposition of a universal culture including an artificial new morality is anti-evolutionary because it increasingly narrows the scope of variability, differentiation and selection; it is regressive.
- It entails the dissolution of natural biologically grounded entities, especially nations and families; thus it eliminates factors of integration, isolates individuals and causes general alienation.
- It goes against the basic nature of life — life's nature to grow; therefore it is more than unnatural, it is hostile to nature.
- It must be imposed from above, therefore, by force, economic or military; its basis — Western nations — is already too small to fulfill such a role and it is shrinking faster than the shrinkage of the rest of the world.

While the progressing implementation of the elitist ideology cannot succeed, it can wreck (and already is wrecking) the existing civilization in the same way in which communist totalitarianism failed to impose its values, but left behind anomie, anarchy, criminality; the attempt to implement economic and biological materialism as basis of an international legal system must have even farther reaching consequences. Communism tried to implement a program within the limits of European culture; elitism attempts to implement a project outside of European culture. Communism caused its own collapse; elitism could create the collapse of the entire (and at present the only) civilization and everything a collapse of civilization involves: wars, famine, epidemics, technical and scientific retrogression. (The collapse of the civilization of antiquity gives an appropriate example.)

The movement derives its strength from tapping into the strength of the United States (which, at the same time, it undermines through its domestic policies); therefore, it is by interrupting or severing this flow of power that the descent towards the collapse of the western civilization can be blocked. (Some attempts were made under the presidency of Ronald Reagan. They were reversed under President Clinton, but are an indication that such policies are possible and attainable.)

The conditions of public debate and political decision making in the United States have changed under elitist influence so that its progress is assured; these changes would have to be removed or replaced if power is to be restored to democratic processes; from such rectification can originate an alternative program for domestic and international policies, democratic and civilized.

CHAPTER 27

THE UNITED STATES

The State

From an evolutionary standpoint, the structure of the United States at its inception was a masterpiece providing for progress and development. The arrangement of the federation guaranteed variability and selection resulting in flexibility and adaptability.

Most public affairs, mainly those affecting the people directly, were decided locally, by communities. *Local self-government* had a very wide scope of authority which went as far as trials and execution of sentences by the public ("lynching") and expulsion of undesirable individuals (sometimes tarred and feathered). All general affairs were handled by the *states* through elected organs, with the exception of specific enumerated matters reserved to the *federal government*.

The federal government was divided into three branches — legislative, executive and judicial — organized on the principle of checks and balances so that none of them can amass overwhelming power; the legislature and the head of the executive branch (the President) were subjected to regular elections by all citizens; the judicial branch was appointed by the President subject to approval of the legislature; was to be independent, its members were therefore appointed for life and normally not responsible to anyone.

The differentiation of spiritual life was therefore thoroughly ensured.

Centrifugal tendencies were limited by the majority principle and the main integration of the state was provided by religion, specifically Christianity of the Protestant variety. In legal theory, this importance of religion was represented by deriving the validity of laws from natural law which in turn was valid because it emanated from God, "nature's Creator," and consequently complementary or coincidental with God's revelation, therefore fixed, objective, recognizable and unalienable. People in general considered their country as a sort of a new promised land, their personal freedom and relative material security as God's gift and as their country's mission to promote in world affairs the government of the people, by the people and for the people, i.e., democracy.

As long as this consensus prevailed over differentiation, the United States experienced unique economic and political expansion. It started to break up between the fifties and the sixties under the influence of a newly emerging class of intellectuals who ridiculed it as primitive and constricting, but until the Soviet break-through in producing the Sputnik, the influence of intellectuals on politics was quite limited; the public called them "eggheads" and the rugged individual, self-made man and person of practical experience enjoyed greater prestige than a person dealing in and with abstractions and symbols. It was after the upheaval of the sixties triggered by the war resisters that the intellectuals and some of their ideas and ideals prevailed through extra-legal avenues — civil disobedience, violence, defiance of sexual morality of the established civic religion. Coinciding with racial unrest and merging with the "sexual revolution" the war resistance found support and gave support to the embryonic elitist movement. The state and its democratic order survived the spontaneous rebellion, but a systematic dismantling of the traditional consensus began.

The principal agent of change became the judicial branch of the federal government. Peopled with a new generation of activist judges the federal judiciary and mainly the Supreme Court began to transform the United States. In trying to prevent a power grab by the legislature or the executive and to guard a system of checks and balances its constitution failed to provide sufficient checks on the misuse of the independence of the judiciary. When the restraining influence of the public consensus started to dissipate, the new generation of judges used their independence to dismantle the existing consensus and to impose on the state parts of the elitists' ideology. By freewheeling interpretations of the constitution the courts started to overrule democratically legislated local regulations, state laws and referendums and to extend their jurisdiction down to the micromanagement of school systems, individual schools, building codes, zoning and management of prisons. By claiming not to be able to discern obscenity from art, immorality from privacy of consenting adults, killing from assistance at suicide, and the beginning of life of a human embryo the courts struck down the walls guarding against disruptive abuse of sex and threw up a "wall of separation" between religion and the state.

As the method of imposing parts of its program against the will of the majority of the people, the movement worked out a pattern: shy away from legislatures and appeal to courts; after several favorable court decisions the public will (a) become accustomed to the new breach of the given civic religion, and (b) realize the futility of efforts to block the change (or effect another change) through the political system because no matter how many referendums are won and how many laws are passed — if they represent an obstacle to the movement's program, they will be overturned by the federal judiciary (where state courts are elective, with a limited tenure of judges, they are visibly less radical and reckless than federal judges).

Another great accomplishment of the movement is the introduction of sex education in public and most private schools. Mostly misnamed as family education or health education and presented under the disguise of objective, clinical approach, this education introduces to children and adolescents the notion that sex is for pleasure and fun, that it is not a grave matter, but a pastime to which they are entitled. Pupils and students learn all types of sexual abnormalities while being admonished to maintain a "non-judgmental" attitude to all of them, and learn that the only limitation to sex is that it be be used "responsibly" which is identical with avoiding venereal diseases and — mainly — pregnancy; nevertheless, should they fail they are given the opportunity to fall back counselling in school clinics without the knowledge of parents and on abortion. The results of this indoctrination are captured under Appendix 6. The main agents of this innovation were NEA and other the teachers unions with the federal Department of Education. This department is a strange institution: it has no jurisdiction over schools; its function is to allocate federal funds to support educational programs which schools would not, on their own, introduce and which parents and local school boards might not approve, at least not in the form mandated by the Department, such as courses on teen suicide, parental (sexual) abuse, value clarification and other similar programs like *Here is Looking at You, 2000.* (A thorough and brief study of recent trends in public education appeared in *U.S. News and World Report*, June 16, 1997, in the article "Don't listen to Miranda" by John Leo.)

Another way of controlling the population without its consent is the proliferation of federal departments and their resulting bureaucracies by decisions of federal legislature without consent of the states, although such bureaucracies impinge on and chip away the autonomy of lower bodies and are not among the powers ceded to the federal jurisdiction. Such departments are always created at the request of the executive branch and approved under the pretext of serving social needs. The Department of Education affects the autonomy of local school board. The Department of Housing and Development encroaches on the jurisdiction of local self-government. The Department of Agriculture has, through its local offices, a firmer grip on agriculture than the Soviet government ever had: on the basis of aerial photographs, it determines which fields are allowed to produce and which not, what kind of crops will be grown and which ones are restricted. The Environmental Protection Agency exempts from development and utilization large areas for the protection of endangered species without regard on the impact on human families whose livelihood is endangered by its actions. And it takes action by Congress or difficult judicial action to correct excesses and errors of the regulators and bureacracies every time when they exceed the limits of rationality and their jurisdiction. The Endowment for Arts resists successfully the exclusion of producers of obscenities from the list of its beneficiaries. While the justification for new agencies is always rooted in real needs, the authority given them is necessarily broad, and is then articulated by members of the elitist movement who give it their own interpretation supported by the mass media in conflict with the citizenry, communities, states and Congress.

Nation

The object of care of politics should be the nation as the bearer of spiritual development. The pledge of allegiance describes the nation of the United States as "one nation under God, indivisible."

Unlike European nations which arose by violent amalgamation of tribes, the nation of the United States (the "Americans") was formed originally from families or religious groups of Anglo-Saxon origin to which later were peacefully added families of all European nations and languages in the process described traditionally as the "melting pot." The various ethnic groups retained elements of their culture and — in their neighborhoods and settlements — also their languages which did not prevent them from become and consider themselves Americans. From the melting process were excluded two large groups: one willingly, the other unwillingly. By their own will native Indians excluded themselves as "sovereign nations," actually tribes segregated in their reservations and preserving their own cultures from the "white man's" influences. The other group was African Negroes brought to the United States by force, segregated first as slaves, later as "equals" until the last decades when full integration was won by them, opened to them and partly forced upon them (against endeavors to become a separate Moslem nation and establish their own language) by the courts and legislation. Originally, also persons of Asian origin, especially those of the "yellow" race, were kept apart, but this barrier gradually disappeared without any formal intervention.

The source of cohesion of the people (not peoples) of the United States was their allegiance to the Constitution and the Bill of Rights and their common Christian faith and ethos combined with the willingness to use English as their common language.

These bonds making a nation from so many diverse elements ("e pluribus unum") began to crumble under the impact of two factors: the distortion of the Constitution and the Bill of Rights by the courts alienated many against whose convictions the new content of all norms, and the growing impact of the new civic religion were forced upon the nation by the elites. A theory of multiculturalism took the place of the emphasis on "patriotism" and the designation of the population as "a people" started to be changed into "peoples" by new theories of history and the new ideology. The ideology of individualism and especially the new sexual mores try to replace as the new element of cohesion the integrating influence of the original Constitution and religion so far with only partial success. Even the last bond between all segments of the population is under attack. From various sides, English, its grammar and orthography is being criticized as kind of oppression and there is a movement to replace it in schools with expression untrammelled by any rules. There is no more a general agreement on very basic practical values governing life, children, marriage, welfare, religion; America is in the midst of a culture war. This means a crisis, a dangerous crisis. Such a war never is limited to the sphere of culture; ultimately it boils over into power struggle and power struggle into violent contest.

The country is now held together by the wisdom of the authors of its constitutional system and the skill of the elites in using instruments of power. In spite of this, disintegration is apparent in the high level of violence and the widespread use of protective devices. Most apartment houses and condominiums bar access to strangers, often with the help of armed guards. Most homes have alarm systems or at least chains and bolts. The tide of crime is such that in many places, the police do not ever investigate minor crimes such as burglaries, thefts or muggings; it is too busy dealing with murders, killings and drug trafficking.

In addition to privately motivated violence there is group violence. The pro-life movement having exhausted all possibilities of the legal process, picketing and sloganeering, and having its political achievements reversed by the courts, elected the method of peaceful civil disobedience successfully used by the civil rights movement: blocking access to and/or occupying abortion facilities; this attempt, initially bringing results even against police force, was finally squashed by emergency laws and local regulations protecting abortionists in their neighborhood and their facilities and by litigations requesting millions of dollars damages from pro-life organizations and even their individual contributors. The frustration then occasionally explodes in violence, such as bombing of abortion clinics and/or murders of their employees followed by punishments stricter than for same crimes committed by ordinary criminals.

The feeling of frustration and helplessness is at the root of the growth of civilian extremist groups who arm themselves against the expected break-down of society and consider the government as an enemy. They do not shy from terrorist acts, such as armed resistance to federal intervention or bombings of federal buildings; others perform group suicide.

More successful are violent outbreaks of racial unrest connected with looting and vandalism; they are prevented from spreading by political and social concessions, their originators are not sought and their perpetrators rarely or lightly punished: court decisions are visibly influenced by threats and fear of new upheavals. This appeasement manages to smother violence, at the same time it strengthens the feeling that some groups are more equal than others and that the government is not responsive to the will of the electorate. The result is contempt for politics and politicians and apathy towards public affairs and elections.

Because of the cultural crisis, the cohesiveness of the population is weakened; without a common culture, value system and consensus, the concept of being an American is attenuated to its legal aspect, i.e., citizenship, and the elites' ideology of individualism and egocenteredness is not able to transform the citizenry from contending interest groups into a nation — which requires a generally accepted common goal.

Economy

In a society which lacks a common culture, violence can be contained provided that all its parts have a minimum of economic security and no larger group suffers misery combined with hopelessness or despair. American economy has been able to provide such security so far, but certain danger signals indicate this situation might not be sustainable forever.

While spanning the globe American economy is losing its domestic basis. For decades, it was unable to balance a single federal budget; the burden of an ever growing bureaucracy is increasing, the deficit in foreign trade is permanent; illegal immigration of millions of persons continues; production is moving abroad; foreign interests are buying American assets. By abolishing trade barriers, the United States is creating larger markets (NAFTA, GATT); this in turn opens its own market to cheaper labor and the largest American corporations lose their national character and establish close ties or merge with similar foreign corporations. The United States is able to impose its own standards (especially environmental standards) on other states, but loses in exchange the full control of its own economy.

The overall result of this development is the existence of a permanent welfare class whose members have little or no chance to escape the status of poverty. Poverty levels in the United States are of course equal or superior to economic well-being in most areas of the world; but this does not change the frustration of its citizens who are excluded from active participation in the economy. Redistribution of incomes does buy social peace, but remains a permanent problem financially and morally.

Because of the culture war, there is no overarching concept of a purpose which the economy would serve. The dynamics of economy are provided by the market, and it is commonly assumed that the market ("the invisible hand") provides the best and most efficient distribution of resources; by one's choices, everyone influences the outcome, "has a vote" on the economy's direction. This is true, except that there is no equality between various "voters:" each one has as many votes as dollars. Therefore, the market serves primarily the purposes of those with the most votes, i.e., most money, and as it proceeds by the elimination of the middle class towards the hourglass society, its serves more and more in the first place the purposes of a smaller and smaller group of people. The rest must be sustained and entertained to be kept docile; this is not a situation conducive to spiritual development and in the long run, can be maintained, if at all, only by demographic manipulation (reduction of population) and reverse solidarism (elimination of the unproductive members — the old, subnormal, ill).

Foreign Policy and International Relations

Because of its position as the only superpower, the United States' relations with other countries are subject to its international policy design, and not the other way around. It follows several correct principles:

— Its hegemony can be retained only through the establishment of a genuine international legal order, i.e., an enforceable order. However, the enforcement of such an order is beyond the means, strength and will of Americans, therefore

— to enforce an international legal order, the United States creates case-to-case coalitions in which other states add their power to that of the United States under its leadership. One of the most advantageous ways of doing so is

— through the United Nations in which, therefore, the United States, with its most reliable allies, must maintain a dominant position.

— Such policy requires creating closer ties with nations having or accepting the same general purposes as the United States. These are democratic industrialized nations.

— It aims to quench by economic and/or military means the rise of any dissenting power or group of powers especially in the strategic areas, i.e., the Near East and the Far East; it is less urgent to maintain peace in Africa which appears unmanageable and impervious to the means available to the United States, its allies and to the world community.

The weaknesses of this policy are:

— The policy of depopulation works against the United States and its allies; they are starting from a numerically much lower base and this policy affects this smaller basis proportionally more than it does the rest of the world. It therefore undercuts their own power base. faster than it does that of their potential adversaries.

— The resources of the United States together with their allies are still not sufficient to police the entire world. Even military technical superiority does not suffice, as the results in Somalia, Bosnia and the Middle East indicate.The revolt against western dominance in Iraq has been suppressed, but apparently not extinguished. If any nation is willing to take severe and sustained punishment, it can resist indefinitely any pressure short of annihilation.

— The United States does not have the power to prevent China from becoming another superpower. The attempts to gain its cooperation (actually integration in the West-dominated new world order) through concessions will fail; the Chinese are too clever to fall into such a trap; on the contrary, they will extract all possible advantages provided they strengthen their position.

— The United States and its allies (and clients) are a minority in the United Nations. Sooner or later, the majority will assert itself and make economic demands the industrialized nations will be unable to fulfill. Then the umbrella of the United Nations so useful for American policy will be lost and their machinery turned against it with a vengeance.

On balance, the strategy of the Western power is doomed to fail; it must be doomed because its aims are contrary to the laws of life and evolution; it attempts to restrain the forces of life and nature rather than support them and invigorate them through human ingenuity and strength.

Political System

The United States is a pluralistic democracy; its citizens form organizations freely to pursue their various objectives. In view of the concentration of power in the hands of the government, all such organizations interact with the government in various degrees of intensity. The organizations whose primary purpose is to transform the will of the citizens into the will of the state, are political parties. They fulfill this role by providing input and feedback by their members as well as their leaders, with the final decision belonging to the membership.

American political parties perform this role very well on the local level, satisfactorily on the state level and very poorly, if at all, on the federal level. For decades, prior to all federal elections, all political parties included in their programs to balance the budget, to reduce the federal bureaucracy, to simplify the tax system, to reform welfare and health care, to improve public schools; the fact that the same promises are made over and over and the same objectives repeated, proves that none of them has been kept or attained. The last and most obvious failure was the attempt at the so-called republican revolution: in spite of majority in both houses, the impetus was spent in one election period — and things remained basically as before.

According to theory, the governing in the United States should be effective and responsible. The country has a majority system which leads towards the majority of one party, and if pre-election promises are not kept and/or the majority party's policy fails, the responsibility is obvious and the failing party should be defeated in the next elections. Therefore, a majority electoral system is supposed to guarantee efficiency. The fact that it does not perform as it should, is due to several causes, external and internal.

The main external cause is the structure of the federal government, i.e., its checks and balances. They were introduced in order to prevent the federal government from turning into a tyranny by arranging it so that each of its three branches actually got into the way of the others whenever any would try to exceed its powers. This type of government by mutual obstruction worked well as long as the federal government's authority was strictly limited; it became a road towards deadlock, when its jurisdiction outgrew by far the jurisdiction of the states (which was not the assumption under which the constitution was written). Especially if the President and the majority of Congress belong to different political parties or when each body of Congress has a majority of a different political party, there is, with rare exceptions, no way that any thorough change can be effected, no matter how urgent or beneficial. When the executive branch and the legislature are deadlocked, the judiciary assumes, or more precisely: usurps parts of their authority, since it is independent from voters and does not have to fear the authority of an indecisive Congress. And the judges decide according to their own ideology which, at present, is predominantly the ideology of the elitist movement.

The other external cause is the importance of pressure groups among which the strongest ones excluded from influence weaker ones as well as individual voters. Politics shifted from a competition of programs to a struggle between "special interests" which use means other than only elections ("lobbying") to obtain financial (subsidies, tax breaks) and legal (relaxation or introduction of regulations) advantages.

The first internal cause of irrelevance of political parties is that, on the federal level, they are for most of the time an empty shell. Between elections, there is no interaction between the members of a party and the professional politicians who represent it; for all practical purposes, the party *is* the professional politicians, the membership is superfluous. The party program is also prepared without the participation of the membership; at best, they receive a questionnaire (whose questions were carefully prepared by experts in public relations to ensure a predetermined outcome) with the request for "a most generous" contribution. When elections near, the professional politicians organized into a national committee select and hire a public relations firm which operates on a commercial basis. These experts determine, by polling the public, what are the priorities and preferences of the party's constituency and those of independent voters whose votes are necessary for an electoral victory. On the basis of these two is composed a program, and a representative is elected who can, by the impact of his personality, with obvious sincerity convince voters that the given party will indeed this time implement it. At this point, groups of volunteers are recruited who man the telephone banks, distribute leaflets, go visiting from door to door; when the election is over, won or lost, they receive public thanks by the candidate — and are forgotten until the next election. There are no organized communications between their candidate and themselves and even less between themselves as a group and the candidate. A large part of the public considers this process a comedy, and the most difficult part of the campaign is to wake up as many as possible from this lethargy.

Directly related to this type of political life is the kind of financing. Because between the campaigns the party is practically non-existent, no funds are needed for its functioning; but vast sums of it are needed for the elections. To awaken interest and allegiance for the candidates, a massive campaign is necessary, such a campaign must be conducted through the mass media and mass media are very expensive. Therefore, amassing a "war chest" for elections is one of the main tasks of every politician. How pressing a need it is is illustrated by the facts that a President rented to rich individuals for large donations historical rooms in the White House and accepted huge contributions from foreign governments with which his country was at that time in political conflict.

Professional politicians especially on the federal level are actually responsible only to large contributors, individuals or organizations who by the possibility of denying financial support can effect tangible pressure on an elected official. Professional politicians on the federal level are not responsible to any body which would regularly meet to discuss politics and which would include also, for instance, governors or legislators of large states; even less can such bodies include party leaders who are not professional politicians and who rose through the organizational hierarchy of the party — because such organization does not exist. The isolation of the "Beltway" or of "Washingtonians" is generally recognized, pointed out and deplored as a serious shortcoming of the existing system.

These gaps and shortcomings of the American political structure and system enable the elites to implement parts of their ideology by circumventing democracy without the consent or even awareness of the people.

CHAPTER 28

SOME CONCLUSIONS

When the theoretical principles of politics are applied to the actual political situation in the United States some practical conclusions follow. Rekindling the spiritual development in the United States requires both the opening of room for differentiation (variability and competition) and firming up integration. This does not mean a return to the past; the changes effected by the Movement make it impossible and attempts at it are futile; but the past represents a solid and correct foundation on which it is possible to build and which it is desirable to develop.

The State

Differentiation

The general rule of promoting spiritual growth through adjustments in the structure of the state is to *strengthen and widen democracy*.

Democracy consists in an arrangement in which subjects of duty bound by a norm are also, to the largest extent, the normgivers. This principle is based on the recognition that the so-called ordinary people know best what is good — that when they reason on the basis of the diversity of their lives' experience using their common sense and with assistance of tradition and religion, and when they have sufficient knowledge on the issues to be decided, they arrive in their majority conclusions at more correct decisions than specialists and experts who judge things from their limited viewpoint. Therefore, the principle of subsidiarity is a strong contribution to democracy: it brings normgiving to those who are closest to the issue to be decided, are familiar with it and know best the consequences of their decision, especially in matters of morals and education. "Ordinary people" are also those who are more willing to subordinate their individual interest to the common good than any other sector of the population. Therefore the strengthening of local self-government and its insulation from interference by federal institutions, especially the arbitrariness of the federal judiciary, represents the strengthening of democracy.

In the same direction aims the transfer to the states of jurisdictions accumulated by the federal government and not covered by the original contract between the states, and especially the exemption of state matters from the jurisdiction of federal courts. It is necessary for the protection of the remaining sovereignty of states that federal judiciary be inhibited from overturning legislative acts and especially results of referendums as unconstitutional by an inventive interpretation of the Constitution. The failure of the assumption by the federal government of jurisdiction over matters reserved by the states is clearly demonstrated on the example of abortion: as long as abortion was a matter under the jurisdiction of states, it did not represent a serious political problem; once it was "federalized" by the Supreme Court, it divided the nation like nothing since slavery.

The other branches of the federal government, i.e., the legislature and the executive, have also the duty and right to protect the Constitution and therefore the obligation and duty to counteract arbitrary judicial decisions which are, by common sense and logical reasoning, against or outside the plain wording of the Constitution; best constitutional lawyers defend against "activist" judges the integrity of "original intent" of the Constitution and their expert opinion would support corrective measures by Congress and the President.

The principle of subsidiarity is applicable also to the raising of taxes, principally to federal taxation when its proceeds are used for purposes other than those entrusted to the Federation by the Constitution. Introduction of subsidiarity would mean that the main institution taxing individuals would be the states; increase of their jurisdiction demands inevitably additional revenues whose collection can be accomplished only if outweighted by lowering of federal taxes. The administration of tax proceeds by the federal government is notoriously wasteful and all attempts to curb the wastefulness have been in vain; due to its size, complexity and ramification, federal bureaucracy is unmanageable; states' administrations are under closer control and therefore more efficient. If Congress finds that the taxing system managed by states is incapable of redressing significant social disparities between states, it would be much more efficient and democratic to impose on states equalization contributions into a common fund from which they would be redistributed to the needy states from the wealthy states. Individual states would be free to defray or to spend this assessment in any way they would find best. Federal grants with strings attached restrict the jurisdiction of lower administrative units including states, and should not be included in the federal budget. This would also decrease radically the need and opportunity for corruption at the federal level. All agencies dealing with matters not reserved by the Constitution to the federal government should legally be abolished. Only such a reform will bring bureaucracy under control.

Such a radical democratization of the legal structure would significantly reduce the elites' near monopoly on intellectual leadership executed through the system of public schools.

Integration

The American legal system was built as a system of rights and was balanced by Christianity which is a system of duties — no man has rights against God. Since the balancing power of Christianity has been legally eliminated by the so-called wall of separation between Church and state, certain integrating elements have to be included into the legal system to restore the balance.

The Constitution lists certain inalienable rights attaching to each human being as self-evident because stemming from nature and its Creator and not dependent on the individuals' will; from the same source flow self-evident obligations attaching to each human being independently of individuals' will or consent. These obligations are ("self-evident") duties towards self, duties towards others, obligations towards the community, obligations toward the nation, towards humanity, and nature.

— Towards *self*, man has the obligation to procure means necessary to develop his potentialities into actualities which includes protection of his life and his health. A body is a cooperative of millions of cells; each of them gains safer and longer life. As man's mind and will coordinate them, he is bound to direct them towards this end.

— Corporally closest to each are one's relatives, i.e., parents and grandparents, siblings, children and their children, and the person with whom one forms "one flesh" in the transfer of life, and this person's relatives. From this bond flows the duty to care and provide for this group — the *family* — on the basis of solidarity, and also to extend the solidarity to their families if need be.

— In a wider sense, and on an increasingly cultural basis, one has obligations towards one's *nation,* an entity based on common ancestry and common culture, especially language, to protect its independence, work for its well-being and to increase its numbers and its spiritual and material wealth.

— Towards *humanity* as the carrier of life's evolution man has the duty to ensure and multiply its life, expand its horizons, contribute towards maintaining peace and establishing an international law based on principles of individual rights, freedoms and obligations as well as the principle of national independence and state sovereignty, and to resist and suppress attempts at subverting or endangering these values.

— Towards the *environment,* man has the duty to avoid actions or omissions which endanger or destroy life, natural resources and species for reasons and in ways not indispensable for the life of humanity. Man has also the duty to change the environment in ways which moderate its natural destructiveness and increase its harmony and beauty.

— Towards *others,* man has the natural duty to exercise his rights in a manner which does not violate their rights and which respects their dignity and sensibilities.

— Towards the *state* in which he lives, man has the duty to observe its laws (he should have the right to leave it as long as he does not intend to obey). The same applies to other *organizations or associations* to which he belongs.

Certain formulations of natural duties are contained in the pledge of allegiance: Americans pledge allegiance to the Republic, to its nation, submission to God, to liberty and justice for all. The incorporation of such natural obligations appropriately formulated into individual states' legal systems, even if overruled by the federal judiciary and retained only as non-binding declaration of the will of a state's citizenry, can serve as interpretative guidelines for the state's courts and for political decisions in order to redress the supremacy of integrating elements over disintegration.

Another integrating factor inherent to democracy is the principle that the majority creates the will of the state in so far as it does not subverts the right of the minority to become a majority and the inalienable rights and civil liberties protected by international treaties and agreements, and in the United States also by its constitution. The majority principle loses its integrative power if the majority must respect in all its decisions the peculiarities, sensitivities and special interests of minorities beyond the equal status before the law. The principle of equality of groups regardless of their numerical strength is not compatible with democracy because it involves the creation of a permanently privileged number of people; beyond a certain point, legally enforced preferences for individuals based on their minority character exceeds individual equality and approaches equality of groups. This might be acceptable and agreed upon by the majority under exceptional circumstances as a temporary remedy. As a permanent arrangement or a permanent "temporary" arrangement it is contrary to democratic principles and has disintegrating consequences. Government against the will of the majority can be maintained only by open or disguised liquidation of democracy.

Nation

The Pledge of Allegiance (now under attack) describes the population of the United States as "one nation under God, indivisible, with liberty and justice for all." Enthusiastically recited by multitudes at all public gatherings, it expressed the overarching national consensus. This consensus is now vanishing.

The unity of this purportedly indivisible American nation was not anchored in common national or racial origin, but in the religious identity ("under God") and adherence to its constitution and especially its Bill of Rights ("with liberty and justice for all") of its citizens. This attitude — patriotism as a form of nationalism — is incompatible with the individualism of the elitist ideology; their movement therefore pioneers multiculturalism, introduction of alternative official languages and racially adjusted history which separate a people into groups of individuals rather than uniting them into a nation. Experience shows that usually states with a population divided by a multitude of cultures, languages and histories do not last and, often bloodily, break up into nation states. In the United States, the slide on this slippery slope has already started.

The elitist ideology is by its very nature unable to form a nation, and is unable to do so especially in the United States whose majority is religious and will not accept killing as means of public policy, even if disguised as compassion (abortion, euthanasia, assisted suicide), and without killing the proven practices of animal husbandry cannot be applied. The population of the United States can be re-formed into a nation if presented with a mission in line with its main characteristics: generosity, true compassion, freedom and a pioneering spirit. This means assuming leadership in activating the resources of the planet and the potential of the human race for ensuring its growth and for pushing humanity's "frontiers" past the limits of this planet — into space. Only the United States has, in this historical period, the means and opportunity to do so, provided it undertakes this as its objectives in the same spirit, in which it secured the dominance of democracy worldwide.

Economy

Disappearance of the middle class resulting in the forming of an hourglass type society is detrimental to democracy; democracy was strongest in America, when the majority of its population owned means of production and could, with their help, provide for itself. The forces of the free market and progress of technology reversed this relationship: at present, only a minority owns means of production and the majority is dependent on wages, salaries and welfare payments.

This majority of the population has been entangled into a web of material dependency on the federal government: through reliance on unemployment compensation, welfare payments, Social Security, Medicare and Medicaid, agricultural subsidies, scholarships, payments to one-parent families, disaster assistance. This dependency influences the votes of the recipients, pits each group of beneficiaries against others and makes a needed reform unlikely. To return to this majority its economic, and therefore political, independence, two reforms suggest themselves:

— Transfer and entrust the creation and management of the safety nets to individual families by encouraging or coercing them to establish and hold funds for future expected expenses: on education, for illness, for retirement, and/or insurance coverages for unexpected outlays: unemployment, disaster, accident. This would relieve the government from collecting and dispensing the funds for all these purposes, necessary subsidies be the responsibility of states and self-government.

— Rather then transfer income, transfer ownership of means of production. This approach has been partly tried by various states (Mexico, Chile) and is successful. Its substance is: corporations pay taxes in the form of their stocks; taxpayers obtain vouchers, conceivably in amounts in reverse order of income. The vouchers enable them to bid for shares of companies from the above mentioned created fund; successful bidders pay the price and this payment flows in the coffers of the government instead of individuals' taxes. The purchasers of these shares have all the rights of regular shareholders except one: they can not (until certain age) sell them; they can only exchange them for shares of other companies from the same fund. In time, each taxpayer would accumulate enough shares to obtain from their dividends the necessary support payments which are now obtained from the government. Every citizen would thus share in the wealth of the entire nation — also in profits obtained by multinational corporations in other countries. He would also bear his share in economic difficulties; such share would necessarily be less than the share now borne by non-owners of means of production: they are the ones who are affected first and foremost and bear the brunt of any economic slump.

Foreign Policy and International Relations

The United States as the most powerful nation is by its position forced to engender a certain world order which would embody its leading ideas. The obvious instrument of the establishment of such an order is the United Nations Organization even if it is very poorly qualified to take up such a role. To be able to play it, it needs to undergo a number of changes.

The United Nations Organization was created for the purpose of maintaining peace; this original purpose has become a side issue; the organization sprouted a number of agencies in various fields having nothing to do with its original objective. They deal with culture, health, children, housing, women rights, environment, and while they interfere in internal matters of states they are practically out of anyone's control. Led by members or imitators of the Western elitist movement, they are endeavoring the impose on the world a uniform, i.e., western elitist culture. No matter what official aims the sundry agencies have, their agenda always boils down to one objective: to prevent more people to be born. The abolishment of all these accretions would render the operations of UNO much less expensive and would disrupt the efforts of its bureaucracy to create a world government without an agreement of the member states and their peoples and beyond their control.

As the source of a world legal order, equipped therefore also with an enforcement force, UNO's agenda and activities would need to be strictly limited and its day-to-day operations put under consistent control. This means the policy of the U.S. as the leading member would apply to UNO the same principle as mentioned under the subsection on the state: democratization. This application could take on various forms, but it has to address the following points: (1) the principle of "one state, one vote" is not democratic because states are not equal; to make the UNO credible, the number of representatives or of votes of each state should also reflect the number of its citizens as well as other criteria — economic power, education, stability; (2) the institution of the Security Council has become obsolete, the composition of its permanent members does not reflect power relationships which were the deciding criterion at the time when UNO was founded; a procedure for their rotation or recall is overdue; (3) the organization needs a small permanent elective body supervising the functioning of UNO's bureaucracy.

By restricting its objectives to matters more closely related to its original peace keeping mission, UNO could become efficient and meaningful. In addition to its present interventions in areas of conflict, such objectives are: (a) to organize and perform worldwide interdiction of drug trade; drug traffickers profit from the fact that their business reaches across state boundaries and is prosecuted under different legal systems; (b) to keep track of production of arms of mass destruction and report findings to the Security Council or other supervisory body; (c) to take over the administration ("mandate") of countries incapable of governing themselves either due to a protracted civil war or a repeated famine, (d) organize space exploration and exploitation, (e) secure sufficient food production for a growing world population (rather than pushing life-prevention measures). By following these objectives, the U.S. would be building the foundations of a world legal system because all participating states would have to surrender to the UNO some elements of their sovereignty relating to these projects (and only these elements); this surrender would be made easier and more palatable, if the organization taking over these fractions of sovereignty had significant democratic elements in its structure. By taking initiative in any of these projects, the United States could assure itself world leadership longer than by financing depopulation measures and creating anomie around the world — measures which will reap it enemies and turmoil caused by breakdown of the various national cultures and religions.

To sustain its international mission, the United States needs to rely on the support of states which are closest. There are two regions of them. Geographically and geopolitically closest are the states of North and Central America; geopolitically and culturally closest are the states of Western and Central Europe.

The basis of closer cooperation is economic interpenetration and integration. This cannot avoid bringing with it certain sacrifices to be borne by U.S. citizens; these sacrifices are justifiable, as long as U.S. foreign policy manages to transform economic closeness into political cooperation solidified by supra-national institutions following identical aims of member states; such organization must not fall into the hands of self-governing bureaucracies which chip away at member states' sovereignty. In both areas, the conditions for such organizations being under democratic control of member states are much more favorable than are conditions worldwide, because the economic, educational and political (democratic) levels are almost identical. The regional institutions do not have to be composed only by government representatives, but some can be (in Europe they already are) elected directly by the people of the member states. In order to prevent managerization the elected normgiving (policy making) regional bodies must not be shunted aside to a "consultative" role; they have to have also a supervisory and controlling function and effectively perform it. Such regional organizations are also a fallback position if and when another power center attains superpower status allowing it to compete with the United Stats in building a global legal system.

To remain a superpower, the United States needs moreover to maintain bilateral ties with reliable allies in other areas and maintain its presence it their regional organizations to exert a balancing and peace keeping (i.e., war preventive) influence.

In order to maintain a leadership position without or with minimal use of force (economic, military or political pressure), the US must avoid coming as a promoter of the elitist ideology inimical to national sovereignty, religion, family, and children of other countries, such policy being against "the laws of nature and nature's God" its long term effects cannot fail being disastrous.

Political System

The American political system is fundamentally a two-party system; attempts to create a third party have never been successful since the creation of the Republican Party. The two contending parties are at present the Democratic Party and the Republican Party.

Their election programs are almost identical; they differ somewhat in methods, but not too much in goals. There is only one issue that divides them sharply and defies attempts at compromise; it is the issue of abortion. Through the instrumentality of the two parties there takes place a clash of two irreconcilable movements described as "pro-life- and "pro-choice", the first one defending the "sanctity of life", the other the "quality of life" when relating to preborn human beings.

The designation "pro-life" is accurate; the designation "pro-choice" is a misnomer; its adherents concentrate on the right to abortion and have not yet expressed any concern, help or assistance to women who choose to have children. Therefore in the interest of accuracy, the term "pro-abortion" will be used, although the issue of abortion is the most visible and critical, but not the only one. Each of the two movements is the result of two different ideologies, the elitist one (see Chapter 23) with an articulated program of managing humanity (biomaterialism) and the opposing one with no systematic positive program, and therefore in constant defensive. The two conflicting positions then permeate the two movements' attitudes toward almost all political issues which, not having a political solution due to the unyielding stand of both, end before the courts — and with another victory of the pro-abortion movement not only in matters related to abortion, but also concerning euthanasia, assisted suicide, homosexuality, pornography, public schools, libraries and an entire progeny of more or less related matters.

The preceding analyses conclude that the pro-abortion movement and its background philosophy are mistaken and fatal. The American political scene will now be evaluated on the basis of this conclusion starting with the recognition that the elitist movement has the initiative and is on the way to creating a decentralized totalitarian political system (Chapter 7) by having attained in part the necessary near-monopolies of communications, intellectual leadership and organization.This emerging political system is wedded with strong elements of the reverse solidarism economic system (Chapter 9).

The near-monopoly of communications is almost complete; all opinion polls indicate that over 80% of reporters, commentators and managers of the nation-wide TV corporations and other media agree with the pro-abortion movement in all issues. On the pro-life side are ranged dozens of local radio stations belonging to the evangelical and biblical "fundamentalist" churches, which devote all their time to religious programs. On the Catholic side, there is one explicitly pro-life TV station which also has an almost exclusively religious character (Masses, rosaries, homilies). For information on politics, economy, science and entertainment, their listeners have to turn to the gigantic corporations which mostly propagate the elitist world view covertly, but consistently; this cannot remain without effect. Among the subtle suggestions, there are explicit plays, movies and panels to break society's "taboos" and immunize it against biases and prejudices of the traditional civic religion. The result is that the ideology of the elitist movement penetrates into the ranks of its opponents, but there is no movement in the opposite direction. Lately, new technology, namely Internet, seems to have alleviated this isolation. Even so, the pro-life movement needs its own "secular" TV corporation which would provide its listeners with the same material as the pro-abortion corporations without their onesided perspectives.

In the world of publications, the situation is similar. All popular periodicals are favorable to the elites; there exist some good magazines on the pro-life side, but they represent a small fraction of the total output. They are more or less boxed in to the readers of their persuasion. The selection of magazines in public places is typical. In waiting rooms of doctors, dentists, lawyers, in restaurants and most libraries, on stands in grocery chains a pro-life publication is never found; nor are they advertised by the most powerful advertiser of magazines, the Publishers' Clearing House or in the samplers distributed by banks to their charge card customers.

Among plays and novels, whether science fiction, spy stories or detective stories, there is practically none that would not take a critical stand towards marriage and family life and would not depict in detail a sexual act or preferably a perversion. This is so although the rare stories which do not follow this fashion, become best-sellers (like the Hobbitt saga) and reruns of old films on TV like the series "I love Lucy" are highly popular, which would indicate that the public still retains its old preferences of decency. Popular songs for the young generation went so far that they became the subject of parental protests so strong that some publishing houses agreed to adopt a rating system similar to that existing in movies.

The near-monopoly of intellectual leadership is completed on the prestigious universities, and in public schools at least to the extent that favorable mentions of Christianity are expunged from history books and readers. Research into fields which are "politically incorrect" or "culturally incorrect" is not funded, not welcome and seldom published. Universities of Christian Protestant churches mostly concentrate on theology and are not esteemed for their natural sciences. The Catholic Church had a few prestigious universities, but they declared their independence from Church authorities and ignored recent papal instructions to submit to their diocesan bishops. Intellectually, they are sources of support for the elitist values. One or two new ones of high quality have been opened and operate successfully, but the results of their efforts are not yet felt.

The biggest battle between the elitists and their opponents was and is being fought on the subject of sex (renamed "family") education in grammar schools and high schools; the battles fought school district by school district mainly by the "extreme religious right" were occasionally won and often lost. In Catholic schools, the clinical sex education was frequently introduced by sympathizers (nuns) of the pro-abortion movement. The graphic presentation of the various types of sex combined with education to tolerance and equivalency of all the practices and life-styles to pupils and students of the most impressionable age destroys their natural modesty and introduces them to experimentation which renders them receptive to the entire message of the elitist ideology; the authority of the school offsets the authority of parents from whom the children are cautioned to keep hidden their schoolbooks on sexual education and its contents. By requesting children to report "incorrect" behavior of parents some schools have assumed a control function over private lives similar to that of schools in totalitarian regimes. The dissatisfaction of parents has called forth a growth of private (mostly religion-affiliated) schools and a movement towards home schooling.

The near-monopoly of organization is not complete, but is successful in the most important area — in politics. Of the two political parties, the Democratic Party is firmly under control of the elitist movement; the control is such that not even one of pro-lifers among the delegates of the Party's convention was permitted to speak. The situation is different in the Republican Party. The pro-abortion forces in the party endeavored to nominate a "pro-choicer" for President and to remove the party's commitment to the pro-life position from the its platform. They did not succeed, but they have enough power in the party that in the conflict between the pro-life and pro-abortion movements in Congress the pro-life forces in the party are effectively paralyzed.

The political organizations of the pro-life movement, the Christian Coalition and the Moral Majority, are strong enough to prevent the Republican Party from moving into the pro-choice ranks, but they are evidently not able to exert political power. But without gaining sufficient political power ("clout"), the pro-life movement will remain helpless. The progress from a moral and religious movement to a political movement and from a political movement to a political party is for the survival of democracy in the United States necessary. It will be speeded up because members of the elitist movement will sooner or later abandon and actually already began to abandon their movements main strength: invisibility of oppression and tolerance of helpless dissent ([41]). Certain anti-religious steps as inimical to Christianity as the communist regimes had been, are pushing the pro-life movement nilly-willy to political action (Appendix 8). In such occasions, a political personality has he opportunity to translate into political action the indignation of people who realize that they are themselves denigrated on a personal, intimate level. Such opportunities might, but might not arise again.

To attain direct political power, the pro-life movement is forced to attempt the creation of its own instrument which transforms voters' will into the State's will, i.e., a political party translating the objectives of the movement into political will: a legislative program, its implementation by the executive branch and its respect by the judiciary.

There appear only two scenarios for the pro-life movement in this respect. One is to obtain control of the Republican Party even at the price of losing its pro-choice segment and its desertion making it a minority party again. In spite of the fact that its last National Convention retained, in its plank, the party's commitment to the pro-life cause and specifically its anti-abortion stand, these and other related moral issues did not appear on any of the insistent appeals for help and activity with which the party's adherents were inundated by the Republican National Committee and the corresponding Senate and House of Representative's as well as local committees in preparation for the 1998 elections. Detailed questionnaires centered on economic issues (which are of little interest to citizens without taxable incomes: tax cuts, balanced budget, "big labor bosses") and remained silent on issues which do interest every citizen: partial birth abortion, condoms and sex propaganda in schools, same sex marriages, special privileges for homosexuals, euthanasia/assisted suicide. Since there is no probability that the Democratic Party would take them up, by this simple maneuver these items were swept off the political agenda.

The other option for the pro-life movement is to create its own party with an uncompromisingly pro-life program. To succeed under this scenario, such a party would have to fulfill three conditions: (1) It would have to join its pro-life platform with a consistent program opposing the elitist ideology in all its points, especially in its unobtrusive circumvention of democratic political processes, and combine this program with a new economic program barring reverse solidarism and including tax reform, welfare reform and reform of financing elections. The program would have to articulate clearly the attitude towards abortion: no compromise concerning its illegality, but admitting alleviating circumstances (same as in ordinary murder cases); (2) it would have to be a party of a type new in American politics: a party based on small local organizations as a foundation for a hierarchical structure through which would constantly flow (by inexpensive internal communications — internet, broadcasts, tapes, videos, leaflets or brochures) input and feedback between the leadership and the membership; a prototype of such local organizations can be the assemblies of local Christian churches in the South and regular meetings of local pro-life groups in the Midwest; joining the forces of the Christian churches in the South with local pro-life Catholic parish groups and gaining the support of the (local) Catholic hierarchy would increase tremendously its change of success; (3) it would have to extend its economic foundation beyond the small contributions of members to financial support of larger economic entities; the first steps in this respect were taken by certain long distance telephone lines and charge card issuers ("Lifeline")who deliver a certain percentage of their income to pro-life organizations (other business could follow: they have an assured customer basis); (4) it would have to concentrate its efforts and resources on one state in which it could win a visible victory in the first elections: governor, senator or congressman. It could then target cutting off the flow of funds from public coffers into the coffers of anti-life organizations, domestic and international or at least balance such contributions with contributions to truly pro-family and pro-life organizations. With related publicity (which would be unavoidable) it could then expect to enter the next elections with confidence, and even its minimal victory would have worldwide repercussions: it would give the pro-life forces in all the beleaguered countries a rallying point and hope. Its opponents would use a strong weapon against effective pro-life political action: the attempt (already initiated by some anti-life groups) : to use the overlapping membership of political pro-life supporters with membership of Chritsian churches to accuse churches of political activity and deprive them of their tax privileges.

Without a political success, the pro-life movement will continue to lose ground; so far, no concerted political effort has been made by its components. Under normal circumstances,the American political system makes the success of a new party very difficult, but the circumstances change by the steadily decreasing voters' participation in elections. (According to newspapers, during the last election 36% of the electorate cast their votes; of the 36% only 49% elected the President; this means that the decision about the Presidency was made by less than 19% of voters.) In this situation, a party of disciplined members convinced of the vital importance of its program can overcome the difficulties for new parties imbedded in the majority electoral system. This would seem to be an overwhelming task, but with the Creator's blessing, it would succeed; after all, it would be in harmony with his rationally recognizable plan for humanity.

APPENDICES
Appendix 1

— Mass Communications Media

a.

By presenting one-sided pictures of the Vietnam war, TV forced the U.S.government to capitulate in spite of military successes. Pictures from Somalia and Burundi forced the American government to undertake extensive humanitarian actions. A typical example of the influence of television was the fate of the tobacco industry. When television took up the theme of smoking as a health problem, within weeks smoking was prohibited on air planes, trains, public premises, work places, each cigarette carton bears a warning against smoking and representatives of the tobacco industry were subjected to investigation by a Congressional committee about an alleged intention to convert the American youth into addicts by increasing the nicotine strength in cigarettes. The industry was forced to pay medical expenses for inveterate smokers who are considered victims rather than culprits.

b.

Terrifying pictures of victims of famine and civil wars in Africa evoked a surge of public compassion and forced the American government (and through it the world opinion) to take action. But no less terrifying pictures of mutilated, dismembered and burned remnants of abortion victims and their insensitive disposal as garbage has during the twenty years of legalized abortion never been shown on television screens, although these horrors take place right at home in America and the number of victims, some one and a half million annually, with a total exceeding 20,000,000 by far surpasses the number of the homeless, of the unemployed and even of the victims of famine and war elsewhere in the world.

c.

The best example is the comparison of the way the media handled police brutality in the case of Rodney King and in the case of the Philadelphia pro-life protesters. In the first case, the video of the beating by the police of Rodney King, a notorious criminal resisting arrest after a car chase lasting many minutes, was on all screens, it started a short uprising in Los Angeles and ended by incarceration of the responsible officers (even after he had been found not guilty by a jury). In the other case, the videos of Philadelphia police atrocities against nonviolent protesters blocking the access to an abortion clinic, got nowhere. The video and subsequent witness depositions recorded breaking of fingers, dislocation of arms and elbows, kicking, beatings, humiliating personal inspections of arrested women by policemen, i.e., behavior which would have caused a storm of TV indignation had it been directed against any other movement. The victims were not criminals, but peaceful law-abiding citizens using in a nonviolent way their right to free expression. In spite of their efforts at prosecution of the perpetrators, in three years they have not yet obtained any satisfaction, not one of the perpetrators was punished and the entire episode is mentioned only in letters begging for financial help to cover the legal expenses of their litigation. If such were a fate of a movement favored by the media, the screens and front pages of prominent newspapers would be full of pictures and editorials whipping up general indignation. Their reporting and/or silence on discriminatory legal and judicial measures aimed against this movement keep the public in ignorance and apathy concerning acts which otherwise cause public outcry and outrage. On the other hand, isolated acts of violence against abortion clinics and their personnel get immediate and widespread attention so that Congress voted a law granting abortion clinics unique protection even against peaceful presence of protesters, something not granted to any other institution in the United States.

d.

A reader of spy stories could not fail to observe how the era of the Vietnam war produced a flood of novels in which members of American secret services were depicted as murderers, cheats and blackmailers in the services of the industrial-military complex while a Soviet (later an Israeli) secret agent represented a fearless fighter for truth and justice. Science fiction and detective stories, underwent the same cycle. Years after the end of the Vietnam war, fiction still ridicules Vietnam veterans as dull and hopelessly outdated clods — members of the anti-war movement never. Similar floods of tendentious literature arose around the questions of nuclear disarmament, the sexual revolution, population growth, ecology, feminism, any theme whose advocacy was adopted by the elitist movement.

Appendix 2

— Doctors as Veterinarians of the Human Race

Summary of the now famous editorial "The Traditional Ethic. . ." published in California Medicine, the official journal of the California Medical Association [Sept. 1970, Vol.0113, No. 3]. The article now sometimes dubbed as "prophetic" is a very clear representation of the method applied by the Movement. Most of its recommendations, some worded as conclusions, have been implemented fully, others partially, without the need for any conspiracy behind this success. All that was needed was the spontaneous positive response of the many adherents of the Movement among the knowledge class and the media, whose opinions the article expressed clearly and comprehensibly, but its significance escaped the attention of the others. Only Human Life Review *reprinted it twice.*

The article acknowledges that "the traditional Western ethics" (not only Christianity) "always" demanded from the medical profession to "preserve, protect, repair, prolong and enhance" the life of every patient. In 1970, more than a year before the Roe vs. Wade decision, *California Medicine* refutes this ethics on the basis of "certain new facts and social realities" originating from technological advancement whose impact will not fail to displace this irrational limitless devotion to everyone's life. The tension between the growth of the world population and the demand for the "quality of life" will result in the necessity to discard this "Judeo-Christian" ethic and replace it with a new scientific ethic which will require "placing relative values on human lives."

The new ethics will lead not only to "birth control and birth selection," but also to "death selection and death control" to be performed primarily by physicians. The progress towards this enlightened state will be delayed by the inertia of people who have not yet managed to free themselves from the allegiance to the old ethics, but it will be impossible to stop. This is most apparent by the public's negative attitude towards abortion: although everyone knows that it is killing, the public prefers to avoid "the scientific fact, which everyone really knows, that human life begins at conception and is continuous whether intro- or extrauterine till death." Nevertheless, under the leadership of the enlightened elites and especially the medical profession this attitude is gradually changing and the impact of the new problems which are basically biological and ecological, will complete this development. The article closes with the following sentence: "It is not too early for our profession to examine this new ethic . . . and prepare to apply it in a rational development for the fulfillment and betterment of mankind in what is almost to be a biologically-oriented world society."

The reasoning behind ideology, goals and methods of the breeding of all humanity and their implementation were explained here unequivocally and are being consistently pursued.

Appendix 3

— The Case of Roe v. Wade

In the very beginning of the feminist movement in the United States, its leadership (Bella Abzug, Gloria Steinem, Betty Friedan and other very intelligent, educated and affluent ladies) concluded that having children is an obstacle to self-fulfillment in their artistic, scientific, professional, social or sexual life and that elective abortion is the way to remove this obstacle. But the democratic character of the United States did not allow it.

According to the Constitution, all powers not specifically granted to the federal government by the Constitution are reserved to the individual states. The Constitution does not mention abortion, therefore it was regulated by the laws of the individual states; most of them prohibited it outright and others surrounded it with extensive restrictions. To gain a majority for an unlimited right to abortion was politically preposterous. Its proponents therefore searched for ways to circumvent the democratic process. Dissenting from from the citizenry, a tight, but sufficient majority of the Justices on the Supreme Court belonged to a philosophical movement whose ideology included the right to abort. In order to legalize abortion, it was therefore necessary to bring a case centering on this issue before the Supreme Court.

This occurred when a young brilliant lawyer Sarrah Weddington was approached by Norma McCorvey, an abandoned young women in a desperate situation, occasional prostitute, drug addict, with one child, pregnant again, who was seeking help in procuring an illegal abortion. Ms.Weddington promised help and sued the state on behalf of Miss McCorvey under the name of "Roe" (to protect her privacy). The substance of the complaint was that state laws prohibiting abortion violate constitutional rights of Ms. Roe and of all women and that her pregnancy was caused by rape. After expenditure of large amounts of money provided by feminist organizations, the case landed before the Supreme Court which decided by a majority of 5:4 that constitutionally protected human rights produce emanations of a right to privacy in turn producing penumbras which include the right of women to decide whether they wish to be pregnant or not. This right, then, in turn included the right to abort the "fetus" because "fetuses" were not persons in the sense of law. This decision was justified by uncertainty about the moment when life begins, and the blob of cells forming a fetus is therefore not protected by the constitutionally guaranteed right to life.

By this legal trickery, the right to decide questions concerning the "fetus" was exempted from the jurisdiction of the states, laws of all 50 states concerning abortion became unconstitutional and the right to abortion came under the jurisdiction of the Supreme Court. And the Supreme Court has since declared unconstitutional all the numerous attempts by referendums and legislation to narrow down the right of abortion (e.g., laws requesting a permission of parents prior performing an abortion on minors, laws subjecting abortion clinics to health inspections, and so on). In order to reverse a decision of the Supreme Court, it is necessary to amend the Constitution, a process so complicated and difficult as to be practically hopeless.

During the litigation which lasted some two years, the plaintiff bore a girl. Her "protectors" abandoned her after the successful conclusion of the litigation as soon as her usefulness as an instrument of policy ended and she sank back into misery. She described her role and experience in a book where she also published the fact that she had not been raped and that the father of the "fetus" was the man who lived with her at that time. This disclosure had no effect; the Supreme Court ruled that the litigation was a class action and became a precedent; therefore cannot be reversed. An accusation of perjury (with penalties up to 20 years of prison) was never raised; Miss McCorvey became an anti-abortion activist, but the "inalienable right" to unlimited abortion remained on the books as a constitutionally protected liberty even after incontrovertible determination by biology and medicine that life beings at the moment of conception and some 1,500,000 preborn human beings are aborted annually.

Appendix 4

— "Brave new World — or Is It?"

Margaret White in Human Life Review, spring 1994 (Summary)

This practice is applied not only in the United States. In an interesting article Margaret White describes the same practice in Great Britain. When the British government intends to adopt a decision which would provoke popular discontent, it delegates the matter to a "Royal Commission" or a "Committee of Enquiry" given "long grandiose names." Such names selected to disguise rather than disclose the subject and task assigned to this body, creates the impression of "a group of disinterested and erudite people," experts who can be relied upon to research the given subject thoroughly and objectively and arrive at a reliable opinion and recommendation. Actually, the outcome is decided in advance and the members are selected from experts whose opinion is known to agree with the desired outcome. Among them, like raisins in a pudding, are interspersed persons of differing opinions in numbers which will be sure to be always outvoted — other such experts are disqualified as prejudiced, biased or not sufficiently erudite (like omitting spokesmen of the "extreme religious right" from debates on prayer in public schools in the United States). — This practice of selecting members became a rule in nominating commissions of the UNO.

Appendix 5

— Courts v. the People

The history of the United States is replete with examples when the Supreme Court in the guise of interpretations of the Constitution managed to implement policies in contradiction to a clearly expressed will of the electorate and thwarted certain policies of the legislature and/or the executive.

By a referendum, the people of the state of Colorado amended in 1996 their state's constitution to the effect that homosexuals should not be given special privileges because they are covered by rights and laws protecting them equally with other citizens. The Supreme Court of the United States declared this equality of rights to be discrimination and in 1997 declared it to be in violation of the United States constitution. In his dissent, one Justice (A. Scalia) stated:

> When the Court takes sides in the culture wars, it tends to be . . . reflecting the views and values of the lawyers class from which the Court's Members are drawn. How that class feels about homosexuality, will be evident to anyone. . . Today's opinion has no foundation in American constitutional law, and barely pretends to. The people of Colorado have adopted an entirely reasonable provision which does not even disfavor homosexuals in any substantive sense, but merely denies them preferential treatment. . . . Striking it down is an act, not of judicial judgement, but of political will.

Similar situations arose in 1996 when the states of Washington and New York enacted laws banning medical assistance in suicides; within one month, the respective Circuit Courts declared both of them unconstitutional (each on different grounds). One of the New York judges justified his dissent from the Court's decision by declaring that the framers of the Constitution did not erect such painstaking structure of legislating in order to have legislatures decide only trivia while all the basic and substantive questions are decided by the Courts. However, as Justice Scaglia pointed out (above), the members of the "lawyers class" have their ideology, and do not let the Constitution stand in their ways. By "interpreting" its provisions, the Courts have finally derived the right to kill the old, the sick and the unborn from a constitution which places the right to life in the first place.

Appendix 6

— Decline of an Individualistic State

William K. Bennett, former Secretary of Education during the presidency of Ronald Reagan and subsequently entrusted with the "war on drugs" worked out an index of the main cultural indicators capturing the development of society. He compared the indicators of 1960 with a civic religion having a strong preponderance of duties towards various groups (family, church, country) with the civic religion of the nineties having an absolute preponderance of individualism and found the following:

violent crimes	increase by 560%
out of wedlock births	increase by 400%
divorce	increase by 300%
one parent families	increase by 200%
juvenile suicides	increase by 100%.
Tests of college graduates	down by 80 points.

According to the Institute of Health there appeared during the same period 16 new venereal diseases, syphilis reappeared and spread, AIDS is growing.

Productivity is declining, foreign trade has been continuously in the red, the federal budget has not been balanced once during the last thirty years, bureaucracy has grown steadily.

Ann Landers, undoubtedly the most influential American commentator (her column appeared in 1200 U.S. newspapers and magazines), a radical individualist, stated during an interview with *New York Times* in spring of 1994 that the majority of marriages end in a divorce, the problem of drugs is terrible and seems to worsen; "Let us face it — America is sick."

A U.S. Senate report records the following changes concerning teenagers: 600% rise in pregnancies, a 300% rise in suicides, a 232% rise in homicides, and 400,000 surgical abortions annually (from *HLI Reports*, March 1997).

Towards the end of 1995, *The Washington Post* conducted a public opinion poll concerning the degree of trust American citizens have in each other and in public institutions and compared it with the results of an identical poll in 1960. (The year 1960 is usually considered a standard of comparisons because it was the year when the values of individualism — the sexual revolution., the intellectuals' rejection of anti-communism, civil disobedience, war resistance — began to take the upper hand over traditional values.) According to the research, in 1960, two thirds of citizens trusted others not to cheat them and to a varied extent, but always in a majority, they trusted various public institutions (the unions, newspapers, politics, government). In 1995, two thirds of the public declared as a matter of principle that they did not believe others would not cheat them and the distrust was even higher with regard to public institutions; as the least trustworthy were considered politics, the government and the media. At the root of this distrust was the conviction that everybody is his own "Number One" and pursues his own self-fulfillment without regard to any other values or persons.

Appendix 7

— Individual Prevails against Community

Four examples illustrate the situation:

Each year prior to Christmas, the Utah University Choir had a presentation of Christmas carols. It was a traditional, joyous and famous happening. Prior to Christmas 1996, one Jewish member of the choir protested against the concert because the celebration of Christ offended her religious convictions. She refused to be excused from participating in the presentation on the basis that she had the right to be a member of the choir and to attend all its performances; she also had the religious right to object to the contents of the program; therefore, the concert had to be cancelled.

In the suburbs of Chicago, a certain Mr. Sherman as an atheist objected to the fact that the historical seal of Palatine pictured a cross, and started a litigation to have the cross removed as a violation of the separation of state and religion. Explanations that the cross had only a historical significance and as such should be preserved, were rejected; the village had to change its seal. Thereafter, Mr. Sherman moved from one suburb which had a cross in its seal, to another and forced all of them to delete the cross.

Traditionally, classes in public schools started with a prayer for the United States, the President and the school's teachers/professors and pupils/students. A Mrs. Madelyn Murry O'Haire, an activist atheist, moved from one state to another, enrolled her son in a public school and then sued the state for violating the separation of Church and state by allowing prayer in schools. When the case came before the courts, they refused to accept any compromise: that participation in the prayer would be voluntary; that students would be excused from praying, that students who wished to pray, would be allowed to pray silently, and finally even that there would a minute of silence for recollection without any official connection with religion. All state laws to this effect were struck down as unconstitutional. This one woman, with the connivance of the courts, managed to overturn the laws of all the states of the Union against the legally expressed will of their citizens and to prohibit prayer — in the name of the freedom of religion. Later, she attempted (in vain) to stop religious broadcasts and TV programs on the airways of America and Christmas songs and carols from public schools.

Nationwide attention was attracted by one woman's insistence to be enrolled in a state military school for men only, named the Citadel. The school, the state and the public defended this centennial tradition. With the help of the courts, the school was finally forced to accept the female candidate, who shortly after enrollment resigned satisfied that she managed to break the tradition and forced the community to bow to her will; she was really not interested in acquiring the education or submitting to the training. A similar situation developed in connection with the Virginia Military Institute. Because one female applicant refused to attend a close-by coeducational military facility and insisted on admission to VMI, its entire structure, program and standards of performance would have to be adjusted.

Appendix 8

— Anti-Christian Bias

A perpetual battlefield of Christians of all denominations are public schools where teachers enforce the "wall between Church and state" beyond legal limits, in dress, speech, association; to obtain redress, parents have to engage in lengthy litigations. Such redress, when obtained, is only local.

In February 1996, the Supreme Court of the State of Wisconsin voided Good Friday as a state holiday. According to the Court, observance of Good Friday violated the constitutionally guaranteed free exercise of religion.

The Postal Administration publishes each year special stamps to commemorate Christmas. In 1995, the inscription "Christmas" was left out; due to protests, it was reinstated in 1996.

The traditional Christmas exposition of the manger with the holy family may be displayed in public places only if symbols of other religions are also displayed (in practice, this means the Jewish menora) or if the exposition means either folklore or commercial advertisement, i.e, at least Santa Claus with reindeer and sleight must also be displayed. The complaints against the display of Christmas trees have not yet been decided by the courts.

Framed Ten Commandments, crosses as well as all pictures with Christian motifs had to be removed from public schools. A County Circuit judge in Alabama was ordered by another Circuit Judge to remove a wooden plaque with carved Ten Commandments from his chamber; he refused, the case is pending.

In a number of decisions, Courts approved the removal of children from religious parents; observation of religious precepts was considered as child abuse. In divorce cases, some judges assigned children preferentially to a homosexual or lesbian parent over the claims of a Christian mother or father.

Appendix 9

— Behavior of Social Animals

Two concrete observations will illustrate the difference better than a theoretical dissertation:

If a person enters a pasture where a herd of cattle is grazing, the first thing he sees is the bull pushing the calves and the cows to the farther area of the pasture; if the intruder proceeds, the bull will either block or attack him. The behavior of all the members of the herd is inevitable because it is caused by instinct. Were it possible to attribute to them reason and will, it would be proper to explain their behavior to the effect that the bull had an obligation to defend the herd and the right to order the other members of the herd to the location of his choice, and that they had the obligation to obey him.

In a gutter among the refuse was found a dying baby pigeon hit by a car. The founder took it home and it grew into a surprisingly domesticated creature which it was possible to let go free; it returned when called, picked its food from a hand, allowed itself to be grabbed, held, petted and teased. Later a mate was found for him in the same way, they built a nest in their small pigeon house and started a family. The pigeon's attitude did not change except in one regard: he defended the entrance to the nest with all his pathetic strength: he pecked, beat with his wings and pushed away with his body. One morning he was found dead, torn to pieces, but his female and their offspring were sitting safe on the roof. A cat managed to climb up to the nest and the pigeon defended his family until he was torn apart. This little pigeon was a hero. But he did not have a choice. His nature forced him to act as he did. It is the same with all animals: their instinct bids them to prefer the preservation of their progeny and their species at all costs.

A basic change occurs when an individual can refuse to act in the way his instinct tells him to act. A man could run away from his endangered family and abandon it to save his own life. The general opinion of mankind would not approve such behavior, rather it would condemn it. The human community would exalt a mother who would sacrifice her life to save her child from drowning. It would not exalt a mother who would let a child drown in order to save her own life. Human consensus bows down before the inscription in Thermopylae "You who pass by, let my country know that we lay here dead, as the laws commanded us to do." The inscription commemorates the fight during which the defenders of the Thermopylae pass prevented the Persian army from penetrating into the heart of Greece. They fell, they thus saved the Greek civilization with its budding democracy, and changed the progress of European and world history. With lesser awe would the human consensus admire an inscription that "you who pass by, let my country know that we ran away in time and thus saved our lives." Rooted deeply in such judgments are human customs and traditions; they resonate human nature, show the way towards the survival of the whole and are a moral norm for the actions of individuals. It takes a considerable indoctrination for them to be abandoned even if they serve to save the life of an individual to the detriment of the group to which he belongs. This leads to a paradox, that an American president who ran away from his nation's war, bows with respect and glorification before the graves of those who did not act like he did, rather than to describe the dead as obtuse and his own behavior as enlightened.

Appendix 10

— Resistance to Abortions

USA

In the United States, both the public and the legislators attempted to outlaw a new method of birth control, the so-called partial birth abortion. During the hearings about law banning partial birth abortions, registered nurse Brenda P. Shafer gave the following description of the procedure to House committee preparing the legislation:

> "Dr. Haskell delivered the baby's body and arms, everything but the head. The baby's little fingers were clasping and unclasping and his legs were kicking. Then the doctor stuck the scissors through the back of his head, and the baby's arms jerked out in a flinch. The doctor opened up the scissors, stuck a high-powered suction tube into the opening and sucked the baby's brains out."

The procedure is used on "fetuses" 20 weeks or more old; the abortionists reach in the womb with tongs, turn the baby around, pull it out by its feet except for the last couple inches of the head, and then kill it by forcing the surgical scissors in the same spot as Nazi and Stalinist killers shot there victims. The law prohibiting this procedure passed by Congress was vetoed by a President who was reelected by a 49% "majority" of the 36% of registered voters who participated in the election, and his veto failed subsequently to be overturned in the Senate.

China

In 1995 a report on the manner of birth control practiced in China was smuggled out and (in January 1996) published by Human Life International.

All Chinese women have to undergo a monthly inspection to check whether they are "illegally pregnant." In the reported case, Wu Chen was found to be pregnant with her second child. She was immediately seized by two "health care workers", forced on the operating table, her hands tied above her head and, after a fight, also her legs were spread and fastened; in spite of her begging, protests and calling "No, no, you must not kill my child" the doctor inserted the hose of a powerful vacuum cleaner into her body and in a few minutes, the child's heart stopped beating.

Appendix 11

— Coercive Depopulation Measures

Brazil

In Brazil (like in other Latin American countries) the most effective depopulation measure was the introduction of free health care in the countryside. Many women who used its services in birth were sterilized without their knowledge and consent. In 1991, the minister of health of Brazil published a report according to which 7.5 million women were sterilized during the previous five years although sterilization is legally prohibited. These illegal activities practiced quite openly were conducted mostly by U.S. non-governmental organizations such as IPPF, the Population Council, Pathfinder, and financed by them with the help of private foundations (Ford, Rockefeller). To start this program, 32 million US dollars were contributed by private organizations and the World Bank, 47 million by UNO.

India

For a time, India became the testing ground of birth control practices. The original method consisted in individual financial subsidies paid and/or gifts of food to men and women who submitted to sterilization; in many instances, the alternatives were famine for the family or sterilization. Because this method although effective, provoked mass discontent (which contributed largely to the election defeat of Indira Gandhi), the method of collective subsidies was substituted, after its success in Indonesia.

Indonesia

In Indonesia, in about 30,000 communities, AID created a network of "operational units" for the collecting of information on the extent of contraceptive practices; only communities which met the prescribed quota, obtained increased deliveries of food, health care and various other advantages. This method (copied from China) was found as the most effective means of birth control including enforced abortions.

Philippines

An official government study discovered that anti-tetanus vaccines provided by the WHO are "contaminated" by a chemical preventing or interrupting pregnancy. The same vaccines were used in Mexico.

South Korea

The depopulation program in South Korea has been extremely successful: the fertility index fell from 6 in 1961 to 1.7 in 1995. In addition to the usual anti-natality measures against unruly parents (including priority in lotteries for apartments for sterilized persons) South Korea has discriminated also against third and additional children by denying them medical insurance and scholarships. By 1995, the number of surgical abortions (illegal, but not prosecuted) reached about 1,500,000 annually. In 1996, the government realized some undesirable outcomes of its breeding program: the shifts in numeric relationships between old and young generations and between "males" and "females" created problems. So brakes were applied and measures strengthened to correct the discrepancies: public health clinics introduced fertility treatments, prenatal gender tests and abortions are discouraged and discrimination measures against "unapproved" children abolished. So far, South Korea has come closest among all countries to the scientific breeding of the human race; in correcting its errors by government action, it is indeed treating its population as a herd.

Thailand

The support of the depopulation plan prepared for Thailand originates with its Ministry of Health which operates through a "non-governmental" organization — the Population Development Association (PDA) with branches in more than 16,000 villages. The organization uses mass media to tie population growth to the low standard of living, various forms of festivities (carnivals for birth control including contests in inflating condoms, marathons of vasectomies effected on the spot free of charge in local or mobile units of PDA) and financial incentives: hiring buffalos to contraceptive families for half the going price, buying their agricultural products at prices about one third above the market prices and selling agricultural supplies at one third below prevailing cost. ([30])

USA

In October 1970, the Planned Parenthood Federation published an action program of 33 measures for decreasing the population in the United States. Among the proposed measures were: direct the economy so that it forces women to seek and hold gainful jobs, at the same time reduce the number of nursing care centers; limit or refuse free medical care, educational grants, loans and subsidies to families with more than the approved number of children; introduce obligatory abortions for unwed pregnant women and obligatory sterilization for women with two children; disqualify families with many children for publicly supported housing, reduce or abolish maternity leave, add contraceptives to drinking water, increase fees for marriage licenses, propagate a new understanding of marriage and promote homosexuality.

Since that time, the following recommendations have been completely or almost completely adopted: legalization of abortion, incorporation of women into the work force, taxes discriminating against families, protection and expansion of homosexuality; others could not be implemented due to public resistance or legislation in the opposite direction was adopted: child care centers were expanded, maternity leave was increased, some tax relief for large families was enacted, educational subsidies maintained or increased, the population decrease was offset by legal and illegal immigration.

China

China occasionally presented as a model in elitist literature goes even farther than other Asian nations: it punishes entire communities or groups, f.i., all employees of a factory, for violation of the anti-population provisions by individuals. The brutal methods used in China were revealed in a scholarly publication by Steven Mosher who researched them in loco under a grant provided by a university. (The publication whose accuracy has never be disputed, marked the end of his academic career, he has been pushed to the margins of the academic community and is active as President of the Population Research Institute publishing articles or making speeches for pro-life magazines or organizations in North America.)

Appendix 12

— "Too Many People"

(Excerpts and translation from *Budování státu*, Brno, Czechoslovakia, 3rd special issue, Vol. 1993.)

Declassification of secret documents of the U.S. Government usually provokes an eager interest of the media. An extraordinary exception is the declassification of documents concerning American population policies from 1974 to 1975, which took place in the years 1989 and 1990. Only in 1993 did there appear articles concerning these revelations, by Antonio Gaspari, Italian expert in demography, François Dumont, professor of demography at the Sorbonne in Paris, and Jacqueline R. Kasun, professor on the Humboldt State University in the U.S., on pages of the international monthly *The Catholic World Report*, April 1993, pp.23 ff.

The foundation of American Foreign Policy concerning international relations is a two hundred page long study of the National Security Council of the United States under the chairmanship of Henry Kissinger. . . .This study is based on projections of global population growth. Its main characteristics are indicated as follows: (1) A dramatic increase of the population caused mainly by the decline of mortality and the doubling of average life expectancy reached almost 2% annually which is four times the average increase of the years 1750—1900. As a consequence, the number of people doubles every 35 years rather than the preceding 100 years, the yearly increase is almost 80 million rather than the 10 million in the year 1900. (2) In the year 2075 the number of people on Earth will reach 12 billion. (3) The population growth is unequal — in the rich countries it is 0 to 1.5%, in "poor" countries 2 to 3.5%. Until 2075, the population of south and southeast

Asia and in South America will have quintupled, the population of Africa septupled, in east Asia doubled and in so-called developed countries increased by 0.4%.

Consequences: The fast growth of the population threatens to produce famine mainly in the poorest countries. On the other hand, it does not have any visible effect on the consumption of raw materials and fuels because this consumption depends on the size of industrial production (United States with 6% of the world population consumes about one third of raw material resources), and therefore the industrialized world depends increasingly on raw material resources in the undeveloped countries. Should precipitate population growth interfere with their development plans and threaten their stability, the supply of raw materials to the United States and other industrialized countries would be seriously endangered. A fast population growth in the poor countries results in internal migration from rural areas to cities, the need to provide employment for the maturing youths, to secure schools, shelter, health care and security from the limited resources which are at the disposal of the governments of poor countries. The failure of governments leads to abandonment of children, juvenile criminality, lasting and growing unemployment, organized crime, separatist movements, massacres, revolutions and counterrevolutions and expropriation of foreign investments. It is therefore desirable for the United States to prevent such a development especially in countries in which it has a strategic (military, political and economic) interest.

*Conclusions.*The strategy of the United States in this regard must contain the following elements: (1) measures to deal with the population growth to 6 billion individuals in the year 2000 and to 8-9 billion until the middle of the 21st century; to hold the final status as close to 8 billion as possible and not permit the growth to 10 or more billions; (3) to compel the world to stabilize its population, i.e., to accept the system of two children per family (which would mean a deficit of 500 million towards the end of this century and about 3 billion people in the year 2050), (4) concentrate on countries whose population and industrial growth are the fastest and where the United States has special political and strategic interests; these countries are, in the order of urgency: India, Bangladesh, Pakistan, Nigeria, Mexico, Indonesia, Brazil, The Philippines, Thailand, Egypt, Turkey, Ethiopia and Colombia, which represent 47% of the human increase in the world.

Means: It is typical for American reasoning to solve problems through technology. This applies also to the population control: the principal instruments are mechanical and chemical contraceptives and surgical interventions — sterilization and abortion. The memorandum recommended that subsidies for biomedical research be increased by 60 million dollars annually to discover "simple, cheap, effective, safe, long-lasting and acceptable" ways of fertility control. (Wherever the memorandum mentions "planning," "control" and "responsibility" in connection with human fertility, in always means reduction of the number of births.)

In addition to the manufacture of these means, it is necessary to teach the people of undeveloped nations how to use them, and compel them to use them. As the basis of this strategy it is necessary to create a political and popular global commitment in favor of the stabilization of the number of people. For this purpose it is necessary to gain the support of governments of the undeveloped nations and to avoid carefully the appearance of a policy aimed against the undeveloped countries by the industrial countries.

Execution: This plan is successful. . . If one person sneezes, it is negligible; if ten billion people sneeze, it is a hurricane. The same applies to all human activities. The principal obstacles of the "World Population Plan of Action" is the natural inclination of mainly simple people to have children, tradition and religion. . . .The World Population Plan of Action is the first attempt to solve them systematically. The error is that it has been kept secret for decades, that it was prepared by elites secretly, that it has not been subject to public debate and competition of opinions and that little is known and written about it, although its consequences change the face of the whole of humanity and of the planet on which it lives.

NOTES

1. Wars were fought and scholars debated about how best to achieve the former and avoid the latter. Until WW I, in many countries prayer books in the hands of ordinary people still reminded them of the eternal consequences of mortal life: there were morning prayers and evening prayers, prayers before and after meals, prayers for all occasions of life, joyous and tragic, prayers of adoration, of thanksgiving and of petition.
2. The breakfast cereals must meet specifications decided upon by politics and bear labels with information and warnings decreed by politics. The car that takes people to work is to be made according to government specifications, and so must be the gasoline used. Politics decides whether the fence posts on the market are imported from China or from Mexico, whether the TV set is from Japan or USA. Politics decides questions of life (contraception, abortion) or death (right to die, assisted suicide), politics decides the rate of inflation and unemployment and the size of budget deficits, the fate of other nations.
3. This explains why members of an organization act differently than they would, if the organization were not there. In modern society, actions of individuals would be largely inexplicable without the existence of organizations to which they belong. Why would thousands of people leave in the morning their homes and travel in discomfort to places where they spend their time and energy in a manner unpleasant to them? Why would they distribute printed pieces of paper from house to house to people who do not welcome them and sometimes behave rudely, in other words why would they participate in electoral campaigns? Why would they pay taxes? Only because they belong to organizations to which

they have surrendered a portion of their freedom in exchange for the pursuit of a common goal: earning money, have a candidate elected, ensure security and order.

4. In history, there existed side by side the principle of territoriality with the principle of personality; the state's subjects "carried with them" the duty to observe the law of the place from which they came and be exempt from the law of the state on whose territory they were. Remnants of the legal principle of personality survive in the immunity of embassies and their personnel; also United States observes some of its provisions: children born to U.S. citizens acquire American citizenship no matter where born, American laws assume the right to impose legal duties on subsidiaries of U.S. firms in foreign countries and enterprises which belong to U.S. citizens abroad.
5. For instance, a freeway planned by the national government might be compromised by the refusal of a community through whose recreation area the freeway would lead. The proclamation of a city as a nuclear free zone may hamper the construction of a port facility for nuclear submarines.
6. In the United States, the right to refuse residency has been taken away from communities by the Supreme Court; in Europe, the same process is taking place by provisions of Europe's supra-state institutions. In the United States, communities protect their character and traditions by other means, such as building codes, taxation, various types of permits, etc.
7. Assuming ten electoral districts with the same number of voters; if one political party gains victory in two of them by a relationship of 80 to 20% and the other party is victorious in the remaining districts by the relationship of 55 to 45%, then the latter party obtains 8 mandates to 2, i.e., 80% to 20%, in spite of having received only 48% of votes while the defeated party obtained 52%. The key to the defeat of the majority lies in the distribution of voters; if the districts were delineated so that the majority is spread more equally across all districts, the results could correspond to the numeric proportions of votes. Therefore, one precondition for victory in a majority system is the determination of boundaries of electoral districts. Modern technology makes it possible to estimate very accurately which groups of voters will prefer a given party, candidate or program, and to ascertain their territorial distribution. The political party which accordingly decides the boundaries of electoral districts, is ensured political victory or at least advantage in elections for a long time. (This is the reason why electoral districts

in the United States resemble the pieces of a very complicated puzzle.)

8. A somewhat similar situation happens in the United States when one political party is victorious in the elections of the President (he is selected on the basis of his position on nationwide matters) and the other political party obtains a majority of congressmen or senators (they are elected on the basis of local interests and issues).

9. Lenin, *Works*, Russian edition vol. vii, pp. 355 and 361.

10. Organizations in favor of abortion, organizations promoting euthanasia, organizations of feminists, of homosexuals, radical environmentalists, for preferential status of certain minorities, for women priests usually participate in each others' manifestations although, for instance, the interest of homosexuals in the right to abortion or the involvement of radical ecologists in the advocacy of women priests is less than obvious. — During the debate concerning the release of funds by US AID for worldwide "health services" (which include depopulation measures) the following organizations kept up the campaign in favor of immediate release: IPPF, NOW, National Wildlife Federation, NARAL, PPFA, Feminist Majority, ZPG, InterActivism and about a dozen of smaller groups.

11. "Under pressure from the Department of Education's Civil Rights office to boost girls' scores on the PSAT, the College Board announced that it would add a multiple-choice section on writing and language structure to the test. It has long been known that boys do better than girls on standardized tests, particularly on the math sections. . . . This is a "problem" because these tests play a large role in determining National Merit Scholarships, and as a result boys have an 'unfair' advantage in the competition for these awards. The 'solution' is to de-emphasize the math section. This is already accomplished by counting the verbal score twice in the Merit selection process; the new verbal section will further decrease the importance of a high math score." (Excerpt from "The Week," *National Review*, October 28, 1996.)

12. Historically perhaps the strongest impact had the Marxist use of the expression "exploitation" originally conceived as a technical economic term. American politics is especially fecund in this manipulation of terms. Terms like "gay" have replaced "homosexual," "homophobe" is used instead of "heterosexual," "pro-choice" has replaced "proabortion" and "anti-abortion" has replaced "pro-life."

"Critical" has become in selected instances "judgmental," approval of vice has become "compassion." To abandon one's principles in favor of "politically correct" opinions is "maturing" or "growing," faithfulness to opposing principles is "rigidity." In questions concerning human life: euthanasia is "death with dignity," "assisted suicide" or "medicide," an aborted fetus is "uterine tissue," pro-life opinions are always "extreme right" or "religious right" whereas opposite, anti-life opinions are never "left," they are "moderate." Introduction of these biased terms into the public discourse would have been impossible without the control of the media.

13. The Soviet Union managed to surmount German technical superiority and the element of surprise thanks to the numbers and self-sacrifice of its population. On the other hand, Great Britain was unable to maintain the tranquility of its world-wide empire and to protect it from disruption without sufficient numbers of its own soldiers, sailors, administrators and security forces. In Central Europe, the relationship between Czechoslovaks and Germans was 1 to 8; if it had been 3 to 8, Czechoslovakia would not have accepted Munich without fighting.

14. Such a location are the Balkans. When, after the First World War, the great powers were pushed out of that area, the center of tensions became Central Europe where a number of small and weak states replaced the previous great powers of Austria-Hungary, Russia and Germany.

15. An exception in international law is the so-called "live pursuit," i.e., an armed pursuit of retreating insurgents or terrorists across a border provided the army does not penetrate deeply into foreign territory and withdraws immediately after the conclusion of its action.

16. For instance, lately a new infringement on human rights was discovered in California under the designation of "lookism," lookism being avoidance or disapproval of people on the basis of their disgusting looks, offensive habits, careless appearance, obesity, eccentric jewelry.

17. Nonviolence succeeded in India and was crushed in China, nonviolent methods succeeded in the United States when used by the black civil rights movement, and were crushed when applied by the pro-life movement. Self-immolation of opponents of the regime toppled the military government in South Vietnam and utterly failed to shake the communist government in Czechoslovakia.

18. Mr. Feierabend, member of the central organ of Czech anti-Nazi resistance in the first year of occupation and later minister in the exile government, describes how information about the places, dates, and participants of the Center's meeting was bandied around in Prague's cafés by society ladies. Not dissimilar was the situation surrounding the group of the (later executed) Milada Horáková during the first years after communist seizure of power. One of the key resistance groups against communism in Czechoslovakia used to keep minutes of its meetings including lists of participants; when they were seized by the secret police, they constituted indisputable proof of illegal activities.

19. Unless an illegal organization has access to professionally created codes, its safest method of coded communication is the use of books (most often, the bible or a dictionary are used). An indication placed somewhere in the message indicates the page and line which is the key to the code; over such line, the alphabet is superimposed. Every message is then coded on a different basis.

20. In view of these circumstances, the Czech anti-Nazi resistance developed certain rules for the behavior of an arrested member of the underground. An arrested key member of the resistance or any member having information endangering the organization is to commit suicide by swallowing a poison tablet he is supposed to carry with him all the time in an easily accessible place. This is usually possible only shortly after arrest, because secret police agents are expecting such attempts. If suicide is impossible or if the arrested person has no information fatal to the organization, he is supposed to deny guilt, deny any relevant knowledge, and give out false information during initial interrogations in order to learn at least approximately what the security organs already know. He should then at an appropriate moment, such as torture, exhaustion and blatant impossibility to persist in his denials fake a break-down and confess, respectively betray the minimum, mostly things he had identified as already known to or easily discoverable by the interrogators, and then to deny to the end knowledge of any information of key importance. He may embellish, but must not change his story, because it would then lose credibility and the interrogations, i.e., torture, would continue past his endurance. Other rules apply in different circumstances, but the basics are generally identical.

21. Argentina suppressed its guerillas only by mass annihilation of actual or suspected sympathizers; they were arrested and disappeared forever; later investigation indicated that some of them were

dumped alive from airplanes into volcanoes. By somewhat less drastic measures did Chile rid itself of a communist underground. Iraq applied extermination methods — use of nerve gas — to entire villages suspected of supporting Kurdish insurgents. Stalin initiated mass famine in the Ukraine is in this category.

22. During the occupation of Czechoslovakia, German Reichsprotektor Karl Herrman Frank kept in a concentration camp a leader of the Czech resistance Vladimír Krajina and when the collapse of Germany became evident, he tried to induce Krajina to form a Czech government which would assume power from the Germans and thus prevent the takeover by the Czech government in exile. Frank hoped this move would save his life and block the influence of communism in Central Europe. (The plan failed, Krajina refused the offer and Frank was later sentenced and executed.) In Yugoslavia, German authorities used the conflict between resistance forces under Mihajlovic loyal to the exiled king and pro-communist ones led by Tito to strengthen the former which in turn occasionally helped the Gestapo to destroy the latter.

23. Literature: E.J. Dionne, *Why Americans Hate Politics*, New York, 1991; Alvin Gouldner, *The Future of Intellectuals and the Rise of the New Class*, New York, 1979; Mickey Kraus, *The End of Equality*, New York, 1992; Roger Kimball, *Tenured Radicals;* Christopher Lasch, *The Revolt of the Elites and the Betrayal of Democracy*, New York, 1995, Robert B. Reich, *The Work of Nations*, New York, 1992.

24. "An Economic Workout," by W.J.Holstein, Dan McGraw and Viva Hardigg, in *U.S. News and World Report*, November 1996. Geographic and social isolation narrows down the choice of marriage partners: members of the elite marry among themselves and not with members of other social strata — they are choosing someone whose income is equal or higher, who has a promising career or a well paid job. M. Kraus (in *The End of Equality*) mentions the example of a lawyer with an income of $60,000 who, in the past, might have married his secretary with an income of $20,000, but at present marries a lady lawyer whose income is also $60,000, while his secretary marries a clerk with an income equal to hers; the disparity between the two families has now increased: $120,000 against $40,000. (The wife's career is a necessary condition for the comfortable, sometimes conspicuous life-style of the elites.)

    Christopher Lash sees the final stage of this development in Hollywood: on one hand film stars and film moguls, on the other hand an army of individuals providing to them personal services: teachers of fencing, dancing, singing, trainers in posture and sports, suppliers of the latest in videos, televisions, telephones, computers and luxury cars, yachts, motor boats and private planes, caretakers of their personal needs, travel and entertainment, all of whose existence depends on the pleasure of their masters. The relationship of these servants towards their customers lacks the personal relationship between servants and masters of the past; it is depersonalized, commercialized, courteous to deferential, in reality personally indifferent and often salacious.

25. One of such processes elevated above other values is *self-expression* whose extreme examples appear mainly in art. Among them are the "Piss on Christ" sculpture consisting of a plastic crucifix in a bottle filled with the artist's urine, the scene in a New York production where the actress urinates in front of the public, a display in a Chicago museum necessitating that the viewer step on the U.S. Flag — creations of persons supported by the Endowment for Arts. Another process to which supreme value is attributed, is *choice*, regardless of outcome.

    The personal lives of Congressman Barnes, the Kennedys and President Clinton are generally known and publicly displayed; this does not prevent them from aspiring for public office — and attaining it. Still better known are the affairs and scandals of movie and sport stars, singers and actors — they even have publicity and monetaray value, same as "kiss and tell" books which are bestsellers.

26. In view of the pervasiveness and importance of the use of sex for pleasure and entertainment in elitist culture, it is necessary to state that its separation from reproduction constitutes waste of the most important, because life-giving, material and of nervous energy whose control and spiritualization provides an irreplaceable source of refinement in human culture — in manners, literature, music and arts. It is argued that this sublimation of the sexual impulse causes neuroses. It does, but its dissipation has much more serious consequences as roots of the coarsening of western culture, growth of venereal diseases, break-up of family, criminality, drug abuse, loss of respect for women, neuroses in children, juvenile suicides.

27. In some schools, the pupils are requested to describe to the class their erotic dreams, phantasies or sexual experimentation, as well as to debate their observing the intimacy of their parents.

28. According to two prestigious Hong Kong dailies the consumption of bodies of aborted fetuses in communist China was reported

and verified by United Press International. According to these articles, many Chinese doctors recommend the eating of aborted babies as health food cooked in the soup or stew. Their ingestion helps skin to be smoother, the body stronger and kidneys better. The supply of this health food is sufficient due to the government policy of one child per family. Prices are between $1.28 and 1.50 per piece. Dr. Zou Quin from the Luo Hu Clinic consumed, per her own estimates, more than 100 bodies during the past six months and commented matter-of-factly they would be wasted, if not eaten. According to her opinion, the first babies of young women are the best. (From *Human Life International Report* of January 1996.)

29. *Culture Wars* , Vol. I, No. 9 (February 1996) p.19, commented on a complaint by Ms.Kimberly DuBont against doctor Ricardo Asch from the University of California published in *Washington Post.* She alleged he stole from the infertility center her fertilized ova and gave them to a research institute for dissection. Ms.DuBont's complaint was that the doctor kidnapped her babies and caused them to be murdered.

    In this connection, it is worthwhile to mention a conversation of Bernard Shaw with a famous actress. She offered to have his child which would combine his brains and her beauty. Shaw's rejoinder: "But what if it has my beauty and your brains?"

30. In 1968 the government of Thailand refused to introduce a birth control program against pressure exerted by a delegation of the World Bank. Pressure continued through refusal of grants, loans or development assistance both from the World Bank and the United States. In 1974, Thailand caved in and within a short time obtained from the two sources assistance amounting to one billion dollars. Since that time, fertility decreased by more than 50%.

31. Some of the most preposterous predictions are in the famous work by Ehrlich, *The Population Explosion.* Although proven wrong, his thesis of population explosion remains an article of faith by the intellectuals of the movement.

32. In Florida, protected alligators multiplied so that they started to hunt dogs and cats in peoples' gardens. A similar situation developed in Inverness, a rich suburb of Chicago. Coyotes introduced in the local wooded areas took to killing dogs of the residents, and when they endangered some infants, the citizens decided to hire an exterminator to reduce their numbers. This brought about indignant protests from local environmentalists arguing that it is up to the house owners to take measures for protection of their prop-

erty and children rather than exterminating the coyotes which, after all, did only what was natural to them.

The fund raising literature of organizations for protection of endangered species boasts that their efforts prevented the extinction of "the majestic Bengal tiger." Since the tiger is a beast of prey, it is questionable whether the wildlife, cattle and peasantry of Bengal felt the salvaging of tigers as a benefit. Anecdotical evidence of similar conflicts abounds.

33. Two glaring examples of this approach are the case of the snail darter, a two inch fish which feeds by snapping off the extruded eyes of snails; their survival required arresting the completion of a dam which already cost about hundreds of millions of dollars. The other case is that of the spotted owl: to allow some 60 pairs of them to multiply, about 6000 acres of forest were closed to harvesting. Local instances when agricultural activities were forbidden and housing developments stopped in the interest of bird watching or landing of migrating geese are too frequent to be listed. Also some animals, especially birds, laboriously collected and transported to other areas, have the ability and preference to return to their original habitat. The public TV in the Chicago area presented a documentary featuring pictures of protected vultures crowding on roofs of farm houses, depositing their dirt everywhere and protected from extermination. To prevent them from landing on the roofs, the farmer was advised to string wires which would prevent the vultures from gripping the roof tops and landing. The result: the vultures acquired the habit of plucking the wires with their beaks adding a concerto to the bird droppings.

34. Literature: Michel Schooyans, *The Totalitarian Trend of Liberalism*, St.Louis: Central Bureau, 1997, *Bioethics and Population: The Choice of Life* , St. Louis, Central Bureau, 1997, V. J. Chalupa: *Catholic Politics? an Examination*, Ed.Regnery Books, Chicago, 1970, *Tri roky*, ed.Melantrich, Prague, 1990, *Human Life International* 1976-1997, *HLI Reports* 1979-1997.

35. For instance, in 1983, IPPF received an allocation of 28 million dollars from the U.S. federal budget and grants were made since then regularly in increasing amounts through the State Department's Agency for International Development until 1996 (575 million dollars) decreased to 385 million in 1997. About 50% of these amounts earmarked for health were spent for depoplation measures; during the debate about release of funds AID claimed that any delay would deprive the developing countries of

50,000.000 condoms and several millions of abortifacients, most of these funds disbursed through the International Planned Parenthood Federation.

36. At the UN FAO (UN Food and Agriculture Organization) World Food Summit (November 1996), U.S. Agriculture Secretary Dan Glickman voiced a thinly disguised threat that the U.S. stands ready to help those nations that demonstrate the political will necessary to achieve food security, "achieving food security" being a new euphemism for depopulation.

37. Between 1952 and 1991, the amount spent for this purpose totalled 11,123.7 million in constant US dollars of which the 17 developed countries contributed 8194.4, UN specialized agencies 454.1, and the World Bank 1,404.4, which does not include amounts spent by the UNPF. The most comprehensive and accurate study of this matter is the authoritative *The Totalitarian Trend of Liberalism* by Michel Schooyans, St.Louis: Central Bureau, 1997.

38. At the Cairo Conference, some delegates from the underdeveloped countries protested during the sessions that the entire agenda was devoted to depopulation while the conference's main theme, namely development, was completely ignored. A similar confrontation developed at the Istanbul Conference on the Habitat for Humanity.

39. UNPF executes and coordinates some 2000 birth control programs with an annual expense exceeding 100 million dollars (122.7 million in 1983) to which the United States contributes 25%, and it finances NGOs promoting birth control such as the those listed below in the section on private organizations. In its report on population for the year 1991, UNPF requested an increase in subsidies for global contraceptive activities from 4.5 billion to 9 billion dollars as the only way of reducing the fertility of the Third World countries from 3.7 children to 3.3 by the year 2000.

40. "Awake Ups" in East Africa, "And the Nile Flows On" in Egypt, "The Equatorial Trilogy" in Indonesia with measurable increases in the use of contraceptives. About the general tendency of future "soap operas" there can be little doubt in view of the composition of the participants of the above "television summit." A 1983 study of American "TV elite" disclosed that 97% of Hollywood's actors, screenwriters, producers and directors supported abortion, and later polls have shown similar results. All major TV networks have gradually increased the pace of breaking traditional moral norms of the majority, representing them as mindless taboos and preju-

dices and featurimg the ideology of this "herd of independent minds" under the heading of entertainment .

41. Such a step was the attempt to force a judge in Montgomery to remove the Ten Commandments from his chambers. The pettiness of this obvious personal degradation of the victim's religion evoked more indignation than the inexorable progress of the elitist political program through invisible oppression. It provoked the refusal of the State of Alabama to allow the forced removal and to open a fundamental question of the limits of jurisdiction of federal organs and especially the federal judiciary.

Index

F

G

I

J

L

R

S

T

U

V

W